MY VISION SERIES

Reimagining Policing in Pakistan

Problems & Prospects of Change, Innovation & Reform

Abbreviations

ADRM-Alternative Dispute Resolution Mechanism

AJPSC-Azad Kashmir Public Service Commission

AKP-Azad Kashmir Police

ANF-Anti Narcotics Force

ASF-Airport Security Force

ASI-Assistant Sub Inspector

ASP-Assistant Superintendent of Police

BCP-Bird-Cage Policing

BDP-Big-Data Policing

BP-Balochistan Police

BPSC-Balochistan Public Service Commission

BSF-Border Security Force

CCPO-Capital City Police Officer

CJCC-Criminal Justice Coordination Committee

COP-Community-Oriented Policing

CPLC-Citizen Police Liaison Committee

CPO-City Police Officer

CS-Chief Secretary

CSS-Central Superior Services

CTD-Counterterrorism Department

CTP-Common Training programme

DIGP-Deputy Inspector General of Police

DP-Democratic Policing

DPO-District Police Officer

DPSC-District Public Safety Commission

DSP-Deputy Superintendent of Police

EBP Evidence-Based Policing

ED-Establishment Division

FC-Frontier Constabulary

FIA-Federal Investigation Agency

FPSC-Federal Public Service Commission

GBP-Gilgit Baltistan Police

GBPSC-Gilgit Baltistan Public Service Commission

HC-Head Constable

HSP-Hot-Spot Policing

IB-Intelligence Bureau

ICTP-Islamabad Capital Territory Police

IGP-Inspector General of Police

ILP Intelligence-Led Policing

IP-Inspector Police

IPS-Indian Police Service

ISI-Inter Services Intelligence

KPP-Khyber Pakhtunkhwa Police

KPPSC-Khyber Pakhtunkhwa Public Service Commission

LJCP-Law and Justice Commission of Pakistan

MI-Military Intelligence

NACTA-National Counterterrorism Authority

NAP-National Action Plan

NFSA-National Forensic Science Agency

NH&MP-National Highways and Motorways Police

NIM-National Institute of Management

NPA-National Police Academy

NPB-National Police Bureau

NPF-National Police Foundation

NPMB-National Police Management Board

NPSC-National Public Safety Commission

Reimagining Policing in Pakistan

- NR3C-National Response Centre for Cyber Crime

  NSPP-National School of Public Policy

  PA-Police Act

  PAS-Pakistan Administrative Service

  PCA-Police Complaint Authority

  PFSA-Punjab Forensic Science Agency

  PLP-Pulling Levers Policing

  PO-Police Order

  POP-Problem-Oriented Policing

  PPO-Provincial Police Officer

  PP-Predictive Policing

  PP-Punjab Police

  PPSC-Provincial Public Safety Commission

  PPSC-Punjab Public Service Commission

  PRC-Police Reform Committee

  PRCR-Police Reform Committee Report

  PRP-Pakistan Railway Police

  PSCP-Punjab Safe City Project

  PSP-Police service of Pakistan

  RPO-Regional Police Officer

  SDPO-Sub-Divisional Police Officer

  SIP-Sub Inspector Police

  SMP-Social Media Policing

  SPM-Strategic Policing Model

  SPSC-Sindh Public Service Commission

  SP-Sindh Police

  SP-Superintendent of Police

  SSP-Senior Superintendent of Police

  STP-Specialised Training Programme

  TPP- Third-Party Policing

4

Table of Contents

Foreword by Dr Zoha Waseem (PhD)

About the Author

Abstract

Foreword

Policing in Pakistan has been a problematic and challenging endeavour, but there is yet to be an exhaustive volume that captures various policing perspectives and issues. Academics and professionals alike have given little attention to the plethora of policing-related challenges in the country. There is, therefore, an urgent need for researchers to develop new approaches for dealing with existing and future policing and police-related challenges. A cursory glance at the literature on policing in Pakistan reveals an absence of innovative analysis; what is available are newspaper articles or editorials by journalists, lawyers, and former police officers. In this regard, academic literature on policing lags behind that produced in other countries of the global South, not to mention police research produced in developed countries. This book fills a crucial empirical gap in global debates and research on policing by producing an extensive volume on policing in Pakistan.

Javed Jiskani Baloch is a reputed and decorated police officer and a leading scholar of policing, criminal justice, and counterterrorism in Pakistan. He routinely contributes to these fields of research and debate through his academic and non-academic writings. In this book, Baloch merges a practitioner's perspective, grounded in the everyday realities of policing in Pakistan, with critical and contemporary debates from policing scholarship. *Reimagining Policing in Pakistan* thus offers a valuable and original contribution to the existing literature on law enforcement, policing, counterterrorism and security. This book will spark fresh debates on postmodern strategic policing and may be a valuable resource for future research and conversation on transforming policing and police reform in Pakistan. It will also serve as a helpful, informative, and readable text for future scholars of policing.

The book's structure is primarily clear, coherent, and divided into four parts. Each part contains three chapters. The book's first part introduces the overall project structure, purpose, methodology, scope, and the research questions under consideration (Chapter 01). Chapter 02 describes the conceptual perspective and the system of police formations in Pakistan at federal and provincial levels, highlighting gaps in institutional networking. Chapter 03 offers a theoretical foundation guiding the research in this book. The second part of the book examines the historical attempts at police reforms before Police Order 2002 discusses police reorganisations under the Police Order 2002 and K.P. Police Act of 2017 evaluates the extent of its implementation (Chapters 04 and 05). Chapter 06 explains innovations in police governance, technology adoption, forensic science, gender demographics, and cybercrime and their effects on national security and public safety. The book's third part identifies the challenges of terrorism, community relations, and police governance in Pakistan (Chapters 07-09). The final section evaluates Pakistan's experience with police reforms in light of existing literature. It puts forward a strategic policing model that combines "the best of all policing strategies, innovations, and practices of new police professionalism" (Chapter 10). In Chapter 11, the author reimagines the possibilities and workable aspects of transforming policing in Pakistan by recommending specific measures in this connection. The author concludes the discussion in Chapter 12 and analyses the problems and prospects of transforming policing in Pakistan in light of the findings of this inquiry. The book is generally well structured and covers critical aspects of understanding policing in Pakistan. It outlines the fundamental problems and offers a way forward for potentially transforming policing in Pakistan.

The arguments made, themes explored, and the multidisciplinary approach adopted by the author makes it an exciting read for local and international students and practitioners interested in police studies, criminology, criminal justice policy, and governance. This book stands out and provides a unique contribution to broader debates on policing and police reform in the developing world.

Dr Zoha Waseem (PhD) Assistant Professor of Criminology

Department of Sociology | University of Warwick,
Co-coordinator, Urban Violence Research Network
Email: Zoha.Waseem@warwick.ac.uk | zo.waseem@gmail.com
Website: www.zohawaseem.com, Twitter: @ZohaWaseem
London, United Kingdom, 20th November 2021

About the Author

Baloch is an enlightened scholar, novelist, blogger, law enforcement educator, and the senior police officer (DIG) at the Police Service of Pakistan. Academically, Baloch, J.J. is the MSc Criminal Justice Policy from the London School of Economics, London, UK, and has made his two masters in sociology and International Relations from the University of Sindh Jamshoro, Pakistan, with distinctions. Recently, he has done his LLM in international security from the University of Manchester U.K. (2019-20 Academic year as a Chevening Scholar) with Merit Class.

Mr Javed Jiskani has Twenty-two years of policing experience in Pakistan. He is currently a regional police officer, the Makran Division in Gwadar Balochistan province of Pakistan. He has served as Director Capacity Building at the Federal Investigation Agency and Course Commander at NPA, Islamabad. J.J. Baloch has vast and multi-agency experience working in different police formations in Pakistan, including the Punjab Police, National Highways & Motorway Police, Forensic Agency of Sindh, National Police Academy, Federal Investigation Agency, and now Balochistan Police.

Baloch is the author of seven books: Understanding English Grammar, Introduction to sociology, On the Art of Writing Essays, The Power of social media and Policing Challenges, Whiter than White-a Novel and Sociology in the 21st Century: A Perspective of Pakistan and Policing Insights: Articles on policing and Police. He is an Alumnus of LSE UK, UoM UK, IVLP USA, CSA, NPA, and many other educational and law enforcement networks in Pakistan and abroad. One can reach him at jiskanijavedpsp@gmail.com.

By J.J. Baloch (2022)

Abstract

Worldwide, police departments undergo drastic transformations. The challenges of terrorism, democracy, technology, innovation, social media, and the rule of law emphasise reimagining the values, models, approaches, and strategies of policing for dealing with crime, disorder, and violence in society. The leading concern of democratic nations is to explore the ways and means of balancing police authority with civil liberty and crime control with justice. Despite the importance of this conversation, hardly anyone has made a significant effort to contextualise the discourse to postmodern developments in societies and Policing. This book embarks upon finding the answer to the question as to 'why and how transforming police-for-the-government into police-for-the-people has become a significant goal and existential challenge for struggling democracy in Pakistan'. Mr J. J. Baloch, being a veteran police officer and an accomplished author, adventures this task. Primarily, 'Reimagining Policing in Pakistan' aims at examining the possibilities and prospects of transforming policing in 21st century Pakistan. Book follows the doctrinal approach, inductive reasoning, and the Harvard referencing pattern. Drawing on theory, law, jurisprudence, scholarship, and participant observation by the author, this discourse makes a case for postmodern strategic policing for Pakistan. The author argues that the strategic model allows margins to adopt diversified strategies to accommodate various requirements, conditioned by cultural, social, economic, political, and civil factors from a given perspective. Pakistan has unique political, social, and cultural conditions. Therefore, the strategic policing approach, being diversified, dynamic, holistic, and adoptive, can arguably sit well in transforming policing in Pakistan.

Javed Jiskani Baloch (PSP, QMP)

Deputy Inspector General at Police Service of Pakistan (28th CTP)

MSc Criminal Justice Policy, LSE, London, UK (2007-8)

LLM Security and International Law, UoM, Manchester, U.K. (2019-20)

Karachi, Pakistan, 17 March 2022

Chapter: 01

Introduction

Chapter Brief

The introductory chapter deals with the overall scheme and structure of the book. It defines the title-Reimagining Policing in Pakistan by arguing the need to transform policing from colonial models to postmodern strategic models based on service delivery and protection of the people's fundamental rights. Defining the terms of police and policing, this chapter explains postmodern policing and emphasises postmodern changes in human civilisation, particularly in policing approaches. Focusing on the developments and dynamics of police and policing, police reform, innovation, and reorganisation in the context of Pakistan, this chapter not only hints at the challenges and opportunities for policing transformations to postmodern settings but also identifies the objectives, scope, importance, and methodology of inquiry that it undertakes. Both national and international scholarships on policing receive sufficient coverage in this opening.

Since the beginning of the twenty-first century, policing in Pakistan has been at the centre of debates on public policy, governance, terrorism and security (Waseem 2019). These debates have taken place in the media, courtrooms, bureaucratic circles, executive meetings and legislative sessions, civil society congregations and the public domain (Baloch 2019). The debate frequently reverts to 2002, when the first successful attempt to reform the police through the Police Order 2002, which promised to transform the colonial structure of police, made headlines. The currency of this inquiry gains credence from the prevailing predicament of policing in Pakistan and relevant conversation on the subject both in Pakistan and abroad.

The *question* which this book attempts to answer is:

Why and how transforming police for the government into police for the people has become an important goal and existential challenge for struggling democracy in Pakistan?

This book utilises a combination of research methods and approaches such as case studies, analysis of primary and secondary sources, and participant observation. Qualitative arguments receive extensive coverage in the discussion here. To explore and frame this project theoretically, this book engages with a contemporary policing scholarship to evaluate the challenges and opportunities of transforming policing in Pakistan. In this way, the forthcoming book attempts to provide practical solutions for reforming the police in Pakistan by examining the legal foundations, theoretical perspectives and policy reforms since the creation of Pakistan. The discourse brings forth new and emerging global scholarship and research on policing to study the under-explored policing landscape in Pakistan.

This study adopts a doctrinal approach and inductive reasoning, following the Harvard referencing method. Relying mainly on primary sources such as policing laws in Pakistan, this study attempts to use the latest literature on the issue of policing under scrutiny. It attempts to apply the postmodern theoretical criteria to the policing context of Pakistan. It argues in favour of the transformation of policing strategies in Pakistan from the colonial model of coercion to the democratic approaches based on consent. The theoretical scrutiny of policing in Pakistan draws on relevant academic texts, police laws, jurisprudence, scholarly works, and reports of international jurists, human rights organisations, criminologists in police studies and international relations experts in police reform, change, and innovation. In summary, this book is a case study of policing in Pakistan with a particular focus on the prevailing crisis of policing, a diagnosis of its causes, recommendations for remedies, and underscoring the need to reimagine policing in Pakistan as a way forward.

This introduction sets the contextual perspective of the book and makes the roadmap of discourse clearer. The discourse here evolves and rotates in postmodern theoretical settings, emphasising change in traditional policing and opposing the forces of the status-quo resisting police reform in Pakistan. This book has extensively used constitutive laws of police organisations, rules on police practice, websites on police departments and agencies, and reports of police reform commissions and committees in Pakistan as primary sources for analysis. However, contemporary police scholarship, jurisprudence and expert commentaries on policing constitute the secondary sources of this discourse. Chapters on policing landscape and theory are descriptive, while chapters on police reform, reorganisation, and innovation are analytical. Part III, containing three chapters on policing, contains policing terrorism, community relations and police governance. This part uses terrorism, technological innovation and democracy as variables to justify arguments favouring change and reform in colonial police modalities and methodologies of coercive policing into consensual, inclusive and strategic policing in the postmodern era. Last part IV stipulates and construes roadmap arguing for specific strategic measures to improve police service delivery through new police professionalism. Most of the arguments in this part get credence from secondary sources such as contemporary scholarship on policing and takeaways from the discussion in the first three parts of this book.

Reimagining Policing in Pakistan

The book's scope examines the possibilities and prospects of transforming civilian policing in Pakistan from coercive policing to policing by consent. Although, the book's focus remains circled on recent developments in the areas of police reform, innovation, and reorganisation. This book analyses the challenges and opportunities for policing transformation to newer settings and explores the 'strategic policing approaches' as a way forward. Strategic approaches stipulate an efficient ecosystem of networked policing partnerships contextualised in diversified police and non-police actors at local, national, and transnational levels (Hendrix et al., 2017). This book highlights the softer components of strategic or matrix-policing models that focus on lesser use of force, avoiding zero-tolerance barcodes and other coercive methods. The strategic policing model calls for professional, communitarian, intelligence-led, digital, proactive, and problem-oriented approaches juxtaposed to form strategic approaches. 'Reimagining Policing in Pakistan' does not claim to bring core subject matters of police studies such as legal powers, work ethics, recruitment process, occupational dynamics, career progression, crime control, police culture and many other traditional aspects of policing. Police Studies have produced many volumes on these conventional issues. The defining concern of this book focusses on the rationale, reasons, justifications, and importance of transforming police and policing in Pakistan in the light of postmodern changes at local, national and international levels in the areas of society, communication, connectivity, human interaction, political relations, governance, accountability, the rule of law, democracy and globalisation. The previous works on transformative policing at home and abroad have been instrumental in developing this book's conceptual tools and foundations. However, this work claims its original contribution to policing studies by bringing the contemporary policing literature to Pakistan for the first time. Moreover, transformative policing literature merged with a practitioner's perspective add high value to this discourse. These combinations signify the worth of 'Reimagining Policing in Pakistan'.

Mclaughlin and Murji (1999) maintain that the digital revolution, characterised by information and media marathon growth, embarks upon transforming international politics, society, economies, cultures, institutional configurations and individual self and identity. In the wake of these developments, McLaughlin and Murji (1999) emphasise 'theoretical revitalisation of police studies' through the lenses of postmodern values and analysis.

> "Amongst criminologists, there is a heightened sense that alongside radically different forms of risk, uncertainty and instability, and the way they are perceived, an incisive re-ordering of the techniques and logics of social control is taking place. As a result, at various moments during the last decade, there has been a recognition of the urgent need to rethink the assumptions and registers on which police studies, as a sub-field of criminological knowledge, has been premised. For certain academic

commentators, the surest way to get to grips with these fins de siècle transformations is to utilise the general theory of 'late modernity. More recently, the discussion has moved on to cross-examining the relationship between policing and the risk society" (McLaughlin & Murji 1999).

The central argument in this discourse signifies that policing, as an instrument of power, authority, and control, has become a contested function of the state. Policing no longer remains the exclusive domain of the state in contemporary free societies where restorative methods take precedence over the old retributive approaches (Vitale 2017). In this context, law enforcement organisations worldwide are increasingly democratic (Diamond 2008) due to transparency and intensive global connectivity spearheaded by technology and innovation. Societal advances and complexities underscore the need for policing innovation and reform (Weisburd & Braga, 2006). Theoretical developments in policing also unfold the globalisation theory of policing (Bowling and Sheptycki 2014), the integrated models of police (Hunter 1990), and the age of collaborative research on policing (Reiner 2010), which we discuss in the chapter on theoretical perspectives in this book, confirm and correspond to postmodern strategic policing dispensation (Hendrix 2017).

Therefore, policing in Pakistan needs to transform from an authoritarian model of policing to a postmodern dispensation. The deliberate and inclusive partnerships with local, national, and international stakeholders, both private and public or governmental, characterise postmodern policing with civilian democratic oversight mechanisms (Lint 1999). This book contextualises the contemporary discourse on policing in Pakistan, using the postmodern theoretical framework in chapter three. This approach acknowledges the police as a 'cultural phenomenon' (Wakefield & Fleming 2008) and (McLaughlin & Murji 1999).

The central discourse centres around the gaps between police capacity and police performance, between police culture and the magnitude of change, between innovation in society and police reform. This book is a unique effort to explore ways to fill the strategic gaps between contemporary developments, both theoretical and practical, in Pakistani society and policing. At present, policing in Pakistan is undergoing a normative crisis and organisational ineffectiveness. Therefore, this state of policing in Pakistan calls for reimagining policing in the context of twenty-first-century challenges and developments in human civilisation (Lyons 2002).

1.1. Policing Crisis in Pakistan

Today, Pakistan represents a model of the so-called risk society, which is diversified, fragmented, divided, polarised, digitalised as depicted by Beck (1992) and radicalised as observed by Abbass

Reimagining Policing in Pakistan

(2012). Indeed, this calls for a strategic policing response. Pakistan has faced a grave security predicament since the 1980s, given its proximity and participation in both the Afghan War and the Global War on terrorism (Rana 2017). Only military responses cannot provide permanent solutions to the problems of terrorism, extremism, and radicalism. Efficient and effective law enforcement based on the value of policing by consent must be the best criminal justice solution to the challenges of disorder, insecurity, violence, and extremism (Abbass, 2012).

During the mid-19th century, the British Empire in India built Pakistan's present police structure to dominate the masses and not serve and protect them. In the 1840s, British India provided its first police legislation in the 1861 Police Act (Constantine Report 1960-61). At India's partition in 1947, Pakistan inherited a colonial police system under the 1861 Police Act. The primary missions of the colonial police were crowd control and the maintenance of law and order in the wake of the 1857 War of independence. In the Indian subcontinent, British colonialists faced public political resistance owing to their political occupation and the establishment of colonies in South Asia.

Moreover, the class distance between the rich and the poor steadily increased due to the new industrial economy and political slavery created by colonial political dispensations (Arnold, 1986). The police under the Daroga system were the coercive arm of the state tasked with protecting the regime in power and collecting revenue for the Moghul Empire. In a way, the police were a symbol of tyranny and regime security, not the emblem of public safety or protector of fundamental rights and civil liberties (Kolsky, 2010).

However, post-independence political dispensation underwent drastic changes in the political, societal, economic, and criminal justice sectors. The police maintained order, managed crime, and provided better public services. This fundamental mission of policing did not transpire since the Police Act 1861- based on 'rule-concept' instead of 'service-concept', remained intact (PRCR, 1985, p.1). Pakistan has failed to change its policies in line with societal changes. Pakistan's failure to tread the path of democracy is primarily due to governments' extra-constitutionalism in the 1950s and the 1960s, authoritarian military regimes (McGrath 1996), and a lack of political and institutional ownership of police organisations. The military dictators used the police to quench dissent and opposition during the three periods of military rule. The approach of civilian leaders in democracies is no better (Khosa, 2019). Therefore, a lack of political will to reform the police has remained a dominant factor in police progression (Khosa 2017).

14

By J.J. Baloch (2022)

There are many daunting challenges for policing in Pakistan. First, the policing stands politicised. Second, policing in Pakistan has not adopted this technology at an optimum level. Police still follows the old military model since both the police and military are altogether different institutions. Third, police in Pakistan work under the influence of bureaucracy, which is not a favoured practice in the developed world. Any effort of police reformers to focus on the modernist legacy of the one-size-fits-all approach is unsustainable (Waters 2007). Policing scholars, researchers, practitioners, and analysts should explore innovative ways to align policy reforms with the postmodern context of diversity and difference.

Among the severe initial problems faced by the nascent state of Pakistan, transferring power to the 'real sovereign' (the people) through a well-defined constitutional system remained an illusion until the separation of East Pakistan, leading to the creation of Bangladesh in 1971. Until the framing of the 1973 Constitution of Pakistan, the country tackled the existential problem of statehood and statecraft (McGrath 1996). Policing, such as development and justice, is one of the fundamental duties of the state (Hof and Groothuis 2011). Still, it remained neglected despite the constitution of more than two dozen commissions and committees on police reform in Pakistan before the 2002 Police Order. New Police Order adopted a new police system on democratic lines, breaking free (at least in theory) from the authoritarian dispensation of police under the 1861 Police Act, which had long lost its appeal and usefulness to the citizenry (Abbass 2012).

However, before Police Order 2002 could mark realigning public policing with contemporary developments in Pakistani society and global policing, the bureaucratic and political elements hampered the implementation of PO 2002 through amendments from 2004 to 2006 (PRC Report 2018). The provincial police departments in Pakistan have been following different frameworks for administration, resulting in a lack of uniformity and raising questions about the constitutionality of policing (see chapters on police reforms and reorganisation in Pakistan for more details). Peoples in Pakistan continue to ask questions regarding the viability and validity of police as trusted and reliable guardians of fundamental rights to life, liberty, property, and security (Reiner 2010). Pakistan also represents a grim picture of the police governance crisis that resembles what Britons called their police "the plague of blue locusts' (Reiner, 1992) during the Sixties. In this state of affairs, reimagining policing in Pakistan attempts to bring together the challenges and opportunities for transforming policing in Pakistan.

15

1.2. Police and Policing

Understanding police and policing is vital. Bowling and Sheptycki (2012) differentiate these terms describing "science of police as referring to a broad set of practices intended to order, to control, to organise and to regulate" (p.11). To Bowling and Sheptycki, "the idea of police is a modern one. It came to political parlance during European Enlightenment' (p.11). In their groundbreaking work on "Global Policing," Bowling and Sheptycki (2012) consider police something more than 'mere criminal law enforcement. Their work further claims that police powers constitute the core of more extraordinary governmental authorities through which the police can regulate that which is otherwise unregulated.

Regarding the science of policing, both authors explain that policing implies the set of activities charged with ensuring social order and maintaining public peace in society. Policing requires police to obtain statistical information and data about the people living in their areas of responsibility, their properties, occupations, and the conditions of their health, prosperity, and happiness. They believe that policing traces not only the misdeeds of the past but also predicts future threats and risks (p.12).

> "Policing is part of a family of words which includes: politics, policy, and polity. It pertains to authoritative intervention into situational difficulties, which cannot be predicted in advance. Policing refers to a practical policy of social ordering. Its core feature [of policing] is the capacity to muster the coercive force to maintain a particular or general social order. It [policing also] involves the surveillance of populations and territory to intervene against past wrongs and pre-empt future problems. Democratic policing is undertaken on behalf of a citizenry that both understand and endorse the police mission," pinning legitimacy to police actions (Westmarland & Conway 2020).

Differentiating between the police and policing, Reiner (1992) remarks that police refer to a particular kind of institution ', while the policing alludes to a 'set of the specific activity or process. He further elaborates that policing is universal, but not police, because many societies do not have police even in the 21st century. Instead, Reiner defines policing as a composite of social control processes involving sanctions and surveillance to maintain peace and social order (Reiner, 1992).

Policing has a broader scope, with far-reaching impacts on human social life. Moran and Newburn (1997) summarise policing from different sources in various ways. Policing refers to a law enforcement activity that highlights strategies for preventing and detecting crime, developing a social environment where crime and disorder do not flourish (Baloch 2016), and provides an antidote to violations of any kind such as laws, rules, norms, and values. Moran and Newburn (1997) define policing as a form of state coercion and the use of force. According to the postmodern critics of public policing, like Vitale

16

(2017), policing should be more than merely a coercive tool of the state to control the population. It should offer social and civic services such as help in public safety matters to the locals, and good police officers should be easily reachable for those in the middle of trouble. Vitale's (2017) best policing approach is restoring the victim and an offender to societal and cultural normalcy through therapeutic measures. Instead, he rejects punitive measures as the government's modern paradigm rests on massive incarcerations and harsh penal policies. As part of retributive criminal justice policies, policing involves coercion.

Critical sociologists and criminologists argue that policing is nothing more than merely a service for a privileged class. Resultantly, policing favours only a few and misuses authority against the rest of the populace. Referring to the Marxist or conflict view, Reiner (2010) maintains that plenty of literature describes policing as an upper-class security service that protects and saves the life and property of the wealthy class, not of the ordinary person. Since its independence, this discriminatory and exclusive policing has been truer in Pakistan, so claims Abbass (2012). This state of policing affairs is more relevant to the context of predominantly authoritarian societies and, thus, dominated by the state apparatus. To control violations of law, to regulate public peace, and to maintain social order by using the police authority of arresting, interrogating, investigating, and presenting the offenders before the court of law for prosecution, and the trial is total of what we have come to understand about policing (Bittner 1970).

Contemporary policing is envisaged as an organised and balanced interaction between the police and the public, reflecting the community's values, government policies, organisational constraints, and individual decisions of the police leaders (Lang-worthy & Travis, 1994). Managing risk by analysing the threat and strategising a response to it is one of the leading policing activities in postmodern times (Stone and Travis 2011). Ericson and Haggerty (2008) argue that police officers have become information brokers for health, welfare, insurance companies, and other organisations. The race among people to have control of information technology refers to the value-added expertise of police organisations because they possess CCTV records and crime data. Making police repositories of the complete information (Ferguson 2016) and the partners with international biotech and infotech (Harari 2018) through INTERPOL give them the edge of having super quality information (Bowling and Sheptycki 2012). Ericson and Haggerty (2008) bring forth the basic tenants of risk society and policing risk society. The contemporary notions of risk society and high policing had impacts on the police thinking of managing information technology in the postmodern age. New social challenges demonstrate that policing is an essential socio-political institution and is a challenging profession (Maguire and Okada 2011).

Analysts in the 21st century maintain that it is essential to understand the context and perspective of the subject in point for studying anything. The police are vital legal, social, and political institutions tasked by the law to protect the social order, public peace, and fundamental rights of the citizenry. Therefore, it is critical to scrutinise the mandate, capacity, performance, and impacts of policing within the context of the society at that particular point of time and its cultural contours that characterise the shape of things as true and correct (Chaudhry, 1990). The 21st century, accompanied by postmodern narratives, is versatile, dynamic, and diverse. It highly values diversity, difference, pluralism, inclusiveness, partnerships, collaborations, legitimacy, individual liberty, privacy, and integrity.

On the contrary, the modernist theory's ideas have lost their appeal to postmodern theorists. For example, the notions the unity, hegemony, racism, nationalism, capitalism, structuralism, scientific fixing of truths, and statutory determinism of narratives no longer exist. Instead of believing in one 'grand theory' as the solution to all human problems, postmodern theorists believe in different approaches for various issues in disparate fields and diverse contexts (Waters, 2007). Police being the core component of the state, is under more scrutiny today than ever before because policing in Pakistan remains aligned with the 19th and 20th-century modernist ideas. At the same time, our society has embraced the soul of the 21st century in many of its areas.

Uncertainty, turmoil, important power battles, and political discord define Pakistan's present law enforcement apparatus. Policing needs reimagining through the postmodernist lenses that remain enveloped in our contemporary political heritage and societal culture. Nonetheless, postmodernism is conceivably a helpful philosophical way to understand current global policing phenomena (Reiner, 1992). For example, the globalisation impinged upon the social relationships of the people, the conduct of the police with the communities, police relationships with other law enforcement organisations, police collaboration with intelligence networks, and police equations with media, academia, civil society, and nongovernmental organisations.

1.3.1. Policing as a fundamental Statutory Function

The primary functions of any state or government are to establish peace, dispense justice, and cinch progress. Police play an instrumental and central role in all three core areas of polity and governance. The police are the foundation and the first gate of the criminal justice system (Newburn, eds. 2004).

Together with crime management, law and order are among the primary responsibilities of the police (Foucault, 1980). No society can ever progress if its government fails to provide justice and peace to its citizenry (Fukuyama 2014). Therefore, no government can claim to ensure good governance unless its police are efficient and effective in public service delivery and in enforcing the spirit of the law. Hence, reforming and innovating police and policing must be the cardinal part of all sensible governments and visionary political leadership (Jones & Newburn 2001). However, the constant crisis of statehood in Pakistan continues to knock at the minds of our leaders to make their police capable of policing the independent and democratic society of Pakistan in a procedurally correct and qualified way (Chaudhry 1990). The Report of the Police Reform Implementation Committee 1990, headed by Chaudhry M.A.K, reads:

> "The image of a government is linked critically with the quality of law-and-order milieu it provides. Law and order, in turn, are part of the overall criminal justice system. Many erroneously believe that it is the be-all and end-all of the system. It is no wonder that whenever crime gets out of control or public peace is repeatedly disturbed, both government and the public hold police responsible' (Chaudhry, 1990).

1.4.2. Policing as an Essential Component of Criminal Justice

Police is an essential component of the criminal justice system in any country. However, public expectations with the police and police responsibility towards the public in terms of maintaining peace and order within society do not sit with the professional role played by the police (PRC 2018). The fact remains that the public renders police responsible for everything crime, including its underlying causes and remedies such as speedy justice. In fact, in the entire criminal justice system, police only play the role of one component (Joyce, 2011). The primary function of the police is the management of the crime committed or its prevention and detection, which starts mostly when a crime incident occurs or when police get information about certain heinous crimes that are to take place (Jobard, 2003). When a crime occurs, police register the First Information Report-FIR at the police station with jurisdiction, and the police start an investigation (CRPC 1898). The police take 14 days to complete the investigation process of the case as per the criminal procedure (Section 154 CRPC). After completion of the investigation, the core job of the police ends because police have a marginal role beyond the collection of evidence except for facilitation of the justice system, such as bringing witnesses, case files, and prisoners to the court of law.

After the investigation completes, the prosecution of the case begins, which is not the job of the police; instead, it constitutes the second component of the criminal justice system. The third component or pillar of criminal justice is adjudication carried out by the court. In contrast, the fourth component is the prison or correction facility, where the police transport the convict after the accused gets sentenced. In this way, the ability of the police to act exclusively or in isolation against crime is limited (McLaughlin, 2007). Police as a law enforcement agency cannot deal with the full range of causes and circumstances conducive to the occurrence of crimes (ibid). Police have little control over the socio-economic and political conditions within the broader context of the country (Ibid).

> "Police is only one part of the criminal Justice system. The criminal Justice system is only one part of society. As crime is a social phenomenon, its prevention should be the responsibility of every part of the society' (Chaudhry, 1990).

Thus, even crime prevention police always need public support and assistance from all stakeholders within society. Despite all limitations and dependencies, failure in policing causes more significant anxiety to the government, resulting in higher unrest among the public by diminishing the spirit of the law. Enhancing effectiveness is, perhaps, why every government wants to reform the police by appointing police reform commissions and committees to make police more effective, active, result-oriented, and people-friendly.

1.5. The Postmodern Policing

Postmodern policing refers to policing methods and approaches that suit the policing requirements of the complex, risky, vulnerable, and highly connected pluralistic and globalised society of the 21st century. The postmodern policing thesis reveals that policing no longer remains a state monopoly but has somewhat shifted to its commodification (Newburn 2001). Nothing is more important for police leaders than the quality of service they provide, in addition to satisfying the end-user (O'Malley, 1997). For building an image as the deliverer, police make annual strategic policing plans with a stated vision, mission, and goals to be achieved within its resources, besides funds for specific welfare projects within the force (Judge 2002). This trend has led to privatisation, corporatisation, and marketisation of policing under the postmodern paradigm (Lint, 1999). Thus, persuasion and consent are essential cornerstones of postmodern policing.

James Sheptycki (1998) defines postmodern policing in the transnationalisation of police which is characterised by what he describes as four postulates under the marketisation of insecurity, social control, policing, and international black markets (cybercrime-currency and trade). He argues that postmodern policing stands embedded in broad changes in global state systems (Sheptycki 1998). He suggests that Policing Studies and practitioners should play a leading role in framing theoretical and practical solutions for postmodern policing. Adopting postmodern policing is seemingly a problematic and challenging domain in changing the dynamics of state systems and emerging globalisation trends (Ibid). Sheptycki (2007) indicates that in the contemporary world, stricken by fear, terror, and insecurity, advocates of technological surveillance cannot ignore the likely infringements of individual privacy in the name of security and crime control. Postmodern policing stands for promoting the human security paradigm as an alternative to new organisational pathologies of security-driven high policing dispensation, which he considers deeply problematic in fostering security and sustainable peace (Sheptycki 2007).

Postmodern policing emphasises maximising community engagement in the police; it strengthens police-community relations and helps control police discretion and coercion (Jones 2009). However, Jones finds that police organisations can transform themselves into legitimate institutions with legal authority by providing effective services to the people. Jones (2009) recommends three steps for the police to achieve the goal of transformation. First, police should limit and rationalise the use of arbitrary force. Second, police organisations have to make institutional arrangements for being accessible and responsive when people need help and successful problem-solving. Third, Police leaders need to cultivate public trust in their police by procedural transparency, character building and integrity of police officers.

Postmodern thinking impacts policing from four main fronts: the mission and mandate of police, police strategies to achieve their goals/missions, guardian or warrior role of police, and the aggressive, hierarchical, and bureaucratic model of authority. Ericson and Haggerty (1997) explain that four factors have played a crucial role in developing postmodern notions of policing. These factors include fragmenting traditional values, global connectivity, erosion of state sovereignty, the emergence of risk society, human security concepts, service delivery and partnerships in maintaining social order and public peace. Waters (2007) argues that modern reforms should be consistent with postmodern policing requirements. Miller (2007) underscores the need for fairness and non-discrimination in responding to the public in difficulty and requiring help. Bowling and Sheptycki (2010) refer to the 'glocalisation' of policing wherein one state's sovereign power centre gets diluted into global and local systems. For security matters and local communities for street-level policing and criminal justice affairs. Service delivery and public satisfaction replace the use of force and coercion employment. Postmodern political settings emphasise the police being answerable to people instead of the leviathan state.

21

Reimagining Policing in Pakistan

Judge (2002) argues that considering policing as a state-centric activity is problematic in the postmodern era. O'Malley (1997) maintains that the state loses its monopoly on (public) police and the use of legitimate force, and many non-state actors and other state agents share this core function of policing with the public police. Besides this, postmodern policing literature identifies colossal restructuring of policing and developments in police strategies worldwide (Albrow 1996). Sheptycki (2002) argues that the latest changes in politics include the dissolution of the state, the power of local communities, popular culture and consensual policy from violence to restoration, and the breakdown of the traditional order. Policing gets globalised through Interpol and UN peace missions and the search for international criminal assistance. In addition, the rise of private non-government police and security agencies, diversification of police role through specialist police services, the involvement of different partners in policing, emphasis on police service delivery to the citizen, cooperation of police with local, national and international police and non-police powers (Lint 1999) constitute the foundations of postmodern policing. Besides this, many managerial and political influences shape postmodern policing and recent shifts in policing worldwide (O'Malley 1997). Newburn (2001) calls 'far-reaching changes in nature and form of policing including massive expansion in private policing and proliferation of electronic form of surveillance' (p.829) to reflect postmodern policing developments.

Postmodern policing models refer to strategic and matrix policing networks that signify 'transnational policing' (Goldsmith and Sheptycki 2007), democratic policing (Bayley 2006), restorative policing (Clamp & Paterson 2017), and plural policing (Rogers 2017). In postmodern policing dispensation, police play the role of the guardian of the people's fundamental rights rather than a coercive arm to control people (Sheptycki 2007). The debate on postmodern policing in this book is essentially rooted in the failure of modern policing ideas of authoritarianism, coercion and state-monopolised 'arbitrary use of force for protecting the tyrannical governments or silencing the dissent and opposition' (Lawrence 2000). Therefore, the primary reasons for framing the conversation on policing in Pakistan within the intellectual framework of the postmodern policing paradigm alludes to its pluralistic and inclusive nature.

Police are now service providers, and their efficiency can be gauged by 'citizen satisfaction' (O'Malley 1997). They no longer remain merely the organisations authorised to use legitimate force to maintain public order and prevent crime (Judge 2002). Nash (2000) refers to Foucault's concept of 'power-knowledge. Reiner (1992) develops this notion designating police officers as 'knowledge workers' and

Wright Mills (2002) as 'image workers', Sheptycki (1996 p6) as 'information workers', Ferguson (2016) as data analysts, Christopher (2016) as social media experts, and Loader (1994) service providers to the public. Harari (2018) argues that those who control information and data will rule the world. Ferguson (2016) confirms that police will be an instrumental department for health, insurance, immigration, intelligence (both human and artificial), politics (electioneering), and other business corporations. All business enterprises would need data regarding peoples' brands, fashion, ideology, and trends.

Policing partnerships with other state and non-state actors to maintain order, respond to threats, and provide security to citizens are the fundamental characteristics of postmodern policing dispensation. O'Malley (1997) quotes Avery (1981-p.3) as stating, "preventing crime, detecting cases, arresting offenders, protecting life, property and liberty of the people, preserving public order, and managing risks are the joint duties of the community and police. These are the obligations of the public, aided by the police and not police occasionally aided by some public-spirited citizens." Policing partnerships under the postmodern narrative of police cannot be limited to citizens and communities. Networks of partners extend to other law enforcement networks, intelligence agencies, academia, media, criminal justice organs and security providers (including private agencies), the legal community, financial/tax departments, foreign counterparts, global platforms both interstate (Interpol, UNO, etc.), and different non-states (multinational corporations such as infotech and biotech (Google, Apple, Microsoft, Facebook, etc.) (Goodman 2015).

Lint (1999) indicates postmodern developments in policing that have undermined the modern version of police ethics, normative order, and authority. The postmodern policing approach is grounded in the pragmatic ground realities of ethnographies. Thus, Lint believes that the top-down synthesis of modern policing counters the postmodern ground-up thesis, enabling the constabulary to rise to top police leadership. For us in Pakistan to learn from what Lint tries to imply is to transform the focus of police reforms from the top echelons of the police to the constabulary, who are to help the people in times of difficulty and emergency.

From the perspective of Pakistan, this book examines policing from three postmodern perspectives, including how the developments in postmodern society influence police and policing. Second, what does the state's liquidation as a political power centre means for police and policing in the globalised world? Third, what changes/reforms and innovations the police and policing need to transform in the 'liquid times' (Bauman 2007) of the 21st century, where mass technology and easy accessibility to information to the people have reduced governmental controls and eroded their monopolies?

1.6. Challenges and Opportunities

The following paragraphs detail the challenges and opportunities related to terrorism, accountability, democracy, and technology and their link to developing new police professionalism based on strategic policing ideals in Pakistan.

Mihailescu and Murkami (2018), in their groundbreaking work: "Policing Literary Theory", refers to "the age of omnipresent terrorism" wherein the police witnesses "the era of ever-expanding policing". Weisburd and Braga (2006) also admit that terrorism is a new challenge and recognise counterterrorism as a unique opportunity for the police to expand their primary mission and mandate from crime-fighting to countering terror, militancy, and multiple forms of violence in society. Pakistan has witnessed a surge in terrorist attacks since 2001; hence, the police developed ideological and structural frameworks (e.g., the National Action Plan, National Counterterrorism Authority, Counterterrorism Departments under provincial police organisations) to deal with this change. Still, these structures need review, realignment, and innovation. In a later chapter on policing terrorism, different aspects of terrorism and counterterrorism in Pakistan receive critical scrutiny, and the chapter proposes a roadmap for effective counterterrorism policing in Pakistan.

Like terrorism, police corruption or misuse of authority is one of the most significant challenges for police reform and police legitimacy. However, Punch (2003) believes that most of the literature on police corruption and abuse revolves around the metaphors of bad apples, black sheep, or rotten orchards. Khalid (2017) argues that police conduct or integrity has always been a cherished theme of both scholarship and gossip in Pakistan. Such public perceptions of police corruption and brutality persist despite the falling of many police officers in the line of duty. Robert and Sarah (2017) examined police legitimacy through a procedural justice model that emphasises treating civilians with fairness and openness, enhancing public trust in the police. The chapter on police governance ahead exclusively discusses the importance of internal and external accountability mechanisms as tools for making the police in Pakistan more procedurally.

When speaking of police accountability, we must underscore the need for a democratic state, under which the police can be answerable to the people, not the government (Manning 2015). Pakistan is a constitutional, Islamic republic wherein sovereignty, which originally belongs to Allah alone, is delegated to the people of Pakistan through their elected representatives under the parliamentary form of government (Preamble of the 1973 Constitution of Pakistan). Since Pakistan's independence in 1947, there have been numerous demands for transforming the colonial police (and the criminal justice system) into institutions capable of policing democratic societies. However, due to the repeated and periodic impositions of martial laws in Pakistan, the democratic process remained handicapped, disallowing state institutions to reform themselves to become more democratic (McGrath, 1997). As a result, reforms and reorganisations in all public sectors, including criminal justice and the police, have remained unsuccessful. Wiatrowski and Pino (2016) underscore the need to adopt democratic policing in their peculiar authoritarian environments wherein justice, equity, human rights, openness, change, innovation, and accountability skip the eye of the critic. Bayley (2005) also advises that the police must respect human rights, especially those related to political activity and expression and civil liberties, which are the hallmarks of democracy. Therefore, this discourse calls for institutionalising democratic ideals within the criminal justice system in Pakistan to reorient the police to serve the public, not state authorities. Community relations are essential in this connection, and a separate chapter deals with this theme in detail.

Furthermore, institutional innovations and technological advancements are well-recognised goals for reforming policing organisations worldwide to make them more effective, transparent, and accountable (Ferguson 2017). In Pakistan, police are still fully adopting the technology necessary for effective policing in the age of social media and encrypted communications. Without data, it is difficult to analyse and predict the possible occurrence of crime or terrorist incidents. The mapping of such associational interaction and networking data further guides police to comprehend crime patterns and trends. Therefore, the appropriate use of technology in policing is one of the most significant challenges in Pakistan today. Any reform can hardly earn good results unless it focuses on adopting technology in Pakistan. This book contains two separate and elaborate chapters on the themes of innovation and technology.

1.7. The Structure of the Book

The author bifurcates the book into four parts and twelve chapters. This introductory chapter deals with the overall picture of the entire scheme of the book project, an explanation of police and policing the relevant literature on defining postmodern policing, and the state of policing in the Pakistani context. Chapter Two sketches the landscape of police organisations in Pakistan from the perspective of this study. Finally, Chapter Three discusses the theoretical perspectives of postmodern policing.

In Part Two, this book addresses developments in the public policing sector in Pakistan. Chapter four focuses on the history of police reforms, while Chapter Five deals with the implementation of reforms and the reorganisation of the police under Police Order 2002. Finally, Chapter six critically analyses policing innovations in five key areas: governance, forensics, urban security, community policing, and gender demographics within the Pakistani police.

The third part sheds light on the challenges and opportunities to policing in Pakistan under three chapters. Chapter seven discusses policing and counterterrorism, Chapter eight on police-community relations, and Chapter nine on police governance. Part three is important because it justifies our hypothesis of transforming policing in Pakistan in the light of developments such as terrorism, community policing and democratic accountability of the police.

Finally, part four sums up the way forward in three chapters on reimagining policing as a way forward. Chapter ten makes the adoption of strategic policing in Pakistan. Chapter 11 draws on reimaging areas and offers recommendations to reform the police. Finally, chapter 12 concludes that although policing transformation, as advised in Chapter 11, seems to be an arduous task owing to problems and challenges in its way, it is a doable project.

1.8. Conclusion

Drawing on theory, law, jurisprudence, scholarship, and participant observation by the author, this discourse makes a case for Pakistan's postmodern strategic policing model. Strategic policing allows margins to adopt diversified strategies and space to accommodate various strategic measures in different contexts as per requirements conditioned by cultural, social, economic, political, and civil factors from a given perspective. Pakistan has unique political, social, and cultural conditions. Therefore, the strategic policing approach, being diversified, dynamic, holistic, and adoptive, can arguably sit well in this book's core narrative of transforming the police and policing in Pakistan.

By J.J. Baloch (2022)

Chapter: 02

Policing Landscape

Chapter Brief

This chapter describes the fundamental architecture of police formations in Pakistan at both the federal and provincial levels. Contextualising the case study perspective of the Pakistan Police, this chapter unfolds weak institutional links, a lack of coherent police practices, and conflicts in the cultural environment of working among different law enforcement and police organisations in Pakistan. Ineffective institutional networking among police organisations emphasises the need to realign policing goals through reform and innovation. Pakistan's law enforcement landscape suggests that Pakistan has an integrated model, neither centralised nor decentralised. It concludes that Pakistan's policing landscape remains colonial in all respects due to the marginal implementation of reform and innovation and calls for review and revision. The primary sources are constitutive documents and legislation on police and policing in Pakistan.

2.1. Pakistan's Policing Landscape

The institutional framework of policing in Pakistan is two-layered at the federal and provincial levels. There are federal forces and agencies for law enforcement, and there are provincial police departments in every Province, including Azad Kashmir and Gilgit-Baltistan. The Police Service of Pakistan offers a permanent and consistent institutional link between the provincial and federal law enforcement organisations and among the federal law enforcement departments and within the provincial forces. PSP officers fill the common leadership positions and roles for almost all civilian law enforcement agencies, including Intelligence Bureau-IB and the Federal Investigation Agency-FIA.

However, the jurisdictions and administrative affairs of the police in Pakistan, under both Police Act 1861 and Police Order 2002, as well as refined and perverted versions in practice in different provinces, are organised at the provincial level. "Police in Pakistan is organised at the provincial level, and there are seven Police forces in the country totalling approximately 450,000 personnel (giving an average of one Police Officer for 450 persons). The largest police force is in the Province of Punjab (over 177,000), and the smallest is Gilgit Baltistan 5000" (Parvez, 2015). Abbas (2011) maintains that provincial police departments fall into the second category of the law enforcement landscape, including Punjab, Sindh, Khyber Pakhtunkhwa (KP), Balochistan, Gilgit-Baltistan (GB), and Azad Kashmir (AK).

Abbass (2011) further elaborates law enforcement organisations on the federal level as:

"There are two sets of law enforcement organisations in Pakistan: those that operate under the federal government and the provincial police organisations. Nineteen major organisations operate directly under the federal government, dealing with various law enforcement responsibilities (including intelligence gathering, border and coast surveillance, and policing) and answering different authorities. The total strength of all law enforcement and intelligence service officials at the federal government's disposal (with cross-provincial jurisdiction) is approximately 210,000. Rarely do these organisations coordinate their plans, activities, and strategies together. The organisations' chain of command varies, complicating coordination and collaborative policy planning. As a result, decisions are often poorly implemented."

Abbass (2011) classifies 18 Federal Law enforcement organisations into four broad categories: 1. Forces under the Ministry of Interior, two police planning and management organisations under the Ministry of Interior, three other federal organisations, and four Intelligence Organisations.

However, I can group law enforcement apparatus into federal, provincial, police, and non-police organisations for simplification. For example, the Police Service of Pakistan commanded all provincial forces, while at the federal level, PSP shares command and control with serving officers of the armed forces and, in a few cases, by the officers of the Pakistan Administrative Service. The list of federal law enforcement formations, which PSP officers head, includes Islamabad Capital Territory Police, Federal Investigation Agency, Frontier Constabulary, Intelligence Bureau, National Police Bureau, National Police Management Board, National Police Foundation, National Highways and Motorways Police (Under Ministry of Communications), and Pakistan Railway Police (Under Ministry of Railways).

Civilian law enforcement agencies, which operate under the direct and exclusive command of armed forces, include Pakistan rangers (the Indian Police Service- IPS in India heads border security force as Inspectors General). However, coast guards, maritime security agencies under the command of Pakistani naval officers, and airport security force (under the Ministry of Defence) in Pakistan. In India, the same arrangements are under the control of the interior ministry through the IPS. Similarly, the anti-narcotics control force (under the Ministry of Narcotics Control) and Inter-Services Intelligence-ISI are led by a serving lieutenant general with federal, provincial, regional, and international offices in Pakistan. While in India, Raw operates under the IPS command.

2.2. The Federal Law Enforcement

Before detailing each federal law enforcement department, it is necessary to comprehend the Police Service of Pakistan.

2.2.1 Police Service of Pakistan (PSP)

The Police Service of Pakistan (PSP) is all Pakistan Service and a body of more than 801 (2017) police officers from Assistant Superintendent of Police-ASP to the Inspector General of Police- IGP. In consultation with the provinces, the government of Pakistan constituted the PSP as a service common to the Federation and the Provinces in 1950. Presently, the PSP comprises cadres on a provincial and federal basis. The government of Pakistan, Ministry of Interior Home Division vide letter No.10/1/50-Police dated 11.3.1950, established the Police Service of Pakistan.

Police Service of Pakistan, comprising police officers in BS-17 (ASP) to BS-22 (IGP), is an all-Pakistan service. Accordingly, the Provincial Police Officers, on reaching BPS-18, enter the All-Pakistan Services and are to be governed under the Civil Servants Act of 1973 and the Police Service of Pakistan Composition, Cadre and Seniority Rules, 1985. The Police Service of Pakistan (PSP) derives its origin from Article 240 of the Constitution of Pakistan[1]. It is an all-Pakistan service, which is common to the Federation and the Provinces. The Act of the Parliament called the Civil Servants Act of 1973 regulates the service conditions of all Pakistan services. In exercise of the powers conferred by Section 25 of the Civil Servants Act, 1973, Police Service of Pakistan (Composition, Cadre & Seniority) Rules, 1985 have been framed' (Writ Petition No.3151-P/2014).

The essential features of the service are as follows. First, the name of the service is the police service of Pakistan (PSP). Second, the central government will recruit services through the Federal Public Service Commission on all Pakistani bases. Third, the service cadres will be on a regional basis, as in pre-partition India, and an officer once allotted to a province will be required to serve in that Province for the whole period of his service. Fourth, twenty-five per cent of the excellent posts of the service, called the listed posts, will be reserved for provincial police officers, who, on confirmation of their promotion in grade 18, will be inducted to the Police Service of Pakistan (PSP). Finally, the service members shall retain the same seniority as shown in the gradation list maintained by the establishment division, cabinet secretariat, and government of Pakistan.

---

[1] Article 240 of the Constitution of Pakistan 1973 specifies the conditions of the all-Pakistan services which it defines as "common to both federation and provinces. It also details the appointments of the chairman and members of public service commissions at federal and provincial levels. President of Pakistan appoints chairman of FPSC on advice of Prime Minister while governor in the provinces appoint Provincial public service commissions on the advice of their respective chief ministers. However, this article authorises Pakistan's Parliament and provincial legislative assemblies to have final say in matters of rulemaking about all-Pakistan and all-provincial services as the case may be.

The development of the Police Service of Pakistan over the last six and half decades reveals that it is an all-Pakistan service and invites the encadrement of provincial police officers. It is striking to note is that the rules of 1969, repealed by Rules of 1985, were provided with a constitutional cover under Article 241[2] of the Constitution of 1973 by expressly protecting and preserving all 'Rules and Orders', which were enforced immediately before April 12, 1973 (Writ Petition No.3151-P/2014).

The Police Service of Pakistan is a lead service pool for providing leadership for almost all civilian law enforcement agencies, both uniform and non-uniform. PSP officers are sent to provincial police departments or federal law enforcement agencies such as the Intelligence Bureau (IB), Federal Investigation Agency (FIA), National Police Foundation (NPF), Frontier Constabulary (FC), National Counterterrorism Authority (NACTA), National Police Academy (NPA), National Police Bureau (NPB), National Highways and Motorways Police (NH&MP), and many other departments such as Secretariat and anti-narcotics forces (ANF).

The PSP officers are selected through a combined competitive examination conducted every year by the Federal Public Service Commission (FPSC) for the Central Superior Services of Pakistan-CSSP. The Police Service of Pakistan is one of Pakistan's top three executive services, and only those who top the CSS exam are considered eligible for appointment to police service. A 10% quota is reserved for the induction of officers from the armed forces of Pakistan in three services: Pakistan Administrative Service (PAS), Police Service of Pakistan (PSP), and Foreign Service of Pakistan (FSP). Officers from armed forces do not opt for eight other service groups such as Pakistan customs, Inland Revenue service, Audit and Accounts, Pakistan Railways, Information group, Pakistan Postal Services, Military land and Cantonment, and Pakistan Secretariat Group. GHQ nominates three officers against one seat for being considered in an interview by FPSC, which conducts only a psychological test and interview of nominee officers who do not appear in written exams for the CSS.

2.2.2. National Police Academy (NPA)

The National Police Academy is the premier federal law enforcement training institute primarily tasked with carrying out the 72 weeks long initial command course (ICC) or specialised training programme (STP) for the officers of the Police Service of Pakistan each year. The academy is located in the H/11 sector of Islamabad. In Pakistan's independence, the Police Service of Pakistan was born

---

[2] Until federal parliament in case of federal services and provincial government in case of provincial services amend or replace under article 240 the existing service rules will continue in force under article 241 of the constitution of Pakistan 1973.

from the Indian Police service after partition; police officers, that is, ASPs, were to be trained initially at Police College Sardah. Sardah is a policy training facility located in Bangladesh, followed by East Pakistan. The Sardah police institution was established in 1913. After the breakup of East Pakistan and the creation of Bangladesh in 1971, temporary arrangements to train PSP officers were made at the Sihala Police Training College located near Rawalpindi District of Punjab. This institution belongs to the Punjab police (NPA official website).

The NPA came into existence in 1978. Its headquarters is located in Islamabad and a training facility at Soawn Camp in Pindi, 31 km away from the commandants' office at Islamabad. The officers mess at Soawn with a stationed Course Commander was an insignificant and insufficient place to impart police training befittingly. As a result, the course commander had to rely on all practical training purposes at Sihala College, the nearest training facility. The National Police Academy always remained hand-to-mouth in terms of having sufficient training resources, including facilities, funds, and human resources, until they built a state-of-the-art facility at the H/11 sector in Islamabad. Although the building is pompous, the training suffers from resource constraints even after 18 years of establishment. Ours was the first batch (28the Common) at a new facility to join in 2001. After 16 years, I joined as a Course Commander to train the batches of 44th and 43rd Commons-PSPs (NPA official website).

New policing strategies for using technology in policing and policing terrorism and democratic societies formed the underlying themes of new training materials that we introduced in ICC training schedules. For the first time, the academy ran the introductory course of six months for the newly appointed assistant directors of FIA, whom I trained as a course commander. The introduction of this training made NPA come out of PSP exclusivity and expand its training base by offering other law enforcement agencies as an opportunity to avail the best environment for grooming officers.

2.2.3 Islamabad Capital Territory Police (ICTP)

Initially established in 1981 under Presidential Orders No. 17 and 18 with 3,484 personnel, the Islamabad Capital Territory Police has grown to 10,333 and is tasked with policing the capital of Pakistan. Although the Police Order, 2002, has not come into force in Islamabad, it is still considered one of the leading police forces in the country. With the best salary packages among all police forces and policy to reduce police torture cases, the Islamabad Police claims that no petition for habeas corpus was filed in 2009. Since the local government laws do not apply to Islamabad, the Police Act, 1861 remains the policing law for Islamabad. Consequently, Islamabad Police, theoretically, works under the general control of the district magistrate; however, for practical reasons, it works under the direct supervision of the Ministry of Interior. It is noteworthy that the Islamabad Police was the first police force to introduce human rights officers' positions to reduce the number of public complaints due to police excesses (IP official website).

2.2.4. Federal Investigation Agency (FIA)
Federal Investigation Agency-FIA is a premier Federal law enforcement agency of Pakistan. It is equivalent to the Federal Bureau of Investigation-FBI in the USA, National Crime Agency of the UK and Central Bureau of Investigation-CBI in India, to name a few. FIA is the successor of the pre-independence Special Police Establishment-SPE established in 1941. At present, it is the lead agency to investigate a range of transnational organised crime, white-collar crime, cybercrime, immigration, Interpol liaison, and many other newer crimes such as terrorism (FIA official website).

Amid World War II, charges of debasement surfaced in the Supplies and Procurement Department of the Indian government. To handle these new issues relating to the graft and embezzlement of government money, the British government established an autonomous law enforcement organisation called the Special Police Establishment (SPE). After the birth of Pakistan, the SPE renamed the Pakistan Special Police Establishment-PSPE. This arrangement and nomenclature continued until 1974. The core responsibility of the agency was to examine graft cases against focal government representatives and officials, the offences charged under the Official Secrets Act of 1923, the Foreign Exchange Regulations Act of 1947, the Passport (Offences) Act of 1952, and the Customs Act of 1958 (Ahmad 2012 pp. 99-103).

The Federal Investigation Agency (FIA) continues to investigate offences committed in connection with matters that concern the federal government, have an interprovincial scope, or involve transnational organised crime. The FIA is a national police entity and statutory body with a total strength approaching 5,500 with a countrywide network. FIA is empowered to investigate and prosecute offences related to corruption in the federal department and organised crime, including terrorism, immigration, human trafficking, money laundering, cybercrimes, white-collar crimes, plastic money fraud, and intellectual property crimes (FIA official website).

Except under exceptional circumstances that do not exceed 12 months, the Director-General (DG) of the FIA has to be a PSP officer who has achieved the IGP rank. The superintendence of the FIA vests in the federal government and the administration of agency vests in the DG. Three additional directors assist the DG in overseeing functional wings. The FIA is headquartered in Islamabad, with five regional directorates in provincial capitals, Islamabad, and several sub-offices in each Province (FIA Act 1974).

In 2018, I worked on the FIA revamping project of our erstwhile director-general of FIA, Mr Bashir Ahmad Memon and his team. The FIA revamping plan sought to expand the organisation's operational network. The new proposed plan envisages the creation of new zones, new directorates, new posts for ADG South and ADG North. The concept emphasised adopting new law enforcement technology international cooperation in human smuggling, cybercrime, money laundering, and terrorism-related cases. Furthermore, the plan continues to reinvent the FIA academy as the centre of excellence for the capacity building of all FIA ranks in conducting complete and trickier investigations relating to money trails, cybercrime, and terrorism. In addition, the restructuring plan needs to establish intelligence and mutual legal assistance directorates for appropriate and befitting financial investigations and international cooperation on criminal matters.

2.2.5. Intelligence Bureau (IB)

The Intelligence Bureau (IB) is a civilian intelligence agency assigned to counterintelligence for internal security. The IB functions under a federal notification, not an act, and operates under the Cabinet Division. Consequently, Pakistan's Prime Minister of Pakistan. A Director-General, a senior officer of the PSP cadre, heads it. However, sometimes army officers have also been appointed to the DG. In recent decades, the IB has played a laudable role in assisting police in fighting terrorism and extremism in Pakistan. Mr Aftab Sultan, PSP, had innovated and equipped the organisation very well during his tenure for about three years (IB Website).

After gathering, the IB disseminate intelligence to law enforcement agencies across the country through the Ministry of Interior. In addition, the Intelligence Bureau keeps an eye on the political activity, community business, and management practices of government servants through intensive surveillance. The IB also manages government censorship programs that monitor foreign and domestic mail. Although the IB has no formal arrest powers, suspects are arrested and detained by law enforcement agencies if the IB makes a request or provides the necessary information.

2.2.6. National Highways and Motorways Police (NH&MP)

Introduced on the eve of the 20th century and the brainchild of PSP legend Iftikhar Rasheed, the National Highways and Motorways Police (NHMP) performs police and traffic control functions on national highways. NHMP functions under the Ministry of Communications. Section 90(2) of the National Highways Safety Ordinance, 2000 mandates the NHMP to maintain order, regulate and control traffic on national highways, maintain law and order, and take cognisance of offences on national highways. This section further provides all possible assistance to national highway commuters, undertaking initial investigations concerning crimes committed on national roads and then transferring the cases to the concerned police station for questioning (Rasheed 2017).

The general public perception is that NHMP is Pakistan's most highly regarded police organisation. In a recent survey conducted by Gallup, 82 per cent of the respondents perceived the NHMP to be less corrupt than other police departments in Pakistan, and 84 per cent recommended that other police forces in Pakistan follow the NHMP model. In a comparison between the NHMP and district police, NHMP officers are better paid better trained, and their morale is higher and is insulated from undue bureaucratic and political pressures. Such pressures lead the force to stop anyone from disobeying motorway rules (including ministers). In addition, the magistrates on site have given them operational autonomy, which saves them from any type of victimisation.

Road safety, which is an alien concept to many of us in Pakistan, is a grave socio-economic problem; hence, it constitutes the core of the culture of motorway police. As a nation lives in a state of denial, but as a matter of record, road safety has emerged as a chronic social problem that severely affects both public health and the national economy. In Pakistan, more than 13000 innocent road users are killed every year, and more than 50000 get injured. The estimated cost of all this unnecessary loss and burden on the national exchequer is more than US$ 5.00 billion every year. It is interesting to note that our Legislature's response and stance towards traffic-related problems is quite forward-looking, but still, a lot is required to be accomplished. Estimates and surveys have revealed that the incidence of people losing lives in road accidents every year in Pakistan is far higher than that of people killed due to natural disasters, terrorists, or other criminal activities (NH&MP official website).

2.2.7. Frontier Constabulary (FC)
The North-West Frontier Constabulary Act, 1915, created "Frontier Constabulary" as an independent force. The force derives its primary law enforcement and policing functions from the Act of 1915 and the Frontier Constabulary Rules of 1958 to enforce the writ of the government of Pakistan primarily in Federally Administered Tribal Areas-FATA, where the jurisdiction of the Khyber Pakhtunkhwa Police does not extend.

The Frontier Constabulary operates as a federal armed police force. Although these frontier regions are a part of Khyber Pakhtunkhwa, the Frontier Constabulary is mandated to work with the consent of the Province. Initially, the Frontier Constabulary served as a line of defence to prevent the incursions and attacks of tribal areas in the settled areas. However, FC now focuses on internal security in Pakistan and protecting vital installations within and outside of Khyber Pakhtunkhwa. FC department's recently announced factsheet reveals that the Frontier Constabulary has about 550 platoons, each having different strengths of 40 to 50 men. Exclusively drawn from the tribes of the Province of Khyber Pakhtunkhwa and the adjacent tribal areas, the Frontier Constabulary is a federal civil armed force with a total strength of more than 25,000 officials.

The functions of Frontier Constabulary include

i. guarding FATA and the frontier regions (areas between the tribal areas and the so-called settled areas/districts of Khyber Pakhtunkhwa);

ii. to stop unlawful activities, including kidnapping and checking tribal disputes on administrative borders between settled and tribal areas.

iii. To act as the second line of defence in an emergency or war.

iv. To assist the local administration in times of need for internal security,

v. to control and eliminate poppy cultivation and growth, check the traffic of narcotics, illegal weapons, and smuggling, and perform any other duties assigned by the federal government (FC Act 1915).

2.2.8. Pakistan Railways Police (PRP)

Controlling crime on railways is the responsibility of the Pakistan Railways Police (PRP). The PRP was reorganised under the Pakistan Railways Police Act, 1977, to provide security to "passengers and goods transported by Pakistan Railways, the protection of Railway property, the prevention, inquiry and investigation of offences committed concerning Pakistan Railways" (PRP ACT 1977). Officers in the IGP rank-supervise PRP. Recently, the jurisdiction of PRP has also been extended to residential colonies (PRP official website).

2.2.9. National Police Bureau (NBP)

The National Police Bureau (NPB) is a statutory body established under Article 162 of the Police Order, 2002, and it is mandated to coordinate and monitor police organisations across Pakistan. A Director-General heads it, not below the rank of the Additional Inspector General of Police, and functions as the permanent Secretariat for the National Public Safety Commission (NPSC) and the National Police Management Board (NPMB). In addition, the NPB performs research and development functions assigned to it by the NPSC and NPMB (PO 2002).

2.2.10. National Public Safety Commission (NPSC)

Article 85 of the Police Order 2002 created the National Public Safety Commission (NPSC), with its permanent Secretariat at the National Police Bureau in Islamabad. Out of the 12 members, six were selected by the Speaker of the National Assembly in consultation with the leader of the house and the leader of the opposition (three each from the treasury and the opposition). The remaining six members are selected by a panel comprising a judge of the Supreme Court (who serves as Chair) and one nominee, each of the President and the Prime Minister (who serve as Members). The functions of the NPSC include

i.   to recommend panels of three police officers to the federal government so that it may choose the heads of the FIA, the NHMP, and the Pakistan Railways Police; and

ii. to oversee the implementation of plans prepared by the head of every Federal Law Enforcement Agency and require every Federal Law Enforcement Agency to submit reports in a prescribed manner.

2.2.11. National Police Management Board (NPMB)

Under Article 158, the Police Order 2002 established the National Police Management Board (NPMB), a body of senior police officials across Pakistan, including the IGP of every provincial police establishment and the DGs of the FIA ANFand NPB. The NPMB's functions include the following:

i.   To advise governments at different levels on general planning and development of policing, which encompasses education, training, recruitment, appointment, promotions, transfers, tenure, and discipline.

ii. To identify and arrange research in criminology, inter-provincial crime, and crime with international dimensions.

iii. to recommend steps to secure intergovernmental and inter-agency assistance to ensure comprehensive and cohesive crime control and internal security arrangements. And

iv. to advise the government on the performance of the National Public Safety Commission and federal law enforcement agencies.

2.2.12. National Counter Terrorism Authority (NACTA)

After obtaining final permission from the president of Pakistan, the parliament of Pakistan published Act No. XIX of 2013, dated March 22, 2013. As a result, the NACTA Act (2013) established the Counter-

Terrorism Authority of Pakistan to coordinate and unify state response to terrorism. As per the mandate, the NACTA got engaged in planning, strategising, combining, and implementing government policies to eliminate the threat of terrorism and extremism, which had become an existential threat to the country.

Section 3, subsection 2 states that "authority will be an independent body answerable directly to Prime Minister" (NACTA Act No. XIX of 2013), and it shall be headquartered in Islamabad. The primary functions as laid down in the NACTA Act include formulating periodical threat assessment by collecting data, information, and intelligence and coordinating among different stakeholders. Section 4 states that NACTA prepares comprehensive and holistic counterterrorism and counter-extremism strategies from time to time. Second, NACTA will research the subject of terrorism and circulate it among all relevant departments. Third, this national body of CT shall liaison with international organisations to facilitate international cooperation, involve counterterrorism experts to make new policies in the mandated job of the authority, and review relevant counterterrorism laws in the country. Finally, the NACTA shall also suggest amendments to them from time to time when necessary (NACTA official website).

Theoretically speaking, NACTA is the central institution in Pakistan to address the strategic and networked policing model this book reimagines as the most viable and effective recipe for responding to new crimes and violence challenges. However, promises on the paper failed to materialise due to internal institutional turf wars, civil-military trust deficit, and blatant disinterest or indifference in political leadership. As a result, the prime minister held not more than a single meeting until now, while eight years have passed since the Act XIX (2013), which created NACTA.

The Army Public School attack in Peshawar in December 2014 led to forming a National Action Plan. All stakeholders envisaged NAP collectively to unify and coordinate counterterrorism efforts of civil and military agencies (Parvez 2015. As a result, the parliament passed the 21st constitutional amendment to enact the National Action Plan. Among so many proper steps, as it suggested, the revival of NACTA was one of the core components of the NAP (The 21st Constitutional Amendment 2014). But unfortunately, the continuous neglect of NACTA has resulted in its institutional dormancy.

2.3. Provincial Police Departments

2.3.1. Punjab Police (PP)

Punjab Police is the largest police department in Pakistan, with a total number of officials around 180,000; correspondingly, their budgetary resources are higher than other police departments. Punjab is also the largest Province of Pakistan, inhabiting 81.8 million, nearly half of Pakistan's total population. The Punjab Police is known for its distinctive police culture, dominated by bureaucratic traditions of the colonial era. However, after Police Order 2002, Punjab Police witnessed many changes in response to new challenges of human rights crimes such as domestic violence and child abuse. Subsequently, they dealt with the waves of sectarianism and terrorism in the province (PP official website).

Policing in Punjab has origins in the "Zamindari System" of Moghul rulers in India. In rural areas, Zamindars had been tasked with maintaining law and order and preventing crime in their lands, fiefs, and the populations living within their areas of influence and holdings. In the villages, village headmen and community notables called Patels assisted zamindars within their landholdings. However, Kotwals carried out policing functions and their local and revenue collection duties (PP official website).

The British rulers replaced Zamindars with their magistrates in Punjab. Initially, there were two types of police: military police and civil detective police. Military police were responsible for dealing with heinous crimes. At the same time, polite detectives dealt with ordinary crimes. Both wings combined to represent the early formation of the Punjab police under British rulers. In 1860, the Police Commission recommended the divorce of military arms of the police from regular civil police and to place police departments under the supervision of the Inspector General of Police at the provincial level and the Superintendent of Police at the district level. However, the Home Secretary and District Magistrates monitored IG at the provincial level and SP at the district level, respectively (PP official website).

The Police Act of 1861 created the Punjab Police, which Pakistan inherited at independence. The detailed Punjab Police Rules 1934 followed the police Act 1861. Police Rule 1934 set the organisational and operational effectiveness of policing in Punjab in Pakistan, as other police departments followed undivided and divided India. Be-that-as-it-may, Police Order 2002 was the first significant reform attempt in the Punjab police after Pakistan's independence in 1947. PO 2002 brought some fundamental and drastic changes by removing the magistrate's control of police and declaring IGP as PPO being the status of ex-officio secretary. PO 2002 also envisaged democratic oversight of police in public safety commissions at district province and federal levels, vesting monitoring of district police with District Nazims. But unfortunately, public safety missions could see the light of the day in Punjab due to bureaucratic and political opposition and resistance (PP official website).

The Punjab police have made many innovations in policing. For example, the adoption of technology and creation of Safe city projects, dolphin force, new colour of uniform (olive green) and much more, yet it is legally still in limbo because of the lack of proper implementation of reforms.

2.3.2. Sindh Police (SP)

Among all provincial forces, Sindh police are the oldest and the second-largest police organisation after Punjab in Pakistan. Karachi, the metropolis of Pakistan and one of the largest cities in the world, is the headquarters of Sindh Police. Karachi hosts approximately 20 million people at the dawn of 2018. Sindh is the most urbanised Province bearing the burden of all internal and external migrations since the inception of Pakistan as an independent country. Sindh police have grown through the rough and tumbles of turbulent times of crisis, conflict, violence, vandalism and terrorism (Mirza 2018).

The Province of Sindh is the wealthiest Province of Pakistan and contributes more than 70% of tax revenues to the country's exchequer; therefore, Peace in Sindh has been the policy priority of every government. Area wise, Sindh is 140,914 Sq Km with roughly 50 million people. The total police force in Sindh is estimated to be 110 400 as per the latest disclosures by the Central Police Office of Sindh Karachi. In my police career of 18 years, I have served more than 12 years in Sindh. For about nine years, I was ASP and then served as an SP investigation, AIG Forensics Sindh, and District Police Officer in 11 districts. Comparatively, I found the Sindh police as the braver force with a strong sense of teamwork propagated in a pleasant environment where the commanders respect each force member. In turn, the constabulary respects police leaders. Moreover, most commands follow therapeutic strategies to build their capacity instead of retributive techniques (SP official website).

Due to urbanised environments, it is the culture of the Sindh police to follow persuasive methodologies, instead of coercive techniques, in establishing order and peace in the province. As a result, the Sindh police have more martyrs than any other police force in Pakistan and almost equal numbers to the martyrs of our armed forces. Sindh Police have been fighting urbanised terrorism, violence, target killings, and unusual mob situations. Sindh has remained a hotbed of political and criminal activities during the 1980s to restore democracy-MRD, 1990s ethnic violence in cities, kidnapping for ransom, tribal conflicts, dacoit culture, and honour killings in interior Sindh. Thus, the Sindh Police has more experience conducting operations of a different nature than any other police department in Pakistan (SP official website).

Sir Charles Napier established the Sindh Police on the Royal Irish Constabulary model through a proclamation after he had conquered Sindh, defeating the Talpur rulers of Sindh in the battle of Miyani in 1843. Napier's police were more disciplined, efficient, and less corrupt because of strict monitoring and hierarchical control. Many other departments in Pakistan, including the Punjab police, imported Napier's Sindh model while raising their police. In 1860, the British government established H. M. Court Commission to bring police forces of the sub-continent on Napier's police model of Sindh, which had earned the reputation of being the most disciplined force under British India. Though civilian forces carrying out civilian policing duties had maintained a discipline similar to military forces, the Court's commission came up with proposals, with few amendments, such as the Police Act 1861 (Constantine 1961).

Crime fiction in Pakistan represents stories of good and bad police officers of Sindh Police. Many TV serials, movies, and novels represent the soul of Sindh police culture. My Debut novel "Whiter than White" (2017) talks about the 'victimisation of women and culturally sanctioned gender violence' (Baloch 201). While the plot of Omar's first novel, "The Prisoner", revolves around the role of police officers who dive deep into the urban culture of politically-cloned crimes and violence (Hamid 2013).

Indeed, saddening that the Sindh police revoked the Police Order 2002 and reverted to the colonial Police Act of 1861. Now functions with all colonial burdens of history on their shoulders, Sindh police's motto; therefore, reads: "Striving to Serve" (SP official website).

2.3.3. Khyber-Pakhtunkhwa Police (KPKP)

Placed at historical and civilisational crossroads, the North Western Province, now known as Khyber-Pakhtunkhwa or KP, has served as a battlefield between many warriors. The people of KP have shown resistance to foreign occupants, including Greeks, Mongols, Afghans, Ghaznavids, Ghauri's, Timurids, Sikhs, Moghuls British, Russian, and American. Therefore, war and weaponry are in the blood of Pakhtoons. British rulers declared NWFP as the Province in 1901 AD and introduced police under the 1861 Police Act model of Irish Constabulary, annexing NWFP to their empire in 1849 AD. Between 1849 and 1901, the British maintained the old policing system of Sikhs and Mughals in the KP.

However, the Police Act of 1861 was extended to frontier territory in 1889. As a result, some armed personnel were placed at the disposal of the district magistrate for police duties. At the same time, the provincial government in KP raised the Frontier Force to maintain permanent and durable peace in the area (KPP official website).

The Governor-General of India posted the Chief Commissioner and his agent in the N-WFP in 1901 when it was declared Province. Two sets of administrations were introduced in the province: settled districts and political agencies. Policing in settled communities, including Hazara, Peshawar, Kohat, Bannu, and Dera Ismail Khan, was a regular Irish Constabulary Model, as it was in other provinces under the Police Act 1861. Similarly, policing in political agencies including Khyber, Mohmand, Kurrum, North Waziristan, and South Waziristan was entirely different from the rest. In political agencies, tribal forces in the shape of Levies called Samana Rifles, Chitral Scouts, Khurram Militia, and Border Military police were to carry out essential policing duties under the command and control of a political agent who happened to be a bureaucrat. Indigenous Maliki and Khasadari systems were in place. In contrast, the Settled Districts were under the Inspector General of Police (IGP) of the N-WFP. Criminal courts were established under the Code of Criminal Procedure in 1889 (KP Government Website).

Like all other police forces in Pakistan, KP police remained deprived of police reform and innovation until 2002. However, PO 2002 revolutionised KP police to a great extent. As a result, the process of making KP Police a democratic, people-friendly, and responsive force began. However, many police and policing changed when Imran Khan's Pakistan Tehrik-e-Insaaf won the 2013 elections in the KP and made their provincial government. The PTI government of KP made paradigmatic changes through revolutionary legislative steps such as the KP Police Act 2017 for building the capacity of KP police through an autonomous institutional network. KP government also focused on additional innovative changes for making the KP police Pakistan's best police organisation in all respects (KPP official website).

2.3.4. Balochistan Police (BP)

Balochistan is the most extended Province in terms of geographical area and borders with Iran, Afghanistan, KP, Punjab, and Sindh and has the most extensive seashore of the Arabian Sea in Pakistan. Balochistan is a nearer Middle Eastern through the Gwadar seaport, another geo-strategically high point, as China is building it under the China Pakistan Economic Corridor (CPEC). This area of Pakistan has become a hotbed of proxy wars between global powers such as the USA, China,

India, and Pakistan. Like the KP, the global war on terror has severely affected this part of Pakistan because it was the transit area of both terrorists and the international forces led by the USA and NATO. Balochistan has provided narcotics, weapons, oil, counterfeit items, and human smuggling routes to criminal syndicates and terrorists in the post-Afghan war period that culminated after 9/11 (Ahmad 2012).

Policing in Balochistan has traditionally been very weak. The province stands administratively divided into areas A (police area) and B (levies area). The regular policing system, created under the 1861 police rule, functions in the regions that constitute not more than 25% of the total area of the province, while the rest of 75% of the Balochistan Levies and Frontiers Corps carry out policing functions. Levies operate in B areas under district administration on the pattern of political agencies of the KP. At the same time, Frontier Corps works under the command of the Pakistan military in both A and B areas. Police in Balochistan has many handicaps, as they cannot carry out the functions of arresting criminals who hide in B areas (BP official website).

General Parvez Musharraf declared Balochistan Province a police area (A-area). However, the PPP government led by Raisani in 2008 undid all the reforms. It reverted the province to the 1861 Police Act that separated B areas from A areas again and handed it to the district administration. This reversion gravely affected the overall efficacy of policing. As a result, Quetta witnessed many terrorist attacks on the Hazara community, law enforcement and security agencies, Chinese workers, lawyers, and innocent citizens in many parts of Balochistan. The deadliest was the Mastung suicide attack of July 2018, killing 149 innocent people, including Balochistan Awami Party-BAP leader Nawabzada Siraj Raisani. Analysts consider this event the third deadliest attack after the Karsaaz Karachi attack on the PPP rally in 2007 and the Army Public School Attack of 2014. In the present scenario, the Balochistan Police needs reforms of the type operative for the KP police, and terrorism is a severe threat that the levies cannot handle. Even in normal circumstances, the Levies are not effective as a force, let alone the spree of violence that grips the province (BP official website).

2.3.5. Gilgit-Baltistan Police (GBP)
GB is located on the northwest top of Pakistan, hosting Asia's most extensive mountain ranges, including the Himalayas, Hindukush, and famous peaks like K2 and Nanga Parbat. GB is one of the world's tourist attractions and beautiful valleys. Once a part of the United Kashmir before Pakistan's birth, GB now has a separate administrative and political status similar to a province but not a full-fledged province due to the lack of a constitutional definition of a particular province. The GB is no

longer a part of Kashmir or India; it is now a part of Pakistan in all possible senses because the region is administered and protected by the Pakistan Army and federal bureaucracy. The GB is not an occupied region or a colony but an autonomous part voluntarily annexed to Pakistan. GB is more like a province, but since the status of Kashmir is yet to be decided and is still a permanent source of tension between India and Pakistan, the final status of the GB area and Azad Kashmir is linked with the final resolution of the Jammu and Kashmir issues (Aafani 2012).

Although crime rates have historically been the lowest in this region and community mechanisms are more robust, in recent decades, sectarian violence and terrorist incidents have raised their heads, which necessitated the formation of a proficient police force. At present, the total working strength of GB police is 6056 against 6354 personnel as against a total population of 1.8 million approximately. In addition, the GB police has ten districts, 28 sub-divisions, 66 police stations, and 14 posts, as per the data provided by the IGP GB office in June 2018. Police and media reports reveal that suicides are primarily prevalent in females in this part of Pakistan (GBP official website). Crimes against persons are higher or almost double than crimes against property. For example, the GB website recorded the common crime against the person from 2014 to 2017 as 440 cases each year. At the same time, the average crime against property was measured as 200 cases each year. However, as per the data available with the IGP GB office, the total offence increased from 1329 registered incidents in 2014 to 1733 recorded cases in 2017 (IGP-GB office records). However, this crime rate is lower than the yearly registered crime of one police station in Punjab and Sindh in many cases.

GB police are organised under the Police Act 1861, and PO 2002 was not extended to GB, Islamabad, and Azad Kashmir. GB adopted the police act 1861 on March 12, 1973. However, the Punjab Police Rules 1934 was extended to the GB on June 22, 1978. Administrative and policing arrangements were made separately for GB after the dissolution of one unit and after the promulgation of the 1973 Constitution of Pakistan. Like all other police departments in Pakistan, which were organised under the Irish Constabulary model of the 1861 Police Act, the head of the GB police is the Inspector General of Police, assisted by Deputy Inspectors General and Superintendents of Police the range and district levels, respectively. GB police badly needs reform and revamping in the wake of new security threats owing to the China Pakistan Economic Corridor-CPEC and hence the redefined geostrategic importance of the region in the 21st century (GBP official website).

2.3.6. Azad Jammu and Kashmir Police (AJKP)

The Azad Kashmir Police is well-reputed in Pakistan. Azad Kashmir is divided into ten districts, including Muzaffarabad as its capital and three divisions, Muzaffarabad, Poonch, and Mirpur. The total area stretches to 13,297 sq. Km. "The State of Azad Jammu and Kashmir is endowed with abundant natural resources and ample human resources dominated by talented and educated youth." The total population of the AJK area is estimated to be 4,045,366. However, the real strength of the police force in Azad Kashmir is approximately 15000, with 46 police stations. The AJK police are organised under the 1861 Police Act and the 1934 Police Rules. Only the IGP comes from PSP, and the rest of the police officials belong to the AJK police (AJKP official website).

Constitutionally a disputed part, Azad Kashmir has its president, prime minister instead of governor, and chief minister, as in other provinces in Pakistan, including GB. The Azad Jammu and Kashmir Police claim to be professionally efficient, politically neutral, people-friendly, non-authoritarian, and democratically controlled. The AJK police have the reputation of playing a very constructive role in providing security to tourists and rescue services during 2005 and other natural disaster events and rehabilitation drives (AJKP official website).

2.4. Conclusion

In 1947, Pakistan inherited a police system that was more than 80 years old from the British under the organised 1861 Police Act. The priority of the colonial government was to use coercion to collect revenue and maintain stability. "Police was designed to be a coercive force, not a public-friendly agency. Service to people was not the objective of this study. "It was designed in response to the social and political realities of the times as seen through the lens of the British Raj" (Suddle 2015). These incompatible functions were vested in a European officer, variously called District Magistrate, exercising judicial authority and acting as a judge in most criminal cases. Britons designed the magistrate office designed by Britons to protect the interests of their middle class responsible for trade and running the administration and politics in the subcontinent. There was no separation of powers between the judiciary and executive, which was the opposite of how the British and the ancient Indian administrative and judicial traditions managed their forces. Although many Europeans criticised the administrative and policing dispensation created under the Police Act 1861 following the Irish model, it was considered inevitable and essential to keep colonies under control. Many critics, including Dr Suddle, believe that police in India was created on the Irish model established through the Constabulary Acts of 1822 and 1836 because, in Ireland, Britishers had a successful experience of curbing resistance of locals against their occupation employing coercive tactics.

Policing in Pakistan has a great diversity of police systems, but its potential has not yet been tapped. Some analysts think that policing diversity is a strength. At the same time, others argue that such diversity is nothing more than mere disunity, disconnectivity, and incoherence. However, in the postmodern era, diversity or diversification in the police stands for strength and energy. In this regard, people have high expectations from the police to make a difference in their lives, at least in Pakistan. There is a need to address the institutional disconnect among departments through procedural and legal standardisation to make our society safer and turn crime back. The continuity of the inherited policing system is shrouded by the doubts and mistrust of the communities. Only change and reform can guarantee continuity, which is why this discourse sets a conversation on why and how to transform policing in Pakistan.

Chapter-03

Theoretical Perspectives

Chapter Brief

This chapter engages with 21st-century research, theory, and ideas on police and policing (Webb, Katz and Flippin, 2020). This chapter opens with theoretical developments in policing, embarking upon the age of collaboration and integration into the healthy ecosystem of partnerships (Katz & Huff, 2020) among different stakeholders of policing, ranging from public and private spheres (Gravelle and Rogers 2014). It further reveals the reasons for the interest of academia and politicians in police research (Reiner, 1992). In addition, this chapter adds the fifth phase in research on policing (Reiner 2010), which signifies the 'postmodern condition' (Lyotard 1984). This section critically analyses three significant theories on policing: state-centric-pre-modern, modernisation-modern, and globalisation-postmodern, and highlights the importance and dynamics of postmodern perspectives in detail (Jones 2009). Finally, it makes a case for Pakistan to adopt a strategic policing model that aligns best with the postmodern age (Clark, 2005) and (Katz & Maguire 2020).

3.1. Introduction

What works well in the 21st Century policing runs at the heart of this conversation. Policing is a vital function of the state; it is existentially central to social order and public peace in any society. Yet, despite the uncertainties and difficulties in policing functioning, many millennials believe that the police are still a Roll-Royce service. Others consider policing a dirty job that involves more risks than offering benefits, except for the sole satisfaction of police officers as a crucial social service provider. In the context of changing dictates of the social structure, its value systems, its body of knowledge, its popular culture, its social order mechanics, and its legal dispensations, including sovereign power balances, policing needs massive readjustments in the postmodern age (Newburn 2001).

There are three significant philosophical streaks on policing: state-centric, modernisation, and globalisation. First, the state-centric model, also called the traditional paramilitary model, accepts the state as a monolithic power actor within society. It acknowledges the coercive authority of the police, with minimum or no limits (Jones 2009). This policing philosophy remains rooted in the unlimited sovereignty of the leviathan, which justifies its powers under the doctrine of the divine rights of kings. Second, the modernisation of the police developed in the enlightenment era of modernity (Reiner 1992). According to historians of policing, modernisation began with Robert Peel when he, as a home secretary of the UK, came up with his nine principles of modern policing and the London Metropolitan

46

Police Act of 1829. The modern police implied that the professional force organised and disciplined under the law to establish political order and social peace (Newburn 2015). Third, globalisation theory addresses the postmodern age that emerged after the end of modernity during the last quarter of the 20th Century (Jones 2009). This theory recommends policing by consent (Kunjappan, 2021), an inclusive approach involving many governmental and non-governmental partners, both at the national and international levels, which work in a network model (Perrott & Trites, 2017). This network model shares power with partners and opposes the erstwhile policing models that concentrate power in the state. Finally, the globalisation theory of policing envisages policing beyond the state of international and pluralistic frontiers (Lobnikar et al., 2021).

Scholars also refer to three models of police and policing networks. These frameworks include centralised, decentralised, and integrated models (Hunter, 1992). Centralised police order means that national police control entire law enforcement from the top to the local level of street policing. The centralised model operates in France. In contrast, American policing systems reflect a decentralised model where policing stands fragmented with disparate police departments. Such a system has been developed based on the belief that lesser authority means greater liberty, and greater liberty signifies democracy and human rights (Reiner 2010). However, others maintain that too much control and freedom fail to work either way. Both systems of police organisations contradict and collide. The only better way out seems to be adopting an integrated policing model. The integrated policing model exists in practice in the UK. Under this model, federal and local police departments integrate their operations and objectives for better service delivery and performance. Overall, the integrated model is the latest in the evolution chain of these models. This model integrates many good things and disparate policing systems into a cohesive policing network (Hunter 1992). It is closer to strategic and postmodern policing that involves partnerships (Jones & Newburn 2006).

3.2. The Evolution of Research on Policing

Research on policing has evolved over the centuries. Research on police to create a body of policing knowledge for developing it as a well-finished profession has always been emotive, sensitive, and engaging for various reasons (Gravelle & Rogers, ed.2014). According to Professor Robert Reiner (2010), four things evoked the interest of academics and non-academic research in the police. The first is the power or privilege that the police enjoy because of their position in the statutory network (ibid). The second important element is the 'political landscape' or the environment in which the police operate to make it a coveting area for investigation (Ibid). Third, the police deal with sensitive

47

and sentimental issues of public grievances and peace that put police officers at the centre of public attention. Finally, the police deal with crime, which has always been the most romantic theme for creative literature and fantasy storytellers (Reiner 2010). Michael Banton, an English sociologist, has been the initiator and founder of research on policing. In 1964 Banton wrote his book, "The Policeman in the Community" (Gravelle & Rogers, ed.2014) and began his series of research articles on 'the sociology of the police in the Police Journal in the 1970s, laying the foundation of controversies in the themes of policing.

Reiner (2010) maintains that research on policing has taken place in four phases and four significant subjects. These subjects of policing research include 'Sociology, Criminology, Psychology, and Law'; however, its stages, as elaborated by Reiner, are also four. (I) Consensus Phase-1960s focuses on success and importance of police in the society; (ii) Controversy Phase-1970s: criticising the police misuse of authority and malpractices including bribes; (iii) Conflict Phase-1980s: merging police and politics, which led to the emergence of critical and radical criminology under the shadow of Marxist or conflict perspective; and (iv) Contradiction Phase-1990s: emphasising on crime control and police effectiveness based on left realism (Ibid).

Gravelle and Rogers (2014) refer to Reiner (2010) for police researchers, which, according to them, include four. The first category of researchers is academic researchers who conduct police research in universities and colleges. The second group involves official police researchers who police and home department bodies of policy and strategy support. Such researcher's groups in Pakistan include NACTA, NPB, and IJCP. The third group is independent think-tank organisations that private and international donors fund for making societies safer. The journalists and media groups constitute the fourth group of researchers who conduct independent research investigations into police malpractice. The fifth group is police practitioners who pen down their experiences by blending them with existing theoretical literature, such as this book.

However, after 9/11, the fifth phase of collaborative research on policing began. The focus was on the collaboration between different stakeholders, both national and international, where practitioners and academics join hands to find the best practices of policing to stabilise societies. Partnerships have received the attention of researchers in this regard. In Pakistan, we divide police reform thinking into three phases: 1860 to 1960, second from 1960 to 2001, and third from 2001 to 2019. The 21st Century policing literature has witnessed drastic changes in the primary mission of the police, its strategies, its relations with the rest of the stakeholders, including the government they report, the community they serve, and the international community they seek collaboration in transnational crime (Bowling and Sheptycki 2010). In the 21st Century, research consortiums collaborated with their research activities and carried out their research inquiries in partnerships with local law enforcement departments (Jones & Newburn 2006). In addition, both practitioners and academicians work together with all other stakeholders, including journalists, NGOs, the judiciary, military, bureaucracy, international community, and other independent Info-Tech giants (Weisburd & Braga 2006).

3.3. Police and Policing Theories

The state-centric (pre-modern) theory of policing has its origin in withering away from pre-political informal social control systems. State-centric idea attained its final shape with the nation-state's emergence in Europe. Levi (2007) maintains that the states needed armed persons for internal security and external defence. Accordingly, the outer protection went to standing armies. At the same time, internal order remained a core police job. Police called "gendarmerie" used coercion and repression to control local populations for colonial empires and quell labour protests against the industrialists in Europe, especially the United Kingdom. Under this theoretical dispensation, the type of state determines the nature of the policing. The authoritarian states envisage authoritative and coercive policing. If the form is democratic, policing will be right-based, service-oriented, and pluralistic.

Modernisation theory (Modern) of policing has its origin in the Peelian nine principles, which call for community-oriented and professional police with the primary task of crime prevention and order maintenance (Newburn 2001). This formal policing began with the London Metropolitan Act 1829, which laid the foundations of professional police and led to the advocacy of police reform in many Anglo-American and Commonwealth countries (Edwards 2005). This theory derives its roots from modernity, based on meta-narratives or one grand theory focusing on a homogeneous and structured society, integrating national politics of unity as the prime value (Lyotard 1984). The available literature suggests that this theory stipulates policing in the bureaucratic Weberian concept of power (Newburn 2015).

The globalisation (postmodern) theory of policing has emerged from the debris of the collapse of state power. Many authors endorse that state sovereignty has been liquidated in the wake of democratisation. Growing democratic awareness stresses shifting power to the people at the local level and global institutions on the international level. The new security paradigms, technology adoption, new social media, the rise of multinationals-Infotech having the monopoly on information, big data, and knowledge define the power of the new world order. Corporations and international organisations such as the UNO, the ICJ, and many other regions such as the EU are more prominent in size, mighty in influence, and richer in finances than most states. The rise of risk society (Ericson and Haggerty 1997), the Commodification of Security and Policing (Sedra 2017), the use of digital technology (Christopher, 2016), consumerism, customer-ism, managerialism, pluralism, and privatisation are some of the features of postmodern policing (Clark, 2005). These changes are inconsistent with the bureaucratic control model based on coercion. Therefore, the rise of such global networks has posed many daunting challenges to police and law enforcement (Jones 2009). Terrill (2020) stipulates that policing needs postmodern fixing through democracy (pluralisation, inclusivity, and diversity as sources of strength, not weaknesses), technology (safeguards against the right to individual privacy against intrusive surveillance), and security or counterterrorism mechanics (rebirth of the state monopoly on the use of coercion and force).

The postmodern theory identifies three significant strands of this emergent trend of postmodern policing perspectives, which include "rise of risk society, Commodification of security and campaigns of international and local non-state security providers" (Ericson and Haggerty 1997). As a whole, this theory endorses the hybrid police governance instituted through the processes of decentralisation and the globalisation of the state's legitimate monopoly on coercive force and its use with network integration (Judge 2002).

3.4. Postmodern Perspective

Reiner (1992) maintains that the end of modernity and the beginning of Postmodernity were first used and indicted by late C. Wright Mills, who was famous for his sociological imagination and the end of the social debate, in his public lecture at the London School of Economics in 1969. Reiner (1992) writes about Wright Mills: "Mills uncanny prophetic ability to predict the shape of things to come gives him a fair claim to be regarded as H.G. Wells or Jules Verne of Social Science, McLaughlin, and Murji (1999) contend as follows:

> "Globalisation of economies and cultures, the advent of new information and telecommunication technologies, unfolding Europeanisation, internal multi-nationalisation, and the 'new individualism' means that the institutional configuration of the United Kingdom is in the process of rapid transformation. Amongst criminologists, there is a heightened sense that alongside radically different forms of risk, uncertainty and instability and the way they are perceived, an incisive re-ordering of the techniques and logics of social control occurs. As a result, at various moments during the last decade, there has been a recognition of the urgent need to rethink the assumptions and registers on which police studies, as a sub-field of criminological knowledge, has been premised. For certain academic commentators, the surest way to get to grips with these fin-de-siècle transformations is to utilise the general theory of 'late modernity. More recently, the discussion has

moved on to cross-examining the relationship between policing and the risk society" (McLaughlin & Murji 1999).

Postmodernity has its soul of civilisation that started to build its foundations on "innovation, knowledge, ideas and their application". Postmodern ideas began to develop in the last three decades of the 20th Century, marking a clear departure from modernism, which started in the late 18th Century after the Industrial, French, and American revolutions. Knowledge is the primary source of wealth, and the economy, such as land, labour, and money, is authentic.

3.4.1. Postmodern Knowledge

The 21st Century is called the "Knowledge Century", which inspires knowledge and emphasises better use. Experts believe that knowledge is no longer considered stuff. Knowledge is not developed and stored in experts' minds, represented in books, and classified into disciplines (Lyotard 1984). Knowledge refers to energy and currency. It is a system of flows and networks that does things or makes things happen. Knowledge is not defined; it is valued not for what it is but for what it can do (Ibid). Individual experts produce knowledge by creativity and 'collectivising intelligence'- groups of people with complementary expertise who collaborate for specific purposes (Ibid)." The biggest challenge for the police is to learn how to use postmodern knowledge about technology, transparency, diversity, the rule of law, human rights, legitimacy, and democracy in policing (Stone & Travis 2011). Experts predict future crime in the digital domain, requiring the police to learn algorithms (Goodman, 2015). Still valuable, for many policing experts, are the knowledge of the societal and cultural context and the understanding of the millennial demographic environments. In such challenging conditions, police need to operate and perform their professional duties of protecting and serving the communities with their consent and not to use coercive authority at the behest of the state (Skogan 2006).

3.4.2. Postmodern Self and Identity

Postmodern culture has transformed the identity and self of individuals (Mclaughlin & Murji 1999). The previous construct of modernism about the self and identity was "separate independent and coherent individuals' (Bauman 2007). In the 21st Century, this idea of individuality has been replaced by the notion that "people have more than one way of being" (Ibid). Mass connectivity, as well as interdependence on others, is increasing to a greater extent. "People are made up of many, often conflicting parts" (Ibid); they think differently in different sets of cultural environs and behave differently in different contexts and cultures (ibid). Knowing the new construct of rules of human behaviour, they construct and reconstruct themselves according to the new requirements of new

51

contexts and situations (Giddens 1991). They developed hybrid personalities in the modern world. Their self and identity are mobile, changing, not fixed, or structured. They are fond of negotiating differences and the boundaries between them and others (Yetman & Wilson 1995). However, in the policing context, the rapidly changing identities and behaviours make it difficult for police officers to develop permanent strategies to deal with the issues of crime and disorder within society (Yetman and Wilson 1995). Unless we get educated well in tracking the change and its different dynamics for which police, too, have to develop multiple professional personalities. The police should think, train, prepare, behave, lead, and live differently in different contexts, cultures, and networks for performing diversified roles (Bauman 2007).

3.4.3. Postmodern Values

Values reflect and inspire a sense of right or wrong, good or bad, just or unjust, fair or unfair, and with such a sense, we grow, develop, and make our future the way we want (Mercer 2019). Understanding the values of the society in which police have mandates to serve and protect is equally crucial for police leadership to make sense of changing versions of equality, justice, unity, freedom, responsibility, accountability, and power (ibid), resulting from the rise of Postmodernity. In the past, ideas about equality, justice, unity, energy, and progress were strictly bound up with reason and knowledge in what is called one-size-fits-all. The one-size-fits-all narrative was coercive, authoritarian, and dictatorial. It never allowed people to think about the best alternatives. This construct expected people to follow as the best available option that the legal mechanism considered fit and suitable in the good name of peace, order, progress, and so on. "In this system, 'equality' means 'the same'. To become equal means measuring up to the norm and assimilating, while inequality implies exclusion (Fukuyama 2014). However, this system is antagonistic to diversity as an obstacle to unity (Ibid). The postmodern world began to expose the inherent flaws in modern structured thinking with different liberation movements during the closing decades of the 20th Century in the shape of feminism, gender equality, anti-racism, and human rights. This activism, of course, did not solve the problem because a person cannot be equal to the same and different-deficient or lacking efficiency at the same time as their recent modern thought (ibid). Freedom, human rights, access to justice, the rule of law, due process, protection of civil liberties, and respect for diversity and disagreement are the values that have gained credence in the postmodern age (Wolin 2016-Classic edn.). Policing is a socio-cultural and sociological phenomenon that aligns with the cultural ethos of value systems (Wakefield & Fleming 2008) for better service delivery and performance.

3.4.4. Postmodern Politics

This debate has eventually produced a new kind of activism in postmodern political theory, known as the 'politics of difference and pluralism' (Fukuyama 2014). In this approach, equality and difference are seen as mutually additional, consistent, and related terms, not antithetical. Moreover, diversity is seen as a power source and strength rather than a disintegrative force (ibid). The pluralistic approaches in postmodern (Guttmann & Thompson 2004) police organisations help police capitalise diversity by acculturating the attitudes of coexistence (Ibid). Law enforcement's pluralistic and inclusive policies also reconcile the state authority with civil liberties of the people into statutory and constitutional dispensations of deliberative government systems (Ibid). This system of governance in the postmodern era allows partners to acknowledge and recognise their differences as differences, not deficiencies (Young, 1990). Justice, in this model, is achieved by working difference together' (Ibid). A simple way for the police is to develop a culture of impartiality, neutrality, integrity, transparency, accountability, easy availability, responsiveness, and professional excellence based on the rule of law, procedural justice, community involvement, and fostering partnerships of diverse segments of society (Yetman 1994). Therefore, police organisations can capitalise on the postmodern conditions derived from diversity, democracy, technology, and Postmodernity to improve service delivery and performance, building a better public image of police in the 21st Century (Lint 1999). However, in Pakistan, developments in these indicators of postmodern drivers are slower, and heightened efforts are required to facilitate transforming policing.

3.4.5. Postmodern Digital Revolution

Due to an expansion of the global digital landscape world is becoming what Thomas L. Friedman (2006) says "flat." Flattening digits and clicks have squeezed the world into chessboard politics and the battleground of new unknown enemies (Friedman 2006). The concepts of crime and war stands were redefined. The scratches of globalisation blur the state boundaries, and state-to-state war gives way to unknown anarchists who inflict terror on innocence and commit violence against the state (Ibid). The age of proxies through non-state actors or colder wars for power, new energy, and technology are commonplace (Katusa 2014). Who to tasks for the counterterrorism military or police? What is terrorism-a war or crime? These questions need to be answered with authority and clarity. Until now, universally accepted constructs or narratives that define terrorism, terrorists, and extremists will continue to operate through new mechanisms and channels of virtuality to radicalise the youth toward hate and intolerance (Majoran 2015). Classifying terrorism is crucial and problematic. However, many experts concur that terrorism is closer to crime than to war, and criminal justice responses, rather than military strategies, work well in combating it (Martin 2013). Obama's Task Force (2015) recommended: "Implementing new technologies can allow police departments to fully engage and educate communities in a dialogue about their expectations for transparency, accountability, and privacy." Terrorists have no state to go for war but have criminal syndicates for militancy and often take shelter under human rights and due process. Therefore, this discourse defines terrorism as politically motivated organised crime and a policing challenge.

3.4.6. Democratic Policing by Consent

For better and effective policing, the daunting challenge for the modern state is to capacitate their police agencies to dominate the space that remains unpoliced. That requires filling the vacuum of public vulnerability to regulate the unregulated (Newman & Clarke 2008). For all this, we need the police who should know to outsmart criminal elements through innovation, energy, and power (ibid). The best way to make policing work is to work out how police should enlist public support and gain public trust, without which policing terrorism would sound like jumping from the aero-plane without a parachute (LaFree 2012). Police should change its organisational and leadership culture from a closed community to a more social and more open communitarian organisation based on service and rights-based approaches to high care for using authority (Newburn 2004). President's Taskforce on the 21st Century policing (2015) made the first recommendation, which reads:

> "People are more likely to obey the law when they believe that those who are enforcing it have the legitimate authority to tell them what to do...The public confers legitimacy only on those whom they believe are acting in procedurally just ways."

3.5. Postmodern Ideas in 21st Century Policing

3.5.1. 21st Century Innovations in Policing

Weisburd and Braga, eds. (2006) focus on three decades of police innovation and changes in the American context. The author claims that in the short period of three decades, policing has changed its fundamental mission, core strategies, and relationship with the community to the extent, intensity, and speed that the police in America or elsewhere could not change even in three centuries since its inception. This book also highlights the dilemmas associated with implementing police policy innovations and could be very useful for building our theoretical design for identifying new thematic domains (Weisburd & Brage 2006). However, Weisburd, as editor of this collection of great criminologists, has not added the latest police strategies such as intelligence-led policing, predictive policing, strategic policing, and social media policing. This book Reimagining Policing does in the context of Pakistan but draws upon the originating countries of those strategies.

3.5.2. Contemporary Global Issues in Policing

Eterno, Verma, Das, and Das, Eds. (2017) in their collection of articles of different contributors from 20 countries compiled and edited under the title: 'Global Issues in Contemporary Policing' dilate upon six themes including "performance management, professional and academic partnerships, preventing and fighting crime and terrorism, immigrant and multicultural populations, policing the police, and cyber-security." The articles in this book address the main challenges faced by contemporary policing. Kratcoski (2017 Chapter-1) discusses continuity and change in policing. He claims that police have sustained potential postmodern attacks led by libertarians, but policing needs to transform in changing circumstances where the state's role of police babysitter has lost its legitimacy owing to community involvement in keeping peace within society. He argues that police cannot continue unless it redefines its role. Perrott and Trites (2017 Chapter-3) argue that issues such as the use of force, exercise of coercive authority, control of corruption and accountability of police leadership require popular mandate through the involvement of private partnerships with different non-state stakeholders. To them, only such private partnerships could help police continue policing. Delahunty and others (2017 Chapter-5) anticipate a solution to policing issues in improving community relations by instituting democratic oversight in policing. Minnaar (2017 Chapter-6) argues that implementing cybersecurity by police is instrumental in redefining the role of police in the postmodern age. Similarly, using digital algorism (technology) to improve police management and public service delivery appears to be an intelligent strategy for policing in the 21st Century (Cofan & Baloi 2017 Chapter-7). Reimagining policing in Pakistan looks into these areas through a case study from the Pakistan Police perspective.

3.5.3. International Police Cooperation in Criminal Matters

The seminal work on international legal cooperation is 'Police Without Borders: The Fading Distinction between Local and Global' by Roberson, Das, and Singer (2010). The book focuses on the need for national and international legal cooperation between the police, the academic community, media, intelligence networks, criminal justice systems, financial institutions, and private law enforcement agencies under the doctrine of policing beyond borders. International legal cooperation between police agencies and non-police is crucial for solving transnational organised crimes, including terrorism. UN agencies' police share the challenges on such collaborative platforms as Interpol. The solution strategies open the dialogue between different global police departments or agencies to learn professional capacity, following international standards (Ibid). The authors discuss postmodern themes in a global context. Book devises methodologies to respond to the challenges of sharing information, intelligence, evidence, and policing experiences of individual nations regarding international and transnational organised crime such as violation of human rights, money laundering, human smuggling, cybercrime, child pornography, intellectual property, public safety, terrorism, and corruption. This global policing methodology of networked cooperation in criminal matters helps police departments understand the need for reform in their respective policing affairs. Another leading book on this theme is *'Global Policing'* by Bowling and Sheptycki (2010), which makes a case for democratic global policing in the wake of the globalisation of crime.

3.5.4. Ideas about Right-based Policing

Asia-Europe Foundation and Hanns Seidel Foundation Indonesia (2011) published the book on international best practices on policing. Police experts from different countries or continents produced the report. The use of force by the police receives close attention. Furthermore, this joint report of AUF highlights and explains the police ethics in dealing with their activities such as stop, search, arrest, detention, investigation, prosecution, and fair trial. After identifying human rights that are likely to be affected by police work, this report recommends some best practices in policing. The best practices include establishing transparency, guaranteeing accountability, offering accessibility, ensuring responsiveness, adopting the technology, framing strategy, finding seasoned leadership, doing a SWOT analysis, capitalising on diversity, introducing proper training and paving the way for professional development. Similar policing models that focus more on community safety and human rights protection than on crime combating and zero tolerance techniques of policing emerged. Another intriguing read on policing undergoing drastic changes across the globe is in the 'Global Environment of Policing', edited by Palmer, Berlin, and Das (2012). Governments worldwide face public pressure to reinvent their policing approaches and cope with funding constraints. Innovations in transnational crime, terrorism, hybrid wars, and socio-political transformations within their societies necessitate a more democratic form of policing that can act as the guardians of human rights and civil liberties.

3.5.5. Demand for Restorative Approaches in Policing

Vitale's book-"*The End of Policing*" (2017), is a newer narrative on policing, which many describe as an obituary of policing. He argues:

> "The problem is not police training, police diversity, or police methods. The problem is the dramatic and unprecedented expansion and intensity of policing in the last forty years, a fundamental shift in the role of policing in society. The problem is policing itself."

He believes that the core of the problem is the 'nature of policing itself. Vitale's thoughts are radical and have generated controversy. In contrast, others think that the problem is not policing itself but rather in policing approaches and strategies to establish order in free societies. Alex has equated police with crime which appears an unsustainable argument where violence and crime are touching unprecedented heights and where everything wrong is not coming out of policing. Most violence and crime result from a lack of proper policing or the absence of police. His critics argue that Vitale's end of the policing project is flawed and inherently contradictory. It is equivalent to rolling societies back to the "Hobbesian state of Nature'–the wildest dream of a theorist in the postmodern age. His argument implicates the state's existence as the agency of order and against the family as a cradle of shaping human behaviour to culture and civilisation. The idea of law and the state loses relevance if people gain absolute freedom without any sanctions, limits, or civility. The argument of establishing order without proper sanctions, necessary regulations, and strong deterrence lose substance in the face of the ground realities of the complex society of the 21st Century.

"The End of Policing" without end of terror, violence, injustice, discrimination, inequality, non-inclusion, and disparity as pre-requisites could land the Planet in total anarchy, chaos and disorder. Alex forgot to devise a new design for the modern policeless society of his thinking as Plato did in his republic, though ideal, yet with an elaborate plan to place philosophers on the throne through a proper system of socio-political filtration via education and communism of family and property. The idea of a society without policing and theory without adequate structure and comprehensive design seems to be a skeleton without flesh and body that lacks muscle, life, and organic substance for workability and sustainability. Therefore, this discourse opts not for the ambitious plan of the end of policing but emphasises transforming police to serve and protect in better ways.

3.5.6. Calls for Procedural Justice and Police Legitimacy

Robert and Sarah (2017) focus on legitimacy in using police authority through a procedural justice model to earn public trust in the police. If adopted, this idea of procedural justice can work wonders in police reforms (Robert & Sarah, 2017). First, procedural justice signifies a fairer, legitimate, and respectful way of making decisions and implementing policies through law enforcement in collaboration, cooperation, and coordination with the community and addressing their genuine concerns as well as considerations. It further suggests that the police should conduct themselves in a dispassionate, impartial, neutral, honest, and professional way with the public. Second, police should make evidence-based decisions that, in turn, will earn goodwill, confidence, trust, and faith for law enforcement agencies in the communities. Third, they make decisions without any preconceived way, fear, or favour.

3.5.7. Police Malpractice and corruption

"Police Corruption and Police Reforms (2015), written by Kempe Ronald[3] Hope Sir, is another essential reading on police reforms. The author admits that developed societies dominate most of the police reform literature. No "significant study has been carried out to understand" the dynamics of corruption, malpractices, and hiccups in the process of police transformation from old models to new models in developing societies. However, Punch (2003) is of the view that most of the literature on police corruption and abuse revolves around "the metaphors of bad apples, black sheep, or rotten orchards' (Punch 2003). In response to police corruption and malpractice, Stone and Travis (2011) came up with the concept of new police professionalism, which emphasises integrity, transparency, legitimacy, democracy, and accountability. The new police professionalism runs through the heart of this discourse as its main artery carrying distilled and filtered concepts into the dysfunctional systems of colonial policing in Pakistan.

3.5.8. Police Culture and Leadership

Caless (2011) views are very telling about what the police leadership is all up for and what they think about themselves, their lives, their working environment, and their mission. This work is classic in the culture of police leadership, which has universal implications. There is a macho culture over long working hours, often over 70 hours a week, although high officials receive no significant compensation. This working culture profoundly affects relationships and marriages, and many officials have mentioned the lack of balance between work and family. In addition, most senior officials classify their role as precarious, often without confidence. Police officers refer to work pressure and external control as possible contributions. Fixed dates seem to play a critical role in this area, reinforcing the feeling that their work is consistently under control. It is, therefore, not surprising that agents are sceptical about their colleagues because of the interview data (Caless 2011). As Caless points out, these issues need appropriate policy response in the face of current developments, politics and "confused amateurism," which will continue to play an essential role in the lives and practices of senior officials. Caless maintains that there is a police culture, there is also a chief of staff' culture.

---

[3] Kempe Ronald Hope, Sr. 'formerly with the United Nations, is the Director of the Policy Division at Development Practice International, Oakville, Ontario, Canada

3.5.9. Increasing Misuse of Police Authority

Heatherton and Camp (2016) focus on expanding police authority to an unnecessary extent, bringing public reactions to encroachment and ingress of police to the fundamental human rights barriers worldwide. The authors explain the broken window policing model, which focuses on the basic premise that zero tolerance should focus on minor offences for controlling significant crimes. Moreover, the book 'Policing the Planet' has a lot for civil libertarians. Critics beat their drums against formal social controls and the infamous extra-legal or moral policing challenges. Moreover, this critique makes a befitting relevance to the context of Pakistani society, which is notorious for its coercive policing methods used more by non-police actors for their political and bureaucratic ends, making policing in Pakistan a very controversial subject. Policing the Planet describes ongoing struggles from New York to Baltimore to Los Angeles, London, San Juan, San Salvador, and beyond (Heatherton & Jordan 2016)." Many incidents in Pakistan, such as the Sahiwal CTD shooting 2019, May 12 Karachi, Model Town Lahore, and much more of a similar nature, has brought much criticism of coercive power by the police in Pakistan.

3.5.10. The Emerging Requirements of Big Data Policing

Hariri (2018), in his book-*21 lessons from the 21st Century,* refers to the postponement of Francis Fukuyama's *"The End of History"* (2004) project, which is closely relevant to this discourse. Noah argues that contemporary scholarship fails to consider the end of the Cold War after the Soviet collapse as the culmination of the historical phenomenon of the 20th Century. However, this was nothing more than a mirage of ideas (Noah 2018). The end of the Cold War and the dominance of capitalist democracies are now showing their inherent contradictions that are more likely to deepen, thereby reaching a new proposition of the perceived collapse of the present capitalistic order. Noah indicates the fundamental challenges to the state's monopolies on power to the power of modern information, communication, and knowledge, arguing that those who control information and data control the world. Not the states, but InfoTech and biotech giants like Google and Facebook regulate the world (Ibid). Cloud computing has alarmed many law enforcement agencies about locating the information since no country claims the clouds that nobody knows where they exactly are and where exactly lies the information sought by the police. Goodman (2015) also warns against the deep and dark web activities of criminals and possibilities of bioterrorism and cyber terrorism, with more focus on what he refers to as the Internet of Things (IoT) (Goodman 2015). Toyama (2015) came up with a new warning about what is happening in the digital frontiers is more likely to pose a potential challenge to governments for policing postmodern societies in the 21st Century. He believes that the society we live in today has become what he calls the "Technological Wild West", where information anarchy and knowledge quacks are but natural consequences (Toyama 2015).

3.5.11. Adoption of social media as Policing Tool

Christopher (2016) focuses on adopting social media as a public management model to ensure social control in Canadian society. As Christopher attempts to answer, the change in communications has changed public life and police work. Christopher, J. S. argues that social media as a form of communication and connection has positively strengthened police and public relationships. Schneider maintains that policing is changing in new ways of influencing the public, cultivating self-promotion, and expanding social control (Ibid). Baloch (2016), focusing on the Pakistani context, argues that how and why they use social media as a policing tool is vital for controlling crime, engaging communities, improving performance, and building public images of the police.

3.6. An Overview

The postmodern theory of policing seeks to analyse the relationship between contemporary policing and Postmodernity (Waters 2007). The police reforms, innovations, and ideas in the 21st Century reflect the postmodern agenda. Analysing policing in a highly diverse, divided, fragmented, and digitalised society under Postmodernity constitutes the core of conversation on policing in the 21st Century. Police leadership and reformers should develop a body of knowledge about policing that could help governments reconcile their policing with their fast-occurring socio-cultural change in the highly connected and globalised world (Ibid).

The discussion in this chapter demonstrates that the audience of police has changed dramatically. The new generation called millennials has unique cultural and mental capacities that urgently require the attention and focus of police leaders and policymakers to confirm and conform to any policing philosophy and draft any policing strategy for their respective societies (Waters 2007). An explosion of technology and the proliferation of social media connecting millennials in real-time is, indeed, an overarching mark of postmodern societies. States and their political dispensations are witnessing decline and liquidation against the emergent globalisation of governance and policing in the backdrop of changed socio-cultural conditions of human civilisation.

Side by side of states, the non-state actors dominate the world order. Global multinational corporations such as Microsoft, Google, Facebook, Apple, other InfoTech and biotech, religious movements and organisations, NGOs, international human rights, and terror networks can operate transnationally. Today, many scholars believe and recognise the global and transnational activities of policing, which are shared by private security, national security, secret services, public police agencies, military, mercenary, and similar other actors to describe what they call the pluralisation of policing (Sheptycki 2000). Walker (2000) warns against what he describes as a sovereignty-trap while ensuring policing as a source of legitimate power that contributes to justice, freedom, and peace, and that should, therefore, correspond to the global narratives of inclusivity, diversity, and difference as sources of new strength and energy.

"In this context, the sovereign out-space is a conceptual space wherein the social power of the sovereign state and of policing is not merely coeval but coessential"' (Sheptycki 2002). In postmodern systems of power arrangements, authoritarian arrangements of police control are not workable. Only inclusive, representative, pluralistic, and legitimate policing dispensations are advisable in liquid times of uncertainty (Bauman, 1997). Police reformers should learn the science of change and innovation taking place in civil, political, economic, social, and cultural relationships of the people and communities to ensure continuity of policing by changing, reforming, innovating, and reinventing it. Realigning policing would be vital to outsmarting criminals and terrorists. The governance of the police no longer remains an exclusivity of the state. The transnational policing regime also plays an instrumental role in influencing the working and organisational culture of police departments across the world and beyond borders. Police, being an essential part of the state, has to redefine their role as the guardians of human rights, street-cleaners of beggars, pesterers, pilferers, and guarantors of public peace (Newburn 2004).

Through tough on crime and the causes, approaches or policies could not work well until the police improved performance, built image, and won public trust through efficient public service delivery. Only new police professionalism based on apolitical and professional police involvement with all stakeholders in the web of partnerships for peace could achieve such strategic goals. The postmodern and diversified policing approaches can work miracles in keeping police relevant and valuable for increasing investors' confidence and building electors' trust in service delivery or good sentiments (Bauman 2000).

3.7. Conclusion

In this context, this book advocates the adoption of postmodern policing culture based on strategic partnerships of state and non-state actors or national and international stakeholders. This book attempts to apply the postmodern theory of policing to transform policing from a traditional coercive tool of the state to a community-oriented service paragon in Pakistan. The fundamental reason behind choosing a postmodern theoretical framework is to find a middle path between state authority and individual liberty and a workable blend of contemporary policing strategies. Balance so achieved could keep policing relevant, current, and legitimate without delinking the role of the state in these critical times of sovereignty-decline, gaps in community relations and the emergence of the globalised world characterised by popular sovereignty and localised authority-a process called glocalisation (Roberson, Das and Singer, 2010). This discourse argues that networked approaches and integrated policing systems could address the challenge of forging policing partnerships for safer societies in the highly connected global world of the 21st Century (Bowling and Sheptycki 2010). It is evident from the above literature review of contemporary policing that human connectivity, information explosions, knowledge boom and new demographics are shaping our millennials in societies and hence require higher levels of policing sensibilities and sensitivities (Bauman 2007). This book undertakes this task from the perspective of Pakistan. Drawn on contemporary postmodern literature on policing, this conversation argues that the Strategic Policing model for Pakistan's police organisations sits well with a changing society and has transformed policing worldwide to deliver its services to communities. The strategic policing model incorporates and accommodates all contemporary policing sensitivities and sensibilities. For policing in Pakistan, the strategic vision of involving all stakeholders, such as communities, business unions, civil society, human rights agencies, judiciary, media, academia, intelligence agencies, security departments, and law firms in a well-defined and integrated mechanism of networked partnerships, has been devised in the last part of the book. The ultimate goal is to make our society safer through efficient, effective, apolitical, and professional police cloned with postmodern policing approaches.

By J.J. Baloch (2022)

Part Two: Policing Developments

Chapter 04: Police Reforms

Chapter 05: Police Reorganizations

Chapter 06: Police Innovations

Chapter: 04

Police Reforms

Chapter Brief

This chapter draws on the history, politics and scope of police reforms in Pakistan. Governments, both civilian and military, have made frequent attempts to reform Police since the creation of Pakistan in 1947. However, in 74 years by now, over 28 Committees/Commissions reports on police reforms, containing many recommendations, continue to get dust in the secretariat files. This chapter refers only to relevant portions of the reform reports, focusing on tensions between different stakeholders and difficulties in implementing reform proposals. The sources of information and data are the original police reform reports borrowed from the National Police Academy Library, Islamabad. The chapter on Police Reforms is descriptive, summarising main recommendations and proposals for police reforms and lists causes of failure to implement them.

4.1. Introduction

This chapter describes the police reform process in Pakistan. Although police reforms started when colonial rulers in India established our modern police forces during the second half of the 19th century, the scope of this chapter is to explain the reforms in Pakistan after its creation in 1947. In addition, this chapter excludes reports prepared by foreign police delegations because of the space here. Not all national police reforms receive attention here for the same space reasons. I have only picked relevant parts of the national reports produced in each decade after the birth of Pakistan.

This reform process began with the first independent police commission report of 1960-61 (precisely after 100 years of the 1860 commission, which came up with the first-ever Police Act of 1861 (in British India). The colonial Police Act 1861 is still valid in many parts of independent Pakistan. Unfortunately, unlike its predecessor, the justice Constantine report 1960-61 could not produce a new Police Act in 1961. However, the Constantine report started the police reform process in Pakistan, which culminated in the P.R.C. report-2019, sponsored by the Law and Justice Commission of Pakistan on police reforms. History of Police signifies a tale of the 159 years Police journey in the Sun-continent and story of over 60 years of police reforms in Pakistan as an independent state.

Governments in Pakistan have been struggling to make Police the rule of law institution based on the democratic aspirations of the people. The idea of transforming the Police from archaic colonial model to the democratic and service-oriented organization has become a difficult task to improve governance in Pakistan. Effective policing is crucial to establish order and enforce the law within a democratic society of an independent nation. Police reforms agenda makes good electoral business and sits at the top of the claims of the governments spearheading Police reforms. During over 74 years of independence, as many as 29 commissions, committees, and delegations have reportedly produced recommendations to reform Police in Pakistan.

The Report of the Pakistan Police Commission, headed by **Justice Constantine**, reads:

"The System introduced in 1860 was, on the whole, an intelligent and efficient system. However, it has failed for many reasons. First, the extent to which village police must cooperate with the regular Police has lost sight of actual work. Second, Police officers are overworked. Third, most bureaucrats underestimate the importance of police work and often take credit for police good work. Fourth, there is no appropriate focus on police training and character building. Fifth, the ill-educated candidates get recruited in the lowest ranks from the lower strata of society. Sixth, the supervision of police stations has been defective owing to the failure to appoint even the staff contemplated by the law and to increase that staff with the growing necessities of the police administration. Seventh, the training and socialization of superior officers within the working environment results in the alienations of the officers. Lastly, the senior officers have lost the sense of responsibility to a greater degree. The measure of interference that the authors of the System never contemplate before the malaise has taken over the entire system" (Constantine 1960-61 p.12).

4.2. Police Reforms in Pakistan

First governor-general of Pakistan, Mr Muhammad Ali Jinnah directed Governor Sindh Mr M. Khuhro, to replace the Irish model policing for Karachi with the London Metropolitan system. Bombay, Chennai, Calcutta, and other urban centres of India had already adopted a very successful design of a police commissioner (Suddle 2015). Unfortunately, due to the sudden death of Khuhro, the matter went into cold storage. After that, many prominent reform bodies got constituted and among them, the following had a national character (Ibid).

4.2.1. Justice Constantine Police Commission 1960-61 Report

President of Pakistan Mr Ayoub Khan constituted the first formal national Commission on police reforms in 1960 under the chairmanship of well-known Mr Justice G.B. Constantine. Mr Constantine was assisted by five other members, including M. W. Abbasi (C.S.P.), K. A. Haqq (PSP), Brigadier Saeed Uddin Khan, Fariduddin Ahmad (Esq), and Ahmad Ebraheem (PSP), who acted as the secretary of the Commission. Resolution No: F. 30/58/59-police (I) of the Ministry of Interior, the government of Pakistan, dated 31 December 1959, constituted the justice Constantine Commission.

The Commission's reference terms included how to improve the organization, strength, infrastructure, training, resources, and equipment of the Police. Second, the Commission focused on building capacity to discharge their duties to maintain law and order and prevent and detect crime efficiently. Third, facilitating police relations with the public and magistracy is also included in its objectives. Fourth, harmony with local bodies, efficient police governance, and uniformity of police laws was T.O.R.s. Fourth, the financial and logistic facilities required for the efficient discharge of duties, bifurcation of the law-and-order and investigation functions of the Police, and enhancement of the standards of integrity maintained by the Police remained the top priorities T.O.R.s. Lastly, to make any other recommendation meant to improve any other branch or its functions that the Commission deems appropriate had been part of the mandate of the Commission (Constantine 1960).

With the mandate explained above, the Commission held its first meeting at Lahore in January 1960. The Commission prepared questionnaires for both the public and government officials. As a result of the distribution of questionnaires, the Commission received 422 replies and examined 317 witnesses during 51 sittings. In addition, the government of Pakistan sent the chairman of the Commission, Mr Justice Constantine, to visit India, France, and the United Kingdom to study their police systems.

4.2.1.1. Constitutional Position

The Justice Constantine Commission recommended seven constitutional measures for police reforms. The constitutional measures included the following:

- constitutional separation of the judiciary from the executive by limiting the role of district magistrates in the direction and control of the police department;
- more authority for the Superintendent of the Police in the district to preserve order and maintain peace under the 144 Criminal Procedure Cod;
- compulsory consultation of D.M. with District S.P. before issuing orders under 144 CRPC.
- D.M. orders without consulting S.P. are not valid and the government cannot call S.P. for account.
- Police, not magistrates, can order the dispersal of unlawful assemblies, and the choice of means to achieve such an end relies solely on Police.
- Though D.M. is in overall control of the maintenance of order but he should abstain strictly from interference of any kind in the internal affairs of the police force.
- the D.I.G. Police, not the D.M., initiates a report of the Superintendent of Police and sends it to Commissioner, who could consult with D.M. if they think such consultation fits.

- Finally, the hierarchical organization of prosecutors under the law department to control the investigation and prosecution as it works in the French System.

4.2.1.2. Recruitment of Police

The Constantine commission has proposed six steps for recruitment in Police.

- Induction through three tiers, e.g., Constable, Sub-Inspector, and Assistant Superintendent of Police;
- District appoints constable, Province Sub-Inspector (S.I.) and Federal Government Assistant Superintendent of Police (A.S.P.);
- For officer cadres such as S.I. and A.S.P., aspirants should qualify competitive exams conducted by respective commissions;
- Qualifying professional courses and performance should determine the prospects of officer's promotion based on merit;
- Districts can retain village Police with minor modifications in employment methods; and
- Finally, police and municipal authorities should ensure close coordination of traffic.

4.2.1.3. Strength of Police

To determine the strength of the Police, the Commission suggested following nine ways.

- Abolishing the post of writer-head Constable (Bara Munshi), particularly in Western Pakistan demanded.
- Village police should perform watch and ward duties in rural areas.
- Ten constables for the rural police station with 75 cognizable offences; however, N.W.F.P. [now K.P.] allowed extra sentries for Police Stations.
- S.I.P.s investigate class V crimes and non-cognizable offences when the magistrate refers.
- The scale of the investigating and scriptory officers was as follows.

Number of cases	Sub-Inspectors	Assistant Sub-Inspectors	Observation/Remarks
75 cases	01	01	
100 cases	01	02	
125 cases	02	01	
175 cases	02	02	
250 cases	03	02	

- When crime exceeds 250 in any police station, except in large cities, police stations need to be split into two or more stations, and by contrast, if crime figures are less than 30 at any police station, they need to be closed.
- In larger towns of two lakhs to five lakh populations, the Commission recommended 01 Constable in watch and ward branch to the 800 to 1000 citizens; 01 Head Constable for 10 Constables; 01 A.S.I. for 05 Head Constables; 01 Sub-Inspector in charge of watch and ward branch or S.H.O. for 100 Constables. Five sub-inspectors assisted him at large police stations where the Station House Officer-SHO was an inspector on the investigation and operation (watch and ward) sides.
- In metropolitan cities, the Commission proposed the constitution of Range Reserves; for example, 300 personnel for Karachi; 200 men for Dacca, Lahore, Peshawar, and Rawalpindi; and 80 men reserved for other smaller ranges.
- For Karachi, Justice Constantine Commission devoted separate chapters VIII and XIV for determining the constitutional position and strength of the Karachi police. The main recommendation includes the amalgamation of the Karachi Police with the rest of the West Pakistan forces organized under the Police Act 1861, with D.I.G. as the head of the Karachi Police, while the Divisional Commissioner is to be responsible for maintaining order.

4.2.1.4. District organization of Police

For police organizations at the district level, the Commission emphasized three steps. First, the Superintendent of the Police should be the head of the district police, and the provincial government should appoint him in consultation with the Inspector General of the Police. One or two superior-ranked officers should assist the S.P. of the district. The reader of district S.P. must be a senior clerk. Second, police stations should get grouped into circles headed by officers not below the rank of the inspectors. Third, the Commission also drew on pay, transport, logistics, maintaining criminal records, leave, amnesties, welfare, and training and recommended forensic laboratories to be established at Karachi, Lahore, Decca, and Sardah.

4.2.1.5. Public-Police Relations

Five initiatives received attention from the Commission. First, the Commission emphasized the importance of the ethical conduct of the Police with the public, especially in times of adversity, difficulty, and emergencies. Second, Commission stressed the values of courtesy, empathy, helpfulness, responsiveness, and goodwill by the Police. Third, the Commission underlined the importance and utility of the press, publication, and broadcasting in enlisting public support for Police and building police images. Fourth, to create an image, Police should consider making documentaries spread specific messages in public to gain trust and confidence. Finally, the Constantine Commission recommended the participation of police officers in local cultural events, sporting activities, and educational fairs to minimize the distance between Police and the public, especially youth.

4.2.2. General Mitha Khan Commission Report 1970

The Police Commission 1969-70 was the second most high-power national and formal Commission on police reforms. The President of Pakistan and the Chief Martial Law Administrator of Pakistan, Mr General Ayoub Khan, constituted this Commission, vide notification no. 9/15/69-BP, dated 23 July 1969. The then government of Pakistan appointed Major General A.O. Mitha S.Q.A. (T.P.K.) as the chairman of the Commission. He was assisted by three vice chairmen i.e., Brigadier Muhammad Jamshed, SJ, MC, Brigadier Malik Abdul Majeed, and Brigadier Ghullam Jilani Khan and one secretary-Mr. Miraj Hussain, PSP. Mitha Khan Commission comprised following ten members:

- Mr. Masrour Hassan Khan, S.Q.A., T.P.K., C.S.P. (Home Secretary, Government of West Pakistan up to 04 August 1969),
- Mr. Salahuddin Ahmad, T.Q.A., C.S.P. (Home Secretary, Government of East Pakistan),
- Mr. A.M.F. Rahman, SK (Home secretary Government of East Pakistan from 05 August 1969),
- Mr. Irfan Ahmad Imtiaz, S.Q.A., C.S.P. (Secretary Finance, Government of West Pakistan),
- Mr. Kafiluddin Mahmood, S.Q.A., C.S.P., (Secretary Finance, Government of East Pakistan up to 04 August 1969),
- Mr. M. Wajid Ali Khan, T.P.K., C.S.P., (Secretary Finance, Government of East Pakistan from 05 August 1969),
- Mr. Saeed Ahmad Khan, PSP, (Additional Inspector General of Police West Pakistan up to 05 December 1969),
- Mr. Tasleemuddin Ahmad, SK, P.P.M., PSP (Additional Inspector General of Police, East Pakistan),
- Mr. Sarfraz Hassan, PSP, (Deputy Inspector General of Police West Pakistan), and
- Mr. Abdul Khalique, T.Q.A., PSP, Deputy Inspector General of Police, East Pakistan

The terms of reference of the Mitha Khan Commission as stated on page 4 and 5 of the commission report include the following:

- to review the recommendations of police commission set up in 1961 under Justice Constantine;
- to suggest the ways and means for the implementation of the 1961 Commission;
- to examine how Police could be enabled to effectively deal with law-and-order situations both under normal conditions as well as in emergencies as the one occurred from November 1968 to March 1969;
- to assess the capacity and efficiency of Police in regards to staff, training, equipment, organization, discipline, welfare, career planning, prevention and detection of crime and suggest improvements;
- to examine the powers and responsibilities of Police and suggest measures for the appropriate use and better discharge;
- to evaluate the level and extent of the relationship between Magistracy and the Police and recommend steps to strengthen coordination and cooperation between them;
- to offer expansion in the classical branches by creating new units, if any, of the Police Department;
- to review and advise on matters relating to finance and budget of the Police Department;
- to examine the relationship between the people and the Police;
- to suggest measures for the prevention of corruption in the Police force;
- to explore the desirability and feasibility of constituting new River Police as well as Highway police; and
- to examine and suggest any other point for reforming Police in Pakistan.

The Mitha Police Commission started work by confessing that police failure owe much to the Police, government, and the public jointly, not to the Police alone, as is a general perception. The Commission could not provide detailed recommendations because of a shortage of time. The Commission admitted in their Report that they avoided indulging in detail, limiting to specificities of proposals. They were given a full range of the terms of reference and the diversity of circumstances prevailing in each province or part of the country, which required different solutions and hence some more commissions with mandate and time to serve the purpose. The Mitha Police Commission offered two recommendations: short -and long-term. The following long and short-term measures reflect the crux of the advice.

Short Term measures for immediate implementation

- Innovation, research, experimentation, and self-criticism should be encouraged by the Police.
- Mitha Khan's Report emphasized reinventing Razakar force on a sound footing.
- Commission envisaged I.G.P. police as overall head of federal Police with standardization and uniformity of police practices and laws.
- Research on radical changes to improve the quality of police training on all levels is crucial effectively and meaningfully
- The problems of corruption and highhandedness in the police force seem vital for improving the police image and performance.
- Mitha Khan's Report demanded the delegation of more financial and administrative powers to the S.P. and D.I.G. for effective management of resources on the ground level, discouraging centralization of financial and operational powers in I.G.P.s.
- Improvements in facilities such as food, accommodation, amenities, and general welfare of force, and enhancement of salary packages and other perks for gazetted and non-gazetted police officers are necessary.
- Honesty and integrity officers should be given a 60% mark in promotions of officers.
- The Report suggested transparency and responsibility in financial procedures and the exercise of authority by police officers.
- Therefore, the annual confidentiality reporting system must be revised.
- The Report recommended supervision and monitoring systems for police performance.
- Police should receive due and timely shares of revenue generated under different heads, including traffic Challan.
- There is an acute need to create new wings such as human resource development, career management, training, research and analysis, publication and public relations, criminal investigation, criminal intelligence, forensics, emergency management, disciple and enforcement, logistics, finances, welfare, statics, etc.
- The Commission recommended separating many services such as investigation, prosecution, watch and ward, process service, C.I.A., C.I.D., and Crime Branch.
- The Commission recommended abolishing many things such as awarding a stipend to intermediate candidates, the System of annual examination for officiating ranks, Baloch Levies in D.G. Khan, and Horsemanship.
- The Commission also proposed amendments in many sections of law and changes in police practices and types of equipment. The examples include PSP officers' Mess Kits, brown belts

and white uniforms of traffic police, and indiscriminate use of discretion or preventive sections of the law to make it more people-friendly and efficient.

Recommendations Long Term Implementation

For a long-term project of police reforms, the Commission recommended abolition of court police, the Assistant Sub-Inspector A.S.I., the rank of the Deputy Superintendent of Police-DSP, and Prosecuting Sub-Inspector P.S.I. Mitha Commission also emphasized the introduction of river traffic police, highway patrol police, fingerprint kits at police stations, cycles to officers on instalments, separate training grants, and new training facilities for specialists. In the same way, report focussed on creating well-paid faculty for research, adequate transport, and accommodation for non-gazetted police officials. Changes in the organization of districts and range reserves into special armed forces at the provincial level, the strength of police human resources, the location of detective schools from Lahore to Sihala, the police academy of Sardah to Dacca, the capacity of wireless school at Bahawalpur and traffic school by expanding them in promotion system of PSPs. Besides, Mitha Khan's report called for rationalizing police equipment, including weapons, vehicles, and communications. Furthermore, the Report required the government to revisit police strength, recruitment process, Police uniform, rank structure, efficiency, discipline rules, promotion systems, police libraries, training curricula, pay structures, and operational laws.

The Mitha Commission report (1970) sets the general guidelines for the improvement of Police. First, the commission report claims were flexible to be adopted according to the local circumstances of each province without any difficulty or adverse consequences. Second, the Commission, keeping in mind the meagre resources in the country, restrained to creating new police practices or building new branches; instead, they tried to preserve and consolidate the old inherited institutions by renovating them. Third, the Commission divided the recommendations into two categories that could be immediately implemented and required no separate funds and budgetary allocations. Reforms could be implemented in long-term duration when funds would be available. On page 2, paragraph 5, the commission report reads:

"The Police will succeed only if the government use them for their proper functions. The police forces are constantly self-critical and determined to keep their own house in order; because, in the final analysis, the

72

ability of Police to carry out the police functions depends entirely on the image which the public has of the Police and therefore the respect they are held in and the willing cooperation they elicit from the citizens. Internal accountability is what makes Police succeed or fail in their duties and not merely numbers, equipment, and organization" (Mitha 1970 Para 5, p.2).

Regarding the Mitha Police Commission report 1970, the 1985 Police Committee Report makes the following observations on page 127 and in Para 198, which read:

"No action was taken on some reports for years, and when these were taken up, these were examined half-heartedly and side-tracked causally. The Report of the Mitha Commission which worked in 1969-70 is a case in point. This Commission examined all the aspects of Police working at length and submitted an exhaustive report in 1970. The Report was examined in 1978 and decisions were taken. As late as 1982, it was brought to the notice of the Federal Cabinet that action on approved recommendations of Mitha Commission had not developed satisfactorily. A committee was, therefore, appointed to look into the state of the implementation of the recommendations of the Mitha Commission. This Committee is still not through with the task (Mitha 1970, Para 198, p. 127)."

The 1985 Police Reforms Committee further brought forth the non-implementation of all reports, including the Mitha Commission. The Report reads:

"The Committee regrets to observe that despite, investment of time, efforts and money in the deliberations of these Commissions/Committees, not much positive came out of these reports...these reports either did not receive serious and prompt attention at the appropriate level or decisions were not followed up...It shows that: a) Reports were not examined for a long time after submission and decisions delayed. b) Recommendations were not implemented faithfully and speedily". (P.R.C. Report 1985, Paras 198-199)

4.2.3. Aslam Hayat (1985) the Police Reform Committee Report

The 1985 Committee, together with examining the previous recommendations made by Commissions/Committees appointed for police reforms since the establishment of Pakistan, insightfully, the underlying causes of the failure of their adoption and implementation, and also forwarded some important proposals for the reorganization of police force on modern and democratic lines. The government of Pakistan realized the tense law and order conditions resulting from the Movement for the Restoration of Democracy-MRD during the first half of the 1980s. As a result, the federal government appointed a police reform committee, including Chairman and Secretary. In this connection, Interior Ministry vide Notification no. 15/14/85-Police dated 24 June 1985 appointed a committee containing five police officers.

The terms of reference of the Committee were

- to examine the relevance and effectiveness of *the 1861 Police Act* in terms of policing an independent nation;

- to assess the feasibility and desirability for the introduction of *Police Commissionerate System* in urban centres of Pakistan on the lines of India;
- to examine as to how to boost *police morale* through effective leadership and policing strategy; to find out the ways for improving *the police-public relationship*;
- to suggest measures to improve the *working conditions* of the police force to facilitate their performance; and
- to recommend improvements of *Police Training* on all levels and to forward *any other suggestion* for making Police working and image better.

After a long workout, with this mandate, the Committee came out with the following recommendations (P.R.C. Report 1985 pp, 149-156) for making Police efficient, effective, and service-oriented.

- First and foremost, the Police *Act of 1861,* based on the 'rule concept' instead of the 'service concept,' is outmoded and needs replacement.
- Second, lateral control of *District Magistrate* over Police is anachronistic, and the police system of accountability based on people's representatives and judiciary should replace it.
- Third, *Police Commissionerate System,* which many scholars consider the standard System for urban policing, should be introduced in cities with 5 lakh or more.
- Fourth, in the first instance, significant cities should adopt in one or more cities in each province on a trial basis.
- Fourth, the Central government in Pakistan should establish *Federal Reserve Police* immediately.
- Fifth, PSP officers of the ranks of grades 20 and 21 should get *appropriate postings* inside and outside the cadre.
- Sixth, the *Inspector General of Police* of the province should be *empowered* and have the Security of his tenure, more purchasing financial powers, administrative autonomy, and the status of ex-officio secretary to the government.
- Finally, the Report recommended deleting Police Rule 1:17 should and instituting *police awards* of meritorious service. In addition to these proposals for reform, the Committee also proposed to improve policing in many other areas.

As regards improving *police-public relationships*, the Committee makes some valid recommendations. First, the Committee proposed the justice of the peace for all elected representatives of the people from councillors to the M.N.A.s so that the public can get their cases registered well in time and their

74

grievances redressed well. Second, District S.P.s and Sub-divisional officers should establish reporting centres in their offices. Third, report offered to install two-digit emergency numbers at public places for emergency calls. Fourth, police officers of all ranks should adopt a code of conduct for better general handling by the Police. Fifth, honest officers should get field assignments to eliminate corruption. Sixth, Police should not take action on miscellaneous complaints but rather forward such complaints to local councils. Seventh, the Committee's recommendations proposed police officers to use results of 'opinion polls' to assess the state of police-public relationships. Lastly, the I.G.P. office should have a separate public relations wing and public relations officer to better relations through engagement, a publicity campaign, and promotion of good police work in consultation with marketing and media experts.

For *improving the working conditions* of the Police, the Committee recommended detailed measures. It emphasized the revision of the pay structure by placing Constable in grade-5, H.C. in grade-7, A.S.I. in grade-9, S.I. in grade-14, and Inspector in grade-16. First, weekly holiday and 8-hour duty shifts for constables ensured. Second, Committee stressed adequate arrangements for residence and accommodation. Third, the establishment of well-organized schools and hospitals at provincial headquarters were for the children of police officials. The committee recommended the treatment of their families with improved medical cover for police officials. Fourth, appropriate financial benefits to be attached to gallantry awards, i.e., Rs. 50,000/- or 12 acres of agricultural land for QPM and Rs. 25, 000/- or a residential plot for P.P.M. Fifth, Report emphasized enhancement of washing allowance and provision of free uniforms for the officers up to the rank of Inspectors. Sixth, the Committee emphasized an extension of a protective cover of 197 CRPC to all police officers. Seventh, an increase in compensation amount in cases of loss, damage, or injury to the life of a police officer or his property was strongly recommended to Rs. 1,00,000/-. Eighth, a uniform maintenance allowance for gazetted officers was recommended to be raised from Rs. 25/- to Rs. 200 per month. Ninth, the provision of transport for S.H.O. was made mandatory. Last, the committee also recommended converting Ministerial Police cadre into Executive Police Cadre to improve their performance.

Committee also made some significant recommendations for the improvements in *Police training.* The recommendations included the following. First, improving the physical facilities of police training institutions is crucial. Second, upgradation of training equipment by replacing old and outdated with modern and more relevant tools could be helpful. Third, placing adequate training grants to the disposal of training institutions for enabling them to deliver quality training is essential for improving

Police. Fourth, equally important is providing sufficient infrastructure and necessary resources to the National Police Academy for performing their functions excellently. Fifth, Inspectors and D.S.P.s should take promotional exams for their promotions. Fourth, it urgently needs to ensure the increase in the number of seats for police officers in their overseas courses. Lastly, Committee called for improvements in the quality of instructors by offering appropriate incentives.

Career Planning for PSP officers by streamlining their promotions, horizontal mobility, and due share in All Pakistan Unified Group pool has been one of the core areas where the Committee report draws detailed recommendations in unequivocal terms. First, revision of the training schedule of A.S.P.s needs consideration, and their posting rotation must include F.C. tenure for at least two years after allowing them to complete their Sub-divisional posting tenures and field learning. Second, those posted as I.G.P.s must be of grade 21 or 22. Third, Central Selection Boards must be represented equally by police officers as the representatives of other unified services do. Fourth, for the promotion of grade 20 police officers, a federal minister should chair the Central Selection Board, and for 18 or 19, the provincial minister should. Fourth, the post of the Establishment Secretary must rotate among all three groups-DMG, O.M.G., and PSP, by turn. Besides these, other posts of the secretariat in grades 20 and 21 should also be offered to police officers the same manner as all other groups in A.P.U.G. have an opportunity. Fifth, the governments should set up the career management and cadre review board for police officers. The board should include, among others, the Inspectors General of Police. Sixth, payments of the same grades in all services (at least in DMG, PSP & O.M.G.) should be equal, and any difference therein tantamount to sheer injustice and discrimination and hence fans group rivalry. Lastly, introducing promotional exams and courses for all ranks of Police to promote meritocracy and fair play is recommended.

Among *other recommendations* included the following, which the Committee forwarded in response to the open term of reference that the Committee can suggest anything that they consider valuable for improving police performance.

- First, establishing a Standing Police Commission to monitor the force's performance and ensure the implementation of various recommendations relating to the Police proposed.
- Second, law enforcement agencies countrywide should hold a National Police Conference every year.
- Third, releasing all outstanding amounts of Police Foundation considered crucial by the Report.

- Fourth, implementing all recommendations of police commissions/committees must receive appropriate attention at all levels.
- Fifth, the constitutional security of service for civil servants should be guaranteed through an amendment.
- Sixth, section 13 of the Civil Service Act is discriminatory and needs immediate removal to guard against arbitrary premature retirement.
- Seventh, service tribunals should provide better and quick relief to Civil Servants.
- Eighth, the Bureau of Police Research and Development should be organized as an autonomous institute.
- Lastly, reforms in the Criminal Justice System of Pakistan along the lines of the Japanese Criminal Justice System stipulated.

4.2.4. Chaudhry M.A.K (1990) the Police Reform Implementation Committee

The government of Pakistan has provided the Cabinet Division Notification NO. DY-104/89-DS (E-1) dated 26 February 1989, appointed the Police Reforms Implementation Committee, comprising M.A.K. Chaudhry-Chairman, SH, Ziauddin Ahmad-Secretary, and Saifullah Khan-Member. The Committee visited India, Bangladesh, and all four provinces of Pakistan. They discussed all the recommendations made by previous committees/commissions with concerned quarters, including I.G.P.s, the Interior Ministry, and police agencies of neighbouring countries. In addition, the Committee made the Bureau of Police Research and Development, Islamabad, their secretariat. The terms of reference of the Committee were: to review the recommendations of all previous Committees and Commissions; to ascertain the extent of their implementation; to suggest, in the light of prior suggestions, how to improve the image and performance of the Police; to examine what measures should be initiated in the present structure of the police service in Pakistan to boost the morale and efficiency of the Police and to assess the career planning and training policies for PSP officers.

The Committee reviewed the state of the implementations of the recommendations of the following Police Commissions/Committees set up by the government of Pakistan between 1960 and 1885.

- Police Commission headed by Mr Justice J. B. Constantine-1961-62
- Police Commission headed by Maj. General A.O. Mitha-1968-70
- One person Committee of Mr G. Ahmad-1972

Reimagining Policing in Pakistan

- Police Station Inquiry Committee headed by Mr M.A.K. Chaudhry-1976

- Law and Order Sub-Committee led by Chaudhry Fazal Haque-1976

- Foreign Experts Committee composed of Romanian Police Officers-1976

- Police Reforms Committee headed by Mr Rafi Raza-1976

- One person Committee of Mr A.J. Giles of U.K. on Training Requirements of Police-1976

- Mr Orkzai Committee on Welfare

- Committee on the Status of Emoluments of the SHO-1982

- Policy Committee headed by Mian Aslam Hayat-1985

The Police Reform Implementation Committee, in the bid to modernize the anachronistic police system of the 19th century, almost agreed with most of the main recommendations of the previous commissions and Committees and suggested an implementation roadmap. In its introductory page, the Committee observes: "It is a pity, however, that despite the elaborate recommendations of these Commissions/Committees, the Police have failed to achieve that degree of professional efficiency and acceptance as a public service which should have earned it a fraction of general approbation...We have endeavoured to identify the causes of this sorry state of policing affairs; Some of these are the following:

- the dichotomy between the political System and the bureaucratic regime in Pakistan,

- the outdated Laws, Rules, and Structure of the force,

- lack of an effective system of police accountability,

- the unsatisfactory System of police training and recruitment methods,

- changing the pattern of crime and police inability to deal with new crimes,

- poor superintendence,

- the slow pace of modernization,

- lack of research and scientific methods,

- poor welfare, low morale and the lowly status of Constable, and

- the bad public image of the Police.

About 1985 Committee Report, the Implementation Committee report 1990 maintains:

"The Report of the Police Committee, 1985, is by far the most important; as the latest of the series, it incorporates and updates most of the pertinent recommendations of previous Commissions/Committees. However, more importantly, it contains several new recommendations calculated to detach the Police from its persisting, oppressive and anti-people role of the colonial era and to bring about a qualitative change in its perspective and approach in line with the psycho-social environment of an independent, democratic Pakistan of today (Chaudhry 1990 p.1)

4.2.5. National Reconstruction Bureau-NRB and Police Reforms

General Parvez Musharraf, after imposing Martial Law in 1999 (and after terrorist threats in the wake of 9/11), established the National Reconstruction Bureau (N.R.B.) to review and change the laws for government reform. The N.R.B. started reviewing the Old Police Act of 1861, and in that consultative process, three police stalwarts–Mr. Zulfiqar Ali Qureshi, Mr Afzal Ali Shigri, and Mr Shoaib Suddle, who were well versed in police affairs, were included. Ultimately, this dedicated team, keeping in mind all the earlier recommendations, came up with a new police law called 'Police Order' 2002. P.O. 2002 promised a paradigmatic change in primary structure, fundamental mission, and overall objectives of the police organization from a regime service to public service controlled through democratic and the rule of law mechanisms instead of colonial-bureaucratic controls.

The Police Order 2002 promised four critical changes in Pakistan's Police. First, the Police will be fully depoliticized; second, the Police will work as a specialized agency with specialized units to attain professional excellence. Third, Police will be a public service and a rule-of-law department instead of a coercive arm of the government; hence, police officers will accept the dictates of none other than the law. Fourth, the Inspector General of Police will act as ex-officio secretaries of their department. Finally, there will be no dual command system for district police officers or superintendents of Police holding police district command, hence, greater administrative and financial autonomy. The law initially got implemented in four provinces of Punjab, Sindh, K.P., and Balochistan, but it did not extend to Gilgit Baltistan, Azad Kashmir, and the Federal Capital Territory Islamabad. The partial adoption of P.O. 2002 has been an unfortunate part and one of the reasons behind its withering away that earlier.

Sindh and Balochistan undid with Police Order 2002. They reverted to the 1861 Act (Jaise thy) soon after the Parvez Musharraf rule ended in 2008. The new civilian government of Pakistan's people's party came into power at the centre and in both provinces, Sindh and Balochistan. However, in Punjab P.M.L. (N) and Khyber Pakhtunkhwa, the PTI formed provincial governments and redo the Police order 2002. Babakhel (2016) expresses dismay on the slow pace of police reforms in Pakistan and believes reforms are more discussed than implemented meaningfully. He further compares the police development phases in many developed countries and sees Pakistan lagging far behind.

4.2.6. Police Reform Committee 2018 under the stewardship of Afzal Ali Shigri (PSP)

On 15 May 2018, the Chief Justice of Pakistan's Supreme Court, Mr. Saqib Nisar, constituted Police Reforms Committee-PRC from the selected retired police officers. Mr. Afzal Ali Shigri convened the police reform committee (2018), the senior-most among all notified members. The announced P.R.C. (2018) members included Dr. Shoaib Suddle, Asad Jahangir, Tariq Khosa, and Tariq Parvez (all retired Inspectors Generals) serving provincial I.G.P.s, including Islamabad capital territory. The Supreme court directed the Government of Pakistan to establish the P.R.C. (2018). The fundamental purposes of P.R.C. (2018) were to make recommendations on internal and external accountability mechanisms of Police; enhance the quality of investigations; modernize urban policing; develop efficient public complaints redressal systems; introduce alternate dispute resolution systems in all the provinces on the lines of Islamabad and K.P., and strengthen the criminal justice model of counterterrorism. The Committee had to make recommendations after perusing court judgments on Police matters and after reviewing the PO-2002 in particular reference to investigations, dispute resolution mechanisms, community policing, political interference, police accountability, autonomy, counterterrorism, transfers/postings, and service delivery issues of the public.

2.6.1. Shigri, A.A. (ed.) (2019) Police Reforms: Way Forward, Police Reform Committee Report

It took P.R.C. 10 months to launch its Report on 14 January 2019 at the Supreme Court Auditorium at 2:00 PM. I had a chance to attend that launching ceremony of P.R.C. (2018) at the Supreme court building Islamabad. A range of police officers, Supreme Court judges, many high courts and session court judges, journalists, academia, foreign delegates, N.G.O. representatives, and other freelance analysts graced the august occasion with their presence.

The P.R.C. 2018 presented a 272-page report containing identification of Police and policing issues, particular reference to the criminal justice context, and made recommendations for implementation. The P.R.C. report (2019) focused on seven areas of police work which constituted seven chapters of its Report; each underlined the need for Police reform. The seven chapters include- proposing model police law, strengthening police accountability, improving the quality of investigations, revamping urban policing, developing alternative dispute resolution, a criminal justice counterterrorism model, and resolving domain controversies through legislative reforms.

2.6.1.1. Police Accountability

The focus of strengthening accountability is internal accountability. The P.R.C. report (2019) suggested the designation of new offices for this purpose at the district, regional, and provincial levels. First, the Committee proposed police departments nominate additional I.G.P at the provincial level, D.I.G. at the regional level, and S.P. at the district level to work as internal departmental Ombudsmen for the exclusive purpose of internal accountability. Second, all concerned governments of the provinces should notify the 'Provincial Police Complaint Authorities.' Lastly, the Committee stresses upon reinvention of provincial justice committees under concerned chief justices of the provinces to act as a robust external accountability mechanism of Police (Shigri 2019).

2.6.1.2. Quality Investigations

The report reads that the quality of investigation is poor and urgently needs to be fixed. The improvement of the investigation, the Report maintains, is crucial in many respects. First, quality investigations will improve the country's justice delivery system by enhancing conviction rates, which shows a dismal picture. Second, active investigations could help redress public grievances by improving service delivery. Third, quality investigations could improve public police relations, and hence, the public will repose confidence and trust in their police forces. Fourth, the quality investigation will improve police efficiency and performance and, therefore, their image. The P.R.C. report (2019) shows concern regarding the negligence of investigation branches and strongly recommends for functional specialization, adequate resource allocation, the constitution of investigation teams, forensic focus, training for skill certifications, and safeguards against abuse of authority that irks the public more than anything else, records the P.R.C. report (2019).

2.6.1.3. Revamping Urban Policing

The second half of the 20th century witnessed the mushroom growth of cities as a benchmark for the shift of societies from traditional agrarian societies to modern urban hubs with their unique culture and diversified demographics. Pakistan is the sixth most populous country in the world. Population growth has led to the proliferation of cities. The National Population Census 2017 confirms that by 2025 more than sixty percent of Pakistan's total population, which must be more than 50 percent in 2021, will be living in the cities. The unregulated growth of Pakistan's cities has resulted in many social, environmental, and political problems. Domestic sectarian violence rank more severe among all the problems

In the wake of the development of unregulated cities in Pakistan, the government and private experts underline the need for better policing and governance of urban centres. Urban boom is perhaps why the P.R.C. report (2019) emphasizes improving urban policing, which has registered a range of innovations worldwide. To achieve policing, the P.R.C. report 2019 recommends declaring ten cities in Pakistan as qualified for urban police setup. These cities include Karachi, Lahore, Faisalabad, Rawalpindi, Gujranwala, Peshawar, Multan, Hyderabad, Islamabad, and Quetta. These ten cities meet the criteria of a minimum population of one million for urban police dispensation in Pakistan. Notably, PO-200 had a nearly identical design. The P.R.C. report (2019) also suggests that urban policing should get organized into eight wings. These eight functional wings include administration, traffic, operation, law and order, investigation, community relations, Security, and communication technology, each headed by an officer, not below the rank of Deputy Inspector General. However, these recommendations need to be implemented in letter and spirit, and each provincial department should establish other committees for implementation (P.R.C. report 2019).

2.6.1.4. Alternate dispute resolutions

The most critical element of postmodern policing is the capacity of the Police to deliver services to the people to enroll mandatory legitimacy for the authority and police officers wield due to their position of power in society. Many non-cognizable problems of civil and domestic nature waste most of the Police and courts' time and energy and cause a deadlock in the smooth functioning of the criminal justice apparatus for better justice service delivery. It is possible to go for less expensive and expeditious systems of traditional dispute resolution mechanisms, which have greater cultural acceptance, viability, validity, and effectiveness in law and order, peacekeeping, and dispensing justice. Therefore, the P.R.C. 2019 report recommends establishing A.D.R. systems throughout the country.

The P.R.C. report suggested many measures for A.D.R. systems. First, the Report recommends extending Pakistan's A.D.R. Act 2017 to the entire country. Second, the Committee emphasizes the training of A.D.R. staff and all concerned (Police and judiciary) for at least three years in a well-crafted curriculum and state-of-the-art national institute for this purpose. Third, every police department should reconcile the A.D.R. system with the centuries-old cultural institution of Jirga or Panchayat. Fourth, each province should establish mediation centres for arbitrators. Fifth, provincial governments must establish the necessary infrastructure with adequate budgetary allocations to establish A.D.R. Sixth, concerned judges should transform matters relating to minor offences to A.D.R. units within their jurisdictions. Seventh, the superior judiciary needs to establish an effective monitoring system to oversee that all actors, that is, federal and provincial governments and judicial authorities, discharge their mandated duties well. Lastly, the Report calls provincial and federal governments to develop elaborate and workable S.O.P. to ensure that the aims and operations of all actors are aligned well to work within the limits of law and code (P.R.C. Report 2019).

2.6.1.5. Criminal Justice Model of Counterterrorism
The P.R.C., in its 2019 report, actively maintains that policing experience worldwide and research on counterterrorism confirms that the most effective way of policing terrorism is by using a criminal justice framework because terrorism is closer to organized crime involving non-state actors than to state-to-state warfare. Therefore, the P.R.C. specifies these steps in this regard. First, the major emphasis is on capacity building of the criminal justice system to counterterrorism as a specialist area. Second, the Committee stresses the uniformity of anti-terror laws and counter-terror policing across all departments dealing with this issue. Third, federal and provincial governments should implement the N.A.C.T.A. Act 2014 in letters and spirit (P.R.C. Report 2019).

2.6.1.6. Legislative Reforms
Legislation signifies the integrity of reforms. What matters in legislation on any issue of public importance is critical consensus among political parties (Shigri 2019). The other most significant dynamics of legislation appear to be the peoples' feedback as to whether the people feel comfortable, happy, and optimistic, regarding legislative capacity of the highest institution (Parliament) of their country. The public in Pakistan rallies around a critical theme of the rule of law today than ever before. Constitutionalism protects the rule of law and declares a report. Implied in the constitutional approach for the rule of law is countrywide uniformity of policing.

The P.R.C. report (2019) holds that police law is relatable to criminal justice law, including evidence and criminal procedural rules, which are predominantly the domain of the federation. The P.R.C. further maintains that the repeal of P.O. 2002 by the provinces violates the core principles of the federation and is contrary to Pakistan's constitution 1973. Therefore, the Committee invites the attention of the superior judiciary to intervene and set things right by emphasizing the adoption of uniform national police laws with no incongruence to the constitution and other parallel laws. Furthermore, such a model law should address police-public relations, police-government relations, and Police and other stakeholders, including criminal justice, for better collaboration and networking.

2.6.1.7. Model Police Law 2018

To achieve all these ends, the P.R.C. report (2019) comes up with model police law, which seems to be more a revival of Police Order 2002 with slighter and minor additions and deletions. The draft law opens those Police will function constitutionally and democratically, not politically or bureaucratically. It further emphasizes the principles of police autonomy, accountability, professional excellence, political neutrality, and efficient public service delivery (P.R.C. Report 2019). The primary duty of the Police is to serve and protect the fundamental rights of the people, as guaranteed in the constitution.

4.3. Conclusion

The lack of implementation of police reforms in Pakistan speaks volumes of more excellent bureaucratic and political resistance for police organizations to attain professional excellence and functional autonomy as a rule of law institution. Instead of implementing the P.R.C. report 2019 recommendations, the government has constituted bureaucratically dominated committees for police reform, hence paying lip service to the recommendations of the P.R.C. 2019 report prepared under the Supreme Court of Pakistan and Law guidance and Justice Commission of Pakistan. As a result, a more profound crisis of identity, uniformity, credibility, and utility prevailed in the Police and policing in Pakistan in the third decade of the 21st century. This unprecedented crisis needs appropriate redressal, failing the forces of chaos and disorder. The prevailing thinking and recurrent theme of reimaging Police in Pakistan are to get police services in Pakistan fully sensitized to the ground realities and fully prepared to respond to such a bleak scenario.

Chapter: 05

Police Reorganisations

Chapter Brief

This chapter discusses the implementation of police reforms, resulting in police reorganisation in Pakistan. Focus remains on Police Order 2002 and other Police Acts envisioned and enacted by different provinces in Pakistan, including the KP Police Act 2017. the section also highlights the underlying political factors behind the quick amendments in PO 2002 and their withdrawal by provinces with no appropriate constitutional considerations. In a nutshell, this chapter offers insights into reversions, conversions, and subversions of police institutions, strategies, and the integrity of their procedures. Finally, this chapter examines the superior and advanced nature of the KP Police Act 2017. instruments seeking amendments in Police Order 2002, published articles, and reports prepared by policing experts from various disciplines constitute the primary content sources.

5.1.

The transformation of policing from a force model to a service model sits nicely at the soul of the entire police-reform process in Pakistan since its independence in 1947. on the essence of the reform recommendations previously made by commissions/committees or individuals, the National Reconstruction Bureau of Pakistan developed a brilliant plan known as the Police Order 2002 for reorganising and restructuring police forces in Pakistan at the beginning of the 21st century. Patel (2008) in "Feudal Forces" opens his thoughts with the acknowledgement that

> "The state of policing in South Asia is abysmal, entirely unsuitable for independent countries that seek to fulfil their democratic promise with their people, who have no confidence and trust in a colonial dispensation of tyrannical police organisation" (Patel 2008).

Patel (2008) drew on the missing links in the colonial police enactment in 1861. to him, the first principal argument on which he relies is that the old legislation fails to address the challenges of free nations under democratic systems. First, the old Act of 1861 made the police answerable to the government instead of the people. In contrast, the reverse was true in democracies. Second, the police were primarily responsible for controlling people using coercion instead of protecting their rights and liberties. Under colonial dispensation, the police organisation remained a chief source of panic for the people instead of being the medium of security and safety. Third, the police were loyal to the rulers in power instead of being faithful to the law because elected members did not make the law at that time.

On the contrary, the law was a word of the ruler. Policing continued as a regime service even after many countries became independent of colonial powers. New police orders took approximately 50 years to shape in 2002 and produce democratic policing. Colonial model police for the government reflects modern age values. At the same time, Patel (2008) refers to the police for the people we need in Pakistan, which spells the postmodern democratic culture of governance.

5.2. the Democratic Policing

Democratic policing, which emerged in the first decade of the 21st century, depicts the attributes of policing as a democracy in which the police serve the general population, not the Government (Sheptycki 2000). a policing order sets out a regularising structure for police organisations in a democratic polity. The frameworks and methodologies for police in one jurisdiction might be unique to another. However, postmodern policing settings, democracy, plurality, diversity, and differences are well-tolerated, accepted, and accommodated against autocracy, centrality, forced unity, and uniformity (Reiner, 1992). provides a standard frame of reference for different communities, strategists, policy specialists, NGOs, benefactors, and police (Guidebook on Democratic Policing, 2008).

According to the guidebook on democratic policing (2008), democratic policing has the following specific characteristics: to serve the community rather than the state; to ensure transparency and accountability of police rather than their impunity; to reflect the demographic aspirations of the people rather than to promote the political agenda of rulers; to function professionally instead of accepting political interference; to perform their duties efficiently and effectively without fear and favour; to follow the rule of law and procedural justice instead of misusing and abusing authority; to be accountable to the people or their representative bodies instead of political machines; and to provide respect, service and assistance to the people instead of using force against them.

Bayley (2006) defined democratic policing as more than mere crime-fighting or order maintenance., it extends to healthy community relations guided by the policing paradigm of the police's guardianship role rather than the conventional warrior concept. The new police mindset is a calculable and responsible exercise of legitimate authority by the police officers.

86

In light of these narratives of democratic policing, it is apt to define the notion of democratic policing as policing that protects fundamental rights instead of impeding freedoms. Democratic policing offers a safe and secure environment where freedom flourishes and authoritarian coercion diminishes. It corresponds to standard policing functions according to law and people's democratic ideals. Democratic policing works as per procedural justice and protects communities from crimes and violence. Po 2002 was the quest for democratic policing that Pakistan, at the outset of the 21st century, came up with a new police Order in 2002, which claims all the features and standards of democratic policing (PRC 2019).

Police Order 2002 was proclaimed on 14 August 2002 as Chief Executive Order No. 22 of 2002 and supplanted the Police Act of 1861. 2002 contained 188 articles with the essential goal of changing the policing to "work as per the Constitution, law, and the expectations of the general population of Pakistan" (PO 2002). addition, it imagines a police organisation that measurably produces outcomes as far as the prevention and detection of crime, maintenance of public order, and service-delivery are concerned (Ibid).

5.3. features of Police Order 2002

The PO 2002 addressed the authoritarian fault lines of the colonial era's anachronistic Police Act (1861). Act (1861) lacked democratic policing, among other things—the PO 2002 welds police and communities in a trusting relationship. The new paradigm of policing seeks to transform and reorganise police organisations in Pakistan from the 'force' to 'Service' model by laying down an elaborate and comprehensive institutional mechanism to control police and the governments who control police in the name of external oversight. Police Order 2002 withdrew all undemocratic and authoritarian policing elements, realigned organisational goals, police missions, and visions, and came up with tangible democratic additions. We focus on democratic additions to the police system under the Police order 2002.

Articles 11 to 18 deal with the postings of the head of police departments at the levels of federal law enforcement agencies such as FIA, FC, NHMP, NPB, provincial, divisional, district, and specialised units such as forensics, investigations, and traffic police heads. 11 explains the role of the National Public Safety Commission in the posting of provincial police officers (PPOs) and leaders of federal law enforcement agencies such as FIA, FC, and NH&MP. National Public Safety Commission (NPSC) serves as a panel to suggest three names to provincial and federal governments, as the case may be, for approval. Governments choose the Provincial Police Officers of their respective provinces, while the Federal Government approves the names of commandants NPA, FC, IGP NH&MP, and DG FIA (Police Order, 2002).

Clause-6 of the same Article gives the provincial police officer (PPO) administrative and financial powers as ex-officio secretary to the provincial government and other authorities under PO 2002 or any additional legal time being in force. Inspector-General of Police (IGP) capital territory enjoys the same financial and administrative powers as provided in clause-6 to PPO. The Capital City Police Officer or any other head of law enforcement agency can delegate their powers to their following junior officers subject to their job description. 11 (PO 2002) fixed the term of office for police officers at three years. The government cannot transfer police officers without reasonable grounds and consultation with NPSCs, PPSCs, or CPSCs.

However, Article 13 mentions the procedure of posting the Additional Inspectors General to assist the PPO in appointing DPOs or CCPOs set to help him manage crime. The provincial government can post Addll IGP as a CCPO based on professional merits and consultation with PPO. 14 lays down the procedure for appointment experts for assistance from the PPO and the CCPO. Thus, the PPSC could appoint one or two experts to assist the PPO or CCPO, as may be the case.

Article 15[4] of the PO 2002 lists city police officers, CPOs, and district police officers (DPOs). PPO can post CPO in the city district and DPO in any district as a general police area consultation with the government. Tenure for both CPO and DPO is three years. However, the government can change it if certain removal circumstances become inevitable due to poor performance or mishaps. The premature transfer of CPO or DPO will occur after District Nazim. DPSC concurs with PPO or Provincial Government on the proposed removal of such an officer before completion of tenure.

Article 17 mentions the provincial government's power and the role of the PPO or CCPO in the posting of the Deputy Inspector General, Senior Superintendent of Police, Superintendent of Police, and Assistant or Deputy Superintendent of Police. Provincial police officer or the capital city police officer

---

[4] Article 16 maintains that CPO and DPO are responsible for the administration of police force in the general area of police they are in charge. However, as per same article DPO can delegate his administrative powers and functions to his next subordinate officer that may be Superintendent, Assistant or deputy Superintendent working in his unit.

shall post senior Superintendents, Superintendents, Assistant and Deputy Superintendents of Police in general (7) police area" (Police Order 2002).

Articles 9 and 10 (PO 2002) elaborate the details of the arrangements about superintendence and the administration of the police. The superintendence of the department must rest with the government. At the same time, the PPO is responsible for the administration of the police force. Section 1 of Article 9 maintains that "the superintendence of the police throughout a general police area shall vest in the appropriate government. Section 2 of Article 9 explains the exercise of superintendence and provides powers to improve police efficiency and accountability.

However, Article 10 clarifies how and who is responsible for the police administration. In this article, the PO (2002) vests the power of the police administration in a general police area to the heads of the DPO, RPO, CCPO, and PPO units. Section 3 of the same article further mentions the powers of the direction and control of the police to be vested in the PPO, RPO, and CCPO, which can issue standing orders necessarily consistent with the order or rules made for the efficient functioning of the police. In addition to this clause, the provincial police officer is responsible for preparing a provincial annual policing plan. Furthermore, the Provincial Public Safety Commission has the mandate to review, approve, reject or suggest some deletions or additions as they deem fit. The annual policing plan is a new addition to Pakistan's policy.

PO 2002 created a separate and specialised investigation branch to improve the quality of investigations. The challenges of new crimes and terrorism were also a step in the right direction, but what was missing in this exercise was undoubtedly the lack of focus on developing independent specialist cadres to investigate different types at all levels. As a result, the investigation from the watch and ward branches was insufficient to attain the goals. Although, DNA, digital forensics, cybercrime, and technology adoption are crucial for better investigation. Despite its loopholes in implementation, envisaging a separate investigation wing was undeniably a leap forward in policing that still struggled despite provincial governments' undoing and redoing of PO 2002.

5.4. and Responsibilities of the Police Redefined

The Police Order 2002 redefines the attitudes, duties, and responsibilities of the police towards the public. Courtesy, promoting amity, protecting vulnerable groups, and rescuing people in danger, under threat, or facing an emergency are some of the new hallmarks of reorganising the police force on democratic and rights-based approaches in Pakistan (PO 2002).

Article 4 of the PO (2002) maintains that the duties of a police officer include protecting the life, property, and liberty of citizens; preserving public peace; and ensuring the rights and privileges of arrested persons. Duties have extended to many new and significant areas. The police must prevent public nuisance, collect and communicate criminal intelligence, and prevent obstruction on public roads, streets, thoroughfares, neighbourhoods, and places of worship. The police should regulate traffic, take charge of all unclaimed property, and prepare an inventory. Police must detect crimes, bring offenders to justice, apprehend all persons required under the law, and communicate the detainee's arrest to the person of their choice. police must enter and inspect public places, shops, gaming houses, alcohol shops, narcotic business compounds, illegal weapons stores, and public places occupied by disorderly characters without warrants., police are the creatures of law, and hence, must obey and execute all lawful orders issued by any statutory body, including the courts. Police must cooperate with other agencies to prevent crime, disorder, vandalism, terrorism, violence, sabotage, and public exploitation., police should take special care of vulnerable groups, including women, children, the elderly, and minorities (Police Order 2002).

5.5. Safety Network

The scheme of the public safety commissions provided in Police Order 2002 is very elaborate and detailed. Scheme structures the four tiers or levels of institutional hierarchy. Original PO 2002 exhaustively dealt with the institutional framework of public safety by devoting five chapters, one for each public safety mechanism, from chapters V to XI. The primary goal behind creating public safety institutional networks is to protect the public from police coercion abuse of authority and safeguard the police against undue external influences, including political and bureaucratic ones. Pakistan borrowed the idea of public safety from the Japanese Police System, which adopted public safety as a core police function during the 1960s as a part of the reform and modernisation of policing in Japan. PO 2002 briefly explain the procedure for establishing PSCs at different levels, criteria for appointment/section, removal of its members and chairman, quorum, and the composition of each commission, their functions, and terms of office.

Federal and provincial governments have the authority to establish public safety commissions within their respective domains. The federal government was competent under PO 2002 to establish the

By J.J. Baloch (2022)

National Public Safety Commission and the Public Safety Commission for Islamabad's capital territory. In addition, governments can establish provincial, capital city, and city districts and all-district public safety commissions within the provincial jurisdictions. The system is well-defined.

PUBLIC SAFETY COMMISSIONS	NOMINATION OR SELECTION
	50% Nomination from assemblies and 50% selection of independent members by the Panels. The Chairperson of PSCs is elected from among its members by majority vote on a rotational basis from nominated and independent members.
DISTRICT	Zila Council and District Selection board headed by District & Session Judge assisted by two members-one a representative of district assembly while the other of Provincial Assembly.
CAPITAL CITY	Governor of province appoints six independent members on the recommendations of the Capital City Selection Panel headed by Chief Justice of High Court. Comparison, three members come from Capital City district Assembly through secret ballot, and the speaker of Provincial Assembly nominates three.
ISLAMABAD	President of Pakistan on recommendations of District Islamabad Panel in case of independent members; the Speaker of National Assembly nominates three members from National Assembly; while Zila Council elects three members through secret ballot from among its councillors.
PROVINCIAL	Speaker of Provincial Assembly and Provincial Selection Panel headed by CJ of HC can appoint.
NATIONAL	Speaker of National Assembly and National Selection Panel headed by CJ Supreme Court can appoint.

PSC	COMPOSITION & MEMBERSHIP

DISTRICT	**8-10 members**, half nominated by *Zila Council* and half independent appointed by Governor on the recommendations of District Selection Panel; however, at least two members should be women.
CAPITAL CITY	**Twelve members**, depending upon the area and population of the district (Article 49). of six nominated members, **three** shall get **elected** by the **Zila Council** from amongst its councillors. Member cast only one vote favouring any contesting candidate through a secret ballot. At the same time, the other **three members** shall get **nominated by the speaker** of the Provincial Assembly from amongst its members, two from the treasury and one from the opposition benches (Article-50). In addition, the Governor shall appoint six independent members from a list of names recommended by the **Capital City District Selection Panel.**
ISLAMABAD CAPITAL TERRITORY	**Twelve members** (ARTICLE-61). Twelve members shall be elected by the District Council, from amongst its councillors, by each member casting only one vote in favour of any contesting candidate through secret ballot. In addition, three members shall get nominated by the speaker of the National Assembly from amongst its members. Furthermore, two members from the treasury and one from the opposition shall get appointed in consultation with the House's Leader and the Opposition's Leader. In addition, the president of Pakistan will appoint six independent members from the list recommended by the Selection Panel headed by the Chief Justice of IHC. of elected and independent members shall be women (Article-62).
PROVINCIAL	**Twelve members**-(Article-73). In addition, (6) were nominated by *speaker* of the provincial assembly, three each from the treasury and the opposition in consultation with the leader of the house and the opposition, provided that at least **two members** shall be women (Article 74).
NATIONAL	**Speaker of the assembly nominates** Twelve **members**- (Article-85). And opposition leaders appoint three each after consultation. In addition, six members will be independent. The president appoints them from a list of names recommended by the *National Selection Panel.* one member will be from each province and Capital Territory of Islamabad (Article-86).

PRIMARY FUNCTIONS OF PUBLIC SAFETY FRAMEWORKS IN PAKISTAN

The primary functions of all the public safety commissions are the same; the only difference is in jurisdictions and levels of operation and administration. functions include: -

1) To help police formulate their policing strategy for adequate crime control, public order maintenance and the protection of fundamental human rights of the people of Pakistan.

2) To assist heads of the police organisations to prepare Annual Policing Plans for more objective, focussed, coherent and result-oriented policing in Pakistan.

3) To safeguard the people of Pakistan from being victimised by the police and their authority misused. Practical and legitimate external oversight of police requires the appropriate means of institutional checks and balances.

4) To protect police from political interference and bureaucratic leg-pulling for ensuring the best practices of police governance and encouraging police to adhere to the rule of law and procedural and a professional working environment.

5) To work as a bridge between the people and the police for reducing the traditional gap created by bad police image based on trust deficit between two critical stakeholders of peace in the society. This way, the role of public safety commissions in establishing Citizen-police liaison Committees is laudable.

6) To facilitate the improvements in police performance by recommending Provincial governments to develop policy guidelines and actionable plans regarding amelioration of better public service delivery at different levels and building police capacity. In addition, The PSC submits annual reports on the performance of PSCs as well as police agencies and departments countrywide.

7) Both the federal as well as provincial, by providing the list of the panel of three police officers for the appointment of DGs (IB, FIA), Commandants (FC, NPA) and IGPs (All provinces, NHMP, Railways). on the levels of their hierarchy, each public safety unit plays the same role for their parallel police commanders, including District Police officers and Regional Police Officers.

8) To coordinate between and among various police agencies and their related departments such as Police Complaint Authorities, Criminal Justice Coordination Committees, and Citizen-Police Liaison Committees at different levels for a holistic approach towards establishing the rule of law cohesive law enforcement policy.

TERM OF OFFICE AND REMOVAL

The term of office for the members of the Public Safety Commission at every level ranging from district to federal levels is the same, which is *three years*; however, there is no provision for the eligibility of second term (Article-45).

Similarly, the **removal procedure and its grounds** are the same with the only difference of invoking body.

- The province governor can remove a member from office either of his own volition or the District Public Safety Commission (Article 46). government or PSC can remove the members of public safety commissions on the grounds of *proving the fake identity, mental illness or physical disability, guilty of misconduct, controversial person, convicted of the criminal offence, a loan defaulter, a tax evader, and a threat to peace, harmony, solidarity and integrity of Pakistan*. In addition, the person who has brought lousy repute to the commission and is a chronic absentee in meetings will also be liable for removal.

- The common grounds for the removal are the reverse of qualifications for the membership of any PSC. Any member has all these qualifications; they can get appointed as a member of PSC of any level. They lack any of these; they will get removed.

- Similarly, *Governor* is also removing authority in cases of CCPSC and PPSC.

- In the case of NPSC and Islamabad PSC, the removing authority will be the *President* of Pakistan.

Selection Panel for NPSC

The selection panel for independent members should consist of the Supreme Court Chief Justice as the chairperson, a nominee of the President of Pakistan, and a nominee of the Prime Minister of Pakistan. Public safety is a unique democratic addition to 21st-century policing in Pakistan. But unfortunately, the concept of public safety commissions neither survived nor thrived; it failed to get implemented at national and provincial levels. Instead, the perverted and politically cloned version came into play at the district level, losing its original objective to immunise the police from political meddling and bureaucratic undertones (see Bayley 2006). Now, the idea of democratic policing in Pakistan remains merely a pipedream.

5.6. Complaint Authority-PCA

Police Order 2002 created a "National Police Complaint Authority" to inquire complaints against federal law enforcement agencies (Article 97). NPCA has one chairperson and six members. The President of Pakistan appoints the body's chairperson, whereas the government appoints members through the Federal Public Service Commission. The term of office for members who hail from diverse backgrounds with relevant knowledge, experience, and expertise, together with impeccable integrity and untainted reputation, is three years. In contrast, no member or chairperson can be eligible for the second term. National police complaint authority receives complaints from police officials serving in the Islamabad Police, FIA, FC, NH&MP or any other federal police department or law enforcement agency. 97 to 108 deal with establishment, appointment, removal, composition, functions, and secretariat of police complaint authorities at district, provincial, and federal levels.

5.7. Police Liaison Committees

"The Government will establish Citizen Police Liaison Committees (CPLCs) in consultation with the National Public Safety Commission or the Provincial Public Safety and Police Complaints Commission. committees will be voluntary," self-financing and autonomous bodies (Police Order 2002); the functions of these committees are: "training and capacity building of members and staff of the commission; developing a mechanism for liaison between aggrieved citizens and" police for providing relief; and assistance to commissions, National Police Complaints Authority and the police for the expeditious and judicious discharge of their duties (Police Order 2002)

5.8. Justice Coordination Committee at District Level

Chapter XI of PO 2002 in article 109, 110, 111 talks about the establishment, composition and functions of the District Criminal Justice Coordination Committee. In each district, the CJCC shall be established. The committee will comprise District and Session Judge as chairman, District Police Officer, District Public Prosecutor, District Superintendent Jail, District Probation Officer, district Parole Officer, and District head of investigation as the Secretary of the Committee.

The primary functions of the CJCC, as enunciated in Article 111 of PO 2002, include many. First, the CJCC reviews the work of police and prosecution. Second, the Criminal Justice Coordination Committee tries to find loopholes in the system, suggesting steps for improvement. Third, the CJCC develops understanding and cooperation among all CJS stakeholders. Fourth, it exchanges the information regarding any issue that affects any of the parts of CJS and prepares an implementation plan for CJS policies. Fourth, it communicates relevant issues to appropriate authorities. This coordinating body promotes the best practices of CJS. Finally, the CJCC follows the decisions taken during its monthly meetings.

5.9. Order 2002 Amendments

Police Order 2002 witnessed amendments in 2004 and 2006. In the following paragraphs, we critically review them.

- **Posting of Provincial Police Officer-PPO:** Article 11 (1) of the PO 2002 provided that the provincial government would post a provincial police officer from a panel of three officers, as proposed by the National Public Safety Commission. The same article got amended, and the NPSC was replaced with the federal government to suggest the panel of three officers to the provincial government., instead of an independent and neutral NPSC body, politics dictate the composition of the panel of the three officers.

- **Tenure of PPO:** Article 12 (6) of PO 2002 provides that the provincial government will not make any premature transfer of a PPO before the expiry of three-year tenure without prior permission from the Provincial Public Safety Commission-PPSC. The federal government can prematurely remove any PPO after seeking agreement from the NPSC. Amendments in article 12 (6), the role of safety commissions in the early transfer of PPOs stands eliminated. As a result, the role of public safety commissions for guarding against police politicisation got diluted to a large extent.

- **Premature transfer of the PPO:** Article 12 (3) provides that the PPO can be prematurely transferred only after explicit and necessary concurrence between the PPSC and PG on legitimate grounds of inefficiency or poor PPO performance. Amendments in article 12 (3) eliminated the promising role of PPSC and PCA.

- **Premature transfer of district police officer:** Article 15 (3) states that DPOs can be transferred prematurely before completion of their tenure only when concurrence between Zila Nazim and the District Public Safety Commission develops purely on the grounds of inefficiency and ineffectiveness. in article 15 (3) incorporated the provincial government could transfer the DPO in the case of necessity, urgency, misconduct, and inefficiency. This amendment eliminated the security of tenure for DPO.

- **Performance Evaluation Report of the DPO:** Under the original PO 2002, District Nazim and the Capital City Mayor had no role in DPO PERs. However, an amendment in Article 33 (3) District Nazim was declared an initiating or reporting officer of DPO. This change put the DPO under the political influence as the DN was not a professional supervisor to keep objectivity in mind to write the PER of DPO and hence politicised.

- **The District Public Safety Commission:** Under Article 38 (1), half of the members of the DPSC were to be the district Councillors, whiles the other half was to be the independent members. of Subsection (a) in Article 38 (1), reduced independent members to 1/3 of the total which was 1/2 before the amendment. As a result, the weight of politics increased through the representation of MPAs and MNAs who could not play a non-partisan role and, hence, more politicisation.

- **A merger of police complaint authorities into DPSC and PPSC:** Article 103-08 provided for establishing separate police complaint authorities at the district and provincial levels. In reality, the government failed to implement relevant articles. However, new amendments in the same articles merged DPCA and PPCA into DPSC and PPSC, respectively, and integrated complaints about police functions. As a result, there is no separate dedicated body to resolve complaints against the police.

- **The composition of the PPSC:** Article 74 (2) states that among the six nominated members of the PPSC, three got selected from the treasury and three from the opposition benches. The amended article included four members from the treasury and two members from the opposition. intrusion of political members misbalances the opposition's role by increasing the policing influence of the government.

Sangay Patil (2008) writes in his *Feudal Forces* Report:

"Even though the Police Order 2002 was not perfect, its proper implementation would have shaken up a morbid system that is in desperate need of reform., since it was promulgated by a dictator that relied heavily on the international donors to resource the initiative, the process of extension of PO 2002 was viewed as illegitimate by the successive political governments like that of PPP and Muslim League (N). a result, the subsequent changes made to the PO 2002 ensured that its progressive elements were neutered and that it would never function effectively" (Patel 2008, p. 60).

5.10. II of Police Reorganisation in Pakistan

The amendments in PO-2002 started within a short period of two years. As a result, amended PO-2002 was implemented in 2004 and 2006, respectively. Amendments focused mainly on police control, where two main interest groups came to the fore: the bureaucracy and political leaders. The impartial institutions of public safety and the role of the bureaucracy in law and order remained focal. More significant is the role of bureaucracy in police, the lesser is the professionalism and legitimacy of police authority, and the conclusion that police leadership had indicated in their interviews while discussing challenges to police reforms in Pakistan.

5.10.1. Constitutional Amendment

The Police Order-2002 was initially a presidential order, yet validated by the 17th amendment, dated 31 December 2003. 17th amendment changed Article 270-AA (1) of the Constitution 1973, validating Police Order 2002. PO 2002 got included in the sixth schedule of the constitution as a part of over 30 laws that could not be amendable except prior permission of the president. 18th constitutional amendment came amid debates on reducing the president's powers and restoring the sovereignty of parliament. Despite their differences over many issues, all political parties were on the same page.

The 18th amendment affected the federal status of the Police Order 2002 in many ways. It affirmed parliament's legislative competence over the PO 2002. The amendment deleted the sixth schedule rendered PO-2002 vulnerable to provincial assemblies. However, parliament had not transferred PO 2002 to the exclusive domain of the provinces, which misunderstood the spirit of the amendment. Another misconception developed because of the elimination of a concurrent legislative list in the constitution containing 47 entries, including criminal law, criminal procedure, and evidence law, to which Police order was relatable. Fourth, doing away with the concurrent list and criminal justice laws, including the PO 2002, conflicted with article 142 (b)., entry number 40, on the contrary, enhanced police officers' jurisdiction to any other province relating to interprovincial coordination on the issues of Council of common interests [Article 154 (1)] reading with entry 18 of Federal Legislative List. Amendment, the 18th amendment brought law enforcement cooperation on criminal matters under international treaties, such as extradition and mutual legal assistance, into the Federal Government's exclusive domain., adding entry number 13, the 18th amendment made it clear for the first time by providing a solid constitutional basis that interprovincial cooperation on law-and-order matters was a function that rested with the federal government., none of these developments had affected the constitutional status of PO 2002 in terms of its concurrent status. Still, the provinces misspelt the 18th

98

Amendment by rushing to dissect policing from the federal domain, which led to a constitutional crisis of policing that continues unresolved (Eighteenth Amendment [Online] 2010).

However, the engineered impacts of the 18th amendment policing remained negative. In this amendment, the provinces made independent decisions regarding Police Order 2002. and Balochistan abandoned and entirely rejected PO 2002, opting to return to the old police formations established under Police Act 1861. Khyber Pakhtunkhwa came up with a new Police Act of 2017, whereas in Punjab, discussions on police reform remained confined to bureaucratic corridors. After returning to the 1861 Police Act, the Punjab government decided to enact a new police act under the framework of the police order. The removal of the roles of the district Nazim and the public safety commission spoke volumes of the attempted revival of magistracy.

5.10.2. Police Reforms & the Issue of "Magistracy" and Police Control

"A justice of peace instead of going under the thumb of the executive brings executive under the thumb of law", beautifully remarks Justice Ejaz Afzal Khan. In Pakistan, things go in their reverse order as the bureaucracy, using their political influence, never misses a chance to grab the powers of the 'justice of the peace from the judiciary. Seasoned law experts unwelcome the Punjab government's move to encroach on the judicial domain and expressed grave concerns. Many experts have declared Punjab's move for the justice-of-peace portfolio as an attack on the independence of the judiciary, the rule of law and civil liberties.

Pakistan's Lawmaking history reveals that the race on justice-of-peace powers between bureaucracy and judiciary dates back to the adoption of the constitution of Pakistan in 1973. Articles 9, 25, 175, 203 provide for the separation of the judiciary from the executive. Constitutionalists envisaged the gradual separation of the judiciary from the executive. Judiciary became independent in the 21st first cbury21st-century. The legal adventures between executive and judicial branches of the government during the Musharraf government imbalanced the governance. Office of the Justice of Peace appeared to have become the most coveted and cherished one for both the bureaucrats and the judges of the courts in the wake of recent efforts to reverse these powers from district and session judge to its former colonial seat of Deputy Commissioner both in Punjab and Sindh. Such efforts by bureaucracy are hard to sustain in the wake of the postmodern criminal justice requirements.

5.11. Overview

Despite the improvement and extension of PO 2002, the KP Police Act (2017) claims many distinguishing democratic and community-centric features that do not parallel the history of police reforms in Pakistan. The new key and distinguishing characteristics of the KP Police Acts (2017) include the following.

Service-oriented: Public service is the soul of the KP Police Act of the 2017 Police and is expected to deliver doorstep services. satisfaction of the citizens is one of the leading characteristics (Section-3) of postmodern policing, and this is how we have incorporated it into our 21st-century police legislation (O'Malley, 1997).

Guardian role: The primary role of the police is to protect the lives, liberty, and property of people and provide them with safety and security against all kinds of human dangers and threats by controlling crime, maintaining order, preventing violence, and countering terrorism. Pakistan's new laws, especially the KP Police Act 2017, identify and emphasise postmodern policing, which seeks to serve the people instead of what James Sheptycki (2000) referred to as protected territories. Instead, KP Police Act focuses on the people, governments, and territories.

Democratic accountability: Police is accountable to the people through well-organised institutional bodies such as police complaint authority, public safety commissions and criminal justice coordination committees. Accountability aligns with police autonomy. Inspector-General of the Police, KP, is competent and independent to post any police officer without external influence. In response to questions regarding what improvements the police urgently need, all the responses can be summarised in the belief that responsibility without freedom is a misnomer. For freedom or autonomy of any organisation, nothing is more important than the 'institutional guarantees, so claims Mr Shigri (2019).

Strategic Planning: The Police Policy Board under the stewardship of the PPO is one of the best examples of strategic decision-making in the police department, which marks a departure from traditional authoritarian decision-making in modern police arrangements Consultations and inclusive approaches in pluralistic settings accommodate diverse viewpoints and accept disagreement or dissent, which is at the heart of what we refer to as the postmodern era Thus, the KP Police Act incorporates strategic planning elements of policing.

By J.J. Baloch (2022)

Redefining the police mandate: Under the KP Police Act of 2017, establishing a counterterrorism department in the province sits well with the emerging requirements for expanded police missions in the 21st century. In national security, policing can rediscover its relevance and vibrance. Contemporary policing faces the daunting challenges of risk society (Beck 1992), black-box society (Pasquale 2015), security threats (Sedra 2017), transnational crime (Madsen 2009), mobile lives (Elliott and Urry 2010), the commodified policing (Newburn 2001), the age of panic (Bowling and Sheptycki 2010) and the threats of nuclear terrorism (Levi 2007). The KP Police Act addresses the challenge of redefining the mandates for policing.

Community-centric Policing: Community policing steps such as Dispute Resolution Councils-DRCs, Police Assistance Lines-PAL, Public Liaison Councils, and online accessibility of police are excellent and rare steps towards democratic and pluralistic policing systems in Pakistan. We will discuss these new institutions of Pakistan police in the chapter on "Community Relations in this volume.

Political Ownership of Police Reform: Section 143 of KP PA 2027 provides for the appointment of the Implementation Commissioner, which speaks of the seriousness and meaningfulness of the government's resolve to implement new police law. The implementation demonstrates the seriousness of this reform.

Adoption of supplementary legislative measures: In addition to the Police Act of 2017, the KP government occasionally implemented many laudable legislative measures after PTI came into power. Legislative measures include Police Act 2017, KP Restriction of Rental Building Act 2014, KP Hotel Restriction (Security) Act 2014, KP Vulnerable and Sensitive Establishment & Places Security Act 2014, and amendments in Punjab Police Rules 1934 as well as in KP Police Efficiency & Discipline Rules (amended in 1914) and much more. These supplementary measures were necessary to ensure that the policy reform strategy was effective and successful.

Adoption of Technology: The KPK police stands ahead of other police departments in Pakistan in technology adoption. These technological initiatives include centralized crime tracking and analysis systems (CCTAS), criminal record verification systems (CRVS), identity verification systems (IVS), and vehicle verification systems (VVS). In addition, tenant and hotel verification systems generate an extensive criminal database that helps in more innovative policing, including easy access and quick response philosophy, which this paper tries to advertise for expanding similar police reforms throughout Pakistan.

Capacity building network: Regarding the capacity building of the force, the reform did not stop with the half-reformed Nowshera School but spread the network of specialized schools in the entire province, which is unprecedented in the history of policing in the subcontinent. The schools included the Police School of Investigation Peshawar, Police School of Intelligence Abbottabad, Police School of Tactics Peshawar, Police School of Explosive Handling at Nowshera, Police School of Public Disorder, Riot Management Mardan, and Police School of Information Technology Peshawar. The up-gradation and expansion of different training schools in KP are remarkable and impactful steps in the right direction. It is important to note that these all-new schools were established in 2014-15, which falls within the PTI government Tenure.

5.12. Conclusion

Based on the above overview, the KP Police Act (2017) was a leap forward from Police Order 2002 in many respects. First, KP PA 2017 involves the strategic vision of policing as a dynamic social process and engages the community to attain societal levels with minimum crimes and a goodwill tool of governance to ensure better public service delivery. Second, KP PA 2017 incorporates more innovative ways of policing, as indicated by expanded police duties and responsibilities and befitting the functional division of force. Third, the KP model emphasises the appropriate use of technology and science in the police. Fourth, KP Act 2017 offers a separate, fully functional counterterrorism department missing in the PO 2002. Fifth, the Office of Implementation Commissioner for Police Reforms was established. Sixth, supplementary legislation influences many KP Police ACT (2017) aspects and ensures better enforcement. Seventh, police specialism has received greater importance in transforming police into an efficient organisation by revamping recruitment, promotion, transfer postings, welfare, pay structure, and capacity-building areas. Eighth, training has been accorded prime and primary importance by establishing separate schools for all necessary police specialisations ranging from investigation, crime prevention, Mob control, crime scene management, and intelligence. Ninth, a provincial police officer got stronger to escape bureaucratic red-tapism in police matters. Tenth, KP policing approach engages the community in policing through dispute resolution committees at the district level to lessen the burden of work on criminal justice institutions, including the judiciary. Eleventh, the KP police have created human rights vigilance wings to notice violations. Finally, institutional police networks in the KP province dilute political and bureaucratic influence. These steps reflect the democratic spirit of the KP policing, which seems to be the best-managed police in Pakistan today.

Chapter: 06

Police Innovations

Chapter Brief

This chapter identifies five types of policing innovations in Pakistan. These five areas of policing innovations include the areas of police governance, technology adoption, forensic science, gender demographics and cybercrime. The innovations that have taken place in NHMP, Lahore Safe City Project, Punjab Safe City project, Punjab Forensic Science Agency, and National Cyber Crime Centre (NR3C) get due scrutiny here. This part also analyses the aggregate impact of such innovations on overall policing in Pakistan. It overviews Pakistan's digital revolution and challenges it poses to policing and also policing innovations made to cope with such challenges. This chapter aims to analyse the effects of policing innovations in Pakistan on national security, public safety, public order, and police capacity to deliver public service, control crime, and combat violence in society. Constitutive documents of these institutions and their performance reports issued internally by these institutions or prepared by freelance authors externally formulate the core of discourse in this chapter.

6.1. Introduction

The use of technology in policing has become commonplace (Palmer et al., 2012). Hanania (2018) believes that the Age of Techno-democracy is afoot, which requires police to reconcile law enforcement with Techno-policing. Policing innovation articulates what the sociologists describe as the 'postmodern condition' of human civilisation (Lyotard 1984). Policing innovations focus on citizen involvement, restorative methodologies, gender streamlining, crime management and proactive policing, forensic investigation techniques, safe city projects, use of technology, Internet of Things (IoT), social media, artificial intelligence, strategic communications, traffic management (Sheldon and Wright 2010), and quick as well as timely police response to the public in an emergency. The cutting-edge technologies have categorically changed the ways police officers perform their job and have also improved police efficiency, accountability, and transparency in protecting the police and the public from any discrimination and distortion (Ferguson 2017).

How has this taken place in Pakistan over the years? The case study analysis into National Highways and Motorways Police (NH&MP), Punjab Safe City Project (PSCP), Punjab Forensic Science Agency (PFSA), and National Response Centre for Cyber Crime (NR3C) reveals much to be understood and learned from the application of technology, science, media and Internet of things in preventing new crimes such as cyber offences, human trafficking, money laundering, street crimes etc. So how could police work to embrace police technology in Pakistan further?

6.2. Police Governance Innovations

6.2.1. Establishment of New Police: NH&MP

The NH&MP is the first tangible milestone in Pakistan's endeavours to innovate policing ideas concerning police governance and professional autonomy. This new organisations' heart is the concept of service and help to road commuters. Serving with a smile sits nicely at the soul of organisational culture, which breaks with traditionally coercive policing conduct in the sub-continent. Mr Iftikhar Rasheed was the first Inspector General who conceived and structured the NHMP in 1997. With human resources of around 12,000, NH&MP oversees the safety of the highway of about 3000 kilometres.

During the 21 years of its existence, NH&MP has established its reputation of modern people-friendly service par-excellence in terms of transparency, public service delivery, professionalism, the rule of law, discipline, and literature of good policing that is always for the public good. Many analysts of policing view this new organisation as a paradigm shift in the ethos of policing in Pakistan. Surveys and Research conducted by scholars acknowledge the success of this police organisation in terms of working environment, workforce capacity, apolitical governance and strategic management and vision.

6.2.1.1. Distinguishing features of Motorway Police

There are many remarkable distinguishing features of this police force (Tahir 2012).

- First, NH&MP marks a break with traditional police forces regarding uniform, public dealing, working environment, governance model and bureaucratic meddling.
- Second, unlike traditional police forces, junior officers of NH&MP take pride in their job and are well educated.
- Third, Motorway police are organised under National Highways and Motorway Police Ordinance (2000), providing a flexible legal and operational framework.
- Fourth, internal decision making of the force is scientific, evidence-based and data-guided and not whimsical nor discretionary.

- Fifth, the application of management and service delivery procedures is homogeneous, non-discriminatory and across-the-board.
- Sixth, highway police follow an empirical and objective performance evaluation system and fully use technology in their operational work to escape error and miscalculation.
- Seventh, the appointment, promotions and transfer/posting are made meritoriously and transparently, following the career planning and welfare guidelines/SOPs.
- Eighth, NH&MP has developed both conventional and social media to engage with the community in more ingenious ways to keep commuters well-informed about road and weather conditions and build their softer and friendly image.
- Ninth, the NH&MP actively participates in community development activities, such as anti-polio, anti-tobacco, flood victims' rehabilitation, anti-pollution, missing child recovery and blood donation, medical camps, and rescue stations did during the 2005 earthquake in Pakistan.
- Tenth, the NH&MP has developed a strong reputation for honesty and fair play, so it is difficult for politicians, bureaucrats, media and other pressure groups to abuse the force.
- Eleventh, the public stand by NH&MP staff for all good reasons, and people react against any disgrace caused to the force in the line of their duty.
- Unlike other traditional forces, motorway police engage the media very meaningfully, especially for informing and educating the masses about road safety and driving ethics. The NHMP also uses its website, public notice boards, seminars, printed handouts, and newsletters for transparency and publicity.
- Thirteenth, NH&MP has developed a very productive system of incentives and rewards for better performance, which go a long way in discouraging corruption and undue favouritism.
- Fourteenth, NH&MP is the only police force in Pakistan that has specified a certain quota of female officers for gender streamlining, an encouraging gesture and act for image building. At present, approximately 4 to 5 per cent force is female, which is a relatively higher ratio.
- Fifteenth, Anti-corruption watchdogs, like Transparency International, have certified NH&MP as one of Pakistan's leading corruption-free public sector organisations.
- Sixteenth, NH&MP runs an emergency ambulance and 24-hour helpline system for medical and mechanical aid people travelling on the roads.
- Seventeenth, the salary structure is very handsome and duty hours reasonable with an impressive infrastructure, transportation and accessible bachelor accommodations for staff.

- Eighteenth, The NH&MP enjoys greater administrative and financial autonomy because it generates revenues, and it is not under any politician to meddle in its affairs, not yet under any magistrate.
- Lastly, NH&MP makes neither arrest nor detains but only helps, facilitates and fines; that is why its conduct has never been objectionable for the public. On the contrary, NH&MP has gradually gained more incredible public accolades.

6.3. The Technological Innovations

6.3.1. Punjab Safe City Project

In Pakistan's Police Innovation history, Punjab Safe City Project is the second-largest and most successful addition after Motorway Police in transforming its police culture and the working environment. Indeed, this change has produced remarkable results in preventing and detecting crime. In the modern-day world, digital technology has revolutionised the way humans live within organised societies. It is one of the fundamental duties of the state to provide security and safety. The provision of safety is the foundation of the 'quality life' of the citizens. Thus, public safety remains a significant challenge to modern governance and policing.

6.3.2. The Safe City Concept

Like many countries, Pakistan police services embrace "a holistic and integrated approach" for ensuring public safety-now known as Safe Cities. The Safe City concept has emerged as a fundamental component of policing the complex urban hubs for citizen security, safety and quality of life using technology, digital infrastructure, skilled police personnel and more innovative processes (Concept Paper PPIC3 2015).

"The Safe City concept can be extended to any physical environment where its citizens require a safe, comfortable environment. It is a system of achieving public safety in modern cities by combining the street patrolman's intuitive approach with state-of-the-art technology for communication and dissemination of information" (Concept Paper PPIC3 2015).

To Jolly Wong, a chief police telecommunications engineer in Hong Kong, "The safe cities concept combines terms such as digital, intelligent, smart and sustainable into initiatives that deploy technologies to enhance security and information flow, (Safe City Index 2018)."

6.3.3. Establishment of Punjab Safe Cities Authority

"In keeping with the Safe Cities concept and making the security challenges of a modern urban environment, the government realised to establish an autonomous authority under the Punjab Safe

106

Cities Ordinance 2015 for the development, construction, installation and maintenance of Integrated Command, Control and Communications Programme throughout the province. The Ordinance was drafted and enacted on 7 July 2015, with its governing body, executive and management setup" (Akbar Nasir Khan Interview 2017).

The Punjab government has introduced the Lahore Safe City Project in 2016. As a result, Lahore announced the first safe city of Pakistan and South Asia in 2018. The cost of the safe city project of Lahore was about Rs 13.5 billion, as reported. The Lahore safe city venture was multiple times bigger than the effectively operational Islamabad safe city project.

Punjab Safe Cities Project is the first-of-its-kind initiative in the entire nation and the most extraordinary venture in Asia. Punjab is the first to present Safe City Project, and now the task covers six different urban areas of Punjab, including Multan, Bahawalpur, Rawalpindi, Gujranwala, Faisalabad and Sargodha. The Punjab Safe Cities Project pursues the "One-Stop-Shop Approach" by working with different agencies and experts in an integrated and networked fashion to manage the crisis circumstances.

Punjab Safe Cities Project is a trademark and flagship project of the Punjab Government. Punjab Safe Cities Authority (PSCA) is Pakistan's unique public safety project with its own advanced 4G-LTE communication system. The venture guarantees the security of urbanites through digitisation of existing policing structures and their integration with other law enforcement, intelligence and other stakeholders in peace.

6.3.3.1. Assessment of previous security Systems in Cities of Punjab

Definite explanations behind the craftsmanship of safe city venture in Punjab Police are grounded in many factors. First, Punjab police had limited capacity to use technology in policing and rescue efforts during emergencies and relied on manuals only. Second, Punjab police did not have a data accumulation and analysis system. Third, Punjab police had no strategic communication network within the department and other strategic partners. Fourth but not least, there was no culture of using material evidence obtained through telemetric devices and forensic instruments in a befitting manner. Last, digital evidence, such as the face or number plat readings, was uncommon.

6.3.4. The PPIC3 Programme

The Safe Cities idea calls for more insight-driven interventions. Along with these lines, the extent of the task extended in 2013 to build up an integrated command, control and communications mechanism with analytic and scientific capability. In this way, the Punjab Police Integrated Command, Control and Communications (PPIC3) Program aims at catering to the safety and security needs of booming urban communities. Accordingly, the Punjab government set up the Project Management Unit (PMU) for PPIC3 in 2014 to improve, develop, and upkeep the first PPIC3 Center (Concept Paper PPIC3 2015).

6.3.4.1. The effectiveness of the PPIC3 Programme
The IC3 Programme could bring together the innovative concept of operations (Concept Paper PPIC3 2015).

- Law-enforcement technology and digital process infrastructure provide real-time information and artificial intelligence for facilitating field commanders in making evidence-based decisions in operationally critical and administratively challenging situations.
- This arrangement will enhance the ability of police to have access to and share information within the Punjab Police and other external agencies in a networked fashion to ensure better service delivery to the public through a timelier response and easier access for effective handling.
- Easy availability of data, information and intelligence could facilitate police to make informed decisions in setting priority and allocating appropriate resources in response to calls for emergency or crime reports in Lahore.
- Adopting technology in law enforcement will make the service delivery system well-oiled and flexible business for police crime control strategies that can evolve with the changing needs and challenges of the cities.
- The Safe Cities project increases police capacity and foreseeable growth beyond any reform.
- Design and implement a consolidated IC3 organisational operating model to enhance cross-agency coordination, communication, integration, and direction that will go a long way in making public safety and emergency services delivery effective and smarter.

6.3.4.2. The scope of the PPIC3 Programme
The Punjab Safe Cities Authority concept is networked and integrated operations through a range of setups and projects which include: 1, facility development 2, development of technology infrastructure within the Centre 3, development of the CCTV infrastructure 4, process development 5, capability and capacity development 6, organisation development 7, business change and cultural transformation of policing.

6.3.4.3. Service delivery potential of the PPIC3 Programme

The safe city literature claims that the system of safe cities will integrate police command and control through five PPIC3 Service areas, including the following.

- Emergency Call Centre (ECC) – ECC will be handling all incoming and outgoing public demands.
- Dispatching Centre (DC) – DC will dispatch, monitor and support operational resources.
- Video Monitoring Center (VCC) – VCC will proactively monitor the public spaces through an integrated CCTV infrastructure.
- Operations Monitoring Center (OMC) – OMC will monitor the location, patrol patterns and status of the police units.
- Crisis Management Centre (CMC) – CMC will plan and manage all the pre-planned and spontaneous major events through a defined escalation process to contain and manage a situation or an event through a clearly defined command structure.
- Media Monitoring Centre (MMC) – MMC will keep an eye on electronic and social media as sources of information for responding to public needs. The MMC will monitor social media to check any suspicious and unlawful acts committed in cyberspace or to check and prevent any rumours so spread to create panic in public.
- Investigation and Intelligence Centre (IIC) – IIC will be responsible for assisting the investigation and intelligence branches of Police and other LEAs in collecting evidence captured through the citywide surveillance system and presenting the evidence in the court of law.
- Police Strategic Command (PSC) – PSC will be responsible for the strategic command of the Center.
- Police Traffic Management System (PTMS) – PTMS will handle traffic-related issues, violations and e-challans.
- Network Operations Control/Security Operations Center (NOC/SOC) - NOC will monitor and maintain the telecommunication network. SOC Will deal with security issues on an organisational and technical level.
- E-Knowledge Center (EKC) - EKC will handle the knowledge database of the PPIC3 Center.
- Access Control Center (ACC) - ACC will manage entry/exit into the PPIC3 Center premises, the security system of the IT system of the project.
- Digital Media Forensics Center (DFC) - DFC will be responsible for manipulating and enhancing video of PPIC3 Center for evidentiary purposes.

- Police Operational Command (POC) - POC will direct operations of the Center.
- Private Automatic Branch Exchange (PABX) Center- Will is responsible for handling and operating fax/telephone.

6.3.4.4. Distinguishing Features of the Project

- **Intensive Surveillance:** The system of Safe Cities involves state-of-the-art surveillance systems, digital cameras, intrusion detection, face recognition and automatic number plate recognition. The surveillance network and equipment collect data in the form of images or video, monitored in real-time through a combination of strategic operations. This arrangement helps agencies make effective decisions. In addition, as part of collaborative monitoring, the PPIC3 Center can collect information from multiple sources and use it to generate a rapid response to incidents of crime, traffic violations, terrorism, and natural disasters.

- **Robust Connectivity:** Network connectivity is an essential part and the backbone of the PPIC3 Programme of the Punjab Safe City Project. Connectivity allows the transmission of information and data from monitors and field sensors to the PPIC3 centre. Connectivity helps commanders make decisions, coordinate response, mitigate the threat and allocate resources. Data Center of Safe City Programme is a warehouse that stores or processes all information and data collected from various surveillance sources.

- **Viable Communications:** PPIC3 is another call dealing system, but instead, it is a radical new model for operational policing. Police in Lahore has received a state-of-the-art wireless solution based on LTE public security technologies (Concept Paper PPIC3 2015). Viable communications address the problems of low signal intensity, sporadic coverage, and lack of facilities by acquiring an extensive communications network that contains high-speed data while maintaining spectrum efficiency in addition to plain-language communication. Therefore, wireless devices are equipped with data functions, built-in cameras, a GPS location service, and a log-in system that allows the user to use automatic resource management systems (ARMS). In addition, all patrol vehicles engaged in operations and investigations, including the Police Emergency Response Unit (PERU), are equipped with mobile data terminals (MDTs). These terminals are permanently connected to the PPIC3 centre via wireless communications and access large databases such as crime data, stolen vehicles, biometric verification systems, and video and voice communications.

- **Smart Traffic Management:** PPIC3 Lahore has a modern, intelligent Traffic Management System. The traffic system offers digital traffic signals of Lahore city, loaded with advanced Automated Number Plate Recognition System (ANPR), Red Light Monitoring System (RLMS), Journey Time Monitoring System (JTMS) and Variable Messaging System (VMS) in line with the most advanced intelligent urban traffic management technologies (Concept Paper PPIC3 2015). This integrated system manages traffic routes and diverts traffic to the shortest ways in case of blockages created by any crowd of protesters or by the occurrence of any untoward incidence.

- **Newer Electronic Enforcement:** In late 2018, automatised traffic violations began in Lahore. Lahore capital city traffic police have adopted a more capable electronic traffic management system, wherein the violators are fined electronically for having digital evidence like videos on record for evidence. The electronic system records violations on video for evidence purposes. It reads vehicle number plates read and generates tickets commensurate with the offence. Traffic police dispatches tickets to the owner's mailing address. This digitalisation of police is accomplished electronically in an error-free manner. In this state of affairs, hardly anyone questions the procedure's integrity (Concept Paper PPIC3 2015).

- **Real-Time Monitoring:** The PPIC3 stands outfitted with uncrewed aeronautical vehicles that will screen the city's movement circumstance and empower the operational authorities to have the eternal perspective of the activity loads and any blocks that require immediate consideration and befitting response. This arrangement also incorporates other field resources to observe unique occasions, dynamic events, and different emergency circumstances. As a result, this system saves significant time and fuel expenses for commuters to a large extent (Concept Paper PPIC3 2015).

- **Constructive Capacity Building:** Capacity building programmes draft standard operating procedures and effective strategies in the wake of making the most of universally prescribed procedures and processes. The designs are likewise confirmed and affirmed by specialists from present-day police organisations throughout the globe.

- **Dynamic Change Management:** The move to the new PP-IC3 Center is a critical change that will affect every operational law enforcement or police officer and the agencies engaged in public safety and peace. Potential change management boards require continued long-haul duty at a senior dimension in the interest of the distinguished partners, agencies, such as the home department, excise and taxation, NADRA, finance, etc. Additionally, training

111

programmes are needed to propel the security officers and encourage their flexibility to adopt the new frameworks and techniques of law enforcement (Concept Paper PPIC3 2015).

- **Stakeholder Engagement Strategy:** The stakeholder engagement strategy incorporates the recognisable proof, investigation and commitment of people who are influenced by, have an enthusiasm for or are fit for affecting the achievement of the PPIC3 Program. It looks for a community-oriented methodology in light of shared comprehension of necessities and concerns. The partnership drive prompts a strong comprehension of the partners' desires. It permits the programme group to guide and bolster the partner destinations that connect to the achievement of the PPIC3 Programme. Comprehensive communication plans are in place to bring the general public on board. Exclusive meetings with all stakeholders, including Army, Police, academia, media, civil society, courts, multi-national corporations and other actors hailing from city business unions, the university as well as school or college associations, banks, and significant international project administrations and others are of vital strategic importance for the networked policing system.

6.3.4.5. Extension of Safe City to other cities

International management experts, research fellows, media, academia, criminal justice and policing stalwarts, sportspersons, celebrities, political leaders and authorised representatives of national and provincial departments share the information, intelligence, and evidence in this high-tech strategic model of policing. Moreover, the management has candidly praised and appreciated the project with solid recommendations to extend this model to the rest of the cities as many research and survey reports suggest that in 2030 more than 70% of Pakistan's booming population would be living in highly complex urban centres. Besides this, crime data analysis of Lahore during 2017 and 2018, carried out by independent organisations and authorities, has recorded a 40% reduction in street crimes in Lahore.

6.4. Forensic Science Innovations in Pakistan

Every physical human contact has a story to tell, so it is right with the criminal activity. Crime is a physical activity whether committed in direct physical contact with the victim or online from a distance using some computer or digital device. Computers and digital devices constitute the newer crime scenes in today's world of technology and innovation. Forensic science signifies the convergence of science with the law for solving a crime more naturally and straightforwardly. After the 9/11 incident in New York, the central government fabricated more labs and redesigned existing ones. A complete 10-year advancement plan was intended for the reason with a dominant and pronounced purpose of transforming police investigations of crime to state-of-the-art methodologies in Pakistan.

6.4.1. Punjab Forensic Science Agency

The Punjab Assembly passed the Punjab Forensic Science Agency Act on 4 October 2007, consented to by the Governor of Punjab on 29 October 2007, and finally published in Punjab Gazette on 30 October 2007. The new forensic Act came in 2007, while the Lab was established in 2011 and started working in 2012 with 14 fully functional forensic disciplines. The government of Punjab funded the project, and no donor from abroad helped as they built the world's second-largest forensic lab PFSL with 2.56 billion rupees cost.

The core service-providing departments of the PFSA include Audio Visual Analysis, Computer Forensics, Crime Scene Investigations, DNA and Serology, Firearms and Tool marks Identification, Forensic Photography, and Finger Prints and Narcotics. In addition, many services are available at each department of the Lab. To expand the project and extend services to all major cities of Punjab, PFSA has established their regional offices in big Punjab cities, including Rawalpindi, Faisalabad, Gujranwala Sargodha, Bahawalpur, Sahiwal, Multan and DG Khan.

In British India first Forensic lab was built in 1905 at Buns Road Lahore by the British government, and this was the only Lab in the Sub-continent catering to the needs of, now, three nations: Pakistan, India and Bangladesh, while America established their first forensic Lab in 1935, 30 years later than us.

6.4.1.1 Functions of the PFSA

According to section 4 of the Punjab Forensic Science Agency Act, the agency has the following functions.

- It undertakes the examination and analysis of all kinds of material evidence sent to it by the police or collected by the Lab staff from the scene of the crime.
- After examining materials collected by the agency, it issues the expert opinion for the prosecution of the case.
- The agency is responsible for procuring, preserving, maintaining and operating forensic equipment to examine material evidence.
- It also initiates proposals for acquiring newer forensic instruments and advanced forensic techniques for better analysis of forensic materials.

- Agency is responsible for ensuring strict adherence to prescribed procedures for collection and safe custody of material evidence.
- Agency also recommends the procedures for collecting, storing, maintaining, preserving and handling forensic materials once in their custody for not less than 35 years.
- Agency is bound to follow specific directives of the government in terms of applying specific scientific methods and particular expertise if required.
- Agency is accountable for maintaining databases for all kinds of records, including identification of persons, DNA information, and forensic materials in their custody correctly as prescribed under the law or directed by the government in exceptional cases.
- Agency should offer training and educational opportunities to the students of law and the law enforcement officials tasked to conduct investigations or affiliated with the criminal justice process (Judges, Prosecutors, Police Officers, lawyers) one way or the other. Agency should also promote forensic awareness among the general public so that their intrusions may not temper the crime scene evidence.
- To perform all the above functions, the agency can also perform any other function connected with accomplishing these listed and mandated functions.

Punjab Forensic Science Agency (PFSA) Lahore is a full-scale forensic laboratory with fourteen forensic disciplines under the Punjab government's home department. It is rendering its services to law enforcement agencies, including police and corruption watchdog National Accountability Bureau. PFSA, for example, accepts physical evidence from law enforcement agencies on criminal and civil cases. It also examines the scientific proof for partners including Apex Courts, Federal Investigating Agencies, Counterterrorism Departments, Prosecutors, and others.

6.4.1.2 Quality of Expertise

The experts working in the agency are qualified scientists and certified experts in their respective areas, having PhDs or at least MPhil degrees in any of the core areas of forensics. Punjab keeps in liaison with the forensic agency of Illinois, which trained our 40 scientists for us initially. Annual proficiency test, the forensic scientists in Punjab have to undergo annual tests, while DNA scientists have to pass a test in 6 months. If any scientist fails two consecutive times, they deserve removal. Around 800 people, including 349 scientists and 370 support staff, work in PFSA, so claims Shahzada Irfan, a columnist in his 11 February 2018, write up titles as "Crime and Forensics" published in Punjab Technology review. The Punjab Forensic Agency has earned a lot of respect and confidence from all stakeholders of justice and peace, including Police, Judiciary, Media, academia, civil society, the human rights community, and international scientific forums.

6.4.1.3. Criminal Justice Innovation

There is a consensus among scholars and practitioners of law that forensic science is critical in revamping the criminal justice system in Pakistan. "The Punjab Forensic Science laboratory helps bring criminals to justice by aiding in analysing what was once a blurred image and non-accessible area of inquiry by changing the prevailing system of assessment of evidence", reports Dawn dated 7 May 2018. The convergence of forensic with the law is a double-edged weapon as, on the one hand, it helps to punish the criminals, and on the other, it ensures to get innocent exonerated.

6.4.1.4. Hallmarks and Success Stories

According to the reports, from 2013 onwards, more than 11000 cases of child abuse and rape have taken place (only 110 cases convicted). Still, the agency was involved only in some of the cases, such as the Quetta blast case of 2017, Zainab case and Asma case of 2018, to name a few which PFSA did perfectly well by getting accused convicted. The accused in the Zainab case was a serial rapist and was involved in many other cases. Zainab and Asma's rape and murder cases underlined the importance of forensic investigations in Pakistan. PFS deals with one hundred thousand cases per year. There is a backlog issue, and courts complain, but Dr Ashraf says that this is only 2% per cent backlog in Pakistan or Punjab, but in the USA, the backlog is 35% per cent. This comparison of the backlog is not the excuse for efficiency but keeping in view the number of cases our laboratory receives every year, this number of cases is the highest in the world, and the percentage of backlog seems one of the lowest in the world.

6.5. Gender Demographics Innovations

6.5.1. gender Streamlining in Policing

The participation and enrolment of women in the police services of Pakistan is a new emergent innovation of 21st century Pakistan. As folklore, policing is considered a masculine job in Pakistan. Traditionally, females have discarded police as an unsuitable job for them in Pakistan, or they have been discouraged and denied by their families to join the police. However, with the Dawn of the 21st century, the women in Pakistan are joining police in large numbers in all ranks ranging from constabulary to high leadership roles as their preferred job to enjoy the thrill and adventure that the policing offers to its practitioners.

Reimagining Policing in Pakistan

Proper women police had been established in 1994 when Benazir Bhutto, the first women head of the Islamic State, established the first-ever women police station in Rawalpindi district of Punjab. It was considered necessary for both women accused and the complainants or female victims to seek their redressal of grievances at the women police station as it was commonplace for female victims and offenders to face further victimisation at the hands of male police officers and male inmates. When the launch of a first-ever police station, Dr Shoaib Suddle was DIG police Pindi Range, and he made his all-out efforts to make it happen. He did it as he played a very instrumental role in the innovation and reforms within the police department. Many Police departments, including Islamabad, Lahore and Karachi, followed the example of Pindi.

Now the situation of female enrolment has increased to a great extent in every nook and corner of Pakistan. The gender gap is narrowing down remarkably not by increasing women police stations but by increased participation of women in male-dominated police stations and workplaces. From constabulary to Additional Inspector General (Helena, PSP), female officers work shoulder to shoulder with their male counterparts. The number of enlightened women is increasing in the police service of Pakistan also. According to recent studies and statistics, more than 4% of the total strength of the police in three central provinces, Punjab, Sindh, and KP, as well as Federal police agencies like IB and FIA, constitute female officers. It will be increased to 10% until 2025 as per the policy of gender mainstreaming in the law enforcement of Pakistan.

During the colonial period, ladies in Pakistan police have had a limited impact. Going back to the British Raj, enrolment of ladies into policing was exceedingly uncommon. For example, seven temporary female Constables and a Head Constable were enrolled for a brief period in 1939 to handle female protesters that were a part of the former movement in Punjab. However, the quantity of ladies' police did not rise altogether until 1952 when 25 Constables, two Head Constables and an ASI got enlisted in Punjab Police.

Even though ladies-only police stations have included the fundamental component of a measure towards gender equality in Pakistan policing, the circumstances seem, by all accounts, to be gradually evolving. Now new incentives for women police officers-place to work- in federal law enforcement agencies like FIA and NH&MP have vastly changed female working conditions. However, the daunting image of police as a male profession and a career unsuitable for women continues to prevent massive entries. Still, newer sensitisation, incentivisation, and policy of gender streamlining in policing have remarkably impacted Pakistan.

6.6. Cybercrime Innovations

6.6.1. Pakistan's Digital Revolution

Pakistan catches gadget revolution in the 21st century. However, only a few are alive to the digital fertility of Pakistan's 200 million population, of which 67% are youth under the age of 25. Since the social media revolution in the first decade of the 21st first century, Pakistanis are fast embracing modern technology in their daily lives. Pakistan, which struggles to come out of the long periods of the 'War on Terror, is advancing with the economic development of 5.8% and enhanced speculator certainty. "In a historic feat, the federal cabinet has approved Pakistan's first digital policy, "Digital Pakistan Policy" which will offer many incentives for the IT sector of the country".

The new 'Digital Pakistan' Policy will catalyse a holistic digital ecosystem with advanced concepts and components to deliver next-generation digital services, applications, and content rapidly. Moreover, the Digital Pakistan Policy will also provide a basic framework to establish incubation centres across Pakistan to nourish technology start-ups to more efficiently work on global trends like IoT, AI, and robotics. Thus, the Digital Pakistan Policy claims to pave the way for the country to drive its growth through the digital economy.

The IT sector claims to generate $3.3 billion in revenues, according to 2016-17, so it records the Economic Survey report for 2017. The IT ministry claims to have achieved the target of raising IT goods and services exports to $10 billion by 2020 by introducing several economic incentives. The China-Pakistan Economic Corridor (CPEC), a noteworthy joint venture between China and Pakistan, has quickly advanced. The effect of the enterprise can be found in the lives of Pakistanis, as reflected in an enhancing Human Development Index 2017. With a range of benefits, the new internet stores a gamut of challenges that have made sleepless many political leaders and policy stalwarts, including governments (Haass 2013).

6.6.1.1. The Telecom Indicators of Pakistan

Pakistan is, perhaps, one of the leading 30 countries in the world, where the use of the Internet and cellular phones (3G, 4G) has recorded a high rise and is likely to increase exponentially in the next few years when Pakistani users anxiously await the arrival of 5G connectivity. 3G and 4G subscribers increased from 14.614 million in 2015 and 31.779 million in 2016 to 100 million at the beginning of 2019. The same is true for the mobile cellular density of annual cellular subscribers in Pakistan, which has increased by 80% in the last ten years. The number of annual cellular subscribers in 2008 was around 50 to 55 million, and now it has crossed 160 million. For example, other telecom indicators in

117

Pakistan, teledensity (number of people who use wired Internet), has recorded a 70% increase during the last ten years.

Connectivity has landed into a new revolutionary phase called "Internet of Things-IoT, " a giant leap ahead of the information technology-IT episode that had long entertained the global community. Similarly, the massive proliferation of connected and connected devices in public spaces and places could cause serious security vulnerabilities and potential crime risks. Black markets would love to make the most of Artificial Intelligence-AI and support malicious actors leading to the sale of malware and the Commodification of cybercrime services. Brian David Johnson, an Intel futurist of Arizona, USA, aptly warns in the Economist, 24 November 2018, that "the big shift is when you start seeing the average person beginning to use the toolkits of Artificial Intelligence" (The Economist 24 November 2018).

6.6.2. Pakistan's National Response Centre for Cyber Crime (NR3C)

The FIA established a high-tech National Response Centre for Cyber Crimes (NR3C) in August 2007 with five notified cyber-crime police stations located at Lahore, Karachi, Peshawar, Quetta and Rawalpindi/Islamabad, having five separate notified Digital Forensic Laboratories. Presently NR3C has a total staff of 160 personnel. The NR3C is primarily responsible for enforcing Electronic/Cyber Crime laws in Pakistan. The fundamental objective of this centre is to ensure the quality of investigation in cybercrimes. In addition, the centre is to make arrangements for establishing reporting centres, digital forensic labs, better prosecution, and cyber tech research and analysis centres. In addition, the centre needs to provide cyber intelligence, investigation and forensic service to other law enforcement agencies and police across the country. Lastly, NR3C has the mandate of developing liaisons with INTERPOL and other international organisations, including UNODC on criminal matters; and representing Pakistan on global cybersecurity forums.

6.6.2.1. Mandate of NR3C

The mandate of the National Response Centre for Cyber Crimes (NR3C) includes the investigations and enquiries of offences defined under Pakistan are following Cyber Laws:

- Pakistan's Electronic Crime Act-PECA of 2016-deals with all kinds of Internet, cyber and social media related crimes
- Telegraph Act of 1885-Dealing with misuse of telephonic devices.
- Pakistan Telecommunication (Re-organization) Act 1996-Deals with licensing for the Provision of Telephonic Services in Pakistan.

- Electronic Transaction Ordinance 2002 (saved by 17th Constitutional Amendment)-primarily addresses the acceptance of electronic documents/data to deal with the privacy of information and its unauthorised modification
- Prevention of Electronic Crime Ordinance 2007 (Lapsed in Nov 2009)-An Ordinance to address all significant types of technology-based crimes

The Prevention of Electronic Crime Act 2016-A Law drafted because of primary foreign legislation to cover all the cyber/electronic crimes. The PECA 2016 imposes high financial penalties but weak imprisonment. Though this Act is in operation, it has not produced promising results due to law enforcement agencies' slow implementation and non-serious response. However, experts of cybercrime concur that the importance of preventing electronic crimes is to increase remarkably in the future.

6.6.2.2. Notified Cyber Offences under Cyber Law

The PECA-2016 notifies and authorises NR3C to investigate a range of crimes or offences. Among the list of such offences include hacking, bullying, pornography, unauthorised access, modification, deletion, generation of objectionable content, misuse of electronic devices. (Credit cards, ATM cards), internet social media networking crimes- (Facebook, WhatsApp, Twitter, Instagram, Snapchat etc.), cyber-stalking (the repeated use of electronic communications to harass or frighten someone), unauthorised use of identity information and illegal voice traffic termination (Grey Traffic) electronic/internet frauds, disseminating hate materials, selling or buying banned items such as weapons, and narcotics online. Besides this, whoever obtains sales, possesses, transmits or uses another person's identity information without authorisation would be liable for punishment under the relevant law (PECA 2016 [Online]).

6.6.2.3. NR3C Capacity

Over the years, the NR3C has developed the capacity to investigate all kinds of electronic crimes, prevent cyber-attacks, perform reverse engineering to trace the attacker, identify hackers, trace complex and suspicious attacks, and prosecute all registered cybercrime cases. The centre has also established remarkable forensic and digital facilities, with world-class hardware and software, including digital device forensics, computer forensics, mobile forensics, network forensics, database forensics, video forensics, audio forensics, image forensics, malware forensics, and wireless forensics.

The skilled human resources and experts working at NR3C have solved technically complex cases. They have continuously been taking training from International Organizations such as AFP/FBI, particularly in "Access Data Systems" and many other technical areas. The experts working at the centre have cyber work experience minimum of eight (08) to fifteen (15) years, having hundreds of hours of hands-on experience. The officials are working at the centre claim to be the country's most experienced digital forensics analysts. These professionals work in a highly motivated working environment with pride in the job. They adhere to civil/criminal guidelines, provide objective analysis, report and interpret digital evidence in a relatively competitive way, proving their expertise during their appearances in high profile cases on trial in superior courts.

6.6.2.4. Cyber Crime Landscape of Pakistan

Though NR3C was established in 2007, it has gained momentum after enacting the Pakistan Electronics Crime Act-PECA of August 2016. Case registered with NR3C under PECA has recorded a gradual increase in the last two years. The figures that I have collected from NR3C data regarding the cases registered under PECA from August 2016 to August 2018 show a regular rise. In 2016 only 47 cases were registered, which increased to 207 in 2017, finally reaching 2034 and making 488 cases of cybercrime for two years. However, regrettably, NR3C was able to get only six cases convicted in which the concerned court had also imposed 2.85 million fines on those sentenced up to seven years imprisonment.

However, during the same period (2 years), NR3C received 21928 complaints which is quite a high figure in terms of the staff and human resources of NR3C, let alone other financial resources to investigate the costlier cybercrime. NR3C conducted 3838 inquiries into more than 2100 complaints because of their limited resources. Besides this, the 7 cases of child pornography and 15 cases of blasphemous and hate materials were registered and investigated during the two years of PECA. Punjab remained ahead of other provinces, including Islamabad Capital Territory-ICT in cybercrimes cases (315 cases) complaints (9151 complaints), while competitions have remained in the second position between ICT and Sindh. In cases, registered ICT with 84 cases won from the second position from Sindh with 30 cases. However, Sindh with 602 complaints stood second against ICT with 416 complaints. Khyber Pakhtunkhwa, with 33 cases and 2193 complaints and Balochistan, with 26 cases and 328 complaints, maintained the same positions being fourth and fifth respectively in all variables during the same period of two years (DD Ayaz 2018).

6.6.2.5. Major Achievements of NR3C

- NR3C successfully averted the estimated loss of Rs. 3358.02 million to the government exchequer by unearthing 273 VoIP exchanges from Jan 2011 to August 2016.

- The Center provided technical assistance for evidence extraction through digital forensic analysis in "Financial Scam of Rs. One hundred three billion of M/s Khanani and Kalia, Financial Scam of Seventy billion rupees of M/S ZARCO money exchange, State Bank of Pakistan to name a few in a very professional manner, which earned them much applause globally.
- NR3C successfully responded to computer emergencies of NTC web-servers, GOP web-portal and NADRA servers and arrested 12 hackers involved in the hacking of various government department websites.
- NR3C technically investigated the Axact degree scandal, which is the world's most significant case in terms of data analysis & forensics, i.e., 700 TB (Tera Bytes). NR3C has submitted 55 x forensic /technical reports in a court of law, including, i.e., Job Portal, IAO International Accreditation Organization created by Axact.
- NR3C has been very forthcoming in helping other government departments. It extended continuous technical assistance/digital forensics to National Accountability Bureau-NAB, ICT, and other Police departments & Intelligence Bureau-IB in different investigations. The NRC3 provides IB, Police, NAB, and Pakistan Customs approximately (197) digital forensic/technical analysis reports. NR3C also investigated the breach of information security and information security audits of different government departments, making recommendations for the design and implementation of information security policies & safeguarding information assets. NR3C also worked on the ministry of interior, the government of Pakistan's sectoral risk assessment required by FATF (DD Ayaz 2018).

6.6.2.6. Challenges to NR3C

The law enforcement frameworks face a range of issues, including cybercrime.

- First, there is always a greater likelihood of losing online business and consumer confidence in the digital economy, which is afoot in Pakistan, as discussed in the digital revolution part of cyber fertility in Pakistan.
- Second, criminal interventions' potential for critical infrastructure to be compromised would affect water supply, health services, national communications, energy distribution, financial services, and transport.
- Third, the loss of personal financial resources and business assets could heavily cause subsequent emotional damage to the business community and country as a whole.
- Fourth, costs to government agencies and businesses in re-establishing credit histories, accounts and identities would remarkably be higher than one can imagine.

- Fifth, the Internet will be accessible in coming years (Facebook Drones, Google's network of balloons travelling on the edge of space). The internet proliferation shall enable hostile states and non-state criminal syndicates to make the most of upcoming opportunities.

- Sixth, the cost of businesses to improve their cybersecurity and enlist international cooperation could not be possible without having a sophisticated, advanced, cutting-edge cybercrime response mechanism of the government.

- Seventh, black markets could utilise new cyber toolkits such as Artificial Intelligence-AI for spoofing data and information from public domains to be utilised for criminal activity.

- Eighth, the advancement in technology expected the arrival of 5G networks. Artificial Intelligence advances appear to be the writing on the wall for all law enforcement agencies. As a result, the LEAs will need to increase their budgets to fight the newer crimes, patterns, and trends, thereby causing a burden on the exchequer.

- Ninth, the law enforcement agencies mandated to prevent and solve cybercrime will face greater capacity and budgetary issues for keeping pace with technological innovations and the growth of cell and broadband user demographics, which are startling even today.

- Tenth, law enforcement agencies like FIA or its NR3C face the daunting issue of disseminating the knowledge, awareness and information among the tech users to take some precautionary measures against falling victim to cyber-attacks.

- Last but not least, eliminating the cybercrime or prevailing on cybercriminals is, indeed, an arduous task because cybercrime offers ease in operation, safety from physical harm, faster action, quicker results and an edge of anonymity.

6.7. Conclusion

Today's task of Pakistan's leaders is to convert problems and Challenges into promising opportunities. Unfortunately, the state of everything-is-fine never produces leaders and visions. The real test for our leaders is their ability to grasp the perspective and carve out a holistic strategy to respond to the new situation where globalisation is on its meteoric rise. State institutions get entangled in the whirlwind of digital revolutions, which means no borders and fast connectivity with lesser controls.

Policing have witnessed significant innovations in Pakistan. In this chapter, I have tried to describe and analyse the dominant and leading innovations which have played a cardinal role in the partial transformation of policing from an authoritative institution of the state to a public service delivery mechanism offering a range of facilities to people. The partial adoption of technology has, to a certain extent, won the public trust and built a public image of police through better performance. These innovations have not been cohesive, and part of anyone's reform agenda but have progressively evolved the federal and provincial governments' policy decisions, thereby adding jewels to policing in Pakistan. The creation of NH&MP, Safe city projects, forensic agencies, cybercrime centre, gender streamlining is all innovative additions to Pakistan's traditional and status-quo-focused policing culture and police organisational structure. The innovations in policing have produced positive results and have secured the confidence of the people in police capacity to deliver and perform. Indeed, these innovations have earned credibility for police to serve and protect.

Part Three: Challenges and Opportunities

Chapter 07: Policing Terrorism (Security and Safety)

Chapter 08: Community Relations (Democracy and Legitimacy)

Chapter 09: Police Governance (Accountability and Integrity)

By J.J. Baloch (2022)

Chapter: 07

Policing Terrorism

Chapter Brief

This chapter considers policing terrorism as the law enforcement challenge of the 21st century (Clarke and Newman 2007). This part illustrates the existing counterterrorism capabilities of police in Pakistan, the problems in law enforcement, and the National Action Plan of 2014 as a case in point. It argues that police can fight terrorism and extremism better than any other law enforcement agency (Mason and Deflem 2004). The police stay close to communities and play a significant role in criminal justice. Here the author articulates policing as an appropriate forum to address the problems and challenges of security (Sheptycki 2007). It argues that policing needs to rediscover its role and relevance (Newburn 2001) in countering terrorism for social ordering in times of shrinking state authority (Baloch 2017c). Overreliance on the militarization of countering violence and extremism has many loopholes. Pakistan needs to build the capacity of its criminal justice institutions, including the police, to deal with this phenomenon (PRC Report 2019). The published views of experts on counterterrorism and Pakistan's legislative documents find space in the bibliography of this part of the discussion.

7.1. Introduction

Terrorism[5] is the postmodern security challenge to policing in the 21st century. Being the epicentre of terrorism and counterterrorism, Pakistan faces serious challenges both from the outlaws and the police abuse of authority (Yusuf 2014). For counterterrorism, the police need to do more than routine policing and go deeper into the psychologist's domains to read the minds of extremists and militants, so advise Clarke and Newman (2007). However, equally valid is the fact that the police cannot fight terrorism alone without connecting to the community and other stakeholders (Ibid). It further endorses the fact that there is no military solution to the problem of terrorism and that terrorism is

---

[5] Terrorism refers to the acts committed with the aim of seriously intimidating a population, forcing a government or international organisation to "abstain from performing any act, or seriously destabilising or destroying the fundamental political, constitutional, economic or social structures of a country or an international organisation (Wiki definitions)." Although the number of different acts encompassed by the word terrorism, it is not as varied as those encompassed by the word crime. Same are also ways as well as the vulnerabilities to defend oneself from crime and terrorism.

more like a form of transnational organized crime rather than a kind of war because terrorism lacks a state-to-state conflict dimension. War on terror could be won by promoting tolerance for others, respect for diversity, and inclusive policies. The police, a civilian law enforcement agency, can curb crime and combat violence under the democratic dispensation only (Mir 2006). Strengthening democratic institutions in Pakistan, including democratic oversight on police, will go a long way in reducing violence and crime in society (Shigri 2012).

7.2. Policing Terrorism

Both academicians and practitioners are engaged in the informed debate on policing terrorism in the 21st century. Among practitioners, knowledgeable members from law enforcement, police services, intelligence agencies, and the security sector actively participate in the simmering conversation on policing terrorism. Similarly, think tanks, social scientists, including criminologists, and experts from the private sector contribute to the body of knowledge on policing terrorism (Clarke and Newman 2007). The critical question at the heart of conversation among the scholars remains: whether terrorism is a criminal act or a form of warfare. This question is a million-dollar question because its answer determines the role of police and the military as the legitimate owners of what we call counterterrorism. The police fight crime, and the military wage war. The latest research on the subject indicates that terrorism skips the generality of both crimes as well as war (Waddington 2007).

Though retaining some of the characteristics of both the organised or cybercrime and proxy war or hybrid war, terrorism, as an asymmetric threat of the 21st century, features its unique stature and identity (Sheptycki (2007). Experts believe that terrorists employ many tactics of war and combatants. Still, their families resort to courts for relief claiming constitutional protections when they get killed or go missing-enforced disappearances. Involvement of court of law brings terrorism closer to crime and terrorists to criminals who, unlike warriors, demand due process and constitutional protections. The experience has taught that the terrorists kill indiscriminately and brutally target non-combatant civilians, including children, women, the elderly, and the poor. Under military ethics and law, non-combatant civilians are not targeted even in enemy land. In Pakistan, the terrorists have spared no place from targeting, whether it is school, Masque, Mausoleum, or any other sacred public place (Rana 2013).

Thus, terrorism is a multi-dimensional threat that calls for a collaborative and networked response from law enforcement, intelligence, paramilitary and armed forces (Manningham-Buller 2007).

However, counterterrorism involves restrictions of human rights and civil liberties that end up in litigations; the criminal justice approach to deal with it is always suggested by academicians and Practitioners (Neyroud 2007). Thus, none but the police are the most suitable agency for countering terrorism in this context (Mason and Deflem 2004). It is perhaps why a range of theoretical literature exists on policing terrorism. Moreover, the ratio decidendi behind the inclusion of this chapter is the rising importance of policing terrorism as a new field of policing. Pakistan, being hard hit by terrorism and extremism, needs to develop a strategic model of policing terrorism.

7.3. Counterterrorism: New Mission of the Police

Since 9/11, policing has recorded massive transformation in many areas, including its primary mission (Weisburd and Braga 2006). The basic mission of police signifies their primary mandate and fundamental duty and the very purpose for which the department is established (Jonathan 2014). In Pakistan, the new police laws have redefined the duties and responsibilities of the police as the institution of social cohesion. Police Order 2002 added public safety dynamics to the primary mission of the police, while the KP Police Act of 2017 added counterterrorism in unambiguous terms as the primary duty of the police. Subsection 3 (i) of Section 13 of the KP Police Act 2017 provides that additional IG rank officers lead a Counter-Terrorism Department. The Provincial Police Officer may determine for a collection of intelligence, surveillance and monitoring, and conduct of operations". The Counterterrorism Department (CTD) shall have its offices in regions, districts, and sub-divisions with notified police stations and detention centres to investigate all such cases relating to terrorism. Traditionally, the Police have been responsible for maintaining order managing crime by preventing and detecting it (Newburn, 2000). The new police mission involves national security, public security and counterterrorism (Weisburd and Braga 2006). Like many other countries, Pakistan has embarked upon reforming and revamping its police organisations in the wake of a newer threat of terrorism (Hussain, 2012).

7.4. The threat of Terrorism in Pakistan

The 21st constitutional amendment 2014, which gave birth to Pakistan's National Action Plan (NAP), describes the magnitude of the terrorist threat in these words:

"There exists grave and unprecedented threat to the integrity of Pakistan...from the terrorist groups using the name of religion or a sect... Extraordinary circumstances exist which demand special measures for speedy trial of certain offences relating to terrorism" (The 21st Amendment 2014).

We have lost more than 70,000 innocent lives due to terrorist acts in the post-war-on-terror period. Despite more significant losses in the war on terror, Pakistan keeps on building communities, state institutions, the education sector, media, academia, and the infrastructure (NACTA Website). The continued prevalence of terrorism and uninterrupted growth of extremism have impacted in multiple ways-all, not in a harmful or destructive sense but instead in some very positive and constructive ways, ranging from state institution building, legal reforms, human rights awareness, democratic awakening, freedom of expression, the rule of law, gender equilibrium, urbanisation, improved literacy rates, police reforms, and much more (Nekokara 2021). The APS Peshawar event of December 2014 proved the 9/11 of Pakistan, which set the process of state to reset its priorities institutional equations and reinvent its governance models and policy based on human rights and technological solutions.

"Despite a 16% decline in terrorist attacks in 2017 and 29% decrease in 2018, Tehreek-e-Taliban Pakistan and its associated groups remained the most potent threat; they were followed by nationalist-insurgent groups, especially Balochistan Liberation Army and Balochistan Liberation Front" (PIPS Security Report 2018). What has been quite alarming are the increasing footprints of Daesh, especially in Balochistan and northern Sindh, carrying out the deadliest attacks? These realities require concerted efforts and a revision of the National Action Plan. However, still, there is no clarity on who is responsible for NAP. It will be much better if parliament provides oversight for the NAP and lays down criteria for mainstreaming militants – which drew debate in 2017 (PIPS Security Report 2017).

7.5. Counterterrorism Challenge

Pakistan faces grave challenges of both terrorism and counterterrorism today than it has encountered ever before in terms of having clarity and credibility about 'what its government wants to do, about what its people need, and about what the global community expects from them in a real sense' (Ahmed, K. 2016). The issues at home and abroad have turned very complex and daunting. At the same time, Pakistan's National Action Plan warrants serious attention on the part of Pakistan to align it with state-of-the-art counterterrorism approaches for ensuring reliability, soundness, credibility, and success amidst the controversies and serious doubts. India has created doubts and controversies regarding Pakistan's counterterrorism agenda among international and regional partners like Afghanistan, Iran and China (Abbass 2012). However, genuine concerns at home remain about across-the-board implementation and adoption of enacted policy lines amidst conflicting interests of different stakeholders and different government organs in Pakistan (Khosa 2017).

Police stalwarts and counterterrorism experts agree that the police departments and agencies need to play different roles and perform varied functions in countering terrorism (Lowe 2015). First and foremost, the counterterrorism functions of police include: collecting information and intelligence regarding terrorist networks patterns, building ideological narratives, and formulating operational strategies (Blake et al., 2012). Secondly, police departments have to establish a terrorist database for research and analysis about the geographical and population demographics of terrorists within the country and their links with regional and international networks (Ibid). Thirdly, police have to keep their civilian-friendly forces proactive to prevent terrorist planning. Fourth, suppose aversion of terrorist activity becomes difficult with softer approaches. In that case, the police should use their coercive force to deter or pre-empt the terrorists from causing damage to the country's people (Ibid). Fourthly, policy should also take necessary measures to mitigate the collateral damage caused by terrorist or counterterrorist actions (Jonathan 2014). Fifthly, police should keep good relations with the community and coordinate well with other stakeholders, including law enforcement actors, intelligence agencies, media, academia, civil society at all the stages of planning, development, and implementation of their counterterrorism strategies (Yusuf 2014). Lastly, police remain the focal, central, imperative, and core actor in all the strategic processes, including calculating, pre-empting, implementing, and mitigating (Lowe 2015).

High policing or big data policing is a product of science and technology. There is no escape from the relevance, currency, and significance of the ingress of science and technology into governance, management, law enforcement, policing, and policy (Brodeur 2011). Marx (2007) argues that the new in police engineering of social order is the globalisation of social engineering? Marx (2007) identifies ways of controlling the environment by targeting, offender, and opportunity. According to his findings, police can prevent crime by removing devaluing and insulating target or victim, incapacitating offender, and excluding offence or offender impunity (Marx 2007).

7.6. Pakistan's Civilian Counterterrorism Framework

In Pakistan, the realization for establishing an institutional counterterrorism framework for Police and civilian law enforcement agencies grew when terrorist offensive did not spare its military, navy, air force, and the personnel of the intelligence agencies (NACTA Website). Such realisation got further fuelled when the terrorist attacks extended to the non-combatant population of the country, taking the targets of schools, airports, markets, public parks, and other public places, sparing not even the mosques (Rana 2013).

The institutional framework of police for counterterrorism developed in three main strands. Pakistan Electronic Crime Act (PECA_2016) and the new 29th constitutional amendment (2016) gave more powers to police. The second strand came with expanding the mandate of civilian intelligence law enforcement apparatus such as provincial Special Branches and Federal Intelligence Bureau and the Federal Investigation Agency to create their counterterrorism wings. The third and the most critical strand resulted in creating National and provincial counterterrorism institutions with broad mandate ranging from policy development, research, coordination, and execution/ enforcement of counterterrorism strategies such as NAP. These institutions include the National Counterterrorism Authority (NACTA), provincial Counterterrorism departments (CTDs), the establishment of anti-terrorism forces such as Special Security Unit SSU in Sindh, Elite and Dolphins in Punjab, Jaguars or Special Combat Unit (SCU) in KPK, and Counterterrorism Force (CTF) Balochistan (PRC 2019). Redefining the primary functions of the police forces in Pakistan, the rise of counterterrorism departments keeps innovating policing in Pakistan. However, perhaps because of the leading and focused role of police, the police department in Pakistan continues to struggle in reinventing its counter-terrorism discourse, role, mechanism, and strategy.

7.7. Pakistan's Counterterrorism Policy: An Autopsy

Pakistan's counterterrorism policy, as well as practice, needs a thorough overhaul. Pakistan needs to revisit its National Acton Plan, which forms the core of its Counterterrorism Policy. The primary objective is to identify the tensions and issues inherent in Pakistan's counterterrorism policy.

Many argue that Pakistan's National Action Plan is not a sufficient and appropriate counterterrorism strategy to deal meaningfully with the magnitude of the terrorist threat to Pakistan and its partners in the 'War on Terror. Second, the excessive militarization of Pakistan's counterterrorism policy can hinder the across-the-board implementation of NAP and affect the capacity-building process of civilian law enforcement and the criminal justice process in Pakistan. Third, popular and international support is vital for Pakistan's counterterrorism policy in attaining its credibility and legitimacy. Khaleda (2016) argues that Pakistan's counterterrorism policy is inherently contradictory and discriminatory at the core in terms of who will do what, why, how, and against whom; therefore, it needs massive resets into its ideals, roles, route, framework, focus, and targets for policing terrorism effectively.

7.7.1. National Action Plan-NAP: A Case Study

Pakistan adopted its National Action Plan with the unprecedented consensus on policing terrorism. However, when it comes to the across-the-board implementation of the NAP, the trust deficit exists among the stakeholders. As a result, the vision of violence-free Pakistan will remain a pipedream unless bringing together is possible.

7.7.1.1. Background

NAP has been a crucial part of counterterrorism (CT) discourse, policy & strategy in Pakistan since the central government adopted the NAP in the wake of the Peshawar Army Public School attack of 16 December 2016. The 21st Amendment in the first schedule of the constitution gave birth to NAP. This time in Pakistan, the CT efforts became part of public debate, a symbol of national consensus, and an emblem of the collective wisdom of all stakeholders. Civil and military leadership supported by the judiciary, media, civil society, and the public, as a whole, came on the same page. Many strategists and national security experts both in Pakistan and abroad agree that NAP has reduced violence in Pakistan. However, freelance circles raise voices and concerns against the government's failure for its inability to implement the NAP in full spirits.

7.7.1.2. Basic Agenda of the NAP

I.   Execution of Extremists: After the Peshawar incident, the government decided to execute extremists convicted in terror-related cases. The Government has already started implementation.

II. Speedy Military Courts: "Special courts, headed by the officers of the armed forces, will be established for the speedy trial of terrorists. These courts will get established for a term of two years".

III. The ban on Armed Militia: Formation of armed militia will not be allowed.

Reimagining Policing in Pakistan

IV.   The revival of NACTA[6]: National Counterterrorism Authority will be revived and made effective

V.   Crackdown Hate Speech: "There will be a crackdown on hate speech, and the LEAs will take action against newspapers, magazines contributing to the spread of such speech".

VI.   Curbing Terror Financing: LEAs will cut financial sources of terrorists and terror organisations.

VII.   Stopping Banned Outfit Activity: banned outfits will not operate under different names.

VIII.   Raising SAF[7]: Governments at federal and provincial levels will raise special anti-terrorism forces.

IX.   Stopping Religious Extremism: LEAs will take measures to stop religious extremism and protect minorities.

X.   Reforming Madrassas: Governments will register, regulate and reform madrassas.

XI.   Disallowing Media Coverage to Terrorists: Government will not allow print and electronic media to give any space to terrorists.

XII.   Rehabilitation of IDPs[8]: Governments will make all-out efforts to rehabilitate internally displaced persons (IDPs) top priority. For this end to achieve governments will expedite administrative reforms and economic development in FATA.

XIII.   Destroying Terrorist Communication: LEAs will destroy the communication systems of terrorist organisations.

XIV.   Controlling social media: "Social media and the Internet will not be allowed to be used by terrorists to spread propaganda and hate speech.

XV.   Containing Extremism in South Punjab: The government will not allow any space for the extremists to operate freely in any part of Punjab.

---

[6] NACTA stands for National Counterterrorism Authority
[7] SAF stands for *Special Anti-Terrorism Force*
[8] IDPs Stand for *Internally Displaced Persons*

XVI.   Continuing Karachi Operation: Operation against terrorists in Karachi will be taken to its logical conclusion.

XVII.   Reconciling Balochistan: In political reconciliation, the Baluchistan government will be given complete authority by all stakeholders.

XVIII.   Reducing Sectarian Violence: Elements spreading sectarian violence will be prosecuted.

XIX.   Registering Afghan Refugees: Comprehensive policy will regulate and govern the registration regime of Afghan refugees.

XX.   Reforming CJS[9]: "To give provincial intelligence agencies access to communication of terrorists and to strengthen anti-terror agencies through necessary reforms in the criminal justice system.

7.7.1.3. NAP Performance

The government of Pakistan claims to have made progress in NAP. The indicators claimed on their website include: first, more than 400 militants hanged. Secondly, 102 Madrassa's sealed & 87 closed down, and 190 received foreign funds. Thirdly, the State Bank of Pakistan froze Rs: 1 billion from 126 bank accounts. Fourthly, LEAs profiled 7,923 clerics in the fourth schedule & 188 in the Exit Control List. Fifthly, over 1500 books containing Hate Material were confiscated, and 71 shops were sealed. Sixthly, 1893 cases were filed against 1961 suspects for hate speech. Seventhly, 97.9 million SIMS were biometrically verified; 5.1 million SIMS were blocked (NAP Statistics 2016). Eighthly, more than 60,000 Afghan Refugees got deported. Ninthly, 80 % of violence was reduced in Karachi due to ongoing operations by LEAs. Tenthly, the Resettlement/rehabilitation process for IDPs began & FATA reforms. Lastly, Geo-tagging of Seminaries completed in Sind, GB, Punjab (Khan 2016). The fourth year of NAP is about to complete, but all parties and institutions have not paid equal attention to all the above challenges. However, all stakeholders had expressed unflinching resolve to act and implement the plan with "iron hand without any discrimination" (Baig 2015). These figures have increased tremendously during recent years. Maliha Afzal (2021) overviews counterterrorism in Pakistan in the following words.

"Over the years, American drone strikes targeted and killed successive TTP leaders, including Baitullah Mehsud in 2009, Hakimullah Mehsud in 2013, and Mullah Fazlullah in 2018. The Pakistani military's Zarb-e-

---

[9] CJS stands for Criminal Justice System

Azb operation (named for the sword of the Prophet Muhammad) began in 2014 — after a TTP attack on the Karachi airport that June — and increased in intensity after the Peshawar Army Public School attack of December that year, which killed more than 130 schoolchildren. Since 2017, having largely routed the TTP (because of limited information access to the area, there are questions about how many terrorists were killed, versus simply displaced across the Pakistan-Afghanistan border), the military's operation entered a new phase of "elimination" of militant groups. The operation is called Radd-ul-Fasaad, which means the elimination of all strife."

The following chart, which shows the latest figures on the counterterrorism campaign of Pakistan, is copied from Maliha Afzal's blog report in Brookings dated 15th January 2021.

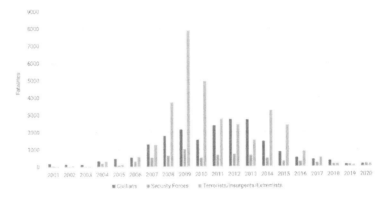

7.7.1.4. Critical Analysis

Despite all these NAP claims, the fact remains that the security situation in our country is riskier and venturesome. It stands to reason that Peshawar attack on Christian colony, Mardan Court Blast on 2nd September 2016, Quetta hospital suicide blast on 12 August 2016, Lahore suicide blast 28 March 2016, all taking more than 250 lives, are question marks on the performance of NAP and agencies implementing it. Indeed, NAP has worked to certain states as 2020 witnessed a remarkable reduction in terrorism-related incidents and deaths (169 deaths). Yet, the loopholes in addressing terrorism and extremism in Pakistan still exist and need a thorough overhaul (Afzal 2021). Critical Analysis of NAP covers its "nature of approach, structure, performance, enabling factors, and enforcement issues.

By J.J. Baloch (2022)

NAP is inherently contradictory, so argues Dr Khaleda Ghous (2016). Many public policy and security experts believe that NAP is against the basic structure of the constitution and fundamental rights (Discussion Club Defence PK 2016). Dr Khaleda Ghous terms it "inherently contradictory" (Ghous 2016). Many argue that military courts and the constitution of Apex Committees in the provinces run counter to the ideals of the rule of law, democracy, and Independence of the Judiciary. It does compromise liberty at the expense of security because of the militarization of the counterterrorism-CT strategy. Others raise their fingers against the legitimately expanded authority of LEAs and the military into the purely civilian domain. They argue that the militarisation of CJS causes injustice and insecurity among the rank and file, which is likely to undermine statehood and encourage extremism in society. Words: "in the name of Religion and Sect" as used in the 21st constitutional amendment is the inappropriate insertion and controversial connotation because this may not be the only reason behind the terrorist activity in Pakistan. The reasons may expand to nationalistic, ethnic, ideological, racial, or other considerations. Maliha Afzal (2021) observes:

"For a brief time after the Peshawar school attack of 2014, there was some clarity in recognizing the homegrown nature of the Pakistan Taliban, and the country devised a National Action Plan to tackle extremism and terrorism. While it was incomplete and never acknowledged the deeper roots of extremism, it was a start. But it has gone by the wayside as the Pakistani state has turned back to blaming India for terrorism in the country. Meanwhile, the underlying roots of extremism — the country's curricula, the way its politics works, and its laws, which have all primed its citizenry to buy into and sympathize with the propaganda of extremist groups — remain intact."

The NAP lacks an appropriate counter-narrative. Lt. Gen (R) Talat Mehmood sees the NAP without a "proper counter-narrative" (Mehmood 2016). In NAP, Pakistan has yet to develop a clear and consistent state narrative for fighting terrorism and extremism. Pakistan needs to develop a counternarrative against the terrorist narrative, failing which terrorist narrative continues to erode its writ of the government and question its authority as legitimate. The absence of counter-narrative causes is the loss of faith in state institutions and narrative, the utility of using violence with impunity, and also glorifying the stature of extremism and terrorist hate ideology. "Radical reform of the education system is required to equip young people with the critical analysis skills to challenge violent extremist narratives" (Peace-Direct 2017). Presentation of alternative moderate points of view and ways of projecting reality of victim's pains would, indeed, be very instrumental in impairing militant ideology, the utility of violence, the stature of the terrorist leaders.

Reimagining Policing in Pakistan

Promoting tolerance and the hybrid coexistence of humanity set within the paradigm of diverse religious and cultural narratives would be less critical. In this regard, print, electronic, and social media could play a pivotal role in evolving such a counter-narrative which seems missing in the NAP scheme. Though NACTA held a three-day Seminar from 13th to 15th January 2017, calling experts from different walks of life to frame what they titled a "National Narrative" to serve as a counter-narrative to the terrorist narrative. The spadework is still underway to reach some definite shape of the national narrative.

The Facts and figures indicate that the NAP has helped reduce terrorist incidents, but it has yet to stop sabotage and violence in Pakistan. The South Asia Terrorism Portal, a website and a research group based in Pakistan, points out the following trends of reduction in violence due to partial implementation of NAP and ongoing military operation, Zarb-e-Azab.

Year	fatalities	Terrorists killed
2013	5,379	1702
2014	5,496	3182
2015	3,682	2403
2016	1770	872
2017	815	524- (16% decline in incidents-370 attacks in 2017)
2018	595	120- (29% decline in incidents-262 attacks in 2018)

Terror-related fatalities have registered a declining trend in Pakistan since the peak of 2009 (South Asian Terrorism Portal [Online]). Balochistan, KP, Punjab, Sindh, and the (FATA) Azad Kashmir also recorded declines, but it does not claim to stop such incidents.

The PIPS Security Reports reveal that in 2018 total of 262 terrorist attacks were executed with the focus on Balochistan, which took the lead, and out of all attacks, 171 were carried out by the TTP splinter group Jamaat-ul-Ahrar, martyring 449 people. The 96 deaths resulted from nationalist groups' attacks in Balochistan and Sindh. The target of terrorists remained law enforcement personnel, diplomats, and political leaders, culminating in terror in July 2018 elections. Though the report claims 29 decreases in terrorist attacks compared to 2017, in 2017, LEAs had killed 524 terrorists compared to 120 in 2018. The report underlines the need to revitalise and redefine the counterterrorism role of NACTA (PIPS Security Report 2018). However, in 2017 the PIPS report for the same year claimed 370 attacks in 64 districts of Pakistan, killing 815 and injuring thousands. Both the reports have identified three main groups having strong roots across the country. These groups are TTP and its splinters, BLA and its splinters, Daish or Islamic State, which, many experts believe, is fast taking deep roots in Balochistan and Sindh alongside nationalist militant groups (PIPS Security Report 2017).

Despite the passage of five long years since we adopted NAP, many non-state actors are at large. Rana (2016) believes that inaction in NAP dominates because of "common confusions and illusions" created to dwindle the implementation process. Many Critics storm Pakistan's counter-terrorism drive with its inaction against non-state actors. Almost all the enemies of Pakistan collectively tag Pakistan as a 'rouge state' standing behind the terrorist networks to fight its 'alleged proxy wars, ' especially in Afghanistan and in Kashmir. Many in American think-tank circles firmly believe that Pakistan supports Haqqani Network and Jaish Muhammad of Mulla Saeed. He allegedly roams freely in Pakistan without any fear of being caught. However, for prosecuting any accused, the country needs evidence against its citizen, which is lacking for those who blame Pakistan for not taking action against the Pakistani Taliban.

Contrary to the above allegations against Pakistan is the capture of an Indian spy (Kulbhushan Jadew) from Balochistan. Indian agent publicly admitted his all sins and crimes. Pakistan's treasury and opposition benches expressed similar concerns in the wake of so-called Indian surgical strikes on the control line. Dawn had reported: "Act against terrorists or face isolation", civilian says military. The story published further stated that Nawaz Sharif, Prime Minister of Pakistan, and his cabinet conveyed this to military leadership and Intelligence networks to do something meaningful against non-state actors. Besides this, Aitzaz Ahsan of Pakistan People's Party raised this issue in Parliament, showing his concerns over non-action against some allegedly favourite (good) militants. However, Pakistan continues to deny offering support to terrorists, some of who are working for foreign intelligence agencies against the integrity of Pakistan; for example, the TTP and Daish. However, the best way to analyse objectivity in analysing such issues of critical nature fairly and squarely.

Others argue that NACTA's dormancy finds it challenging to gain the required legitimacy for the NAP. The NAP promises to revive NACTA, but this central body to implementing NAP remains ineffective to a certain extent. The NACTA appears to be the most neglected institution. Prime Minister, as its head, has to call regular meetings of NACTA as per the schedule. Much freelance analysis gauges the government's importance to the NAP and measures the lack of seriousness in implementing it. More examples of its negligence transpire in the shape of the government's continuous reluctance and denial of releasing the allocated funds to NACTA. Still, the graver is that NACTA lacks human capital, financial resources, physical infrastructure, and networking with multi-agencies. Due to its dumping by the political government and resultant dormancy so caused, hardly any LEA pays heed to its presence or absence. Nekokara suggests a "multi-agency approach for the revival of NACTA" (Naqvi 2016).

The Criminal Justice System of Pakistan, argues Nekokara (2016), is rickety, and NAP's claim of strengthening CJS flies in the face of its viability and public acceptance. Our criminal justice has minimal capacity to bear the burden of Counterterrorism. There exist a profound "mistrust and big disconnect" among different components of the criminal justice system (CJS) (Ibid). The courts blame the police for unprofessionalism in conducting investigations; they also castigate lawyers for seeking endless adjournments, causing scarcity and spoilage of evidence. However, lawyers complain about the unavailability of incentives and rewards for them in facilitating the realisation of justice. Surprisingly, police officers blame the courts and lawyers for their rude, abusive, and violent behaviour; they also grumble about complicated standards of evidence, non-availability of witnesses as well as the absence of witness protection programs. Prosecutors also bemoan their alienation and step-motherly treatment in CJS (Ibid). Besides this, the jail authorities have limitations. They complain about their poverty to feed the inmates and work for their rehabilitation. Therefore, the problem with the CJS is not only the lack of funds, weak laws, and poor skills but also the "dysfunctional relationship", which undoubtedly continues to damage the efficacy of CJS.

The critics point at NAP's inability to have played a promising role in getting the crime-politics nexus disturbed for establishing enduring peace in the society. First, the impunity of criminals from punishment undermines criminal justice more than anything else. Militant wings and extortionists within political parties employ violence to rule the society and influence its political decisions (Iqbal 2016). Secondly, political victimisation caused by the ruling elite against their opponents creates a moral crisis of the legitimacy of statehood and the culture of disobedience to its laws, a condition conducive to producing extremists and anarchists. Finally, announcing general pardons for so-called political prisoners hardly reduces violence (Ibid). This mess again aggravates the already precarious situation. Thus, using power structures for the party's political interests in power and damaging the party, not in power, is commonplace in Pakistan.

As stated in the NAB body of principles, madrassas (seminaries) will get reformed, but the process is slower to the level of disappointment and, sometimes, embarrassment. Many critics condemn the government for spending sizeable funds on madrassas reforms. They allege that despite NAP's claims, many banned outfits collect donations, and student databases and funding sources remain undocumented (Rana 2012). In addition to this, Parallel education systems, i.e., private, government, and religious seminaries, are altogether different and contradictory and unreformed systems. To them, merely Geo-tagging of seminaries cannot do!

Besides, weapons still proliferate in Pakistani society. Governments and LEAs need to take more strict measures against those who keep illegal weapons. Only limited and sporadic recoveries can hardly create any impact on controlling violence. Critics believe that criminals have better weapons than law enforcement agencies. Besides this, governments should keep the process of de-weaponization depoliticised, failing which weapons will continue to increase unchecked. Therefore, bearing unlicensed weapons must be declared a heinous crime without any bail.

Terror financing is another critical area for any counterterrorism strategy, but the NAP has yet to showcase performance in this crucial area (Crisis Group 2017). Reportedly, Donations (Chanda/Bhata) collected by different religious groups goes on unstopped. In addition, Pakistan's government needs to complete the long-awaited documentation of the economy. Also, the strict implementation of money laundering laws is pending. Ironically the black economy accepts no laws and will remain terrorist friendly unless this aspect gets fully addressed. Pakistan faces severe challenges with FATF observations regarding ensuring strict implementation of financial rules to check funds of outlaws. However, in the wake of FATF pressure, the government of Pakistan has taken tangible measures to document the economy-a process that is long term. However, the NAP has yet to overcome all the parallel systems of the criminal cartels, which are essential for counterterrorism in Pakistan.

The NAP coexists with lousy governance (Yousuf 2014). Good governance is central to fighting terrorism. Pakistan suffers from continuous political instability. Corrupt practices pave the way to compromised action, immunity from accountability, selective justice, business not service, personal interests, not national interests, and money laundering, which collectively result in lousy governance and weak national bond (Ibid). Shuja Nawaz (2016) analysis point out:

"[M] many of Pakistan's domestic problems are related to poor governance and the imbalance of power and operational ability between civil institutions and the military. Shortsighted policies of successive civil and military governments and a dynastic political system have hobbled efforts to develop a strong, stable polity and economy. As a result, civil and political institutions remain weak and dysfunctional; a well-organized and disciplined military continues to dominate key strategic sectors related to foreign policy and security…."

This state of affairs is what best defines today's Pakistan. The NAP does not address this issue while it has to when it claims to be all-inclusive.

Pakistan continues to grow radicalised unabatedly in the presence of NAP pomp and show. Political grievances, religious sectarianism, provincialism, ethnic divide, poverty with unequal opportunity, socio-political non-inclusion, political injustice, unequal Development –discrimination, weak writ of law, erosion of family and local culture, easy access to hate material, and also growing religious intolerance allows intolerance take deep roots (Hyder Lecture NIM Karachi 2016). Daud Khattak (2020) refers to Pakistan's situation as:

"A resurgent Tehrik-i-Taliban Pakistan (TTP) could soon again pose a major threat to Pakistan, as underlined by a bomb attack on a luxury hotel in Quetta in April 2021 claimed by the group that narrowly missed endangering China's ambassador. Weakened from 2014 onward by infighting, defections, operations against it, and public disgust at its brutal violence directed at civilians, the group under the leadership of Noor Wali Mehsud has finally escaped the shadow of the Islamic State in Khorasan, which was founded in the last decade by disgruntled TTP figures and threatened to eclipse TTP. After reabsorbing many splinter groups, and addressing internal tensions, TTP has intensified its campaign of terrorism in Pakistan and is again growing in strength. It has made clear its commitment to a long-haul struggle against the Pakistani state and is attempting to grow and broaden its support base, including by trying to co-opt the grievances of Pashtun and Baluchi ethnic groups and curtailing its violence against civilians."

The NAP fails to pass the benchmarks of the state-of-the-art counterterrorism strategy. UN advises a fourfold approach to contain extremism and terrorism. The UN suggests four models. First, the root-cause model signifies poverty, non-inclusion, the rule of law, human rights. Second is the enforcement model, which involves coercive methods. The third is the good governance model, which focuses on state building. The development model is the fourth and the most important because it emphasises inclusive Political, social, and economic development, welding together all marginalized segments of society (UNGA Res. 60/288, 2006). Unfortunately, the NAP focuses mainly on the enforcement model, which avails nothing against the magnitude of the threat.

The NAP stands heavily militarised strategy. The militarisation of counter-terrorism policy is insufficient to stabilise the democratic transition and go for therapeutic approaches. The coercive side of counter-terrorism policy fails to make it more efficient and more promising in terms of measurable outcomes. Coercive approaches undermine the credibility and authority of the government and writ of the law (ICG Report 2015). The current emphasis on revenge and retribution and the emasculation of fundamental rights and the rule of law are undermining citizen confidence in the state to deliver justice, a flawed approach that also fuels grievances that benefit the violent extremists, the NAP aims at combating" (Ibid). Therefore, an empowered and resourced police force remains the most credible tool for enforcing a sustained and successful counter-terrorism strategy (Abbas 2012).

Whether by default or by design, the militarisation of the government's criminal justice and security apparatus goes a long way in undermining capacity-building drive in the police department, questioning the credibility and efficacy of the courts, eroding criminal justice professionals (PRC Report 2019). The militarisation of Criminal Justice overburdens the military, exempting civilian law enforcement agencies from ownership and responsibility of counterterrorism (Shuja 2016), keeping criminal justice reforms in cold storage, and excusing the implementation of the National Action Plan (NAP). However, there is no doubt that terrorism knows no military solutions (Abbas 2009). Neither has it proved, nor yet a counterterrorism expert has ever recommended or approved this paradigm of using brute force alone can root out terrorism (Chaudhry 2021). Therefore, terrorism seems closer to crime than war, and CJS should better deal with it as a criminal justice affair.

In the light of the above loopholes, this piece argues for a more significant police role in fighting terrorism for two reasons. First, terrorism is not much different from conventional crime. Secondly, local police can better coordinate intelligence and local response to terrorist attacks (Perito & Parvez 2016). First, however, it needs the clarity that no police officer or researcher of different police models argues that police alone is enough to counter-terror. On the contrary, renowned experts consider the police a primary law enforcement agency fighting terrorism. In comparison, other agencies should play their specific role in a more networked way of partnerships with all stakeholders, including media and the public (Ibid).

Exercise of coercion produces criminals in society instead of working well in building peace (Peace-Direct 2017). The supply of offenders in such conditions of authoritarianism never ends. According to reports, with each generation of youth, five to ten per cent will become regular offenders (Newburn 2004). In practice, the present system of policing terrorism in Pakistan creates more criminals than it contains or restores them (Yousuf 2014). High imprisonment rates carry high economic and social costs, both for society in general and prisoners and their families in particular. Killing terrorists carries even higher costs. First, it creates more bitterness among already hostile populations, making the conflicts that underlie terrorist acts even harder to resolve (Marx 2014). It justifies violence and supports the claim that they are fighting ruthless enemies (Ibid). Finally, it turns them into martyrs

141

and, therefore, into potent recruiting symbols among the impressionable young men and women terrorists seek to attract.

Above all, the NAP needs policy priority and political ownership. Merely setting goals is not sufficient but evolving an appropriate mechanism to achieve them is of cardinal importance in building the capacity of police to overcome the challenge of terrorism. Therefore, the future of the NAP depends mainly on establishing a well-crafted mechanism to implement it.

7.8. Recommended Measures

"No silver bullet can address global terrorism in all its complexity," writes Maleeha Lodhi in "The Threat of all Threats" (Lodhi 2011). However, since there is a method to the madness, there must be counterterrorism at all levels. In this connection, the experts suggest a variety of measures.

First, "political authority must claim ownership" of counterterrorism (Khosa 2016). Moreover, overburdening our armed forces at a time when external threats to our national existence abound would not be the strategic approach. The letter and spirit implementation of NAP has become an existential challenge for Pakistan. NAP is crucial because LEAs could balance the outcomes accomplished by military operations (Abbas 2009). Secondly, police must be depoliticised and reinforce its fundamental unit: the Police Station, which many accept as the nursery of intelligence gathering at the grass-roots level (Perito & Parvez 2014). Perito & Parvez (2014) maintain:

"An effective program for police station reform would begin with assigning priority to the police for controlling terrorism. Then, it would include developing new organizational structures, positions, and standard operating procedures to ensure that local police understand their enhanced role and mission. It would also include improving police-public relations and networking police stations into a national information-sharing network with anti-terrorist agencies. Creating high-profile specialized units appears to offer a quick fix to a complex and increasingly pervasive problem. However, the real solution lies in empowering Pakistan's police stations to protect their communities from criminal and extremist violence through modernization and reform."

Third, we need to create a national counter-narrative for countering the radical worldview. We need a research culture for developing our narrative. The narrative is the essential standard for strategic conversation. Today, we desperately need research organisations to cultivate a peace proposition for policing that works well. Despite colossal losses of life, property, and culture, critical sections of society and certain political elements in Pakistan still extend their support and sympathies to extremist groups. The highly changed religious discourses experienced in Pakistan feed the prevailing chaos rooted in confusion over the explicit meaning of jihad and the definition of terrorism. Corman (2015) finds the reasons behind extremism-friendly environs, and his article reads:

"Most Pakistanis draw distinct boundaries between the forms of violence attributed to their affiliations with various schools of jurisprudence and confessional doctrines. Analogously, the youths in the poor and upper-middle classes throughout the country tend to view the world through a strict black and white lens, developing their radicalized beliefs from the clash of civilization paradigm'. As a result, they embrace radicalism "not necessarily because they understand the underlying ideology or comprehend the religious principles, but because such ideas have become popular in society and are not challenged by an alternative discourse. Also, there are clear divisions among political parties concerning the definition of terrorism and how best to counter its expansion. Some support a general war on terror but concurrently hesitate to categorize the subsequent violence due to terrorist's ethnicities. The result is many conflicting viewpoints that make it impossible for society to develop a cohesive narrative to counter the growth of extremism and fight terrorist activities within the country (Corman 2015)."

Thus, 'Pakistan's attempts to craft a scientifically-structured counter-narrative are neither traditional nor within the country's current CT capability', and the lack of coherent and fully functional counter-narrative limits Pakistan's ability to combat terrorism effectively.

Fourth, for the government to effectively improve policing to counter-terrorism, it is essential to reform the justice delivery mechanism or criminal justice. Without improving all components of criminal justice, including police, prosecution, judiciary, and prisons, it is impossible to bring significant change in policing. Police reforms in isolation could hardly be productive. Criminal justice reforms are integral to policing terrorism. For aligning counterterrorism policy with constitutional provisions regarding the protection of fundamental rights of all citizens, including the accused persons, it is essential to engage parliament and the superior judiciary in the monitoring of the National Action plan. The engagement of these leading institutions will add legitimacy, transparency, accountability, and integrity to policing terrorism in Pakistan.

Fifth, the police must enhance their digital capacity by properly adopting law-enforcement technology to manage the response to terrorism. For this end in view, police training must focus on counter-terrorism intelligence, operations, specialisms, and psychological methods to demotivate the extremists. In this regard, the best course to follow is seeking assistance from international partners like UNODC, Interpol, ICITAP, INL, ICMPD, NCA, FBI, AFP, and many others.

Sixth, good governance is crucial for policing terrorism effectively. Corruption and efficiency do not go together. Correspondingly, the rule of law and money or coercion cannot coexist. Good governance could ensure politically neutral and professional police, essential for policing terrorism. The political conditions of the hybrid state of Pakistan combine struggle and tension between civil and military institutions and perpetual politics as a business in few selected hands who use it more for their aggrandisement rather than nation-building and wellbeing of the oppressed have alienated the people from their statehood. Durdana Najam (2021) aptly observes.

"A state is not merely a collection of people who need to be herded to some direction. A state is a living entity relying on its people. A state is not merely a collection of a few, riding the big horse of leadership, whipping their people to submission along the way to rule and reign. There is a marked difference between a state and a zoo. People are not born to be chained but to be directed towards the ultimate good that benefits the world. It is the duty of those sitting at the helm of affairs to work out what suits best for whom... It is for the state to find out, layout opportunities, and define and design ways to enrich its people's potential. Eventually, the state, the people, and its leadership achieve the objectives of an authentic life toward the ultimate truth. However, this reality about the state's mission could not be accomplished if those running the affair, i.e., the leaders, were not suitable for the job. When the state's system is not based on equality or principles, it ultimately leads people to a self-fulfilling life."

Therefore, there are no two opinions that national building through democratic advancements offering protection of fundamental human rights and civil liberties could be instrumental in containing mounting radicalisation and increasing terrorism in Pakistan, struggling for democracy since its birth in 1947.

Seventh, the revival of culture through education for building resilience in society would be a right and timely step. However, we have to unify our mis-directional educational system in the long run. We must develop a uniform educational system promoting moderation, harmony, and tolerance by adopting the Sufi way of life and thought to bring interfaith and sectarian harmony to most central Asian states. For example, Azerbaijan and Uzbekistan promote Sufi thought to inspire their populations for peace and harmony. Besides this, promoting Sufi thought is also part and parcel of American CT strategy to build moderate Muslim societies (RAND Report 2007).

Eighth, the government must enlist public support for fighting terrorism through proper socio-political and economic inclusiveness, which is paramount. CT policy will remain elusive and cosmetic. Consolidation of democracy, the rule of law, and distributions of powers among all the tiers of government as enshrined in the constitution of Pakistan could go a long way in mitigating the reasons behind public resentment and social unrest.

Ninth, a well-defined hierarchical institutional network must be specifically tasked to implement the NAP. For this, no other higher institution than the National Counterterrorism Authority (NACTA) offers relevance and focus. It is a top civilian national institution under the direct and actual command of the Prime Minister of Pakistan. The primary task of this authority is to make counter-terrorism policy and coordinate works of all agencies to keep the prime minister updated on efforts taken at all levels. Therefore, the Prime Minister should allow NACTA all required funds, human resources, and infrastructure to beef up the accomplishments. Raza Rumi (2015) embeds his ideas of inventing a new CT policy for Pakistan in these words.

To effectively counter internal militancy and external terrorism, Pakistan's policymakers will need to harness civilian and military institutions. To do so, they need to develop a multifaceted strategy that incorporates a national intelligence directorate, an internal security adviser, enhanced jurisdiction of the National Counter Terrorism Authority, parliamentary participation in counterterrorism, increased financial commitments, education reform, provincial counterterrorism strategies, and altering public narratives. Such measures need to be implemented in letter and spirit with complementary institutional reforms.

NACTA should be a helpful platform for meaningful collaboration of law enforcement and military components for substantial outcomes in a networked system. Together with reconciling the intelligence reports coming from ISI, IB, MI, and provincial intelligence departments, NACTA must coordinate joint military and police operations against high-value targets in a professional manner to avoid the incidents of the police shooting.

Tenth, working with different non-government organisations, businesses, and private security agencies would serve as instrumental in managing risk, analysing the threat, and controlling terror financing. Our LEAs, like FIA, should employ advanced digital methods, work with financial institutions and banks, and deal with black economy finances in much more innovative ways. Police should cultivate information sources for enhancing performance. Likewise, enlisting popular support has become a mandatory part of our law enforcement culture and public expectations in Pakistan (Rana 2012).

Eleventh, while working in the counterterrorism field, the law enforcement officers, including police, should be well-educated in the mechanics of terrorism, particularly knowing full well how the terrorists think! Thinking like a terrorist will enable cops to decode the terrorist secrets of carrying out the plans of disasters and destructions. Equally valid and vital is taking lone wolf-single terrorism as seriously as we take the groups and networks. Sometimes, the lone wolves play hell to an irrecoverable extent and unamendable level. In this regard, de-radicalisation of youth would be a wise and appropriate strategic step towards preventing the recruitment of suicide bombers (Rana 2012).

Twelfth, terrorism should be policed as an organised crime instead of war. Considering terrorism, a high-profile organised crime based on brute violence would pave the way for finding reliable criminal justice solutions. Instead of laboriously relying on state coercion, gun power, military muscle, and rampant use of force, we should look for inclusive and democratic methods to intimidate and threaten the undaunted terrorists. Fighting terror sets a deadly game that ends in complete nought, blurring a thin line of ethics and law between authority and criminality (Baloch 2016). Abbas (2009) aptly concludes: "It is a globally recognized fact that a state's police and law enforcement agencies play a critical role as the first line of defence against the threats of terrorism and insurgencies. An informative RAND study titled *How Terrorist Groups End* provides evidence that effective police and intelligence work, rather than the use of military force, deliver better counterterrorism results." In his recent article Shahzad Chaudhry (2021) also reaches the same conclusion:

"If there is one lesson that must emerge from twenty-years long US military presence in Afghanistan and its rather symbolic closure is that militaries are most ill-suited to nation-building and must refrain from such ambition. If Americans can't do it with all their wherewithal, no one else too."

Thirteenth, not least valuable, are the target hardening methodologies employed by the police and law enforcement agencies while preparing for countering any possible terrorist attack (Clarke & Newman 2007). In this regard, it is vital to know the terrorist groups, their associations, their links, potential targets, motivation, extraordinary capacity, drivers, funding sources, overall plan, and apparent goals and demands. This knowledge could enable law enforcement officers to shortlist possible targets to minimise the likelihood of striking. The Police taking stringent security measures should adequately address the probabilities and possibilities of terrorist targeting (Ibid).

Fourteenth, developing data and intelligence to monitor immigrant populations is vital in policing terrorism in Pakistan. Pakistan hosts millions of refugees, and it is undeniable that such refugee populations have been a source of violence in the country (Yousuf 2014). Though there is no substitute for human intelligence, the experience educates us that exclusive reliance on professionals in the community for information is not advisable in terrorism. Most importantly, the slum areas and the settlements of internally displaced populations have a greater tendency and likelihood of getting involved in terrorism and crime. Therefore, the documentation of such demography and their profiling should be the primary responsibility of intelligence and the police (Ibid).

Lastly, A collaborative joint strategic network of counterterrorism should involve all stakeholders. Gathering actionable intelligence through joint tasking of intelligence networks could work well for conducting intelligence-based operations against terrorist networks. However, in countering terrorism, no measure could match the joint task force model of intelligence sharing with inventing the ground information inflow and real-time distribution system of information among law enforcement actors for timely pre-emption and prevention of any untowardly incident. Technological sources of information like cameras have limits as they show what is happening in front of them; they become blind to explaining what is happening where they do not watch or where their range ends. More importantly, Police operate cameras manually. Therefore, only joint tasking and responsibility could better separate a dream from reality in gathering actionable intelligence (Baloch 2021).

7.9. Conclusion

Policing terrorism in Pakistan is more daunting a challenge than it is in any other part of the world. However, policing needs innovation in data and intelligence collection. For this end in view, police have to develop a highly professional, objective-oriented, scientific, responsible, capable, resourceful, accountable, communitarian, intelligence-led, futuristic, autonomous, and well-policed police. The invention of highly efficient police would be instrumental in dealing with the challenge of terrorism, extremism, and mega-civil disorders. Therefore, Pakistan should chalk out a new holistic counterterrorism policy and framework by pooling a total of wisdom drawn across different segments of the society and various fields of academia to widen the security vision and broaden the CT base beyond NAP. Experts of CT here and abroad have been calling for reviewing Pakistan's excessive reliance exclusively on the militarisation of its counterterrorism, for building the capacity of the police the criminal justice system, and for establishing a national network of CT through a more formalised mechanism and collaboration of police and non-police actors engaged in counterterrorism one way or the other. For this end to achieve, NACTA could be a centrifugal force and an appropriate to begin. Also, Pakistan needs a national level institute and think tanks to improve the research, legislation, and policy regarding counterterrorism to make it more coherent in terms of policy and practice of policing terrorism. To end with what CIA director James Woolsey's testimony to Congress in 2004 states.

"Only an effective local police establishment that has the confidence of citizens is going to be likely to hear from, say, a local merchant in a part of town containing several new immigrants that a group of young men from abroad have recently moved into a nearby apartment and are acting suspiciously. Local police are best equipped to understand how to protect citizens' liberties and obtain such leads legally (Woolsey 2004)."

Chapter: 08

Community Relations

Chapter Brief

Skogan (2006) maintains that '"whatever be the policing model or framework or philosophy of policing, what matters the most is capacity of police to deliver public service in a friendly, accessible and expeditious manner". Making a case study of citizen-police-liaison-committees CPLC Karachi and Dispute Resolutions Councils in KP province, it argues that police-community platforms help draw principles for building bridges of cooperation and partnerships for peace and in turning crime, violence, and terrorism back. This chapter finds that the police responsiveness to public calls of emergency satisfies the public and cultivates cordial police-public relationships, generating a general sense of self-help and collective responsibility. Moreover, substantial open-source intelligence for police also keeps feeding police officers regarding crimes and illegal activities in their area of responsibility (Skogan 2006). However, police in Pakistan struggle hard to institutionalize police-community relations, which remains strained at this juncture. This chapter looks at how community relations leave marks on police performance and why such relation is essential for transforming policing in this part of the world.

8.1. Introduction

We can analyse Police-community relations from many perspectives. First, a close police-community connection offers people easy access to police as the service provider. Second, easy access to the public enables police to manage quick police responses to emergency calls. Third, the friendly and responsive police improve their efficiency through performing and delivering. Fourth, public satisfaction for police effectiveness in providing service rolls up. When police keep delivering in an organised way, the public image of police gets improved. Fifth, the public dissatisfaction in the current scenario of policing in Pakistan is the root cause of the bad image of the police, and satisfaction of the public with police performance is the only realistic way to refine police image (Skogan 2006). Strategically, the police responsiveness to public calls of emergency satisfies the public and cultivates cordial police-community relations.

Another strand to comprehend the importance of community relations in policing is the proliferation of the democratic governance model worldwide. Democracy signifies the system of governance where people are sovereign. Nothing gets legitimized without the public mandate in a democratic dispensation. The authoritarian regimes are more prone to impose constraints on civil liberties than to allow freedom of expression and movement to the people. Democratic policing protects the people's fundamental rights instead of depriving them by the use of coercive authority. Thus, in democracy, police are rule-bound to build better community relations and secure higher levels of public trust (Weisburd and Braga 2006). Many societies, which have been involving their communities in policing and their police have been very responsive to their communities, have seen a significant reduction in crime rates. Community policing plays a pivotal role in the two defining elements of policing: police-community relations and problem-solving. "First, it should broaden police organisation goals. Secondly, community police changes police organisations, operations, and ideals" (Skogan 2006).

8.2. The issue of the Public Image of Police

The public image of Police is central to building public-police relations. Communities trust and cooperate with their police following. If the image is terrible, people prefer indifference. As explained in the preceding paragraphs, there is no shortcut to building an image of police except ameliorating police performance and public service delivery. In countries like Japan, Germany, France, Italy, the UK, the USA, Canada, Australia, Sweden, India, and many other countries, community policing dispensation has earned greater trust for their respective police departments. In many of these countries, the credibility of police has increased to the levels that "lying to police is a crime" and "statements before the police have higher evidentiary value in the trials courts" (Skogan 2006).

Many studies and surveys have revealed that the majority of the people in Pakistan have little confidence and trust in the police forces, and they hardly take the police role as satisfactory, given their inept attitude and behaviour while dealing with the public. For example, Gallup Pakistan conducted a public survey across the country in May 2014 maintained that only 27% per cent of people repose moderate trust in Police while 77% per cent population have no trust in police. In many of its annual reports on corruption, Transparency International also shares similar conclusions and findings, thereby putting police among the first two, the most corrupt departments in Pakistan.

Human Rights Watch Pakistan report titled "This Crooked System" dated 27 September 2016 reveals startling facts about police corruption, extortion, and highhandedness. According to the report, People fear and distrust the police, and most of the complaints are against police mishandling, torturing, extorting, and killing innocent people in Pakistan. HRW report (2016) identifies critical areas

149

of police malpractices, which create more problems for the general public than solve them. First, marginalised and vulnerable groups cannot get their First Information Report-FIR lodged without an approach and bribes (PRC 2019). Second, investigations also cost the complainant heavily, but he does not get justice even then. Third, illegal custody is commonplace in every nook and corner of the country. Fourth, custodial torture is part of the occupational culture of police in Pakistan (Khalid 2016). Fifth, extra-judicial killings know no abating despite efforts of the superior courts to stop that barbaric practice. Sixth, police implicate innocent people in false criminal cases. Last, there are no reliable mechanisms to redress grievances and accountability for abuses. HRW Report further gets into the pulse by stating that corruption, more impoverished working conditions, lowly status of constable, and abuse of authority characterise policing environs in Pakistan.

8.3. Legal Foundations of Community Relations

8.3.1. Police Act of 1861

The police Act 1861 provides the centralised organisational structure of the police force. British officers retained most senior command positions, which concentrated the decision-making powers. However, the subordinate officials represented the local communities as constables and head constables, who were not in a position to forge some meaningful relationship with the local people. The colonial police were loyal only to the British crown that paid them salaries. Besides that, the police officers were also responsible to the magistrates, who were also British in most cases. The occupiers always suspected local communities, who never allowed their force to get closer to local people.

The community relations received some consideration when Pakistan came into being. But, tragically, Pakistan took too long to make the constitution for a free society. However, hardly any reform commission report or veteran experts of policing in Pakistan have ever missed the importance of community relations while making a point of police reforms. In all 29 police reforms, reports of commission/committee emphasised the significance of police-community relations categorically. The reports observed that improving police image through cordial relations of police with the community is crucial for better public service delivery.

8.3.2. Constitution of Pakistan 1973

Though there is no direct mention of police-community relations in the constitution 1973 of Pakistan, there are specific provisions concerning the fundamental rights and principles of policy. These provisions emphasise the importance of civilised conduct of all state functionaries, which include

150

police also for the rule of law, due process of law, respect for the fundamental liberties, and social justice. The constitutions' preamble that contains objective resolutions reads in Article 2-A: "wherein Islam enunciates democracy, freedom, equality, tolerance, and social justice. Adequate provision for minorities to profess and practice their religion & develop their culture without restrictions. It underscores the fundamental right to equality by guaranteeing the equalities of status, opportunity, fair legal treatment, social, political or economic justice, freedoms of thought, expression, belief, faith, worship, and association subject to the law and public morality". However, Article 25 established the equality of all citizens and reads: "All citizens are equal before the law and are entitled to equal protection of the law...there will be no discrimination on any basis whatsoever" (1973 Constitution of Pakistan). These provisions mandatorily require state functionaries to make all-out efforts for ensuring across the board implementations of all these and such other provisions of subordinate laws from time to time made to organise the police forces in Pakistan.

8.3.3. Police Reforms Committee Report 1985

About the narrative of public trust in the police, Reform Committee of 1985 on Police reads:

"There is no shortcut to police efficiency and effectiveness. Police performance, in the first place, is dependent on conscious public cooperation, and this cooperation flows from the general social and cultural levels of the society, political maturity, commitment to religious and moral values, performance to other criminal justice institutions, most importantly judiciary, the right atmosphere of working and correct policies. We look upon the police as a "service to the community... Freedom from hunger and fear is also one of the fundamental duties of the Islamic state as enunciated in verse 106 of Surah- 'Quraish' of the Holy Quran (Police Reforms Committee-1985 Report, Para 1).

8.3.4. The Police Order 2002

After the independence, the first indigenously evolved police law was Police Order 2002, which has been the outcome of more than 25 commissions and committees. This Law was the first democratic law of police in Pakistan, which provided many brilliant ideas about police-community relationships and policing the police through civilian democratic oversight. PO 2002 provided cooperation mechanisms such as Public Safety Commissions, Police Complaint Authority, and Community Police Liaison Committees. Despite amendments in Police Order 2002 in 2004 and 2006 by different provinces and its revoking by Sindh and Balochistan in 2011, the original law had many provisions directly tasking police to serve and protect the marginalised and vulnerable groups through institutional platforms.

Police duties and responsibilities as defined in Police Order 2002 are to protect life, property, and civil liberties, maintain public order, prevent and investigate crime impartially, arrest criminals and violators of the law, and enforce the law without fear and favour. Police also provide service to the community without discrimination based on status, gender, religion, sect, age, race, disability, political affiliation, and ethnic origin or nationality (PO 2002). Besides this, the Police would remain humble, helpful, courteous, and neutral in discharging their duties and would perform the same with humility, authority, and common sense. This dispensation fits well only under community policing.

8.3.5. Khyber Pakhtunkhwa-KP Police Act of 2017

Almost the same is true in the case of the Police Act 2017 of KP. KP Act reproduces similar duties of the police as enunciated in PO 2002 only with a few additions such as countering militancy and terrorism as the primary job of the police officer. Without indulging in any re-mentioning of the same police duties, it is essential to mention the community policing mechanism as provided in 'Dispute Resolution Committees' (Section 73 KPPA 2017) at the district level and 'Police Assistant Lines' at the police station or circle levels as per population indicators. Public Liaison Councils (Section 47 KPPA 2017) in rural areas mostly, to name a few. These institutions are newer innovations of KP police and were not found even in Police Order 2002. Pakistan attaches the highest importance to these kinds of statutory responsibilities.

8.4. Community Relations Framework of Police in Pakistan

In Pakistan, community relations with their police is yet to grow up. Most of the police departments in Pakistan are still organised and work under Police Act 1861, colonial formations entirely unsuited to today's complex and urbanised society. However, many have demanded community policing in Pakistan, and now the community and political leaders welcome this idea to a certain extent. The 18th constitutional amendment (2010) has decentralised authority to the provinces and transformed power to the people. All stakeholders of public order such as people, police, governments at all levels, civil society, think tanks or specialists of law enforcement, media, academia, and international partners fully concur on the empowerment of the people. Empowering the people in their municipal and police administrations is unbeatable for a thriving democracy.

8.5. Citizen Police Liaison Committee-CPLC Sindh

In 1989 Sindh was the first province to launch CPLC initially in the four police stations of Karachi vide "the Commissioner's Administrative order No. HMS/JUB-1/10(982)89 dated 31.08.89", during the government of Mohtarma Benazir Bhutto's first stint in power (1988-1990). "CPLC's Computerized

Criminal Record Management (CCRM), till March 2013, stored the data of 766,398 FIRs. CCRM was the brainchild of then prime Benazir Bhutto, who provided a grant of Rs five million for the purpose in 1994-95 after her visit to CPLC (CPDI Report 2014). In 1996, governor Sindh Mr Kamal Azfar issued the charter of CPLC. He reorganised and expanded it operationally and made it an apolitical statutory institution. A board of governors, assisted by many community volunteers, was to run its affairs more institutionally and professionally. However, on 24th October 2003, the charter got final approval from the government of Sindh, and permanent institutions of CPLC came into play, targeting heinous crimes such as kidnapping for ransom, dacoities, vehicle snatching, theft, target killings, and other crimes to name a few. "A notification was issued by the Sindh Government amending the Police Rules 26 vide notification 27 dated 15 April 1990, to institutionalise the CPLC concept" (CPDI Report 2014).

Many believe that Governor Sindh Fakhruddin G. Ebrahim created CPLC to cultivate the community's confidence in law enforcement. During the late 1980s and early 1990s, the kidnapping for ransom industry boomed in Karachi, Sindh. Therefore, the Sindh government realised the need to establish an efficient body of volunteers to curb the menace. Besides this, crimes like vehicle snatching/theft, robberies, murders were rampant in Karachi. The wealthy-business class was the target of kidnappers. Therefore, the business community underscored the need for such a specialist body to control Karachi's kidnapping and other heinous crimes. It attracted the business community's interest as they were the prime target of kidnappers because of their wealth. "CPLC was co-founded by Nazim Haji (chief) and Jameel Yusuf (joint chief), both belonging to the business community" (CPDI Report 2014).

8.5.1. Functions of CPLC

The constitutive notification of the CPLC reveals many functions of the agency. Timely registration of FIRs, ensuring quality investigation, developing crime database, helping police in crime management, helping citizens remove illegal social crimes such as drugs, gambling, prostitution and suggesting mechanisms for better public service delivery at police station levels have been the core functions of CPLC. At the heart of CPLC functions is the idea of bringing police and community closer together in fighting crime and social evils.

8.5.2. Achievements of CPLC

CPLC-Sindh's core work areas include anti-Kidnapping, citizen's support, community awareness programme, Nazareth-charged parking, neighbourhood care, police welfare, public toilet scheme, and street crime. CPLC has the following achievements to its credit in available records.

153

Reimagining Policing in Pakistan

i. **High Performance in Anti-kidnapping**: CPLC claims that from 2008 to 2018, they have dealt with 837 kidnapping for ransom cases and have solved 834, achieving success rates of 99.9% through the intelligent use of technology (CPLC Website). However, the recovery success rate of kidnappees from 2003 to 2013 was 98%. Moreover, the CPLC conducted these operations in coordination with police, not independently.

ii. **Street Crime Recoveries:** The records reveal that 861,508 mobile phones had been snatched or stolen since 2005, and with the assistance of mobile phone dealers registered with Karachi Electronics Dealers Association (KEDA) and Pakistan Telecommunication Authority (PTA), CPLC succeeded in recovering only 37, 776 which is not a satisfactory achievement as per crime analysts. "The number of crime incidents increased from 175,286 (the year 2016-17) to 239,405 (2017-18) according to crime statistics compiled by the CPLC" (CPLC Statistics).

iii. **Establishing Effective Response System**: CPLC runs round a clock 24/7 communication system, which works as its name 24 hours and seven days like the 24/7-i system of Interpol, which claims to follow the sun. Fully trained 60 operators equipped with dedicated lines with recording facility managers are available for attending public calls of emergency and verifications of stolen and snatched items. This call centre entertains 25000 calls a day on average, making a total of 7 50,000 to a maximum of 900,000 per month as days in a month vary and daily traffic of calls too (CPLC Statistics).

iv. **Launching Scientific crime management:** CPLC has emerged as an extension of specialised police functions. It has subsequently evolved from a mere public facilitator to a record keeper. CPLC has developed advanced crime mapping skills necessary for analysing and applying crime data analytics for actual crime prevention tactics of modern policing. CPLC announces annual reports regarding an audit of sensitive data, which they share only with LEAs and IAs and associated official platforms, but not with the public. However, crime statistics are shared publicly.

v. **Building Jail Inmates Database:** the CPLC has established fully equipped offices in Central Prison of Karachi for recording and maintaining the record of inmates using biometrics and digital photosystems, which further analyse criminal demographics, crime patterns, prosecution challenges, and the investigation problems by getting questionnaires filled by the inmates. The application of scientific methods helps police in making profiles of criminals.

154

vi. **Making Sketches of Criminals:** Using technology or crime analytics has helped CPLC make accurate sketches of criminals. In this process, they have made more than1500 sketches per year for various cases with an accuracy rate of 85%. This facility that was exclusive with CPLC now extends to police.

vii. **Community Support:** The most important of all roles that CPLC plays is educating the general public in taking precautions to escape criminal victimisation. In this field, CPLC Karachi has seasoned and well-experienced volunteers who play a cardinal role in spreading awareness among the public and keeping them engaged and alert regarding public safety and security issues. Furthermore, CPLC, together with developing advanced skills in negotiating with different kinds of criminals, provides moral and technical support to people who receive threats from kidnappers and extortionists. CPLC has advanced digital facilities to use technology and current guidelines for tracking criminals in this connection.

viii. **Safety Awareness Campaigns:** CPLC continuously organizes numerous safety awareness campaigns. These campaigns include providing relief to victims of natural disasters, i.e., floods, cyclones, earthquakes etc., public service messages, personal safety against kidnapping, extortion, robbery, travel guides, school safety against terrorist attacks, anti-vehicle snatching, and preventions against street crimes.

ix. **Checking Police Abuse of Authority:** "CPLC also monitors police illegalities including arbitrary arrests, torture and ill-treatment, and other malpractices such as taking bribes. For example, CPLC helped police ensure the accountability of 216 defaulter police officials, who got punished with demotion or fines for 1,226 others between November 1998 and July 1999". The number of other police officials, who got punished for minor violations, crosses 5000 from 2000 to date. Here tensions exist between police and CPLC because the police think CPLC is not their oversight body, nor does it have any legitimate mandate.

x. **Supporting Police Technically in Raids:** CPLC-Sindh also conducts joint raids with the police and Anti-Violent Crime Cell (AVCC) to arrest kidnappers and get hostages released. In addition, CPLC has replicated its Community's Dispute Resolutions (DRCs) Mechanisms in other cities central regional headquarter of the Sindh province, including Hyderabad Sukkur, Mirpurkhas, and Larkana.

xi. **Uniting Broken Families:** CPLC has devoted teams to uniting families by bringing back lost / runaway persons from far-flung areas. As a result, people, courts, and media have reposed a higher degree of confidence and trust in CPLC in helping police in social work of uniting broken families. Though figures vary, the number of recovered persons runs in thousands regarding children, women, and the elderly.

xii. **Helping Traffic Police:** CPLC plays a cardinal role in advising and ensuring proper traffic management. CPLC has been able to assist police in improving provincial traffic discipline and snap checking of vehicles to curb crimes by carrying out analytical studies and surveys successfully, mainly due to its extended network all over the province especially having its camp offices in the regional headquarters of Sind.

xiii. **Neighbourhood Care (NC) Projects:** "CPLC has successfully launched 21 neighbourhood care projects in which residents along with CPLC attempts to ensure area security" in close liaison with Police Municipal organisations and Rangers-a networked policing approach. Such a strategic approach has produced remarkable results in reducing heinous crime and street crimes. In addition, CPLC has played a pivotal role in curbing public nuisance, ensuring public safety, maintaining sewerage lines, guaranteeing road safety, planting trees, lighting streets, ensuring water availability in some neglected regions, developing children/ladies parks. This multi-agency coordination has remarkably reduced mugging and street crimes.

xiv. **Providing Community Welfare Service:** CPLC is making sincere efforts to provide relief to masses living in downtrodden areas of Karachi. CPLC launched free schools in 3 areas of Karachi. CPLC claims that it has offered free education packages to over 1,150 students. Schools established for the welfare purposes of backward areas of the city have secured more than 90% results in the matriculation examination in the last three years. These schools are located at 1) Campus- (Khawaja Ajmer Nagri, 2) Campus-II Gulbahar, 3) Campus- III F.B. Industrial Area. Besides schools, CPLC provides Free OPD, Free medication, for instance, hepatitis vaccination, to masses living in low-income areas of Karachi and entire Karachi police at CPLC dispensaries: 1) Federal B. Industrial Area and 2) Khwaja Ajmer Nagri (CPLC Website). Thirdly, CPLC established 42 public toilets at different locations of Karachi, realising their acute need in the city (Ibid).

xv.   **Capacity Building:** CPLC has been continuously conducting training courses for building police capacity in handling Kidnapping cases, CDR analysis using tools, and alternate dispute resolution mechanisms. Besides police and its volunteers, CPLC also offers short courses and orientation courses in community-oriented policing and governance to students of criminology and management enrolled in different academic institutions for their postgraduate studies.

8.6. Dispute Resolution Councils DRCs in KP Province

The document creating DRCs borrows the idea of settling disputes among the Muslim brothers from the holy Quran as a statutory duty and a religious obligation. The vision of the DRCs reads: "And if two factions among the believers fight, then make settlement between the two", Verse 09, Surah Al Hijrat. The mission of these community bodies is "facilitating the common man in getting his petty issues resolved amicably through an alternate process of restorative justice involving members of the community." In 2014 DRC was first established at Peshawar only as a pilot project to transform the rusted and outlived "thana Culture" (Hashmi 2018). Later on, the KPK Police Act of 2017 incorporated the provisions that made it incumbent on the police to establish DRCs on each police station level in all districts. This project of KP police, like their Police Access System and Police Assistant Lines, envisages the transparent system of community policing with the direct involvement of the grassroots community and the local police of their district.

8.6.1. Composition and Structure of DRC

Each DRC is composed of 21 members who hail from varied backgrounds from the community. The aspirants, who have professional backgrounds, for instance, retired judges, retired civil servants, military officers, educationists, religious scholars, journalists, and people in business, are preferably enlisted. Secondly, each police station has a DRC with a minimum of 21 members. Thirdly, there are no permanent members in the DRC membership who can join and leave upon their will. Fourthly, if the DRC feels that any member is not participating fully, the District Police Chief may request to replace him with a new volunteer. Fifthly, the secretary of each DRC is responsible for organising and planning its scheduling and overall working. Sixthly, each DRC is divided into different panels, consisting of three members each. Seventhly, in each police station, a complete room is dedicated to the Jury office of the DRC. Eighthly, for the record-keeping of DRC, a police officer is appointed from the concerned police station. Lastly, though located in each police station, DRCs essential work is to keep close liaison with the sub-divisional Police officer, who is supervisory in charge of two or more than two police stations.

8.6.2. Functions of the DRC

The core function of the DRCs, according to KP Police Act 2017, is assistance to the police station for the amicable resolution of civil disputes within the ambit of the constitution. DRCs send a fact-finding report to Station House Officer-SHO of the concerned police station to file a criminal case when both parties fail to reach any settlement. DRC acts as observer jury in case of contested investigation of the police. If the DRC observers disagree with the police investigation, they will send a dissenting report to District Police Officer. Thus, dispute resolution, getting the case registered, and ensuring merit in investigations are the three primary and mandated functions of the DRCs in the KP province of Pakistan.

There are certain limitations on the discretion of the DRC members. First, DRC cannot take up any case for resolution or cannot interfere, on their own, in any dispute unless the parties concerned express their willingness in writing. Secondly, members have no mandate to get involved in complicated cases or controversial disputes having bearings on law and order. Thirdly, the members will make decisions or recommendations in the cases of culturally sanctioned violence against any age group, gender, minority, especially when it violates human rights or goes against the form or spirit of the constitution or other laws of Pakistan.

8.6.3. Enlistment Procedure of DRC members

The enlistment procedure for DRC members is straightforward. District Police Officer is competent to select members from within the community. However, an eligibility criterion set in the rules tells that an apolitical, seasoned, and well respected in the community can aspire to get enlisted as a member of the DRC of their district. The district police officer, after due diligence, verification of character credentials through different official and unofficial sources, and consultation with the civil society, can issue enlistment notification of DRC members, who then choose their chairman from within themselves on a rotational basis. This DRC job is a voluntary social service for those interested in becoming members of DRC.

8.6.4. Need to Revive Culture through Community involvement

The Khyber Pakhtunkhwa region, described by the 'Pashtunwali' code, has saved its traditions and culture for a considerable length of time. These social characteristics, today, are woven into their social texture. The tradition of settling disputes amicably through the intercession of 'senior citizens' called "Jirga" has been age-old and significantly adored. Be that as it may, the invasion of militancy and fear-based environment of terrorism in KP disturbed the peace and social order and annihilated a robust convention of settling disputes on community levels amicably through compromise. With a mission to revitalize this critical custom of dispute resolution through restorative justice, KP Police took this initiative of Dispute Resolution Council.

Today, the traditional court arrangement of Pakistan is involved in a heap of additional and authoritative issues. The civil courts also are unreasonably "over-loaded and under-resourced". In this manner, the police send cases on petty issues, including non-cognizable offences, to civil courts. As a result, the parties involved in disputes end up following a lengthy and costly procedure of justice. The frequent postponement in the administration of justice causes a sentiment of disappointment, frustration, and melancholy, to name a few. Establishing an alternative dispute resolution mechanism is one of the 21st-century milestones of Community policing in Pakistan.

8.6.5. The idea behind DRCs- Community Engagement in Policing

The idea of community engagement is to sit together relatively in a pleasant atmosphere generated by a balanced cultural approach to make concerned parties feel comfortable and willing to narrate the truth so that a fairer decision to settle the issue defines the soul of DRCs. The unavailability of such an inexpensive dispute settlement mechanism often results in more significant issues like bloodshed and tribal feuds that last for decades. The expensive and cumbersome criminal justice process, where most people complain about having their safety and dignity preserved compromised with no meaningful outcome, underscored the need for an alternative dispute resolution system as provided by DRCs. The system of alternative dispute resolution will achieve great success in this land rational people bound by centuries-old systems of Jirga and Pashtunwali" (Nasir Khan Durrani-Ex IGP KPK-2014)

8.6.6. Performance Achievements of DRCs

The DRCs in KPK received 1436 dispute references and resolved 727 while referring 80 disputes for legal action to relevant forums. DRC Swabi, which amicably settled 195 disputes in the first quarter of 2018, stood first in performance while Buner remained second with 71 settlements and Peshawar third, having worked out 67 referrals. However, the performance of the DRCs in all districts of KP is highly encouraging as it reportedly crossed the 70% problem-solving success rates at the close of the year 2018 (KPP official website). The excellent performance through the general mechanism has brought higher levels of community satisfaction, trust, and confidence in their police force. Besides building an image, the outcomes extend to many economic, political, cultural, and social advantages such as inexpensive justice, comfortable, friendly, and familiar methods, contributive to the maintenance of public order, delinking community support for militants and criminals, and revival of peoples' faith in the writ of the law and state.

8.6. Obstacles in Improving Community Relations

xvi.   **Practical Constraints**: In the end, "community policing is a philosophy, not a program"(Roth, 2000). If all stakeholders do not understand the philosophy of community policing, then the programmes will not succeed. The philosophy of community policing is, consensually, to encourage public police interaction so that the gap and trust deficit may be lessened (Ibid). Unfortunately, the example of CPLC Sindh fails to fit in this theoretical framework of community policing. Both the police and the community are missing in their model. In CPLC, only a handful of business tycoons takes the lead instead of the community. In the CPLC framework, police do not interact with the community; instead, they share their functions with a parallel bureaucratic and politically-cloned network of wealthy people. They focus more on the elitist crimes and who love to act more like a police oversight body than to help police build their capacity to improve police-public interaction or service delivery to the ordinary men.

xvii.   **Partial Implementations**: The community-oriented programmes are only a tiny part of making the community policing model work. The Community facilitation mechanism as established in KP reflects the true spirit of community police with amicable equations. DRCs and PLCs are classic examples of how police should work to facilitate public service delivery and involve the community (KPPA 2017). However, the scope of these bodies is limited and does not extend to all policing functions.

xviii. **Minus Community:** community policing works if the whole community, ethnic, racial, sectarian, religious, political, economic, and social backgrounds and class, together with the police. In KP province, the entire community police framework calls for volunteerism of the community to build peace and cohesion in the society. On the contrary, CPLC Karachi does not represent the community but a business and elitist group, who look for their protections

160

by securing their business and neighbourhoods in a private corporate security firm. Therefore, police organisations in Pakistan are yet to present a nationally coherent model for democratic reflection of community policing.

xix.   **Change Orientation:** The biggest obstacle that the community-based programmes face is the idea of change and transformation. Some conservative communities do not like to get their police involved in culturally sensitive matters and are reluctant to share anything. However, there can hardly be any more conservative and inward-looking community than the KP. Still, the community engagement network is so beautifully envisaged that it covers and respects even their cultural values. Hence, the acceptability levels of new community police arrangements in KP are higher than in any other place. However, policing as a cultural phenomenon is yet to make a promising breakthrough even in KP province.

8.7. Critical Analysis

Many criminologists express their concerns on some grey areas of community policing because this policing model focuses on and influences police-community relations. Correia (2000) highlights the ambiguity in the conceptual definition of "community" because many vested interest groups try to dominate police for reasons other than the objective facilitation of concerned communities, as we have noticed in the case of CPLC Karachi.

Second, it is almost impossible to understand community policing unless the world community is defined in a universally accepted way (Ibid). In Pakistan, we have seen that CPLC, a group of elite industrialists who have taken the shelter under the excellent name of the community for having access to power corridors by self-presuming the functions and authority of police, lack public mandate of the community at large. Their work has no significant impact on the lives of the commoner. Such wealthy and well-equipped bodies should prefer to address the causes of crime within the society. CPLC can help the government reduce poverty and offer shelter, food, and clothes to the poor people of Pakistan's metropolis, where people kill other people just for the meagre amount to make their ends meet.

Third, some critics like Peter Waddington (1984) feel sceptical of the political cloning of community police initiatives. The CPLC office is located in Governor house Sindh where seats of CPLC are distributed among people of certain smaller ethnic and business groups, and every Karachiite avails no such opportunity to serve the community and become part of the CPLC. CPLC is a class-closed body lacking a democratic spirit.

Fourth, Waddington argues that there was never a time when a police officer was always a friend of everyone, nor could this happen anytime in the future. Waddington's concern is genuine, particularly in developing countries, including Pakistan. In countries where democracy has not been able to take its roots properly and where the hybrid nature of polity prevails, the strong authoritarian tendencies tend to resist the transformation of police and policing as a rule-of-law institution tasked to serve and protect.

Fifth, David Bayley (2006) considers community policing "rhetoric more than reality", leading to some significant change in police work. Bayley's concerns do deserve some attention here. When we compare the facilities, equipment, hardware, and resources of CPLC with our police station in Karachi, we find that both are poles apart. Hardly any police station has any of the facilities and resources that CPLC has. The advancement and expansion of CPLC have also prevented the development of police stations from growing full-fledged public service centres because the elite class exercise their influence on political gentry and manage to get funds. Since the elite class has established their private police with policing functions, they do not bother for the police station where largely lower-class people get chained and go for basic services. Thus, here community policing becomes nothing more than mere rhetoric.

Sixth, Steven Herbert (2007) contends that the dynamic and democratic ethos of shared governance runs counter to focal components in police culture, which is authoritarian at best, and increasingly broad understandings of crime and punishment, which are primarily retributive than these are restorative. Policing involves using force in many of its basic functions, such as arrest, detention, prevention, control, and order. In contrast, community policing is designed to minimize the coercive authority of the police by softening the core policing functions. As a result, the chances of the clash between authority and liberty become thick in community policing dispensation. David Bayley (2006) considers that establishing community policing strategies may prompt a decrease in crime control viability, upkeep of order, the increment in authoritarian control over community affairs, particularly civil liberties.

Seventh, Kevin Stinson (1993) believes that police officers in community policing always try to impose their 'particularistic normative standards' on the people. These views of experts of policing bring home the persistent tension within the body politics of community-police relations in which both police and community mutually feel scared of each other for being subjected to the control of one over the other. For example, DRCs involve the voluntary participation of notables who get selected, not elected by the people, by the police authorities. Those who want to play a voluntary role must keep good relations with police authorities, or the prospects of his entry could be dimmer. Though this is not a universal rule, it prevails; hardly anyone can deny it. However, there are, indeed, some exceptions in police leadership.

Thus, some misconceptions come from the criticism that community policing is just a public relations gimmick and a romantic delusion of strict controls in the guise of democratic principles. However, Trojanowicz and Carter (1988) stated that excellent police-community relations are a by-product of community policing. Besides this, Steven Kelly Herbert (2006) argues that bringing change in policing ways would remain a pipedream without the engagement of the community. Unfortunately, the CPLC lacks the essential element of "community", and it pretends more of an oversight body of the police than a framework of community policing.

The police oversight should be strengthened in the public interest, but for the legitimacy of policing, the police require democratic cloning. New police laws in Pakistan have addressed this issue by establishing some particular institutions of police oversight. For example, Public Safety Commissions, Police Complaint Authority, Criminal Justice Coordination Committees, etc. The role of these institutions should not be replicated or duplicated by the PLCs that are neither police nor community. Any model of community policing should have appropriate representation of apolitical community members, who should be responsible to their localities instead of political or bureaucratic bosses. The police should directly enlist such members to directly interact with the community without any irrelevant intermediary, who looks for their interests instead of public interest.

In Pakistan, many experts of policing concur with the views of the advocates of the community policing framework. Perhaps in Pakistan, the old authoritarian model of policing as envisaged by the British colonialists in India continued to service the governments in power rather than the communities. In the 21st century, the old model of policing in Pakistan has become outlived and quite unfit to address new challenges of crime, violence, terrorism, public order, and public safety. Therefore, working for innovative solutions to bridge the gaps between the public and the police through more democratic and fairer models of taking the community on board in police policy, reforms, and implementation has become the strategic policing goal in contemporary Pakistan.

The models of community policing in Pakistan like that of CPLC Karachi need critical democratic scrutiny for their being authoritarian and lacking community elements. However, evolving the standardized community policing in Pakistan has to undergo more experiments like that of Faisalabad CPLC, Islamabad CPLC, and the extension of KP's culturally charged model of community policing. Indeed, these successful models need to expand coherently to all police formations in Pakistan.

8.8. Recommendations

Pakistan needs to develop a standardised community policing model for the entire Country's law enforcement and police agencies in line with its socio-cultural realities. Community policing allows adjustments in structure, process, procedure, and strategic vision of gaining public trust through better public service delivery. We can achieve the goal of better working relationships of trust between the community and the police by following the core values of policing, i.e., transparency, accessibility, responsiveness, accountability, innovation, reliability, due process, democracy, integrity, and honesty. Community policing is the composite of all these ways and values. Therefore, there can hardly be any two opinions regarding the institutionalisation of community policing ethos in our law enforcement landscapes. However, suppose we, police, want to win the public trust and build our image. In that case, the police have to engage and interact with diverse communities living within their areas of responsibility to show their humanity and professional excellence to maintain peace in society.

Police in Pakistan are not stagnant, nor yet fully grown up but struggling to work their ways towards modernisation through innovation, reform, and change. Community policing is one of the globally acknowledged best practices of policing, while its efficacy of operations largely depends on socio-political and cultural dynamics in which particular policing works. The police in Pakistan, as we have seen in the preceding paragraphs, have been trying to make headways in community-oriented policing. However, for their transformation from a force model to a service model, the police in Pakistan need to ensure following community police measures.

I. **Adopting Procedural Justice:** Procedural justice signifies the fairer, legitimate, and respectful way of making decisions and implementing policies by law enforcement in collaboration, cooperation, and coordination with the community and addressing their genuine concerns as well as considerations (Robert & Sarah 2017). It further suggests that the police should conduct themselves in a dispassionate, impartial, neutral, honest, and professional way with the public. Police should make evidence-based decisions that, in turn, will earn goodwill, confidence, trust, and faith for law enforcement agencies that they serve the community and that they make decisions without any preconceived way and any fear or favour (Ibid). Police departments, to enhance their credibility, should develop a culture of transparency and accountability and promote legitimacy by applying procedural justice principles.

II.   **Switching to Guardian Role from warrior mindset:** The policing challenges in the 21st century require policing educators to revisit the basic structure of their training designs which appear to be inherently flawed in the context of emerging socio-political realities. The warrior mentality of the police appears dominant and recurrent theme, filled with great slogans and enthusiasm for waging war on everything-crime, drugs, illegal weapons, and terrorism (Hope 2015). Indeed, it is vital to instil the physical spark in young officers facing the challenges of crime. The moral values of courage, confidence, optimism, cordiality, honesty, service delivery, passion, empathy, impartiality, democracy and the rule of law in building their integrity of character could serve as instrumental in winning the public trust (Newburn 2015). The warrior image of our police has not earned any goodwill for the police. Reform and innovation in Pakistan have redefined to some extent the role of a police officer as a helper, facilitator, supporter, and problem solver rather than a problem creator or fighter (Weisburd & Braga 2006). Guardian mindset helps ensure that officers give people a voice, fair treatment, and respect. They are participating in Open Data Initiatives, an online portal that provides the public with information about practices of particular concern, including the use of force (Robert & Sarah 2017). Police should conduct so that the public feels they are the guardians of their rights rather than their encroachers. Joint and interactive sessions between police and community could work in this connection.

III. **Police must be polite and courteous in Law enforcement:** Police may take all possible steps to refrain from practices requiring officers to issue a determined number of tickets, citations, arrests, or summonses, or to initiate investigative contacts with citizens for reasons not directly related to improving public safety, such as generating revenue (Vitale 2017). Police officers should share the list of names of the individuals they have stopped, along with the reason for the stop, the reason for a search. Similarly, during stop & search, Police should give a card with information on reaching the civilian complaint review board (President's Task

Force on Police Reforms, USA 2016). Moreover, The police should communicate the specific Purpose of stopping and Searching the people and their community (Ibid).

IV. **Regular community meetings are encouraged:** New approaches in policing consider community meetings as a critical element in engaging community members in a dialogue with local police (Maxson, Hennigan & Sloane 2021). Law enforcement organisations have achieved success in smaller, less formal settings than a community centre or other public forum (Ibid). Police should engage communities with high rates of investigative and enforcement involvement. They need to consider the potential damage to public trust while implementing crime-fighting strategies. Police do their best to get public approval in such cases and rack the level of trust in the police similar to changes in crime.

"Police can improve public opinion by increasing their informal contacts with citizens. Residents' opinions of police job performance and officers' demeanour, police can increase residents' approval of their job performance by participating in community meetings, increasing officers' visibility in neighbourhoods, and talking with citizens. Informal contacts with police also lessened the negative impact of residents' formal contacts with police (such as being arrested or questioned by police)" (Maxson, Hennigan & Sloane 2021).

V. **Keeping communities informed:** Homicide and other shooting investigations frequently take place in Pakistan's different parts. Sometimes community members remain uninformed of the processes required for these investigations. The community engagement causes frustration for community members, who feel shut out from significant events in their neighbourhoods. Without disclosing sensitive information, explaining the investigation process may assist community members in feeling connected to the process and lead to higher clearance rates. An action as simple as explaining what happened at the edge of a crime scene to a community member would provide valuable community support for police and may even yield valuable investigative information.

VI. **Building relations with Immigrant Communities:** The police should also capitalise on diversity; create a workforce diverse in race, gender, language, life experience, and cultural background. In Pakistan, many refugees live and are sometimes involved in illegal activities (Yousuf 2014). Therefore, the police must build relationships with immigrant communities based on trust so that police officers may have insights into their problems and issues. Pakistan's main cities such as Karachi, Lahore, Peshawar, Islamabad, and Quetta have hosted over 3.5 million immigrants from Afghanistan, Bangladesh, Behar India, Cambodia, and Iran.

All these Immigrants have different cultural backgrounds and significant sources of violence in Pakistani society. Police should keep them engaged and under a vigilant eye.

VII.   **Intelligence-led Specific Operations:** Besides this, police departments should conduct targeted crime reduction operations such as SWAT operations and service of specific search warrants. Any failure to notify residents of the purpose of the mission can make residents feel subjected. In all, police should follow due process and uphold the rule of law norms in collaborating with community members to develop strategies in communities disproportionately affected by crime for deploying resources and improving community relations.

VIII.   **Use of new Technology and Media**: social media has emerged as a new communication and information tool which has assumed the core of policing operations in the 21st century. "Implementing new technologies can allow police departments to fully engage communities, to educate them in a dialogue about their expectations for transparency, accountability, and privacy and to adopt model policies and best practices for technology-based community engagement that increases community trust and access" (Tulsa Commission 2017). The advent of body-worn cameras or the digital police helmets, as are being acquired by KP police, have provided law enforcement with an opportunity to show the public what an officer experiences, mainly using force. Releasing body-worn camera or digital helmet camera videos can provide a layer of transparency unparalleled in policing (Tulni 2019). Making such videos public as early as possible without compromising any of the necessary administrative, investigative, and legal processes will greatly value all stakeholders. Humans lie but technological and scientific evidence never. This scientific method helps to improve the entire criminal justice process, thereby cultivating more community trust in the police (Ibid).

IX.   **Respect the fundamental Rights of Everyone:** Constitution guarantees all citizens' fundamental rights, including civil liberties. In this connection, police have to collaborate with community members to develop strategies to redress their genuine grievances. For implementing policies on the use of force, police should share clear, concise, and publicly available information with communities regarding training, investigations, prosecutions, and data collection (Maxson, Hennigan & Sloane 2021). Police should collect data regarding shops, schools, mosques, universities, and other sensitive places that are likely to target any criminal activity. In this regard, police have to maintain data for strategic planning involving search, stop frisks, summons, and arrests. The police should implement civilian oversight to strengthen public trust in police in a way as desired by the community. It is also critical for the police to frame policies and standard procedures for policing crowd protestations like Dharnas in Pakistan. Using tactics could need to employ a continuum of managed tactical resources to minimise the chances of using force. Using provocative tactics and equipment would likely undermine community trust (Stone & Travis 2011).

8.9. Conclusion

It stands to reason that community relations have a strategically pivotal position in reimagining policing in the postmodern settings of inclusive, stimulating, and pluralistic policing. The existence and continuance of this social institution of policing could survive and thrive only of the popular mandate. Therefore, the absolute sovereigns in political terminology are the people, not the ruler or their governments. Deflem (2016) believes that police can never attain social and political legitimacy for policing unless they develop good working and trust relations with the people they serve. It is fairer and convincing to argue that the police can remain relevant, responsible, responsive, accessible, practical, current, and legitimate only when they enjoy community confidence and earn their trust. However, there is no shortcut to winning the public trust except showing performance in public service delivery in a more straightforward, simpler, quicker, and more suitable manner. For that end in view, the police in Pakistan should transform through reform, innovation, and change from their traditional ways to the new mechanism of policing community and democracy.

By J.J. Baloch (2022)

Chapter: 09

Police Governance

Chapter Brief

This chapter focuses on police accountability (Stone and Travis 2011), its different forms, politics, and problems. The difficulties pertain to procedural justice, the rule of law, excesses in the use of authority, and politics of police governance in Pakistan (Shigri 2016). This chapter argues that autonomy and accountability can only go together under the dispensation of civilian democratic mechanisms of external accountability. Only democratic accountability could promise political neutrality, legitimacy, democracy, transparency, inclusiveness, fair play, better service delivery, and professional excellence in the police organisations of Pakistan (Babakhel 2021). Different Police Acts and Police Orders (PO 2002 and KP PA 2017, for example), court judgments on political interference in policing, and opinions of the academia provide for democratic police governance in Pakistan. It further expands the main argument that the provisions of democratic accountability of police under PO 2002 and other new police laws have been amended to keep police as the political instrument of control. Consequently, police accountability has not yielded positive results because neither has it controlled police notoriety nor yet reduced political intervention (Riaz 2018). The reform legislation and academic research both in Pakistan and abroad constitute the core of content in this chapter.

9.1. Introduction

As discussed in earlier chapters, the accountability frameworks under the 1861 Police Act and subsequent Police Order 2002 and the KP Police Act of 2017 differ remarkably (Babakhel 2021). Under old police law, the District Magistrate vested primary control or superintendence of police, while under newer laws, the dual control system got diluted. The new laws authorised Provincial Police Officers to wield the authority of police internally. On the other hand, new laws new institutions such as Public Safety Commissions and Police. Moreover, Complaint Authorities Criminal Justice Coordination Committee to ensure democratic oversight of the police instead of bureaucratic and political oversight dispensation (Ibid). Unfortunately, the new democratic dispensation of police oversights, though provided under the new law, could not see the light of the day due to bureaucratic and political resistance. Either new Police laws were not fully implemented or instantly amended before their implementation could begin. However, the emergent new police professionalism worldwide, which consists of four foundational pillars, i.e., accountability, transparency, legitimacy, and national coherence, was the recurrent idea of the new Police Order 2002. Still, unfortunately, this police law could be adopted in its pristine purity and was slightly defaced through amendments limiting its democratic scope. Here we discuss the politics of police governance and find out the reasons behind the failures of new laws to ensure democratic police oversight in Pakistan.

9.2. Policing the Police

Throughout history, the governments in Pakistan have been over-ambitious in controlling police (Shigri 2015) for their political gains instead of controlling the notoriety of police behaviour towards the general public. Most police officers' authority was derived from the federal laws by origin. However, new provincial laws have created duplications, complications, and contradictions by devolving exclusive provincial police domains (PRC 2019). Now, it lies within a realm of provincial governments as it has been confirmed through court decisions that law and order and the police are the provincial domains as per our new legal scheme (CP-7097 Sindh High Court 2016). Without any surprise, this dispensation has never been the same all the time, even under 1861 and 2002. Still, the 18th amendment has created some distortions in governance, which the provincial governments are utilising in Pakistan (Babakhel 2021).

The constitution of the police force and its governance are two different things altogether (PRC 2019). The constitution of the police and making of its fundamental laws such as Criminal Procedure Code, Pakistan Penal Code, Evidence Law, and any other laws governing the constitution and operations of the force and their operational authorities have been federal before and after Pakistan was created.

The constitution of Pakistan entrusted the law-and-order function to provinces. On the contrary, the constitution of the police force and its organisation was the federal government's job. The 18th constitutional amendment, as discussed in earlier chapters, created confusion about the exclusivity of policing domain without clarifying the difference of mandate to federal and provincial governments regarding the criminal procedure (Babakhel 2021). After the 18th Amendment (2010), policing has changed dramatically. Each provincial police have adopted its provincial Police Acts, which have caused many problems for both the public and the police (PRC Report, 2019). There are too many checks on police departments to grow efficient in Policing (Waseem 2018). As a result, police control on crime and police leaders' grip in disciplining the police force keeps losing (Ibid).

The PRC report-2019 envisioned the rule of law, fundamental rights, police accountability, service delivery, quality investigation, operational autonomy, and integrated criminal justice approach as core areas for future reform. The PRC (2019) proposed a well-articulated report to Supreme Court for referring the recommendations to the government for stepping ahead in making police apolitical, transparent, accountable, responsive, responsible, and friendly with administrative, financial, and operational autonomy (Address of CJ SC-Saqib Nisar 14 January 2019). Many insights emphasised the need to engage communities, adopt the technology, apply science (Presentation by Tariq Parvez 14 January 2019), build capacity for specialism, and ensure objectivity, legitimacy, transparency, and due process for revamping police and policing in Pakistan.

9.3. Police Accountability

Accountability of police is a cardinal part of the new police professionalism (Stone and Travis 2011) that sits well in democratic dispensations of society and the polity in the 21st-century postmodern perspective. The policing paradigm suggests that the coercive apparatus of power has transformed into an inclusive mechanism of the welfare of the people. Consequently, the police have to redefine its mandate through widespread acceptance and support on their proportionate exercise of authority.

Walker (2006) defines police accountability in these words:

"Accountability is a vital element of policing...It [accountability] is a fundamental principle of a democratic society that the police should be held to account for their actions. Accountability includes both what the police do and how they perform. Agency-level accountability involves the performance of law enforcement agencies concerning controlling crime and disorder and providing services to the public (National Institute of Justice, 1999). Individual-level accountability involves the conduct of police officers concerning lawful, respectful, and equal treatment of citizens... Effective accountability procedures are essential if the police are to achieve their goals of lawfulness and legitimacy... Lawfulness refers to compliance with the formal requirements of the law, including statutes and court decisions. Legitimacy refers to the perception that police conduct is both lawful and consistent with public expectations (Walker 2006).

On the definition of police accountability, the UN handbook on Police Accountability (2011) reads:

"For the police to be able to take responsibility for actions and wrongdoings, they need to receive proper direction. They also need to be well-prepared and equipped to carry out their functions professionally and need to be assured of proper working conditions. Moreover, effective accountability requires a proper complaints system that is easily accessible to the public, and that can effectively investigate allegations and recommend disciplinary sanctions or refer cases for criminal prosecution. It should also make recommendations that target the underlying causes of misconduct. Effective police accountability involves many different actors representing the different layers of modern-day democracies, including government representatives, the parliament, the judiciary, civil society actors, and independent oversight bodies such as national human rights institutions. But, primarily, it involves the police themselves" (UN Handbook 2011).

171

Reimagining Policing in Pakistan

As a democratic republic, Pakistan has to reorganise its police governance by placing its police as a robust service delivery framework for public facilitation and support by gaining higher levels of public trust and confidence, which appears to have been on the lowest ebb. Resultantly, there is a greater realisation among police leadership to heed to the public demands for responsive, responsible, professional, result-oriented, and people-friendly police service. Hence, democratic institutions for police oversight have been proposed in all police reforms (PO 2002). Thus, ideally, police should be accountable to the people rather than the state or government. The policing experts believe that police can be rendered responsible for three main things, i.e., crime, cost, and conduct-3Cs (Stone & Travis 2011).

First, by accountability for crime, police are tasked to prevent and detect crime and maintain order in the communities (Stone & Travis 2011). It requires clarification on how efficient police are in performing their primary functions of crime management, public safety, and internal security, including counterterrorism, interests every taxpayer, the critic of governance, and progressive analyst (Ibid).

In this regard, remarkable developments have been witnessed in Pakistan in the 21st century due to rising literacy rates, increasing urban cultures, media boom, judicial activism, and the awareness of human rights among the citizens. However, everyone tends to raise fingers against police for their failure to prevent and detect crime and serve and protect the people. Increased crime and violence put police in moral and legal dilemmas (PRC 2019). Thus, police performance is the primary area where police leaders and their forces face severe criticism in all circles of society and are very often punished for such failures. Many police leaders, officers, and constabulary have been punished for not being able to discharge their duties in a befitting manner for one or the other reason (Stone and Travis 2011).

Secondly, accountability for the cost (budgetary expenditure) alludes to the taxpayers' money spent on policing (Stone & Travis 2011). In Pakistan, with the modernisation and expansion in policing due to the challenges of terrorism, extremism, and other newer crimes, police annual budgets keep increasing exponentially. Moreover, the last two decades since 2002 have witnessed the birth of many new policing functions, branches, divisions, and units for performing different duties of the police ranging from counterterrorism, mob handling, crowd management, public safety, forensic tasks, technological challenges, and much more as having been discussed in part II (policing developments) in this book. On the contrary, police departments in the countries like the USA and many other

172

European nations have opted for budgetary cuts cost-cutting strategies, including reductions in human resources (Stone and Travis 2011). Moreover, to minimise the expenses, police departments worldwide look for more innovative technological surveillance of police conduct.

However, in Pakistan, the case is reverse of it. Perhaps, police in Pakistan are expanding where the police technological modernisation is taking place now and which in the Western developed countries happened a century ago. The decrease in the number of sworn officers gives way to the inclusion of civilian and private specialists of different fields in policing. Many experts consider it a welcome move for police to develop as a diversified and dynamic organisation. However, many financial risk observers and analysts in the USA and the other developed nations are rare in Pakistan. Governments spend money on police and policing, and the public feels susceptible. Hence, they keep their governments under pressure to get transparency, integrity, and honesty of police professionals ensured.

Thirdly, conduct accountability is a crucial and critical part of police accountability (Stone & Travis 2011). People forget everything-crime, poor performance, cost of policing, but they never remain silent on the mistreatment and any laxity on police when people need police help and assistance (Ibid). Police accessibility and responsiveness for extending help to the victims means a lot to the people. Good police behaviour in times of adversity is nobler than the detection of crime (Ibid). Police misuse authority by using abusive language, excessive force than required, torture, demanding a bribe, and any form of highhandedness, which becomes unbearable for all citizens. As a result, people react fiercely to such conduct of the police. In media, courts, and political circles, people outcry for fixing police officers involved in such incidents of mistreatment. It is a welcome sign that there is growing realisation among top police leadership to discipline their police forces and change the culture of police working and police mindsets through different modern toolkits and techniques in Pakistan. Such people-friendly policing methodologies are adopted to win public trust for gaining legitimacy for their police profession in a highly charged anti-police environment of our society that asserts to be more democratic than ever.

9.4. Forms of Police Accountability

In all police organisations, there are two forms of accountability, i.e., internal and external. Internal accountability signifies that police officers are responsible for their hierarchical command line within their departments. External accountability refers to political, bureaucratic, and civilian oversight mechanisms. In both cases, police are questioned for their exercise of authority and use of force, increase in crime and expenditures on policing (Clarke 2006). However, more focus of internal accountability remains on crime management and observance of discipline and rules. In contrast, external accountability extends to the exercise of policing powers and budgetary matters together with some concerns about crime rates (Ibid). As a whole, policing experts refer to police accountability as a "conglomerate of processes" wherein diverse players share their joint responsibility of checks and balances in police actions in terms of arrest, detention, use of force, budgetary expenditures, and appropriate utilisation of human resources (Malik 2019). Let us shed some light on each form of police accountability.

I. **Internal Accountability System:** In Pakistan's police accountability systems, both under the old 1861 Police Act as well as Newer Acts in post Police Order 2002 era, the head of the police department (federal or Provincial) or unit (district) is responsible for the internal discipline of the police force. The police heads of the general area oversee whether police work within the bounds of law or commit excesses in terms of exercising their lawful authority (PO 2002). Whether police perform their lawful duties without charging the public for bribes; or whether police fulfil their function of preventing and detecting crime, maintaining public order, and ensuring public safety remains the responsibility of the police chief of that respective unit (Ibid). Most of the thrust of internal accountability remains on lower non-gazetted ranks up to SHO and SDPO levels. Inspectors General as heads of Police departments in Punjab, Sindh, Khyber Pakhtunkhwa-KPK, Balochistan, Islamabad Capital Territory, Gilgit-Baltistan, Azad Kashmir, are responsible for the general control and direction (PO 2002). At the same time, old law PA 1861 provided for "dual control" of magistrates for internal accountability of the police also.

II. **External Accountability System:** External police accountability has a broader framework, and many actors are involved. For the reader's convenience, the components of the external mechanism can be classified under four main heads: statutory, public, independent, and international (Ramsey 2018). First, three branches of the government, namely the executive, the judiciary, and the legislature, carry out external accountability of the police (PRC 2019). As regards executive, police respond to the provincial chief minister through home departments of the concerned provinces (Ibid). Regarding legal accountability, police are responsible to law, judges, and prosecutors on all levels of administration, ranging from the district, provincial, and the federal Supreme Court and the ministry of law. For political or democratic accountability, police on both federal as well as provincial levels are responsible to the public through their representatives in National Assembly, Senate, and prime minister's cabinet minister for interior and to the Nazims in districts or mayors in cities and their respective councils on lower levels (Ibid). Secondly, police are also responsible to the public through community police forums such as CPLCs, DRCs, and other civilian oversight boards represented by media and academia (UN Handbook 2011). Thirdly, police are responsible for independent mechanisms such as Public Safety Commissions, Police Complaint Authorities, and human rights commissions. Finally, the Ombudsmen institution does not represent any particular interest group or stakeholder (PRC 2019). However, impartially work on behalf of the public as constitutional and democratic mechanisms, which are impartial and immune from political and bureaucratic influences, are called civilian oversight. Lastly, police are also responsible to international bodies due to treaty obligations; for example, Pakistan is the signatory to many UNO conventions against transnational organised crime, anti-corruption, money laundering, terrorism, and human rights violations.

"External oversight is complementary to internal mechanisms; it can reinforce them and sustain police managers in their efforts to enhance police integrity and performance...as whoever controls the police are in a powerful position; it is, therefore, important to ensure that no single party dominates" (UN Handbook 2011). UNODC Handbook on Police Accountability lists many advantages of the external accountability mechanisms. First, it is a more credible system in the eyes of the public because it is unaffected by police spirit de corps. Secondly, it is not biased, and its procedures and findings are easily accessible to the public. Lastly, external mechanisms strengthen legitimacy to policing, transparency in procedures, and integrity of the police, which can go a long way in gaining public trust and building police image.

9.5. Police Powers and Discretion in Using Force

The essence of the postmodern law on police accountability, discretion, and use of coercive authority suggests the principle of proportionality even in the authorised use of force. The unauthorised use of force can by no means stand justified in the face of universal human rights awareness and limitations. However, in many parts of the world, the issue of the use of force in law enforcement remains surrounded by serious doubts, controversies, and concerns. The same is true in Pakistan.

175

Reimagining Policing in Pakistan

To start with UN General Assembly resolution 34/169 of December 17, 1979, which suggests a comprehensive code of conduct for police officials to work with extreme care and responsibility while using force. The code's title reads: "Code of Conduct for Law Enforcement Officials", and its articles 1 to 8 deal with police officers, who are defined as the "officers having the power of arrest and detention." However, this obligation extends to all others, which affect arrest and detention, whether military/police officer or a private security agent.

Article 2 emphasises respecting human dignity and protecting human rights by the police officers at all levels in all circumstances. However, article 3 reads: "Law enforcement officials may use force only when 'strictly necessary' and to the extent required for the performance of their duty" (UNGA Resolution 34/169 1979). This principle implies that highly exceptional circumstances for preventing crime and effecting the lawful arrest of a suspect or offender can allow using force. No police officer can use force disproportionate to the objective to be achieved. For example, arresting a motorcycle snatcher does not require bombardment or the use of lethal weapons. In a similar vein, for engaging with a terrorist, regular watch and ward equipment cannot work. The use of firearms involves extreme and extraordinary conditions and cautions, wherein sometimes police face fierce armed resistance on the part of the criminals. There appears to be no other solution in such a situation than a viable and workable use of firearms as a last resort. Violence both on the part of criminals and police is likely to endanger the lives of people and police.

Besides using firearms and lethal weapons for arresting criminals, the issues of custodial torture, cruel, inhuman, and degrading treatment are crucial for calling police officers to account. Except for grave public emergencies such as the state of war, threat to internal security, breakdown of public order, and political instability, the law does not allow police officers to use force unnecessarily, so it underlines Article 5. Police need to take proper medical care of a person in police custody. Law considers custodial death a crime unless proved otherwise that factors other than torture in custody have caused death or agony. Other factors include natural disease and other health problems. Therefore, the treatment of persons who police is to interact and handle in case of criminal investigations should be polite and civilized by the rules which place restrictions on the use of force and discretion on the part of police officers.

Article 7 of the UN Resolution requires every police officer to outperform their duties in combating all kinds of corruption. Any act of corruption is tantamount to abuse of authority. At the same time, article 8 of the resolution calls upon every police officer to respect the rule of law above everything

176

and allow no violations therein at any cost. Thus, the UN code unwraps that police action is rule-bound, not absolute, nor yet an irresponsible one. Furthermore, for neutralising doubt and suspicion, police need to display the highest professionalism in recording reasons and evidence for every act of using force. By so doing, police could defend themselves and their intentions, failing which the police are likely to lose their relevance to public order and safety in the days to come.

9.6. Excesses or Misuse of Police Authority

Excesses in the use of police authority are commonplace in almost all developed and developing societies, let alone Pakistan. Police are still to wash their image of terror engineers and fear mongers. Most people hate police as agents of brutality, and hence many argue that no police department is good police. Suppose ancient societies managed better peace without criminal justice and police. In that case, the highly formalised criminal justice structures seem to be more of a liability and a burden on the public exchequer than a reliable mechanism of building peace across the board in the society. The available literature on policing suggests that the restraint in the use of force and community engagement help build democratic peace (Mello 2015), which is viable and sustainable in all respects.

Since the outset of 2018, the police in Pakistan have come under severe criticism due to Sahiwal shooting by Counter-Terrorism Department (CTD) Punjab. In the recent past, specific incidents of police brutalities came under public scrutiny due to social media activism. First, the "incident of Model Town Lahore took place on 17th June 2014, where Police opened fire on protestors" (Imam 2019). Eleven persons got killed, and around eighty were injured. Secondly, the shocking death of Amal, a school-going girl, killed during an encounter between mobile snatchers and police officers on 14th August 2018 in Karachi sent shockwaves nationwide. Thirdly, on 13th January 2018, Karachi police killed a young man named Naqibullah Mehsud in an allegedly staged encounter. Fourthly, on 20th January 2018, Karachi police claimed to kill a wanted suspect named Maqsood, a young man of 20, who did not allegedly stop his car as per the initial police version. Police changed their version later, disowning the responsibility and saying that some unidentified criminals opened fire on Maqsood. Fifthly, on 13th January 2018, Karachi police killed 19 years old named Intezar Ahmad in a shootout for which they had no reasonable ground to use lethal force. Lastly, on 19th January 2019, Punjab CTD killed Khalil, his wife Nabila, his 13-year daughter Areeba and Khalil's friend Zeeshan at Sahiwal Toll Plaza over the doubt of Khalil's alleged association with the Islamic state as its country-commander in Pakistan (Pakistan Today 2018). Sahiwal incident raised public outcry and media hype without anyone getting into the details of Khalil's profile and acts because police had failed to handle this issue well operationally and professionally. These police shootings have clouded the police reforms based on the paradigm of police autonomy because professional police organisations can never be a guild of mercenaries nor ever create such an impression.

9.7. Politics of the Police Governance

The political power struggles in Pakistan have centred on controlling police by those at the helm of affairs. The police historians believe that police emerged in the first quarter of the 19th century as a legal tool to serve the authoritarian regimes by quenching dissent and controlling the protesting crowds. To them, police became a crime responder lot later as it was raised to control anti-regime populations in Europe, notably the United Kingdom and France (Reiner 2010). However, the knowledge and awareness of the rule of law, due process, human rights, democracy, and other modern developments in human civilisation have raised numerous questions against the existence, relevance, and utility of police wielding such enormous powers (Newburn 2015).

Therefore, the emergence of police institutions is linked with authoritarian political regimes. The exact purpose also served the colonial masters in the sub-continent to raise the police force in British India in the wake of 1857 uprisings followed by the Police Act 1861 (Patel 2008). The colonial government ended after Second World War, and Pakistan became an independent democratic republic. As a result, all the authoritarian legal literature had to be done away with, and new laws suitable for the independent democratic state had to get reframed (PRC Report 1985). Ironically, even after seventy-four years, Pakistan is still to realign policing with contemporary developments in law enforcement. The police in Pakistan search for a newer identity to justify their existence and legitimacy.

Police mandate changes with the reinventions and innovations in politics. The challenges of national security and public safety in the post-terrorism and post-human-rights world have changed the conventional functions of police (Weisburd & Braga 2006). The pluralisation of policing involving the private sector in policing, the end of the state monopoly on policing (Newburn 2015), the emergence of new police professionalism and standards of police integrity and accountability (Stone and Travis 2011) have challenged the police in Pakistan. The pluralisation will go a long way in mending their ways and redefining their role, identity, mission, and restructuring its redundant as well as an outlived colonial policing model that established the police-for-the-state, not a police-for-the-people paradigm.

By J.J. Baloch (2022)

Traditionally appointed deputy commissioners and home departments in Pakistan have been responsible for police oversight, external accountability, and justice of peace functions. However, police order 2002 promulgated by Pervaiz Musharraf regime and separation of judiciary from the executive as a consequence of Supreme Court judgments, police oversight function stood divided among District and Session Judge (Justice of Peace), District Nazim (Funds, ACR of DPO, Annual Policing Plan), Public Safety Commission, and Police Complaint Authority to monitor police discretion and use of force (PO 2002). Such a police oversight system was democratic compared to the previous authoritarian and bureaucratic model of police governance in Pakistan. However, due to the non-implementation of police reforms, Pakistan is yet to realise this goal.

Besides this, expanding mandate from common crime and public order to national security and public safety, police services in Pakistan are pressing for more administrative, financial, and operational autonomy with minor political interference. As a result, the networked and multi-agency dynamics of more innovative policing are gaining ground to transform traditional state-controlled police organisations into apolitical, neutral, impartial, efficient, responsive, professional, and dynamic public service (PRC Report 2019).

However, many controversies about police governance and accountability have emerged due to different provincial governments' undoing and redoing of PO-2002 as per their political interests. Sind and Balochistan have undone PO-2002 and have reverted to the 1861 Police Act. On the other hand, Punjab and Khyber-Pakhtunkhwa (KPK) governments are redoing Police Order (2002) with some additions and deletions. KP province has come up with Police Act 2017, which promises more financial and administrative independence and police professionalism focussed on public service delivery.

While such wave of police autonomy as a specialised and focal agency to deal with crime, public order, public safety, and national security has witnessed severe disruptions in the Punjab Civil Administration Ordinance (PCAO-2017). Section 15 of the PCAO states:

"The Deputy Commissioner on his own, or the request of the head of a local government or head of the District Police, may convene a meeting for purposes of maintaining public order and public safety and safeguarding public or private properties in the district; and, the decisions taken in the meeting shall be executed by all concerned accordingly."

Besides this, Pakistan Administrative Service officers went on a single-agenda strike for Justice of Peace powers delegated to Deputy Commissioners and Assistant Commissioners. Section 16 maintains:

179

"No public meeting, procession, assembly, or gathering shall take place without prior permission in writing of the Deputy Commissioner."

However, officers of the Police Service of Pakistan have taken this move seriously on many counts. First, the PSP stalwarts believe that the police officers are more respected and professional than the officers of the Pakistan Administrative Service as per their professional training and expertise as a specialist in crime, risk, threat, violence, and terrorism fields. Police officers know police better than any other civil servant because they have given their lives to police. Second, the police are not a bureaucracy nor a bureaucracy that can perform as police. So, it implies that police should remain independent in making professional decisions.

Third, the Police service is engaged in a national campaign to eliminate all illegal and undemocratic police governance and oversight channels. PCAO-2917 has opened an unnecessary debate of the closing chapter of district magistracy as a criminal justice oversight body. The 1973 Constitution promised separation of judiciary from the executive. However, in the 1990s Supreme Court of Pakistan issued an order implemented in 2001 by General Parvez Musharraf by creating the third tier of local district government with district Nazism having powers of police oversight.

Fourth, police order 2002 proposed delineation of Deputy Commissioner (DC) from police affairs and came up with democratic alternatives such as elected Nazim and public safety commissions and police complaint authorities at district, provincial and national levels to institutionalise democratic police oversight. Critics see the present move of PCAO-2016 as an attempt to revert police progress in attaining autonomy as a specialised service for maintaining social order and public peace in the wake of the two main steps. The establishment of Pakistan Motorway Police and adoption of Police Order-2002, the two benchmarks that ensured the departure of police from the district magistrate (DM), led to the set-up of autonomous and depoliticised policing with a democratic external oversight system in Pakistan.

Fifthly, the 1973 Constitution of Pakistan provides a complete democratic mechanism for police oversight and accountability. Elected Prime Minister, his federal Cabinet, provincial Chief Ministers, their respective cabinets and superior and lower courts, independent institutions, i.e., Public Safety Commission, Police Complaint Authority, service tribunals, and Ombudsman office offer legislative, executive, judicial and popular democratic methods (including non-governmental pressure groups, civil society, media, etc.) of external police oversight (PRC Report 2019). The non-implementation of democratic civilian oversight as provided in PO-2002, owing to vested bureaucratic and political interests, is being used as the primary argument by opponents of democratic reforms in police to gain leeway in police governance (Suddle 2012). This argument signifies keeping bureaucratic controls over the police.

Sixthly, in the wake of the expansion of police mandate to national security and public safety from conventional crime control and maintenance of public order, policing no longer remains a local subject as it has conventionally been all along (Newburn 2015). National security and public safety are too important for the subjects to be left to the mercy of locals or provincial governments in Pakistan (PRC Report 2019). However, it does need some public input. Therefore, the Police Service of Pakistan (PSP) should constitute a primary mechanism of strategic, networked, and multi-agency, intelligence-led, and evidence-based approaches of policing, counterterrorism, and counter-extremism that is purely a criminal justice policy domain (Ibid).

Lastly, policing is a highly specialised profession; hardly anyone can substitute it with non-police agencies or serve and protect the public if we place police under undemocratic and illegitimate controls. The elected police oversight bodies responsible for appointing/hiring and dismissing police chiefs worldwide have emerged as good international police practice. For example, police and crime commissioner (PACC) in England and Wales, elected Mayor of London Metropolitan Police, Public Safety Canada, Canadian Association of Police Governance, and mayors of the cities who oversee police performance get elected by their people and are not part of the state bureaucracy. However, nobody can interfere in the job of a police chief once he gets notified; the institutions assist, facilitate, support, and supplement him. He takes all administrative decisions as an independent, capable and responsible professional without any external interference. However, he is responsible for his and his department's actions before the democratic oversight bodies that work in a procedurally appropriate manner to fix responsibility and carry out accountability in which law, not whims, rules.

9.8. Politicisation of Police

Over the years, the governments in Pakistan have been more interested in using police for their political gains than in raising it to a public service delivery mechanism (Shigri 2012). Albeit, Police Order 2002 laid down a course of action to curb politicization (Preamble PO-2002). Still, the amendments in PO 2002 in 2004 and 2006 altered the composition of National, provincial, and district public safety commissions which had the authority to work as a board for the appointment of the heads of police departments (DPOs, RPOs, PPOs, and DGs-IB & FIA) at district, regional provincial and

181

federal levels. Thus, the amendments in PO-2002 have compromised the procedure of neutral and civilian external accountability of the police by politicisation (PO-2002-Amendments 2004-6). The Public Safety and Police complaint authority mechanisms of external police oversight was envisaged the democratic oversight, the rule of law, and international standards of good policing in Pakistan (Babakhel 2021). These legislative alterations in PO-2002, further accompanied by the 18th Amendment in 2010, have further impeded the procedure of police accountability to get fairer. Like the judiciary and military, the police should get administratively immunised from politics and bureaucracy (Iqbal 2019). According to Mr Afzal Ali Shigri (2012), a handful of the officers of high moral stature and integrity have a lesser likelihood of making any difference in the ocean of corrupt and abusive environment of outlived police culture in Pakistan. This state of affairs in the police will stay unless political interference in policing gets uprooted through establishing legal civilian police accountability mechanisms in Pakistan (Ibid).

9.9. Autonomy versus Accountability

Responsibility without freedom is a misnomer. Autonomy does not mean an exception to accountability. However, it implies that society, through their statutory laws, allows the police space to make decisions regarding the enforcement of the law and perform any of their primary functions for maintaining order, managing crime, and ensuring public safety. The efficiency of the police in this regard is based on their professional skills, specialist learning, the rule of law, procedural justice, and strategic wisdom without being hampered by external influences of any kind, whether political or bureaucratic (Riaz 2018). Without having the necessary administrative and financial autonomy, police cannot deliver and perform well. Without performing, police can neither win public trust, which is the foundational strategic principle for effective policing, nor transform their autocratic culture to democratic standards.

As a result of too much external interference, the police would merely remain the instruments of control used by other people who control the state, and they would not be able to oppose making ill-conceived demands of those on horseback. Such controlled police, whether under governments or local communities, would be prone to commit excesses in using their authority, thereby violating the laws and rules they are supposed to uphold impartially (Riaz 2018). Any attempt for police autonomy is always foiled and aborted on demands of more accountability. Neither autonomy nor accountability can be established in separation. In accountability is implicit autonomy and autonomy always needs accountability to balance police integrity through transparency, legitimacy, and due process (Ibid).

Society always concedes for police autonomy on certain conditions. First, the police will perform their mandated task following law and procedure, neither in line with their petty interests nor on the dictates of any influential person or interest group. Secondly, police will never extend any favouritism to the powerful and influential lot at any expense, including depriving the vulnerable groups for reasons other than in the course of law and justice. Thirdly, the police will exercise their lawful authority and discretion for establishing peace and protecting the citizens' life, property, and liberty and not for obliging someone, minting money, political engineering, supporting criminals, and getting lucrative postings.

"The accountability, however, is neither possible nor advisable without autonomy. The former holds power to account, and the latter holds *power to perform*. No department or organisation can be asked to account for its action, which does not have the autonomy to perform those actions. The colonial system denied both. Police were just a tool in the hands of the empire and were neither autonomous nor accountable to people. The arrangement suited the empire whose targets were transitory and obligation to the public non-existent. The irony, however, is that the arrangement continued even after the targets have become permanent and obligation to the public, a necessity." (Riaz 2018)

Balancing autonomy with accountability is critical and sensitive for all stakeholders, including the police, the state, and civil society actors. Therefore, the police need to maintain reasonable and acceptable self-control overstepping their mandated job and using force proportionately. In this regard, the police must take good care of public expectations, legal requirements, and professional norms in policing democratic societies (Kumar 2015) like Pakistan. State and society realise the inevitability of policing in society despite police excess of their authority and limits of capacity. The best way out from here is the new police professionalism which society and the state must accommodate, and police should also balance the conflicting trends of both in society and the state (Stone & Travis 2011).

In recent decades, the rise in crime, the proliferation of terrorist activities, and the spread of extremism in Pakistan have glorified public fears. As a result, the governments over the years have granted more leeway to police for doing their job, and many new counterterrorism and public safety mechanisms have seen the light of the day, thereby expanding police mandate remarkably (Weisburd & Braga 2006). Therefore, practical autonomy comes with strict accountability wherein police know full well the limits of their authority. The public is fully aware of their responsibility to respect the law and cooperate with the police by keeping negotiations to balance autonomy and accountability running without any break.

9.10. An Overview

"Police accountability is much discussed but less implemented. It constitutes holding the police responsible for what they do, organisationally or individually, and monitoring their policies and practices, addressing failing to register cases, poor investigations, custodial torture, corruption, and abuse of power. The police have powers to arrest, detain and use force and therefore must be held accountable for violations of this authority. In developing societies, however, a 'blue wall of silence' within police ranks facilitates the concealment of misconduct and abuse" (Babakhel 2021).

In Pakistan, the public image of police stands tainted. The police are considered corrupt, inefficient, coercive, unresponsive, brutish, and unprofessional. As a result, the public shows a lack of trust in the police. The situation gets grimmer when police connivance with those in authority becomes graver in depriving people of their fundamental rights to life, liberty, and property. Carrying out tortures in custody, highhandedness, extortion, illegal detention, extra-judicial killings, land grabbing, shoddy investigations, and inept response to the people in trouble make police working doubtful, controversial and very often criminal.

Equally truer, the police cannot function unless they build their capacity to work and resist external pressures extended by influential and powerful segments within the society. Transforming police in Pakistan will not happen unless police become clean with high standards of professional ethics and integrity. However, for attaining autonomy, the police should accept legitimate checks on their authority. Pakistan is a constitutional democratic republic, and the constitution of 1973 in article 4 acknowledges the right of all individual citizens of Pakistan to be treated following the law. Article 4 admits that every citizen is entitled-"(1) to enjoy the protection of the law and to be treated under the law is the inalienable right of every citizen. (2), a) no action detrimental to any person's life, liberty, body, reputation, and property shall be taken under the law. (b) No person shall be prevented from or be hindered in doing that which is not prohibited by law. (c) Also, no person shall be compelled to do that which the law does not require him to do" (1973 Constitution of Pakistan).

Besides this, articles 9 and 10 are very elaborate and vocal for police to understand while enforcing the law and using force. Article 9 reads: "No person shall be deprived of life and liberty, except under the law". Thus, article 9 promises security for protecting fundamental rights through the rule of law and due process. However, article 10 further takes this responsibility of state and law enforcement or police, remarkably that police should follow only law and procedural justice while exercising their power. The article reads: **"No person who is arrested shall be detained in custody without being informed of the grounds for such arrest, and shall not be denied the right to consult and be defended by a Legal Practitioner of his choice"** (1973 Constitution of Pakistan). If the police fail to abide by the constitution while executing arrest and keeping custody, the law enforcement would be committing the crime of forced disappearance. Such violation of the law is also punishable under the Penal Code of Pakistan as well as Police laws and statutes together with violations of fundamental human rights invoking therein the jurisdiction of superior courts to take notice under 199 articles of the 1973-constitution of Pakistan. Therefore, the misuse of police authority deprives a person of any fundamental rights through coercion violates the supreme law of the land.

Only independent police can claim neutrality and apolitical entity. Similarly, independence does not mean recourse to absolute authority. Still, it implies the elimination of all political pressures, gaining institutional and professional excellence by police, making their decisions under the law, and strategic vision of peace without following illegitimate dictates. However, genuinely autonomous police also signify that they engage and consult communities while chalking out their policing plans and make every action transparent, legal, and legitimate by garnering public support and mandate. Thus, the police should gain public trust by engaging, keeping onboard, informing, consulting, cooperating, and coordinating community regarding policing matters ranging from the stop and search to arrest and detention.

9.11. Towards the New strategic police Governance

Such a dispensation of new strategic police governance for effective policing develops only when police are accountable to the law and the people, which happens beautifully under civilian democratic oversight of the police (Shigri 2012). For this apolitical approach to external police accountability, some measures are recommended hereunder:

I.   Oversight bodies like PCAs and PSCs under PO-2002 should get notified in all provinces and the centre without any delay. In addition, governments at different levels should establish Police Ombudsmen on the lines of tax Ombudsmen, which has been a fruitful experience countrywide. These mechanisms will play a pivotal role in ensuring meritocracy, transparency, and legitimacy in police governance, especially in transfer postings of PPOs and DPOs. Political interference affects police performance and makes it controversial (Babakhel 2021).

185

Reimagining Policing in Pakistan

II.   Provincial governments should institute the efficient public complaint redressal mechanism at the police station level on new facilitation centres in Sindh, Khidmat Centres in Punjab, and Police Assistance Lines in KP. Furthermore, it seems sensible to convert all police stations in the country into facilitation centres with all advanced equipment and infrastructure. Developing duplicate and parallel structures deliver no good to the public and police department except being the burden.

III. Police need innovative, creative, dynamic, predictive, proactive, practical, realistic, systematic, scientific, result-oriented, and visionary police leadership both on the policy and the practice level for ensuring strict internal accountability. Therefore, the only suitable candidate should get recruited at police leadership levels in the Police Service of Pakistan.

IV.   Training/education is at the heart of police transformation and capacity building for changing the ways to post-modernism and innovation. "The potential impact of police education and training on violence reduction is indirect. That is what police do that might affect community violence, not what police know (via education) or what they know how to do (via training)" (Cordner 2021).

"Recent studies show that having a higher education degree tends to have a more significant impact on police officers' knowledge and appreciation of the values and lifestyles of peoples from different cultures, especially minority groups and immigrants" (Shohel, Gias Uddin, McLeod and Silverstone 2020).

Therefore, I suggest the professional academic education programme as a vital tool for developing police forces. Police need training and retraining, and therefore police training institutions in Pakistan which our governments keep neglecting at policy and practice levels should receive due consideration and priority in terms of resources, incentives, and best faculty. Pooling the best talent to impart training and strategic importance could make police responsible and responsive (Fritsvold, E. (2021-a). As a result, not only do police officers get benefitted from the growth of their careers and communities in receiving better services from the Police (Fritsvold, E. (2021-b).

"Since 9/11, the need for new and regular training for law enforcement personnel at all levels of government is ever increasing. Due to the high visibility of police officers and interaction with the public constantly, police officers must practice situational awareness consistently throughout the day. This mindset underscores the need for routine application of training to ensure good investigative technique, officer safety, and efficiency. Law enforcement personnel are responsible for making certain they are up-to-date on modern-day training formal education and become knowledgeable in tactics used by the criminal element. Training and education are more than just sitting in a classroom and earning a certificate. It is also about applying this newfound knowledge and maintaining proficiency" (McHenry 2019).

V.   An inclusive police oversight mechanism stands the test of democracy, transparency, legitimacy, and meritocracy in police accountability (Riaz 2018). The police accountability mechanism should involve the actors like police command, inspectorates, prosecution, judiciary, parliamentary committees, mayoralties or Zila nazmiyat, human rights activists or organisations or ombudspersons, police complaints bodies, public safety institutions, civil society organisations, non-governmental organisations, academia, media, community notables, treaty bodies, peace committees, etc. (Babakhel 2021). The diversity of actors overseeing police work could filter politics and vested interests from creating impediments in the way of building impartial and legitimate police engagement (Gilmour 2007).

VI.   The context of policing in terms of the socio-political and cultural perspectives of concerned police organisations should be given top priority while instituting the accountability mechanism of the police. The enlightened leaders drive organizational change through strategic management, an ongoing process that "seeks opportunities to enhance operational efficiencies by identifying internal issues and external influences that hinder organizational sustainability" (Charrier 2010). However, the police context challenges change in terms of corruption and isolated police reform. Corruption in law enforcement, criminal justice, and security apparatus impede impartial policing and undermine police accountability. Pakistan is a classic example of this context and badly needs to develop the integrity of police in policing strategy and policy (Jones 2009). Our police need to adopt a holistic approach in which criminal justice and security sector reform must form the cardinal part of the improvements in policing (Shigri 2012). Besides this, the country's economic, social, political, cultural, and other challenges facing the country should receive due coverage in analysing the overall security situation in Pakistan.

VII.   Police should serve as a balancing mechanism between the state and its populations. Inclusive and pluralist role of the police is possible only under democratic dispensation and democratic police oversight. Mathew Jones (2009) finds:

"Police organizations can transform themselves into institutions deemed as legitimate legal authorities providing effective service to their recipients through limiting the arbitrary exercise of power, establishing institutional arrangements for successful social problem solving, and cultivating the appropriate character for those who carry out the institutional responsibilities. Through this process, the police organization can find the right balance between a theory of governance and modern policing".

187

Police in Pakistan must maintain balance in multiple stakeholders and offer the due share to all irrespective of their relations with the police department. The oversight system must reflect the appropriate mechanism to allow complaints to reach the members of the bodies or associations established for police accountability. Cultivating police integrity for claiming autonomy and gaining legitimacy through a public trust are critical components of police professionalism. Therefore, the police accountability mechanism in Pakistan should be representative, and it should reflect gender mainstreaming and the voice of vulnerable groups and minorities.

9.12. Conclusion

Police accountability is a big challenge in Pakistan due to the fluid nature of police work and the unavailability of effective monitoring mechanisms for policing. Police governance models in Pakistan are cloned with politics and vested interests. As a result, the police are not autonomous in the sphere of their activity. Equally true is the police reality of being a corrupt and coercive agency, lacking public trust. Thus, police are in dire straits of their profession in present circumstances. The above discussion stands to reason that autonomy and accountability can only go together under the dispensation of civilian democratic mechanisms of external accountability that could promise political neutrality, legitimacy, democracy, transparency, inclusiveness, fair play, better service delivery, and professional service excellence of the police in Pakistan. It is why former Chief Justice of Pakistan, Justice Asif Saeed Khosa, "emphasised the need for ensuring administrative autonomy of police and said the issue is as important as the independence of the judiciary" (Iqbal 2019).

By J.J. Baloch (2022)

Part Four: REIMAGINING POLICING-THE ROADMAP

Chapter: 10

The Strategic Policing

Chapter Brief

This chapter finds that policing changes quickly, and its mandate grows exponentially. The rise in terrorism, extremism, radicalisation, technology, democracy and the rule of law signifies the new role of police officers as guardians of the people's fundamental rights (President's Task Force, USA, 2011). This role of guardian differs drastically from the concept of a police officer as a warrior, protecting political regimes. I argue that we need to go strategic in policing visions, goals, approaches, management, operations, and organisations because the strategic policing model emphasizes on inclusive, dynamic, adaptive and holistic nature of policing approaches (lister & Jones 2016) and (Rogers 2016). While explaining the strategic policing model, this chapter also refers to other policing strategies related to their relationship with the strategic policing model (Weisburd and Braga 2006). It also argues why and how the strategic policing model suits Pakistan. Police practices and theories constitute the core of content and literature in this chapter.

12.1. Introduction

The review of contemporary research on policing suggests that strategic policing is the most suitable model in terms of the contextual, theoretical, and practical aspects of postmodern policing. Strategic policing implies a beautiful convergence of tradition with innovation in policing strategies (Hendrix, 2017). The strategic policing model aims to combine all policing strategies, innovations, and best practices of new police professionalism (Stones & Travis 2011), addressing the necessity and relevance of police within the specific socio-political and cultural environments in postmodern societies (Jones 2009). Policing experts describe this model as a modern and diverse partnership framework for making societies safer, turning crime back, and empowering people through inclusiveness, engagement, democratic dispensations, the rule of law, and procedural justice for serving to protect the fundamental rights of the people (Lobnikar, Mesko, & Modic 2021). The policing we live with and the stage of progression and reform we stand, strategic policing is arguably the most needed and the most suited policing dispensation in the 21st century (Charrier 2010). That is why this book advocates a strategic model for policing in Pakistan.

By J.J. Baloch (2022)

12.2. The Strategic Policing

The strategic policing model seeks to establish partnerships between various actors and stakeholders in policing. Strategic policing attempts to bridge efficiency, trust, transparency, representativeness, inclusion, democracy, legitimacy, integrity, and service delivery (Lister & Jones 2016). This postmodern model adopts a mix of police strategies that are current, relevant, efficient, and productive in terms of acceptability, reliability, efficacy, economy, and technology (Haines 2000). Through a strategic approach, the police build a broad-based mechanism and involve different stakeholders in peace, including community, NGOs, human rights agencies, legal fraternity, medical experts, biologists, social scientists, technocrats, economists, psychologists, criminologists, forensic specialists, financial analysts, law enforcement actors, intelligence agencies, and international law enforcement partners through Interpol and United Nations (Haines 2000).

We can better understand the institutional arrangement of the strategic policing dispensation as a birdcage or a matrix model. Every stakeholder collaborates as an interdependent, inter-supporting, apolitical, professional, objective, and scientific partner. It evaluates the police performance through empirical key performance indicators (Hendrix 2017). Thus, strategic policing models adopt a multi-institutional approach to balancing the state, public, and police (Jones, 2009). "Strategic policing can drive organizational change through strategic management, which is an ongoing process that seeks opportunities to enhance operational efficiencies by identifying internal and external influences that hinder organizational sustainability and progression (Police Chief Magazine 2021).

The strategic policing model, based on the 21st century networked approaches, is referred to as the distilled total of all policing innovations in police strategies made and filtered through scientific inquiry and evidence (Hendrix 2017). This model promises to enhance public service delivery on the ground by utilising crime-mapping analytical techniques, case file management systems, artificial intelligence methods, and newer human resource management skills, by envisaging an innovative and efficient police response to all types of emergencies and by adopting technology as a powerful tool for information, communication, and community safety tools (Glensor & Peak 2005).

Strategic policing has many advantages for police officers (Rogers, 2016). It can help an agency identify and anticipate critical trends and issues that the organization may face now and in the future (Lister & Jones, 2016). The planning process also explores options, sets directions, and helps those involved make appropriate decisions (Hunt, 2006). It facilitates communication between the key stakeholders

191

and keeps companies focused on results as they face daily crises (Stroshine, 2021). Experts use strategic performance standards to measure an agency's efforts and improve performance (Lawson & Wolfe, 2021). Most importantly, strategic planning helps police executives to facilitate change and manage innovation (Kratcoski, 2017).

The 21st-century research on policing has found different policing strategies for different policing contexts. For example, police have begun to use technology, and many police departments and experts are not themselves tech-savvy. Strategic policing envisages taking police out from the black-box approach to adopting technology by police and emphasises learning to create and innovate law enforcement technology (Katz & Maguire 2020). This model advocates technology science for police officers who need to become users and creative producers of technological crime solutions (Hendrix et al., 2017) and become crime scientists and sociologists (Stroshine 2021). Two developments in policing research pose an intellectual challenge for policing practitioners today than ever before. First, most philosophical methodologies overlap and conflict in terms of human rights.

In contrast, others are not universally workable, meaning that specific strategies are most effective in various conditions or contexts but not everywhere. Before going into detail, let us understand the basic requirements of strategic policing (NIJ 2017). Hendrix et al. (2017) expressed their concern about the inappropriate use of technology in these words: **"Police departments that emphasise certain strategic models (e.g., community-oriented policing and problem-oriented policing) [Other models such as evidence-based, intelligence-led, proactive, predictive, CompStat, etc.] may adopt specific types of technology to achieve their core missions better. In contrast, police agencies do not invest strategically in technology; rather, they adopt technology in a black box without a larger plan for how a particular technology fit within the agency's guiding philosophy or operational goals."**

12.3. The Basic Requirements of Strategic Policing

The primary strategic policing requirements are academic research, data-driven analysis, and evidence-based decision-making.

12.3.1. Studying:

Strategic policing starts with studying and assessing the threat or problem of crime or disorder. It also attempts to comprehend the police's capacity to deal with crime challenges. By collecting data and information on crime and policing performance, assessing threats would help identify key policing issues within the jurisdiction and develop their solutions (Webb, Katz, & Flippin, 2020). Many theorists call the 21st century the "knowledge Century" (SCJ 2009). Police, like all other departments, must be well versed in the knowledge of policing, its theoretical and practical dynamics, and procedures (Lint 1999). Many criminologists continue to argue that just knowing a sure thing is not enough but being well-equipped in using that knowledge and joining it with experience for maximum results is something that sits at the heart of strategic policing (Ibid). However, if we look at our training modules, we find that such modules are redundant and irrelevant to the performance of the police in postmodern times (NPA Training Modules). No institute, school, or university exists in Pakistan on essential subjects such as criminal justice, counterterrorism, and policing. We need such institutes and learned faculties to help our police and save the people of Pakistan from recurring violence. Training to gain knowledge and use it smartly and efficiently to build police capacity is one of Pakistan's foundational strategic policing requirements.

12.3.2. Understanding

Sometimes, specific problems warrant police organisations to conduct research or conduct research through academia using different research methodologies such as data analysis, surveys, experiments, and observations on the scientific basis for a better and proper understanding of the problem (Home Office UK 2015). Some social scientists call this approach proactive policing and problem-solving police strategy. Understanding police culture, crime trends, potential threats to peace, and people living within the jurisdiction always constitute a crucial element of strategic policing (Judge, 2002). Not only that, but the uninformed person must sharpen their mental teeth for the proper intellectual bite to the issues, problems, and challenges. Indeed, study and knowledge complement this contention (Webb, Katz, & Flippin, 2020).

12.3.4. Analysing

After the study, understanding the issues or challenges is the key dynamic of strategic policing. Crime and corruption remain the most significant challenges to any police department to varying degrees at any point in time. Crime analysis and policing analysis require an appropriate analysis toolkit. Crime analysis is instrumental in understanding crime trends and patterns that change over time (Jones and Newburn 2001). Ideas such as storing criminal data, collecting intelligence reports, and having access and the ability to make the most of artificial intelligence are a few of the many steps required for effective policing based on the strategic vision of the police department (Ratcliffe 2016). Hardly any police department in Pakistan, whether federal or provincial, is toned and tuned to such a modern trend of strategic policing requirements. Therefore, realigning policing demands reimagining and strategizing.

12.3.5. Strategising

After studying and analysing any crime problem, police leaders and analysts formulate a strategy to deal with it well in time. Strategic means to envisage something through research and analysis and prepare a plan to achieve specific goals with efficiency, economy, objectivity, calculus, and professionalism (Ratcliffe 2018). When we talk about strategising policing, it signifies that we adopt a scientific and evidence-based approach to study, understand, and analyse policing challenges, problems, capacity, and mandate while working out a plan for police departments (Katz and Maguire 2020). High-tech police departments prepare their annual policing plans worldwide and implement them after approval from legitimate police governance bodies to achieve the desired set goals of controlling and reducing crime. The police order 2002 prepares the annual policing plan at the district, provincial, and federal levels. However, due to the non-implementation of PO 2002, this practice was discontinued and was never implemented across the board. The police order was implemented partially by some police departments only, so this practice could not be sustained (Abbass 2012). However, this is an essential requirement for strategic policing to get revived in Pakistan. Strategic decision-making is always empirical and objective, based on evidence and data calculus (Katz and Maguire 2020).

12.3.6. Integrating

Strategic policing integrates the efforts of all stakeholders; for example, law enforcement departments, intelligence agencies, civil society, non-governmental organizations, media, ethnic and religious groups, social services, political elements, traders' associations, business communities, academia, and paramilitary forces. Such institutional networking is a prerequisite for a united and multi-agency stance to the challenges of crime, disorder, terrorism, and any similar threat to society (Rogers 2017). Preparing strategic policing plans requires all stakeholders to share, exchange, and discuss their input before, during, and after the policing plan preparation and implementation. Once we work out a consensual policing plan through coordination, reconciliation, and incorporation of all genuine concerns and points of view, such plans need the approval of legitimate police oversight bodies or the concerned provincial and federal government, as the case may be through set-out procedures (Ibid). After the policing plan is approved, all stakeholders join the hands to implement it. To achieve strategic goals, the support and cooperation of all stakeholders are crucial requirements for the implementation and adoption of such a strategic plan. In Pakistan, the culture of JITs and national coordination on countering terrorism has emerged. Still, the institutional disconnect among all stakeholders and the non-availability of joint legal or community forums have deadlocked the process, and it is yet to take proper roots. Therefore, developing procedural and organisational networks among all stakeholders is a way forward in Pakistan to achieve strategic policing goals for better public service delivery.

12.3.7. Connecting

The connectivity of resources and capabilities with strategic policing partners is critical to the effectiveness of the strategic policing model (Perrott & Trites, 2017). For instance, all law enforcement networks, intelligence agencies, forensic science authorities, safe city mechanisms, police departments- local as well federal, security services providers, and other government departments such as banks, Federal Board of Revenue, economic, regulatory authorities, and anti-corruption organisations must share information about sensitive security threats, risk assessments, and prepared levels in more innovative ways within and into themselves (Sedra 2017). These departments, as mentioned above, must offer resource support to their partners because their causes of fighting crime, disorder, violence, and terrorism are common. Thus, connectivity is also a fundamental principle and norm of strategic policing (Home Office, UK, 2015).

12.3.8. Innovating

Policing transforms social and cultural changes (Katz & Maguire, 2020). Society develops, expands, and changes over time. Policing, as an integral part of society, must change through reform and innovation to keep pace with societal changes failing which it would get irrelevant, unproductive, and a burden on the exchequer (Stanko 2009). In Pakistan, society has changed, but its policing has not. The gaps between social change and policing leave space for criminals and terrorists to grow faster, more comfortable, and ultimately become unmanageable (Tylor, 2006). Any police strategy should accommodate changes within society and plan ahead of changes, called policing tomorrow (RAND 2018). Policing preparedness for rising equal to the challenges of peace and order has emerged as an inevitable part of police strategies to fight crime. Police leaders in Pakistan must plan strategies to achieve specific policy goals. The use of technology, social media, and scientific forensic methods to solve crimes and prevent disorder and violence are catalysts for improving policing through strategic measures (Sheldon and Wright 2010).

12.3.9. Specialising

Policing is a specialist job and cannot be conducted in a generalist way, as we have been doing in the Indian subcontinent since the establishment of the police in the 19th century. Policing itself is a specialist in nature and form. Still, it has many expert areas such as crime scene management, emergency response, public order, complex crime investigations (cyber, money laundering, terrorist financing, human trafficking, kidnapping for ransom, target killing, street crime, extortion, corruption, homicide, child abuse, domestic violence, extra-judicial killings and police abuse of authority, transnational organised crime, white-collar crime, etc. In addition, policing specialities include human resource management, protection of witnesses, keeping hidden tactics secret, budgeting resources, using firearms, managing mega-events, managing intelligence, using technology, and many more (Sharkey 2018). Police in Pakistan, despite their tall claims, has only been marginally successful in developing a few specialist units in policing. Moreover, they have focused on providing functional distributions of police work in new legislation, such as the KP Police Act 2017. Moreover, Police Order 2002 needs to be implemented in letters and spirit because the mere separation of function is nothing more than rhetoric. The need is to create a separate cadre for each specialised area. Each police cadre should be equipped with essential toolkits and be fully trained to achieve the standardised skills required to meet the expert criteria, including certifications and other specialist qualifications. In new TORs set for the police reform committee constituted by the Supreme Court of Pakistan on May 15, 2018, specialism in investigations for improving the quality of investigations is one of the crucial areas of police professionalism (PRC Report 2019). The public expects their police to offer them a better quality of investigation. The reform agenda included community relations, new police laws, public service delivery through alternate dispute resolution mechanisms, police accountability, administrative autonomy, urban policing, legislative reforms, and efficient complaint redressal mechanisms (PRC Report 2019). The required specialism mainly focused on using forensic science, digital technology, and biology to trace and detect criminal cases of complex nature is one of the core areas of strategic policing. In Pakistan, strategic policing is on its way on paper, but it needs to streamline the progression process of policing.

12.3.10. Implementing

The capacity of force and ground conditions of the specific environment of the area in terms of its cultural, social, political, and economic aspects should be taken into consideration while envisaging and implementing policing strategies. Police should be mindful that they alone cannot implement a strategic policing model because policing no longer remains an exclusive domain of police in postmodern society. Many partners in the strategic policing plan have their interests, concerns, roles, and functions in this networked system, where everyone participates in implementing his part of the plan. The strategic plan does not produce the desired results unless all the stakeholders fully collaborate. Strategic policing is the partnership of equally weighted and equally essential parts of the whole birdcage (Hendrix et al., 2017).

12.3.11. Contributing

Communities and governments expect their police forces to produce specific, measurable outcomes. The police get paid through taxpayers' money. Policing is an expensive government function per pay index compared to other departments. Police leadership in Pakistan must ensure that their forces can contribute substantially and satisfactorily in reducing crime, maintaining public order, combating terrorism, guarding fundamental human rights, and protecting civil liberties (MacLean et al., 2021). Preparing a strategic policing plan, coordinating well with other security agencies, intelligence networks, law enforcement departments, criminal justice partners, paramilitary forces, media, academia, civil society, independent actors, strategic coordination groups, local resilience forums, and the communities help accomplish the job of strategic policing (Reiner 1992). Good policing is always suitable for the people; the police must perform a mandated task to meet the expectations of the communities (Skogan 2006). There is no better gift for communities from the police except for the establishment of peace and order across the board in society (Katz & Maguire 2020). Therefore, police leadership in Pakistan should work out empirical performance indicators as per the job descriptions of police officers to ensure organizational justice and policing legitimacy as part of the strategic policing ideal (Lawson & Wolfe 2021).

12.3.12. Sustaining

Sustainability is crucial for strategic policing. Police leadership determination and capability remain consistent in identifying, specifying, procuring, implementing, and operating strategic policing plans (Kumar 2017). Such plans must address a range of police functions. The strategy has to address crime reduction, maintenance of public order, assurances of public safety, contribution to national security, counterterrorism, counter-militancy, and counter-extremism (Weisburd & Braga, 2006). Using proportionate force, embracing technology, applying science in police investigations, respecting human rights, making appropriate use of firearms, respecting privacy in surveillance, managing responses in emergencies, and providing adequate public service delivery mechanisms by the police are also part and parcel of a sustainable policing strategy (Jones 2009). Police leadership needs to build the capacity of police personnel to read between the lines in terms of carrying out their policing function with more outstanding care, caution, quality, integrity, transparency, legitimacy, and high standards of professionalism (Stone & Travis, 2011). Such new professionalism could capacitate police

197

to perform their function and meet the standards of professional ethics of police without any interval or gap (Home Office, 2015). Sustaining what police achieve through rigorous decades may not flow down the drain just because of the lacklustre attitude of police leadership and their governments owing to their narrow interests of continuing on lucrative assignments (Kratcoski, 2017). Therefore, police leaders and enlightened politicians need to consider sustaining police reforms by all means and further develop them to achieve strategic policing goals in these turbulent times of the nation.

12.3.13. Getting Feedback

Strategic poling approaches highly value the feedback of all stakeholders, particularly those who implement such a strategy (Hendrix 2017). The effectiveness of policing strategy needs the scrutiny of its impacts. The affected or victim groups giving feedback on whether the police have done or are doing has brought some positive results. The strategy may get revisited and revised (Ibid). It is essential to invite the positive input of all strategic partners, including the people of Pakistan, being the primary stakeholders in policing (Perrott & Trites 2017) for improving policing. Once feedback comes, the next strategic plan should incorporate the suggestions and address the concerns expressed by strategic partners (Ibid). These steps are universally attempted and tested to amend and improve the strategies and performance (Ibid). Such measures require sufficient time to sustain and progress in our secrecy environment. However, embracing strategic policing approaches could fix such deadlocks and hesitations in our society.

12.3.14. Evaluating

Evaluation of outcomes and performance of police for achieving strategic goals as set out in planning, preparing, and implementing stages constitute a substantial area of strategic policing (Hendrix 2017). Strategic policing experts use objective performance indicators to evaluate police working and service delivery. Police strategists assign top priority to objectivity, transparency, and fair play at the top of their analysis benchmarks. They encourage best performers to get incentivised. On the contrary, policing strategists recommend rehabilitative approaches for the mediocre to build their capacity; however, this approach has failed to integrate the below-average officers (Maguire, Somers, & Padilla 2020). Every police officer has a spark and hosts a hero within themselves; what is required is a friendly environment and inspirational police leadership in integrating the disgruntled lot (ibid). For instance, during the initial formative years of the National Highways and Motorways police in Pakistan, mediocre human resources were provided to NH&PM by the provincial police departments. Still, the enabling environment, incentives, and inspirational leadership gave them a mission to fulfil.

This rejected lot proved their mettle by making a huge difference in protecting the commuters' lives (Rasheed 2017). Therefore, a performance evaluation system should be empirical, objective, fair, and transparent for the adaptability, sustainability, and quality outcomes of strategic policing in Pakistan.

12.4. Why go for Strategic Policing

Strategic policing refers to the juxtaposition of several leading policing strategies such as community policing, problem-oriented policing, big-data policing, hotspot policing, evidence-based policing, third-party policing, intelligence-led policing, pulling-levers policing, broken-window policing, social-media policing, and proactive or predictive policing models (Hendrix 2017). All these models contain essential elements of strategic policing as their core values and focal norms, standing out in different strategic domains of policing. Here, we discuss all these major innovations in policing strategies in terms of their link with strategic policing in postmodern settings. This section also debates the relevance and impacts of the relationship between policing strategies and attempts to justify strategic policing in Pakistan as a postmodern product in law enforcement.

12.4.1. Community-Oriented Policing-COP

The core value of community policing is to ensure community participation in policing. Community policing is a prevalent theme in police innovation (Skogan, 2006). Community policing is closer to democratic policing approaches that empower people over public servants and accept no space in their privacies. Some scholars think it is a policing strategy in which the community is tasked with policing. However, some people maintain that the police and the community work in partnership to build peace in society. There are still others who describe the responsibilities and obligations of the police towards their respective communities. Skogan (2006) refers to community policing as "an organisational strategy that leaves setting priorities and means of achieving them largely to residents and the police who serve in their neighbourhoods". He further maintains, "Community policing is a process rather than a product. It has three core elements: citizen involvement, problem-solving, and decentralisation. In practice, these three elements are densely interrelated (Ibid)."

This approach can coexist with strategic policing in many ways. Weisburd and Braga (2006) argue that the democratic element of community policing and community engagement and sharing reducing crime campaigns by the people refers to postmodern conditions in which statutory monopolies have lost monopolies. Hendrix (2017) maintains that strategic policing idealises community engagement as part of the doctrine of policing by consent. Second, the outcomes of community policing in reforming

199

the police and reducing crime have been disappointing for many critics of community policing. To the sceptics, the benefits of community policing are 'zero' especially for the disadvantaged class, but rather its' reaps are specific to those influential, who use community platforms to influence policing (Skogan 2006). Community Policing, as a form of the decentralised and fragmented policing model, disconnects national policing policies (ibid). Third, community policing increases crime fears with the excessive sensitisation of communities with magnified threat perceptions (Ibid). Fourth, community policing's claim to reduce crime is doubtful and lacks evidence (Ibid). Fifth, community policing has proven wishful thinking as a bulwark of defence against the asymmetric threat of terrorism. Lastly, Stephen (2010) concludes that community policing is nothing more than mere rhetoric. Here, the association of strategic policing with community policing can defend against the vulnerabilities of community policing and balance the public fear of violence and terrorism through new police professionalism, adoption of technologies, and creation of specialised police units for different policing functions.

In Pakistan, community policing has lost its charm and appeal. In the old days of Mughals and Britishers in united India, Kotwals and Zamindars, who were allotted lands to control local populations, gave birth to feudalism, which widened the gap between the government and the governed (Arnold 1986). Such dispensation came under severe scholarly and popular attacks (Kolsky, 2010) after Pakistan's independence in 1947 to make police more professional, democratic, and service-oriented. However, Police Order 2002 decentralised policing and incorporated community checks on police discretion and performance by putting it under district Nazims. Yet, it hardly produced any meaningful result except the politicisation of police, perhaps because it was never implemented in letter and spirit.

At present, we have discussed in the community relation chapter the role of CPLC in Sindh, DRCs and PALs in Khyber Pakhtunkhwa but have found their impacts and outcomes are negligible. Recently the police reform committee constituted by the Supreme Court also advocated "Alternative Dispute Resolution Mechanism (ADRM) at district levels to deal with non-cognizable nature of complaints about reducing the burden of litigations. However, we do not have statistical data to assess their impacts. Still, they are instrumental in resolving the conflicts and irritants that lead to crime and violence. The community policing paradigm is the present and future of policing if aligned with strategic policing goals. For example, scholars of policing concur that using the community as an open-source of intelligence has dramatically helped garner popular support against kinetic threats such as terrorism and proxy wars. Only the strategic policing model can balance and blend the community-relation potentials and strengths by converting them as strategic sources to combat terrorism and violence in society. Hendrix (2017) considers community engagement part of strategic policing on these grounds.

12.4.2. Broken Windows Policing (BWP)

Broken-window policing focuses on minor crimes and calls for the use of excessive authority, which is hardly needed. New York ex-Mayor, Rudolph Giuliani, was the founder of the broken window paradigm. He invented it when New Yorkers was in the grip of street crimes of heinous nature. The Economist (27th January 2015) claims that broken window dispensation is the invention of Kelling, a criminologist, and Wilson, a sociologist. The latter developed the proposition that if one broken window goes unnoticed by the house owner and takes no cognisance, breaking the rest of the house's windows will follow (Kelling & Wilson 1982). Whether small or big, police leaders cannot ignore crime because minor offences build confidence and career, which begins to believe that no one cares and there are no consequences for crime (Ibid). For example, when young people witness that prostitute visibly play and beggars accost passers-by, they are encouraged by such an environment. As a result, heinous street crimes have flourished. For police, the broken window paradigm of Kelling and Wilson implies that police officers should keep streets clean and orderly and must take punitive action against minor misdemeanours. Such zero tolerance could work well as a strong sanction against crime. Strategic policing, however, balances zero tolerance with timely standard action against minor violations and emphasises restorative measures to rehabilitate the offender so that they may not repeat the crime.

The core belief of broken window dispensation was that the crack-down on minor crimes could deter significant crimes such as terrorism, serial killing, and severe street crimes. No police can control heinous crime if they ignore the abnormal street behaviour of muggers, beggars, drug sellers, gamblers, and Manipuri or Gutka in the case of Pakistan and India. However, such a link between beggars and terrorists lacks empirical evidence and seems to be based only on assumptions. Moreover, it is pretty tricky for police organisations to take action against non cognizable offices because the law does not allow police officers to indulge in misuse of their authority, and moral policing is considered a crime in professional terms (Reisig, 2020). Here, strategic policing emphasises the non-use of force and community-oriented measures to deviate back to normalcy (Terrill, 2020). Thus, strategic policing is less prone to controversy.

12.4.3. Problem-Oriented Policing (POP)

POP targets both crime and non-crime without going into the depths of its origin and cause of criminality. POP overburdens the already fatigued forces. There must be some support for sworn officers in solving such non-police problems and sharing such responsibilities within society. In 1979, Herman Goldstein predicted that in the future, police will not only be dealing with common crime but also with so many forms of the disorder. He critically stated that the police practices addressed the means of policing rather than its ends (Eck 2006). Goldstein advocated the replacement of the primarily reactive, incident-driven "standard model of policing" with a proactive approach focusing on alleviating the root causes of crime (Ibid). He termed "problem-oriented policing " to this paradigm shift, " which targeted problems instead of mere crime incidents. He also called for the police to expand their toolbox to address social problems other than classical crime-related issues.

Skogan et al. (1999) described a five-step model for a problem solution under the Chicago Alternative Policing Strategy (CAPS). The first recognition and prioritisation of recurring problems are essential; second, analysing diverse data, designing response strategies, converting strategies into doable actions, and assessing the outcomes. Eck (2006) believes that POP redefines policing in the postmodern complex age, where people demand more police to address their multiple problems. To him, "logical," "scientific," "surprising, " and effective (Ibid).

Critics of this philosophy (Braga and Weisburd 2006) raise many objections regarding the effectiveness of this model. First, a drawback of this model is arguably the possible inaccuracy of the data and the community bias reflected in the scanned and analysed information (Ibid). Second, POP's multifaceted operations and their different interpretations and implementations hardly leave us to reach any meaningful result in terms of its effectiveness. The same is true for assessing monetary outcomes, which have not been well developed (Joyce, 2011). Third, dealing with significant crimes is the core function of the police. However, the law discourages police from getting involved in minor offences like pissing in the streets. If cops become busy in the running after minor deviant acts, then who will take care of significant crimes like robberies, murders, and street crimes, to name a few (Braga and Weisburd 2006). Fourth, police culture is another drawback of police forces (Reiner, 2017). Most officers believe in the principle of using force to solve crimes and disorders (Ibid). If officers follow this belief, police can hardly solve any problem because the root cause or origin of crime will not receive appropriate attention (Ibid). Offenders will keep committing the same offence, and officers will take action by using enforcement and not engagement.

Here, the strategic model saves POP because, as a part of the strategic model, the stakeholders in policing share the burden of responsibility with police officers who stand protected and controlled in terms of using excessive force, as is the case under POP theory and practice. Second, police mandates are limited and do not extend to all problems under the sun. Third, contemporary societies face multiple problems of different nature. Chasing problems with their causes leads police officers to off-track and lose focus on their core crime control function. Fourth, the engagement of different stakeholders under the SPM model could offer a range of ideas and skills to deal with non-police matters of daily routines, primarily by partners across society (Katz & Maguire 2020).

12.4.4. Pulling Levers Policing (PLP)

PLP adopts a surgical and cosmetic approach to policing and crime. The pulling lever model focuses on offenders rather than places, offences, and causes (Braga, 2014). This model advocates deterrence strategies based on certainty and the severity of publishment. A criminal must get reminded that crime has grave consequences, and he will surely get punished. The certainty of punishment is far more effective than its severity; therefore, it articulates social scientists. Pulling-levers dispensation helps reduce severe violent crimes committed by gangs. Problem-oriented and third-party policing dispensations stand closer to PLP, so far as concerns their approach to situational crime prevention (Ibid). This paradigm uses offender behaviour and the fundamental factors as an intervening variable while analysing crime and prevention strategies (Braga and Weisburd 2012). Pulling levers policing, such as problem oriented and third party policing strategies, tend to blend community services with a refreshing approach in addition to pure law enforcement. Community mobilisation, as well as social service orientation, characterises pulling levers (Braga 2014).

The PLP centres its strategies around deterrence in many ways. First, the PLP model selects a particular crime problem, such as street crime in cities. Second, it liaises with law enforcement, social service groups, and community-based practitioners. Third, the PLP develops a response to offenders or gangs of offenders using a variety of sanctions to stop continued violence. Fourth, the focus of PLP policing remains on the involvement of community resources and other social services for targeting offenders. Fifth, unbroken communication with offenders to make them realise that they are under the spotlight is a core strategy of the PLP paradigm (Braga and Weisburd 2012). Lastly, in many areas of focused deterrence and forging partnerships with community groups, PLP overlaps with CP, POP, and TPP, and in some ways with strategic policing. However, this model is also a by-product of the desire to use force excessively. Like many other strategies, it lacks balance, and its focus is narrow in terms of police mandates and policing functions. This strategy lacks universal appeal and cannot be effective in different cultural situations. Strategic policing can support PLP with adjustability, acceptability, viability, and achieve workability and efficacy (Hendrix 2017).

12.4.5. Third-Party Policing (TPP)

TPP involves a third party between the police and the criminals, seeking assistance either by using force or convincing through persuasion (Buerger and Mazerolle 1998). TPP emphasises non-police stakeholders, bringing this model close to the strategic policing model. Specifically, the police know that parents, teachers, friends, neighbourhood notables, social workers, peace activists, people in business, and other civil society have stakes in the socialisation of youth and the maintenance of public peace (Ibid). Hardly anyone likes to see their children, students, friends, and neighbourhood youth growing in crime and violence. As a result, visionary police leaders make the most common proposition for enlisting public support against crime and violence in society as a strategic measure. As a result of police efforts, some or all stakeholders take responsibility for working together with the police to reduce crime and other recurring social problems such as street crime (Ibid). Thus, the TPP cultivates a control guardianship, free of financial costs.

At the heart of the TPP runs the partnership or collaboration idea, which brings this model close to strategic policing. Like the strategic policing paradigm, forging partnerships with other stakeholders is crucial for establishing peace in postmodern society (Reiss, 1992). In such associations, every partner can get equal say, attention, and response in controlling crime and solving social problems (Perrott & Trites 2017). Volunteers in such collaboration for peace hail from different backgrounds and professions, including people in business, traders, community notables, local government representatives, feminists, minority members, refugees' spokespersons, and other inspectors from different departments, join to work with the police (Mazerolle and Ransley 2002). In Pakistani society, the well-educated middle class is very responsive and helps police, citizens, Police Liaison Committees-CPLCs in Karachi, Dispute Resolution Committees in Khyber-Pakhtunkhwa, Local Panchayats in Punjab, and *Rajoni* Councils for dispute resolution in Sindh are some of the leading examples. Owing to its narrow scope and overreliance on non-police actors, this model is not a substitute for strategic policing, nor is it dynamic and as versatile as the strategic model. The strategic model involves a variety of networks, stakeholders, and strategies to support a single cause of policing, with police being in the driver's seat (Lobnikar, Mesko, & Modic, 2021).

12.4.6. Hot Spots Policing (HSP)

HSP focuses on small geographic areas or places where crime incidents concentrate and repeat (PERF, May 2008). This policing model is useful in urban settings, particularly in large metropolises like Karachi, Lahore, and Islamabad, where crime creates clusters. Hotspots refer to places on a crime map that shows high crime intensity and density (Weisburd 2011). Crime reporting analysis by the police creates data with place time, type of crime, victim and offender demographics, type of weapon used, and type of property targeted (Portland State University 2013). Such data offer deep insight to the researchers and analysts to formulate adequate police responses to the crimes and enable local area police to gain deep insight into the state of affairs and preparedness the police need to effectively handle different crimes (Taylor, Koper & Woods 2011). This approach aggregates crime in a geographic location. It contextualises analysis into small micro-units such as addresses, registration numbers, faces, and street segments to identify crime patterns, trends, and offender-victim demographics (CrimeSolutions.gov.).

Theoretically, the hotspot paradigm comes from routine activity theory. This theory unravels the existence of opportunities for crime (victim), the absence of capable guardians (police), and the presence of potential offenders (criminal) produce crime (Kochel 2011). The hot spots approach has to disturb the devil's alliance between the offender and victim through a guardian intervention (Ibid). David Weisburd (2011) suggests that, in HSP, 'places' receive more attention than people. The police should also attach importance to hot spots as strategic components of databases and research materials for crime mapping to fight disorder more effectively (Ibid). Research evidence suggests that the hot-spots approach has undoubtedly reduced crime, regardless of whether it is enforced adequately (Braga et al., Papachristos and Hureau 2012). Pakistan, though trying to adopt policing technologies through IT initiatives in different police departments, leading to Punjab, Islamabad, and KP, is still developing a proper crime mapping system in its metropolis and other urban hubs.

They are focusing on crime maps in places where crime makes clusters and where crime repeats are one of the core components of strategic policing, which attaches more importance to objective targets of reducing opportunities for crime and increasing the risks of committing it (Hendrix 2017). Therefore, strategic policing imbibes the hot-spot approach, but SPM is not limited to it because the strategic policing model incorporates many innovative policing approaches in contemporary postmodern times. For this reason, policing scholars describe strategic policing as a cluster of the best policing strategies-build like a birdcage through a networked procedure followed by many policing partners. Given the challenges and problems, Pakistan needs to construct a comprehensive policing response in an integrated strategic policing model.

12.4.7. Big-Data Policing (BDP)

Experts maintain that this dispensation of big data policing alludes to the police use of digital algorism and technology. Statistics on crime and police strategies sit nicely at the heart of this policing strategy (Cofan & Baloi, 2017). This strategy involves a computer comparison of statistics (operational and organizational data) regarding crime and policing (Stroshine 2021). As a whole, a computer comparison of statistics about crime pales, offender demographics, and resources of police for allocation to deal with crime defines this policing strategy. This proactive strategy guides police leaders to analyse crime and its trends and fix police officers found inefficient in discharging their duties regarding crime reduction and order maintenance (Bond 2016). These core components of big-data policing align with problem-solving approaches of community policing (Ferguson 2017). The police leader knows the problem and its environmental causes; they make plans based on the predictive outcomes of their perceived interventions (Henry 2002). Scholars call big-data policing a new way of managing police resources and tactics and "the single most important organisational innovation in policing" in the contemporary age (Ibid).

The rapid proliferation of technology from IT to IoT and 5G has made the future of digital policing bright and somewhat promising (Goodman 2015). Digital policing is likely to continue evolving with policing innovations and technological advances. Advances in information systems and digital technology will impact police agencies' ability to quickly and accurately identify crime problems and deploy resources (Ferguson 2017). Managing the enormous quantities of available information will probably require agencies to prioritise investing in crime analysis. It includes hiring professional crime analysts, providing them with training to stay abreast of the latest developments, and fully utilising their skills to perform sophisticated analyses (Henry 2002).

Shrinking public sector budgets require more efficient and more competent policing, and the use of technology can help ensure that police resources are monitored and used effectively (Ferguson 2017). Like most policing strategies, this strategy appears narrow in scope and invalid in all circumstances. For example, underdeveloped countries can hardly afford and manage this, nor developing or developed countries can exclusively rely on the digital solutions of crime and violence because there is much beyond technology to blend with it for practical police work. However, this strategy can work well when tied to the POP and CP models under the umbrella of the strategic policing model (Hendrix 2017). In Pakistan, this model could be very impactful because, when aligned with strategic policing approaches, it could improve public service delivery and police performance (Geoghegan2006).

12.4.8. Evidence-Based Policing (EBP)

The EBP allows police leaders to make informed decisions based on evidence that helps them avoid operational mistakes in common sense and the gut (Katz & Maguire 2020). This model attempts to apply research outcomes and findings regarding the best police practice for policing. During the last decade, the novel policing concept termed 'evidence-based' emerged from police leaders and academicians-criminologists, sociologists, and policy experts (Telep & Bottema 2020). Evidence-based policing refers to contemporary research and practice in policing that enables police leaders to base their field, policy, and strategy decisions on scientific research evidence, findings, and guidelines instead of information, gut, and intelligence (Ibid). The EBP also facilitates academics to hear police practitioners' voices as the primary source of their research methodologies (Huey & Mitchell, 2019).

Policing grows costlier every other day. Police departments worldwide are worried about the rising costs of policing (Lobnikar et al., 2021). Police researchers now look for more thoughtful and less expensive policing (Ibid). The fiscal challenges to the governments at all levels, especially the local city administrations, underline the need to balance crime-fighting with policing costs (Ibid). However, public safety is so severe that no government can take risks without finding reliable and measurable alternatives (Sherman, 2009). Things get worse, especially when communities face the threat of terrorism, a new style of warfare and crime almost found in every part of the world in varying degrees (Katz & Huff 2020). The threat of terrorism may be why social scientists and criminologists, such as Lawrence Sherman, have developed scientific, more imaginative, and digital criminal justice solutions, focusing on adopting science and technology as a reliable and effective alternative for costly policing (Bueermann 2012). This model, therefore, represents what Sherman (2009) calls "the field's most powerful force for change'.

We need to devote more funds to policing and criminal justice research than to unnecessary expansion and focus on what does not work. Sherman (2009) describes evidence-based policing as "the use of the best available research on the outcomes of police work to implement guidelines and evaluate agencies, units and officers." Research link evaluation of police performance to improve public safety outcomes. This approach enables police organisations to move beyond a reactive, response-driven approach to the strategic and more ingenious ways of crime management (Bueermann 2012).

It is crucial for police leaders to make research findings readable and understandable for police officers with minimum qualifications in science and modern technology (Huey and Mitchell 2019). In an evidence-based policing approach, police officers and staff create, review, and use the best available evidence to inform and challenge policies, practices, and decisions (Telep & Bottema 2020). As a way of working, it can be supported by collaboration with academics and other partners (What Works Centre for Policing 2017). The strategic policing model envisages smarter, cost-effective ways involving feedback from all partners, particularly academia and research circles. Pakistan faces severe financial deficits. Therefore, police leaders in Pakistan encourage policing research to make evidence-based decisions as a strategic measure to improve police performance and legitimacy (Telep & Bottema 2020).

12.4.9. Intelligence-Led Policing (ILP)

The ILP focuses on assessing and managing risks and threats (Ratcliffe, 2016). This model emerged in the 1990s in the UK and the USA (Ibid). In this strategy, intelligence officers serve as guides for police operations. A pre-operation knowledge and information scheme governs the operation mechanics (Ibid). Criminologist Lawrence Sherman founded this strategy in 1998 and claimed Ratcliffe (2016). Police everywhere have intelligence networks; for example, in the Pakistan Special Branch in the provinces and Intelligence Bureau at the federal level are lead civilian intelligence networks of police. "Intelligence-led policing is crime-fighting by effective intelligence gathering and analysis—and it has the potential to be the most important law enforcement innovation of the twenty-first century" (Kelling and Bratton 2006). It is closest to problem-oriented police, and to some degree, the accountability mechanism of policing with the technology model, yet ILP is distinct from both (Wells 2009). Moreover, intelligence-led policing appears to be relatively fluid as the police services experiment with different organizational philosophies, priorities, and configurations and attempt to integrate community issues into police decision-making to enforce the law across the board.

Having our home scenarios regarding crimes, forms of violence, social problems, economic regression, and political uncertainty in mind, in the post 9/11 era, police and armed forces have carried out thousands of successful intelligence-led operations in Pakistan (Babakhel 2015).

"Without credible intelligence, policing recedes to a ceremonial status and leads to wastage of resources. The price for the continued romance with a colonial, bureaucratic, autocratic, stagnant, and inhuman policing model is paid by the victims of terrorism and crime. Those who are involved in this romance derive the maximum benefits."

Elahi (2017) observed the following:

"The modus operandi is to increase the use of intelligence, surveillance and informants to target major offenders so that police could pre-emptively fight crime rather than responding to it. ILP can help develop strategy and priorities through a more objective analysis of the criminal environment... Our police force is designed to come into action after a crime is committed or at times when it's taking place. The yardstick of success is to arrest the culprit or recover the looted articles. The police do not have the training, capacity, or mandates to take pre-emptive action. The watch and ward system, considered to be meant for pre-emptive action to deter criminals, is also in the doldrums."

Elahi (2017) also lauded the historical role of Special Branches and the CIA in detecting crime during the colonial period. Police in Pakistan is well acquainted with intelligence-led policing, which is part of the strategic partnerships of police with intelligence networks to share critical information regarding crime and terrorism. Although ILPs have become part of counterterrorism in Pakistan, they are yet to be fully adopted by classical policing at the police station level. Counter-terrorism departments (CTDs) have embraced the intelligence-based operations-IBOs culture. ILP is also a cardinal part of the strategic policing model because doing targeted operations produces better results and improves police performance to a great extent.

12.4.10. Social Media Policing (SMP)

Social media policing depends on the Internet of Things (IoT) and online connectivity. This policy has gained currency in the wake of the proliferation of cybercrime. Social media connectivity is the core of this postmodern miracle and social revolution in real-time. It has magical powers to neutralise physical distances and gather the entire global population in just one small chat room or social network. "A fascinating new human phenomenon of the twenty-first century, the social media dictates and facilitates a remarkable change in human social life and so, no less than a global social revolution" (Baloch, 2016). Everything is online; even marriages, education, interaction, and human relationships of all types go social on media. Therefore, it is time for police services in Pakistan to adopt social media policing as an international best practice of policing (Ibid).

Internet arrival in the late 1980s accompanied by email and other social networks prepared the ground for social networks such as Facebook, Twitter, WhatsApp, Instagram, LinkedIn, Tic-tac, YouTube, and others in the first decade of the twenty-first century (Ibid). Today, more than half of the global population, including all age groups, use social media to post, exchange, share, share, follow, tweet, tweet ideas, research, knowledge, news, information, feelings, and emotion. As a result, social media constitutes an open source of information, intelligence, and valuable evidence for police.

In the wake of increasing cybercrime, it is advisable for police organisations in Pakistan to learn to use social media as a policing tool (Baloch 2016). Many police organisations have adopted social media as their policing policy and strategy to control crime, violence, disorder, and extremism. The Constable Scott Mills of the Toronto Police Department is the founder of social media policing. Mill laid the foundation for the social media strategy of policing in 2007 in response to managing massive mob demonstrations in Toronto, Canada (Ibid). Afterwards, many police departments, including the New York, London Metropolitan, Boston, Helsinki, Philadelphia, and many other leading police organisations across the globe, have adopted social media policing as one of the best practices of 21st century policing. The main highlights of the research findings of Baloch (2016) are as follows: First, for police to stay away from social media is dangerous. Second, the adoption of social media as a policing tool is inevitable. Third, using social media in policing reduces the financial cost of policing. Fourth, many departments worldwide have adopted social media policing. Fifth, social media is a source of high power and progress, improving police performance. Sixth, no use or underuse can be counterproductive. Finally, the national social media policy for law enforcement agencies in Pakistan is fundamental and necessary (Baloch, 2016).

Social media policing based on the connectivity principle is essential for strategic policing (Home Office, UK 2015). In Pakistan, this policing strategy is yet to take its roots in an organized policy and practice domain of policing. Pakistan is one of the countries in the world, such as India, Indonesia, Brazil, Malaysia, and many other Middle Eastern countries, where social media use is on a meteoric rise. Social media statistics and demographics reveal that the number of social media users in these countries is likely to increase by up to seventy per cent of their total population by 2025 (Christopher, 2016). This discourse recommends the adoption of social media as part and parcel of postmodern strategic policing in Pakistan.

12.4.11. Predictive Policing (PP)

The predictive approach emphasises 'criminal activity and is closer to data-driven, hotspots and intelligence-led policing models (Perry, McInnis, Price, Smith, & Hollywood 2013). Predictive policing anticipates and forecasts criminal activity using mathematical, predictive, and analytical techniques in law enforcement (Ibid). "Predictive policing involves using algorithms to analyse massive amounts of information to predict and help prevent potential future crimes" (Lau 2020). Predictive policing leverages computer models for law enforcement. For example, artificial intelligence and business intelligence in the business industry can anticipate how market conditions, industry trends, and customer considerations will evolve. Similarly, law enforcement agencies have new knowledge and skills.

Predictive models assess criminal activity and its different dynamics relating to specific gangs and their area of criminal activity and their repeat timings like hot-spot mechanisms. However, unlike hotspot policing, the predictive approach ties crimes to people and places (Lau, 2020). The creation of risk profiles of suspect individuals is a critical component of predictive policing. Offender-based modelling by age, criminal record, employment history, and social affiliations in the criminal justice system help police pre-empt crimes before happening (Perry et al., 2013). Predictive policing is an approach of police to manage crime and make communities safer by harnessing the power of information, geospatial technologies, and evidence-based intervention models.

211

Reimagining Policing in Pakistan

Criminologists, crime analysts, police leaders, and policing experts are fancied with police science of palmistry, experimenting with using predictive analytics in forecasting future crimes like Mark Goodman (2015) have done in his seminal work: "Future Crimes." Surveillance technologies help reduce crime and reduce police abuse (Ferguson 2018). However, civil rights and social justice groups are unhappy with intrusive techniques for privacy issues that are likely to arise with the application of such monitoring mechanics (Kochel 2011). Moreover, many critics of this policing model show their serious concerns that offender-based predictions are likely to promote racial biases in the criminal justice system and police investigations with engineered evidence, undermining the principle of presumed innocence (Wallace et al., 2020). Therefore, it transpires that equating locations, ethnicity, creed, genealogy, and other preconceived considerations with criminality create more policing and crime management problems than they reduce, thereby amplifying problematic policing patterns.

Criminologists have contrasting perspectives on predictive policing. Advocates of predictive policing argue that computer algorithms can predict future crimes with greater precision and objectivity than police officers who rely solely on instincts (Lau 2020). Some also argue that predictive policing can provide a cost-effective model for police to fight crime more efficiently (Ibid). Proponents also maintain that crime statistics, community relations, and the legitimacy of public servants can help police improve their public image and performance. On the contrary, critics warn about the authorities' lack of transparency that administer predictive police programs (Ibid). They also highlight many concerns regarding civil liberties and human rights, including the possibility that algorithms may reinforce racial bias in the criminal justice system (Ibid). These audit concerns have resulted in significant law enforcement agencies, including Los Angeles and Chicago, phasing out or restricting their predictive policing programs after the audit (Ibid). There are three reasons for rejecting this "great big data hubris' (Ferguson 2017). First, the public has no access to investigating the classifier behaviour of police officers. Second, strict monitoring of police behaviour during the arrest and the search for suspect citizens through their departments will expose their ethics to prosecution. Third, proponents of the predictive police hide the racial and biased behaviour of police officers that could justify and legitimise coercion and discrimination (Lau 2020).

The strategic policing model allows technology and information to solve the crime, but it discourages police officers' roles as warriors and violators of human rights. In contrast, strategic policing incorporates democratic and rights-based approaches that define the role of police officers as guardians of human rights rather than their violators. Strategic policing narratives are rooted in police

212

approaches to protect and serve. The normative format of predictive policing does not align with strategic policing because the fundamental element of procedural justice, which is the soul of strategic policing, is missing in the predictive policing narrative. Therefore, the chances of misuse of authority are thicker in predictive policing. There are already many complaints of the misuse of authority by police, particularly in developing countries [such as Pakistan] (Terrill 2020).

12.5. Going Strategic in Policing

To go strategic in policing implies specific measures that police departments must take. First and foremost is to adopt the innovation that has taken place in the wake of technological applications in everything police and policing (Hendrix 2017). Pakistan has adopted only a fraction of innovations in policing and therefore needs more additions given the crime, disorder, and violence in society (refer to chapter-6 of this book). Second, the police departments in Pakistan should improve relations with the community as the core strategic partner and stakeholders in policing and peace (see Chapter 8). Third, partnerships with all other stakeholders, both domestic and international, are vital strategic importance to the police in Pakistan. Lastly, the combination of strategies should be in line with the contextual and cultural realities of the police (Reiner, 2017).

There is a central question behind the silver bullet or what police pioneers call "it depends' (Ratcliffe 2018). A system's legitimacy or usage viability is essential when performing in the police. Strategic validity includes the adequacy of the technique, similar to its external validity (ibid). Effectiveness is imperative because there are a few strategies that, for the most part, do not work (Hendrix 2017). External validity signifies the degree to which a police strategy that worked in one place would ever work at another (RAND 2018). The few strategies have more prominent relevance to a more extensive scope of police departments and their services to the communities (Ibid). Although fewer departments have investigated air crash cases, most places have tried different things with various strategies. The external validity of a strategy is, like this, a factor to consider when evaluating likely achievement (Hendrix, 2017).

The second most vital factor is usage viability or implementation effectiveness. Any police officer can use Google as a strategy supported by another police leader. This dependence on Google produces similar results. There is a significant difference in operational execution, and it is difficult to predict the achievement. Since your specialisation may receive a procedure that is on a fundamental level imperfect or is not fitting for your condition, or you probably would not execute it viable, no one can state for sure whether it will succeed. On the off chance that some police departments, like ours, have a weak organisational culture, putting resources into body-worn cameras will have to end up in failure (Ratcliffe 2018).

Strategic policing converges all these meanings and mandates into one integrated networked system of strategic partnerships (Webb et al., 2020). Police strategists should always know what policing is while strategising policing goals and methods. In this connection, police leaders need two essential things, without which it is difficult to achieve strategic policing in Pakistan. These include strategic frameworks with leadership dynamism (RAND, 2018). Leadership dynamism implies certain qualities of a police leader: positivity, capacity, vision, will, action, pragmatism, persistence, evaluation, feedback, innovation, and change.

While chalking our strategic framework of policing for establishing peace and order in society, community priority should always be at the centre of strategy (Hendrix 2017). The community is a primary stakeholder and the end-user of policing products, such as procedural justice, due process, and peace. In this, the community will follow the strategy so developed and make such strategy a success or failure by cooperating to provide information, logistics, resources, and legitimacy to police action. Above all, the public image of police gets crafted at the place where the community votes for or against whether police are good or bad, or they deliver service or cause problems. Strategic policing, being closer to democracy, accountability, and technology, is a multidimensional approach to law enforcement that has great potential to transform police and policing into the real art of Peace-craft in Pakistan. This discourse draws the following policy vision and mission as starters:

12.5.1. Strategic Policing Vision
Transforming police from a coercive model to a professional, apolitical, autonomous, accountable, service-oriented, and democratic organisation through a change, reform, and innovation so that the police could act as the guardian of human rights in Pakistan constitutes the core of our policing vision.

12.5.2. Strategic policing mission
Turning crime and violence back and making society safer through strategic policing in line with new police professionalism based on the core values of integrity, specialism, legitimacy, accountability, autonomy, innovation, partnerships, and national coherence in Pakistan's police organisations by blending diversity signifies our policing mission of the 21sr century.

12.5.3. National Strategic Plan for Policing

Contemporary Police leadership should formulate a national strategic policing plan to transform the police in Pakistan. Police officers should obtain the necessary training and education to serve and protect the communities rather than serve the political governments. Instituting a democratic oversight model for ensuring administrative and financial autonomy of the police world help instrumentalise change and reform in the police. Security of service and tenure for police leaders is essential to follow the rule of law, procedural justice, organisational justice, role specialism, human rights values, technological embrace, and community engagement in a strategic partnership.

12.6. Conclusion

To realise this vision, police leadership needs to rethink and reimagine the roadmap involving legal, social, political, economic, and cultural perspectives. For many police leaders, this might be an arduous task to achieve. Still, this book argues that this phenomenal objective is realisable if we embrace the strategic policing model in Pakistan. In this connection, police leaders must focus on recruitment at all levels, career planning, capacity building, meritocracy in reward and punishment, professional integrity, care and caution in the use of force, strategic communication, quality of public service delivery, adoption of technology, and close collaboration with the communities and other stakeholders to address the gaps in contemporary policing. Among these, recruitment, training, career planning, and organizational justice are the key and core components to work out. No one other than police leadership can accomplish this task befittingly. Neither the bureaucrats nor the politicians are responsible for this. Still, police leadership need to come out of the shallows of their persona and try sincerely to promote institutional and collective thinking in the public interest.

If we need to make the most of science, technology, inclusivity, and democracy for policing in Pakistan, we must work on strategic policing. The first step towards strategic policing would be to develop ten years of policing vision plans and draw the mechanism for implementation and goal achievement. Such a policing vision must incorporate our plan to transform the police from force models to service paragons with more explicit details about the financial and human resources required to make communities safer. Then, a consortium of researchers, academics, journalists, and law enforcement practitioners led by AFIGP veterans may get together outside the government circles to formulate plans and policy recommendations on transformation to postmodern strategic policing in Pakistan. Thus, the strategic ecosystem of policing partnerships should continue to work on policing research to facilitate police transformation (Katz & Maguire). Police alone cannot do this job because policing no longer remains an exclusive domain of the police.

By J.J. Baloch (2022)

Chapter: 11

Policing Reimagined

Chapter Brief

This chapter highlights the key areas I have tried to reimagine policing. The reimagined areas include developing a strategic policing (Hendrix 2017), cultivating effective police leadership (Sutton), introducing police officers' bill of rights (Tan 2020), developing constabulary ethics, resolving the constitutionality of policing (PRC Report 2019), de-bureaucratizing policing (Meares 2017), developing a professional specialism in police (Westmarland & Conway 2020), adoption of police technology (Chapman 2016) and (Davies 2021), framing media strategy (Christopher 2016) and (Jewkes 2011), focusing diversity and pluralism (Rogers 2016), and transforming police (Katz & Maguire 2020) to new police professionalism (Stone & Travis 2011). This chapter argues that in the 21st-century, police alone cannot perform policing functions in isolation, but they direly need the engagement of other stakeholders (Lyons 2002). Therefore, the police in Pakistan need to 'forge partnerships with other law enforcement and community groups for better performance' (Ibid). The relevant writings on policing by Hendrix (2017), Bowling and Sheptycki (2011), Reiner (1992), Newburn (2001), O'Malley (1997), Wills (2010), Sutton (2012), Jones and Newburn (2013) (2006), Katz & Maguire (2020), Vitale (2017) and Pakistan's experience with reforms (PRC Report 2019) make up the core of analysis here.

11.1. Introduction

The traditional hardcore of the paramilitary model in policing is not too hard to break if we embrace change and innovation (Kratcoski, 2017). Given this, we should reimagine policing culture, organization, mission, and strategies that could help transform policing in Pakistan from coercive models to democratic approaches. Arguably, police leadership alone cannot affect good change and institute propitious reform in policing because bureaucrats and politicians make policing-policy decisions in Pakistan. However, non-police actors see our strategic visions as daydreams. Few beneficiaries of the status-quo in police service, connected to top decision-makers, think about themselves, their perks, comforts, and interests more than they bother about police reforms. Only a few and far between PSP officers keep trying to bring good homes. The police officers' efforts to get the Supreme Court of Pakistan engaged in police reforms have been laudable. Police officers' efforts brought the police reform committee report to the limelight through Pakistan's Law and Justice Commission (PRC Report 2019). Unfortunately, the government has put the report in cold storage where it keeps getting dust and needs a political push to beef up the police reform process.

Triggering police reforms significantly on policy and legislative levels is, indeed, a difficult task in Pakistan, at least for PSP echelons. However, police leaders can play an instrumental role in the maximum utilisation of resources, creating specialised units, adopting police technology, improving police training, resisting political interference, focusing on welfare, changing working culture and building the professional capacity of the police (David et al., 2008). Similarly, accountability at all levels is crucial, and there should not be sacred cows or untouchables in the police department.

The most fundamental aspect of this conversation on reimagining policing is to involve millennials (generation-Z) constructively. Millennials can be more imaginative, creative, innovative, open-minded, and tolerant to coexistence, diversity, difference, and disagreement to accommodate change and innovation. They have a better idea of being and feeling curious, adventurous, ambitious, democratic, progressive, and futuristic than authoritarian stereotypes, strictly hierarchical organizational structures, and archaic environments we were born and grown. The Accenture Report (2018) reveals that the use of contemporary police technologies will accelerate evidence-based decision making and strategic quality actions in policing in years to come (Accenture Report,2018). The openness to new ideas, agility for experimentation, willingness to embrace innovation, the culture of experimentation, appreciation of diversity, the requirement of integrity, emphasis on transparency, and focus on legitimacy appear to be the crucial drivers of change and innovation in the postmodern age of strategic policing (Hendrix et al., 2017). For policing postmodern complexity, a networked approach to forging partnerships would be a befitting response (Crank, 2003).

11.2. The Rationale Behind the Strategic Policing

Following presumptions endorse this discourse's advocacy for the strategic policing model-SPM. First, SPM is grounded in the postmodern theory of policing that seeks to build policing strategies on the newest notions of police management and operations and absorb the essence of best policing practices tried and tested in many police organisations in the 21st century (Hendrix 2017). Second, SPM addresses the challenges of frequent social change within human social institutions. The SPM does not conform to the status quo but emphasizes change, innovation, and reforms (ibid). Third, the SPM incorporates the practical and pragmatic characteristics of strategic innovations in policing, forming a compelling and dynamic mix to be fitted in the given circumstances of societal frameworks, cultural environments, and political ideologies that are current, relevant, and integrated (see Chapter 10 of this book). Fourth, this model offers an equal opportunity to all stakeholders by discouraging police monopoly on the use of force and on the narratives of peace and order in the society they are to protect, thereby preparing the ground for democracy and the rule of law (Jones 2009). Fifth, the SPM encourages science and technology to solve crime and deliver public services efficiently by reducing communication gaps between the police and the public, promoting public trust and confidence in police forces (Charrier 2010). Sixth, strategic policing promotes good governance through interaction, dialogue, constant engagement, inclusiveness (Hendrix et al., 2017), organizational justice, and legitimacy (Lawson & Wolfe 2021). It opens up fairness, transparency, integrity, social cohesion, and accountability (Gilmour, 2007), which are the foundations of the new police professionalism (Stone & Travis 2011). Lastly, the effectiveness, viability, and validity of this model depend, to a small extent, on the capability and dynamism of police leadership (Sutton, 2012) to push for legislation on the strategic policing model. In addition to across-the-board implementation, the SMP advocates more imaginative ways for operational and financial autonomy of the police and ensures democratic oversight (Decker & Sjarback, 2020). Police autonomy is one of the primary requirements for transforming rule-based colonial police into service-oriented organisations in Pakistan (Babakhel, 2021). The adoption of technology (Stroshine, 2021) and forging partnerships with research consortiums (Webb et al., 2020) to incorporate evidence-based decision-making (Katz & Maguire 2020) in police operational culture is a cardinal part of strategic policing (Hendrix et al., 2017). Above all, strategic policing philosophy seeks to transform police officers' warrior roles of police officers into the guardians of fundamental rights (MacLean et al., 2021). Based on the above rationale, Pakistan should adopt a strategic policing model to transform the police and policing in this world.

11.3. Resolving Constitutional Issues

The constitutionality of policing has emerged as a central question in Pakistan today since the adoption of the Police Order 2002, enactment of the 18th constitutional amendment (2010), and revocations and amendments of PO 2002 by the provinces. Whether policing is a provincial subject or a federal domain has generated heated debates in police circles, courtrooms, public forums, and media channels in Pakistan. The PRC report (2019) acknowledges Pakistan's "federal nature" of police procedural law. The question of the constitutionality of police laws first emerged in the Supreme Court in the case of Zafarullah Khan v. The Federation of Pakistan (2002). In 2010, the 18th Amendment paved the way for provinces to materialise their cherished dream of police control. Provinces revoked PO-2002 without any preparation or consideration of the constitutionality of Police Order (2002) in terms of police role as human rights enforcing agency. Among other good things, PO 2002 included

219

political neutrality, democratic oversight, an effective accountability framework, functional specialization, and many other defining characteristics of postmodern policing. Sindh, Balochistan, and KP completely withdrew from the 2002 Police Order. The Punjab bureaucracy moulded it to suit their interests by inserting many new amendments in which the PO 2002 lost its essence.

The PRC Report (2019) contends that Police laws are "relatable to criminal law, criminal procedure and Evidence Act. Police Laws fall in the concurrent list, which means a common domain for federal and provincial governments, subject to the primacy of federation over the province" (Shigri 2019 p. XV). Article 143 of the constitution of Pakistan 1973 provides for resolving the inconsistency between federal and provincial laws:

"If any provision of the Act of Provincial Assembly is repugnant to any provision of the Act of Parliament (Majlis-e-Shoora) which parliament is competent to enact or to any provision of the existing law concerning any of the matters of Parliament which Parliament is competent to enact, then the Act of Parliament, whether passed before or after the Act of Provincial Assembly, shall prevail and the Act of Provincial Assembly shall, to the extent of repugnancy, be void" (Article 143 Constitution of Pakistan 1973).

The PRC Report (2019) further states that the federation's role in dispensing justice could not be underestimated. Policing is the central part of the criminal justice process and the primary criminal justice instrument to ensure fundamental rights, as enshrined in Chapter One of the Constitutions of Pakistan (1973). Therefore, the PRC (2018) reviewed the Police Order (2002) with a fresh mind taking into consideration various superior court rulings on Police Order (2002) from time to time and came up with Model Police Law 2018, which is an improved version of the Police Order (2002) with some deletion and addition.

In the wake of the presentation of the PRC Report on Police Reforms (2019), the Supreme Court of Pakistan passed a short order of six pages which maintained that "Policing is a concurrent subject and not the exclusivity of the provinces." Therefore, the provinces cannot legislate the police law on their own and are inconsistent with the police law of federation. In response to this short order, all four provinces submitted their replies to the court, claiming their exclusivity of the police domain in the court. In this regard, the views of provincial bureaucracy and the federal government are the same, arguing for provincial exclusivity of police domain. In contrast, the views of PRC (2018) members consisting of veteran police officers and renowned jurists are quite the opposite. However, the constitutional position of the PRC is grounded and well-founded. It would be difficult for the provinces to stand against the structure of the Supreme Court, but we have had a bad experience with the implementation of reforms. Therefore, it is uncertain whether the model police law 2018 chalked out in PRCR-2019 could be translated into reality without the political will of Pakistan's federal and provincial governments.

Uniformity of police laws is essential for reorganising police in Pakistan. The gaps in police laws in Pakistan cause conflicts in governance, which further undermines the cause of peace in society. The diarchy of police laws is good for nothing, except for the criminals and miscreants who can make the most of these missing links to quickly escape the retribution in the courts of law due to the lack of national coherence in policing. Therefore, there must be a uniform law of policing across the provinces. There is a remarkable difference between policing and the maintenance of law and order-only one of the many components of policing- and which is traditional with the provinces, but the constitution, structure, and procedures of police have always been a federal constitutional domain (PRCR 2019). I advocate national coherence in policing laws and stand for policing as a national phenomenon due to new public safety challenges, national security, and counterterrorism. National security and counterterrorism are too important subjects to be left to the narrower jurisdictions of the provinces with many variations in the policing methods. However, street-level policing should remain with local police departments at the provincial level, recommending integrated police systems at the national level. Uniformity is different from unity here because Pakistan is a heterogeneous society and country where many cultural and ethnic groups formulate the socio-political ethos of the nation. However, policing is a component of criminal justice and government, so uniformity will not disturb diversity but adjust it.

11.4. Towards the Strategic Police Leadership

Practical, dynamic, and visionary police leadership could serve as the engine of all police transformations. Police leaders should reimagine policing and translate it into practice by pushing change within police organizations (Kumar, 2017). Dynamic police leaders can strategically manage to convince political leadership for new legislation and obtain new principles incorporated into the rules of newer professionalism in police and adapt the strategic policing paradigm.

However, police leadership in Pakistan is yet to evolve a collective sense of a family to work together on police transformations vehemently. At the same time, there is a remarkable consensus among them on strategic goals. Only a handful of officers succeeded to some extent, but their marginal victories did not have any lasting impact on policing culture inherited from British India (see Policing Development Part). Had there been more like Mr Suddle, Mr Iftikhar, and Mr Durrani, the situation would have been entirely different and better today. We often blame the police are ineffective because they are under-resourced, understaffed, politicized, and bureaucratized. This perception appears to be a lame excuse. First, we have to genuinely play our part and blame others for their natural indifference to policing. Others have nothing to do with the poor conditions of the Police unless we convince and sensitise them after making our maximal efforts to ease them. Our demand for more police autonomy stands justified only when we have made most of the given limited autonomy. Second, we carry out our jobs of superintendence and administration of the police befittingly. In the same way, we follow the rule of law. Third, we should involve external actors who could improve policing in Pakistan.

Police leadership faces a severe legitimacy crisis in Pakistan. Police leadership is an incredibly misunderstood area of public management, where most of us in the police department reserves it for ourselves by position and rank. Here, the problem of present leadership grows. The second crisis of police leadership stems from our presumptions as police chiefs that we know everything better than our contemporaries and the people who work with us. As a result, we developed authoritarian and fascist attitudes and stopped consulting anything either vertically or horizontally. Ultimately, everything stops working in an environment of distrust and ill will (Sutton, 2012). He further (Sutton, 2012) argues that police leadership can make a difference to our staff, department, agency, and communities. This flawed self-perception of police leadership needs to cease if we intend to transform policing in Pakistan because police leaders 'self-obsession is the most pretentious obstacle to police reform.

There are specific criteria associated with effective police leadership, which outlines many of its core elements. First, police leadership is not achieved by dint of position or rank. Even a constable or head constable or any officer wearing a uniform can be a police leader. Only such a leader, who can "think differently, train differently, prepare differently, behave differently, lead differently, and live differently, can make a difference in policing" Wills 2010). Second, the enlightened police officers always keep their work transparent and open to the public to share information about challenges to the police. Police openness also gives them timely awareness of the likely problems that arise. Third, offering easy access and rapid response to the people in the middle of difficulty cultivate the wealth of experience to help, assist, coordinate, and foster cordial relationships with all strategic partners, including the community. We need to institutionalise such organisational culture in our country for better public service delivery.

222

Third, genuine police leaders own their force and represent them reasonably well when the police commit some miscalculated acts in good faith in the line of duty. Such police leaders or commanders never lose their balance in the face of media and public pressure because they know full well the cost of saying "no-comments" in front of the media (Wills 2010). Experience has shown that failure in strategic communications can destroy public trust and the force's morale for being disowned by their leaders. Disowner-ship is commonplace in Pakistan and calls for immediate fixing.

Fourth, leadership refers to a lifestyle rather than role performance. The visionary police leaders always adopt restorative mechanisms to build the capacity and confidence of the force who work with them. Dynamic and strategic police leaders feel reluctant to impose penalties that kill the initiative by questioning the intention of officers working in intolerable and miserable conditions with high spirits (Sutton 2012). An arbitrary culture of police management fails to work in a postmodern organizational setting. Only consensual and consultative approaches to strategic management work well in policing. Therefore, police leadership should adopt restorative approaches to build the capacity of their rank and file rather than opting for retributive methodologies, as has been the case in Pakistan.

Fifth, influential police leaders know the art of winning the heart of their subordinates by cultivating extraordinary volunteerism to get the riskiest and most complicated assignments done by their staff. I have heard police officers confessing: "Sir, we can lay down our lives for our leaders who, we know, will take care of our families as their own families when we are down in the line of duty." After many sacrifices of police officers in the line of duty to make communities safer, many of our police leaders have done an excellent job by getting Shuhda packages enhanced in terms of material and monetary benefits. In contrast, our leaders need to develop a strong culture of care and protection for the families of fallen officers.

Last but not least is the advice of Robert Sutton (2012), who in his thoughts on 'Good Boss & Bad Boss' writes:

"Do not hold grudges after losing an argument. Instead, they help victors and implement their ideas. Imagine revolutionising police culture if we fail to learn from our mistakes. A culture of forgiveness and taking good care of the constabulary would heal many angry cops' {Sutton 2012}.

In this regard, police leadership in Pakistan needs to welcome criticism and follow an open environment, allowing their officials from all ranks to contribute to making communities safer by sharing their own experiences. Such an engaging, inclusive, and consultative working environment is what strategic policing invites. Thomas E. Baker (1941) believes that "strategic leadership anticipates problems" and prepares to pre-empt them by applying strategic and tactical methods. Successful strategic leaders assess and predict crisis scenarios and challenging situations that form 'the foundations of problem-solving policing approaches'. They do not wait until the problem boils down into an unmanageable crisis but timely 'execute effective solutions. For example, TLP processions and Dharnas in Punjab sent home many police officers for their failure to stop them. However, police leaders failed to get justice for police officers who TLP activists badly beat. No balance in actions causes disappointments and loss of the morale of officers. At the same time, physically, police officers couldn't stop such a remarkably outnumbered and largely frenzied procession. It never works and always proves counterproductive. Police leaders in Pakistan should look forward to leading their force by example, making a difference in the lives of people they serve and protecting their rank and file who work with and for them. Only such exemplary acts could help transform the police and policing in Pakistan.

11.5. Towards Police Officers' Bill of Rights

Like all other people, police officers also deserve organisational justice and due process in criminal and departmental proceedings, without which we can never raise a professional and efficient force having faith in the system (Tan 2020). Police cannot conduct quality investigations and follow the rule of law if their leaders and courts do not treat them fairly. Here, it is clear that legal protections for security against illegal orders and organisational justice never mean impunity for police officers (Trinkner & Tyler, 2020). Innocent police officers likely commit bonafide mistakes in the line of duty. Some police leaders impose heavy penalties on them without following the principle of organisational justice. Retribution is quite common police leadership culture in Pakistan (Ibid).

The police officers' bill of rights emerged from "two important U.S. Supreme Court cases (Garrity, v. New Jersey and Gardner v. Broderick"). From the police officers' side, the case had been pleaded by "the Fraternal Order of Police (FOP), arguing that during administrative investigations of the police officer, the constitutional rights of the officers should be protected and a clear distinction should be maintained between the criminal and administrative acts of the officers.

Garrity v. New Jersey (1967)

In this case, the officers were under investigation for the alleged fixing of traffic tickets. During interrogation, the officers were informed that their statements could be used against them in criminal proceedings. They were allowed not to disclose anything that could implicate them in a criminal act. On the contrary, they were also warned that they would be dismissed from their jobs if they refused to answer any question. The officers honestly answered the questions and were incriminated, prosecuted, and convicted of their crimes. As a result, the officers filed an appeal in the US Supreme Court, claiming that they were convicted based on the statements that they were forced to make under the threat of losing their jobs. The court admitted the appeal and ruled that "threatening officers to lose the job for not making statements runs counter to the due process and is violative of protection against the self-incrimination principle guaranteed under the Fifth Amendment of the US Constitution. Hence, the admissibility of these statements for criminal proceedings is unconstitutional (Garrity v. New Jersey 1967).

Gardener v. Broderick (1968)
In this case, the officers were under investigation for bribery allegations. The investigators offered the alleged officer's immunity from the prosecution if they made truthful statements before the grand jury and warned them that they would be fired if they refused to make statements. On the one hand, investigators presented immunity waivers to the alleged police officers. In contrast, on the other, the investigators made the police officers clear about the consequences of refusal to waive their right to immunity. However, Gardner declined the dictates of signing the waiver. Instead, Gardner invoked the fifth amendment in his defence. As a result, his department dismissed Gardner. The Court, taking stock of the forcible testimony of Gardner, declared it wrongful and turned down his dismissal order (Gardner v. Broderick 1968).

In Pakistan, the PSP Association and the Association of Former Inspectors Generals of Police-AFIGP should play the same role in working for the constitutional rights of police officers, as it has become a global trend. Nobody in police wishes to protect bad cops. Still, everyone should be concerned about the good cops or innocent police officers who are unduly punished by their command under pressure and when police officers get severe court punishments without sound legal grounds other than whims. A case in point, for example, is the crime scene wash case of Benazir Bhutto assassination, in which the trial court acquitted the originally alleged persons but awarded a sentence of seventeen years imprisonment just for the alleged official neglect, if any. Organisational and procedural injustice should not happen and will not happen if police officers find their bill of rights (Magliocca, 2016). In Pakistan, many police officers are either killed in the line of duty or sent to jail for self-defence against the criminal elements in the good name of human rights. It is harder to transform the role of police officers from warriors to guardians without offering them a bill of rights (MacLean et al., 2021).

Reimagining Policing in Pakistan

The job of the police is different from the rest of the civil service. Therefore, this discourse suggests that the Police Service of Pakistan should draft their separate service rules in line with international best rules for police. Furthermore, as police leaders, we should ensure organizational justice in the police accountability process and protection against the wrong incrimination of our officers. No other than police leadership can initiate the process of organizational justice in Pakistan (Majid, 2020). Although the police officers' bill of rights varies from one police department to another, the standard provisions that this book recommends for Pakistan include the following:

- The police officers must get timely informed regarding any investigation or inquiry pending against them without violating their integrity.
- In disciplinary matters of any kind, police officers under investigation should know the result of such proceedings that should necessarily be transparent and fair in all senses.
- Police officers, under inquiry or investigation, should not be suspended or punished before such proceedings get completed. Instead, the accused officer should get interviewed while on duty to ensure the proceedings' impartiality and offer a fair environment.
- The alleged police officers should get informed about the inquiry officer's name, rank, and portfolio and an authorised officer supervising such inquiries. If they express dissatisfaction or lack confidence, their inquiries or investigation officers may change.
- The alleged officers must be offered the opportunity to have an attorney or legal assistance during the proceedings and interrogations/interviews.
- No one can threaten alleged police officers for severe consequences, nor can pressure him to make certain proto-type statements, nor should they be incentivised for rewards of any kind in exchange for making such testimony.
- The alleged police officers should be given the complete chance of personal hearing regarding the disposition of such proceedings with complete access to evidence produced against them.
- No alleged police officers are punished just for the sake of setting an example for creating deterrence for maintaining the general discipline of the force on whimsical and personal grounds, nor should their misdeeds be condoned on the grounds of maintaining the morale of the force.
- The information and evidence that the alleged police officer provides written or oral forms that should be recorded and documented and placed in their files with the statement of allegations or any adverse information against them.

- The alleged police officers should not be subject to retaliation to exercise these rights, as guaranteed under the law.
- Police officers should not be criminally charged for functional performance and departmental actions. If police officers commit mistakes in carrying out their lawful duties and mandated functions such as policing, investigations, and counterterrorism, they should not be booked in criminal cases.

All the violations are commonplace in Pakistan, so legislative measures must discourage such outdated practices.

11.6. Capacity-building for Professional Specialism

The developments in policing scholarship and international practices have globally acknowledged and testified that policing is a specialist field (Craig 2011). Professional specialism in police alludes to practical ethics, individual qualities, professional skills, and the typical environment in which the police function in society (Westmarland & Conway 2020). The specialist nature of policing professionalism demands view policing as a skilled and expert profession that requires the police officer to acquire specialised skills, knowledge, and education to discharge his lawful duties in a befitting way (College of Policing UK 2020). Like doctors, pilots, engineers, and other specialised professions, police are not fit for non-specialists or generalists as they need to master a certain level of science, skill, toolkit, strategy, and the art of gut knowledge or common sense (Ibid).

Police in Pakistan were under criticism for recent high-profile shootings in Sahiwal and model town Lahore a few years ago, and technological innovations are taking place in safe city projects and legal landscape countrywide. Police organisations need 'highly educated police officers equipped with certified skills and multitasking capabilities' (Braga and Winship 2006). Now we need leaders who can go beyond traditional police academy training and who can advance police professionalism at all levels through innovation and creativity with substantial knowledge of socio-cultural and technological impacts on highly complex and diverse societies of the 21st century (Caless 2011).

The last few years in Pakistan have been marked with countrywide violent mass protestations and demonstrations (Dharnas), which paralysed the entire nation. Islamabad, the capital city of Pakistan, has remained the centre of demonstration activity (D Chowk and Faizabad Chowk) since 2014, following many other similar demonstrations that continue even in 2021, for example, recent October-November TLP massive precessions. These demonstrations, with many other things, exposed the strategic weaknesses of the police to handle mass riots. It also raised many questions about the professional wisdom and sensibility of the police to exercise discretion and use force. The rioters unleashed the reign of terror on innocent citizens by killing, burning, injuring, blocking, and vandalising everything that one way or the other came in their way. Protesters did not spare police and attacked, injured, and killed many police officers who tried to stop them. This vandalism of protesters and police helplessness, inability and hesitation to use necessary force failed police to handle protesters (Maguire et al., 2020). This poor state of policing affairs frustrated the people who were caught in the crossfire or watching all this on conventional and social media (Gabol 2021).

Second, the rise in violent acts of terrorism during the last decade brought home that police professionally stand at the lowest ebb to prevent terrorism incidents and ensure quality investigations in terrorism cases. As a result, the conviction rate in terrorism cases is 3 per cent, which is significantly lower (PRCR, 2019). Third, the police also failed to prevent human rights crimes against vulnerable groups such as women, children, the elderly, the poor, and minorities. Police's inability to deliver brought a bad name to the police in Pakistan. Many saner circles referred to the police as the most inefficient and unprofessional force, lacking professional integrity and specialism (ibid). Lastly, the rise in extra-judicial killings, custodial torture, and illegal detentions send clear signals to all stakeholders that police are a source of crime and lawlessness. Hence, the police lack specialist skills and toolkits to deal with crime and violence in society.

The colonial and abusive police exercised coercive authority without law, professional rationality, and human sensitivity, developing a bleak scenario. Now the mode of police authority stands transformed into public service through well-articulated reform to raise them to higher levels of professional integrity and law enforcement ethics (Hunt 2007). The police can cultivate public trust only through professionalism, integrity, and specialism by acquiring advanced education in policing (Webb et al., 2020). Police education is, unfortunately, an academic and policy wasteland in Pakistan. Research on policing reveals that police integrity means that the police are functioning within their legal authority under the rule of law, established police procedural practices, and in a fair manner consistent with what community expects' (Katz & Huff 2020). The U.S. The Department of Justice defines police integrity as "resistance against temptations for abusing authority, rights and privileges that the police officers uniquely enjoy in their profession due to their power positions within the society' (Ferguson 2017).

By J.J. Baloch (2022)

Nothing can match advanced police education in professional ethics and specialist skills in this connection. Some specific policing roles, such as carrying out quality investigations, would reduce crime through more imaginative use of science, technology, strategy, resources, and engaging communities. These measures help build trust and deliver public services (Lobnikar et al., 2021) to the people by ensuring easy accessibility and rapid response to those who need help (Joyce 2011). Several countries in the world, including the USA, UK, Japan, China, Australia, Canada, and many others, are investing in police education and criminal justice research to make their societies safer and peaceful because one of the core jobs of the state is peacekeeping in society (Lobnikar et al., 2021). The postmodern era is characterised by blurring borders, high connectivity, diversity, inclusivity, innovation, and globalisation, where statutory dilution has become commonplace (Lint 1999); indifference to building the capacity of police could be a great disaster for countries such as Pakistan.

President Obama's Special Task Force on the 21st Century Policing (2015) underscored the need for "education and training" for police officers as one of the five proposed steps for future policing. The report reads:

"The skills and knowledge required to deal with these issues like international terrorism effectively, evolving technologies, rising immigration, changing laws, new cultural mores and a growing mental health crisis, the police officers need a higher level of education as well as extensive and ongoing training in specific disciplines and professional areas."

On these grounds, the report proposes the establishment of quality law enforcement or criminal justice education at the national level (Final Report of President Obama's Task Force 2015). In addition, the report suggests that for motivating the serving police officers for higher education and rigorous research in policing for better community service, it should be linked with career promotion incentives. This method could go a long way in cultivating competitiveness in police ranks to outperform their best.

In Pakistan, we do not have criminal justice, counterterrorism, and policing studies universities, institutes, and departments to conduct research. Proposing policing policies and strategies, preparing our police officers for real-world challenges and situations (PRC 2019), and talking about outdated training modules available in our National Police Academy Islamabad are crucial components promoting police education. However, the academy neither has resources nor human resources and no strategic planning for developing a state-of-the-art curriculum for police education (NPA Website).

Reimagining Policing in Pakistan

Police officers should develop specialised skills sets. These specialised areas include leadership skills, crowd management procedures, crime scene management, investigative craft, interview and interrogation techniques, strategic communication adeptness, intelligence artistry, cyber expertise, high-wire documentarian instinct, and uniquely innovative crime palmistry (Jones 2009). To develop all these skills, we have to develop on-campus and online exams for certifications and accreditations to be mandatorily obtained by police officers. Specialism through accredited and certified qualifications should be linked to the career progression of police officers (PRCR 2019). This specialisation will improve the quality of policing and the services it promises to provide to the people (Ibid).

There is an urgent need for Policing and Peace University at the national level and its four campuses at all provincial headquarters to promote research and analysis of everything about policing as a science and art of peace. Research is crucial to cultivate professional specialism in police services in Pakistan. However, at the federal level, the resources of separate academies of FIA, IB, Anti-Narcotics, NAB, and FC should be integrated with the National Police Academy as state-of-the-art law enforcement and Policing University for the training of all commissioned cadres of the law enforcement agencies. However, these departmental academies currently train only the lower cadres of their respective departments. To this end, the National Police Academy could also be expanded into a full-fledged university on the patterns of the National Defence University of Pakistan, which is headed by the serving military General.

The National Law Enforcement and Policing University faculty should be permanent, representing all law enforcement specialisms and social scientists or subject specialists with the minimum qualification of Doctorate for this purpose. This qualification could prepare raw material to join the police and finish the half-finished senior police leadership for diversified police roles required for policing the 21st-century complexity, diversity, and innovation in society. In addition, the NPA should also establish a national research and policy centre for policing and law enforcement and publish studies, guidelines, and tutorials for policy, procedures, strategies, curriculum, and skills for specific specialist roles and issues to deal with crime. Thus, establishing such universities to award accreditations and certifications for different law enforcement fields in partnership with the Higher Education Commission of Pakistan and the Science and Technology Ministry of Pakistan is invincible. If we want to make a difference to the many lives and are serious about transforming coercive policing, creating new universities on peace and policing is the only option.

Tracy Meares (2017) suggests that curriculum of police training should be drafted anew and 'police officers' should be referred to as "peace officers" following procedural justice in dealing with the people, which is likely to improve the democratic legitimacy of police as the guardians of fundamental rights. He writes:

"Peace officers [may be] tasked with public safety and concern for individual rights... the social psychology of how people understand-- procedural justice—is one way to understand [police practices of dealing with the public] these practices and their effects, and to improve the relationship between law enforcement and the public. Procedural justice posits that people are likely to comply with the law, cooperate with authorities, and engage with them when treated fairly. The public tends to interpret how they are treated instead of focussing on the outcomes of authorities' decisions. Research suggests that the way police treat people impacts how people think of themselves, especially how they think of themselves as citizens. Positive changes in procedural justice may encourage more democratic participation in government" (Meares 2017)

11.7. Debureaucratising Police

Modern scholarship on policing maintains that the police are not bureaucrats. The bureaucratized policing stands between the bureaucracy and law enforcement and hence no longer remain police in the literal and practical sense. In Pakistan, bureaucratic resistance to police reform remains a significant obstacle in policing transformation (Suddle, 2012). In Part 2 of this book on the Policing developments, we discussed the reasons behind bureaucratic resistance to police reform.

Thomas E. Baker (1941) maintains that contrary to the police leadership,

"Bureaucracies are characterised by control and hierarchies that resist change. Autocratic leadership stifles initiative and creativity. This approach was accepted under the traditional model of policing but not under new community-oriented policing dispensations. Police leaders need flexibility in decision making. Now focus is not on command and control but participation, distribution, and inclusion. The strategic shift from management to leadership will not take place without creativity and innovation" (Baker 1941).

Bureaucratised Policing loses its soul of sociability and effectiveness as an agency of human rights (Huggins, 1997). The bureaucratic dispensation of policing disallows police to be the guardian of the people, tasked with serving and protecting the citizens' life, liberty, and property (Ibid). Somewhat its bureaucratized skin disqualifies the police to attain its strategic goals of working in open democratic environments of partnerships with other stakeholders in a meaningful way (Baker 1941). Therefore, transforming the police from coercive models to consensual models serving and protecting is a catalyst for de-bureaucratise police and policing in Pakistan.

There is a clear difference between law enforcement and bureaucrats armed with guns. If the police follow the whims of politicians, police officers become as dangerous as armed bureaucracy. On the contrary, if police judge themselves on the benchmark of law enforcement, they would be able to resist temptations and personal pursuits for money, nuisance, and power, but rather work well for better public service (Hutta, 2019). Unfortunately, in Pakistan, we have existed with the former dispensation of bureaucrats with guns who do not seem to be willing to disconnect with their guns, which signifies their brutal and unchecked authority.

In Pakistan, police have remained cloned with bureaucracy since their inception under British rule in India back in the early 19th century by working under the non-uniform bureaucratic controls of the Patwari system. Even after the 1861 Police Act, the police have been under the dual control of magistrates who have happened to be bureaucrats (Kolsky 2010). Even after Pakistan's independence in 1947, the bureaucracy continued to control the police. In many parts of Balochistan and KP, political agents, who are bureaucrats and have no training and aptitude for policing, command levies-an an untrained tribal force. The bureaucracy in Pakistan has constantly thwarted any reform effort to convert B-areas (for Levies policing jurisdictions) into A-areas (police jurisdictions). The bureaucratic desires for control and dominance have always kept police-dependent, subservient, under-resourced, and submissive lacking capacity, legitimacy, autonomy, and professionalism.

In addition, the entire recruitment and career planning process of police officers in Pakistan has been under the control of the bureaucracy, even in the case of senior police officers. Police leadership is recruited through competitive exams every year through the same procedure and process as the officers on the same ranks are recruited in other federal departments. The FPSC is overstaffed with bureaucrats, with hardly any police officer being its member. Police officers should go through specialist exams to join the police, and such examinations should be conducted by police officers (retired or serving). Service bias and prejudice dominate the bureaucracy in Pakistan.

The de-bureaucratisation of the police has become a universal trend. For example, the UK Home Office started "the Reducing Bureaucracy Programme" for policing in November 2012 with the aim of de-bureaucratizing policing. The programme has identified man core elements that serve as an obstacle to good policing due to the bureaucracy, which undermines policing. First, the bureaucracy in policing frustrates the police and the public because of excessive delays in simple routine work. Second, it observes that policing is more a job of taking common-sense risks (quick decision-making) than a bureaucracy going for unnecessary paperwork (Letter-Bazi). Third, separating police from bureaucracy will enhance their capacity to serve and protect communities more befittingly (UK Home Office, 2013).

By J.J. Baloch (2022)

Police departments worldwide are going to reduce police bureaucracy. Bureaucratic policing is an outmoded model that has lost relevance and effectiveness in post-modern and complex societies in the 21st century. The Superior Courts have declared "administrative magistracy unconstitutional through many rulings in Pakistan. However, the classical conservative mindsets in bureaucracy in Pakistan struggle to use its political clout to bring in the 29th constitutional amendment for the reintroduction of executive magistracy in Pakistan. The apparent motive behind this legislative move seems to dominate police and assume the office of the Justice of Peace, an administrative domain of the courts.

In one of the recent episodes of bureaucratic grab on policing, the old-timer royal political agents resisted the idea and process of the FATA merger. In response to the merger, the bureaucracy came up with the new Levies Act 2019 to retain the old system of policing there. This law defeats the very purpose of the merger, and the people will live in the same authoritarian system of colonialism under deputy commissioners who pretend to wield all coercive powers in one person or office. The other example includes the amended TORs for police reforms change in the very mission of the police from "administratively and operationally independent police" to the "police for the government", which contradict the government's claim of making police apolitical and autonomous. Moreover, all new police reform committees of the federal government appear to be crowded with PAS officers who continue to express their concerns about police going out of their control. In addition, the comprehensive PRC report (2019) on police reforms produced by retired and serving police officers to the Supreme Court of Pakistan still receive adequate attention due to persistent bureaucratic opposition.

The problem with bureaucracy in Pakistan is the legitimacy of their authority. The bureaucrats self-proclaim that they are both the community and the government. However, they are neither of them. They are not the government because, in democratic systems, elected representatives have a legitimate right to oversee the performance of all government departments as chief executives (President, PM, CM, Minister, Mayor etc.). Their secretaries have no such authority but to run and administer their offices for the elected leaders. Just being without a uniform does not make someone qualify for the community. Therefore, the desire to control and subjugate other departments under any excuse is not justified both legally and normatively.

11.7.1. Divorcing Police from Bureaucracy

For divorcing police from bureaucracy, it is essential to establish the National Police Management and Policy Commission/Secretariat comprising senior police officers for the human resource management of PSP officers with non-bureaucratic pay structures and pay scales such as armed forces and the judiciary. Second, for the recruitment and career planning of PSP officers, including their promotions and postings, this constitutional body must adopt newer strategic management and policy methods. The serving police officers who reach the senior-most grades of 22 or so should constitute the chairman (the senior-most serving police officer) and members in different areas (Directorates with DG as head of each). These new areas include human resource management, policy and strategy, police partnerships (national and international), innovation and reform, science and technology, education and training, media and publications, criminal justice coordination, counterterrorism intelligence collaboration, and police-public relationships.

In addition to the National Police Management Commission, the National Police Services Commission of Pakistan (NPSC) must recruit police officers of grade 14 and above. A similar commission should also be made to recruit constables and ASIs at the provincial level. Like Judges appoint judges, Army officials appoint army officers; only police officers can better appoint police officers. Third, a separate federal police Ministry on the lines of American Homeland Security should be established. Fourth, the National Police Bureau should be developed into a Peace and Policing Research Institute with professional PhDs to carry out research. Only retired police officers with PhDs should be reemployed for the purpose, and no serving police officer should be part of think tanks for police policy and research. The serving police officers should form part of the administration of the bureau.

Jan Barry, who is UK's Home Office Consultant on their "Reducing Bureaucracy in Policing", says meaningful words:

"In a world where trust is in short supply, bureaucratic demands are increasing, greater accountability is demanded, and few are willing to take the risk of not conforming to rigid rules, the fear and implications of getting it wrong are greater than the acceptable tolerances for getting it right. Therefore, to reduce bureaucracy, there is a need to rebuild trust, make rules more flexible, and encourage a proportionate, common-sense approach based on integrity, ethical standards, and professional judgment. Some forces are already adopting such an approach; the challenge is for others to follow. The need to remove and reduce bureaucracy is an ongoing process. While much can be done to tackle existing bureaucracy, one of the long-term goals must be to ensure that future policy and process changes do not add to the burden" (Berry 2009).

The police should be a separate specialised national service with its national police headquarters and Secretariat at Islamabad for the policy and management of all police organisations in Pakistan. This arrangement should be a constitutional body with the constitutional chairman, the senior-most PSP officer, with the separate Ministry of Homeland policing and Peace. Furthermore, the chairman of this national police body should organise research and policy by publishing, getting required legislation passed, when necessary, from the government and maintaining specialised force trained for specialist counterterrorism tasks countrywide. Such a qualified, well-trained, and well-paid force of around 20 thousand strong initially could be used to support provincial CTDs in their targeted operations.

There is a need for Pakistan's National Police Research Council (NPRC), which should be mandated to research all policing areas through highly qualified and hired experts. Furthermore, the national police research body should publish annual guidelines, broachers, SOPs, human resources and training strategies. Furthermore, it should develop strategic police planning and build a national crime record Database-NCRD liaison with the national policing university (NPU) NPA could be raised. In addition, a national implementation commissioner/coordinator-NIC should also be notified by the commission to implement policing policy, reform, and strategy.

11.8. Adoption of Technology in Policing

Post-modern societies demand shifting police officers' roles from traditional crime fighters to problem-solver and guardians of the people's fundamental rights (MacLean et al., 2021). Police cannot transform into postmodernity without adopting law enforcement technology (Katz and Maguire 2020). New police should be equipped with advanced technological knowledge, skills, and toolkits regarding technology applications in policing to make communities safer. Innovative gadgets have greatly empowered police and have made it an action-packed profession, and the police are sworn to serve and protect. Both federal and provincial law enforcement departments in Pakistan must appoint professional technology officers with minimum masters in technology. They develop a training curriculum and a strategy to enhance further the skills and expertise of the practitioners working in the field and acquire law enforcement technology that police departments have adopted in many countries (White et al., 2020). These debates around the law and technology point out that technology outruns the law. This fact has baffled many researchers, policymakers, legislators, and political stalwarts in almost all parts of the world, where people have learned to use cell phones and other gadgets (Vadhwa 2016). Many digital analysts believe a gap and tension exists between the laws and technology. Technology updates in seconds, and laws change over decades or centuries (Toyama, 2015).

Reimagining Policing in Pakistan

The security versus privacy debate caught curious minds when it boiled up to Apple vs. FBI Case-2016 in the US Supreme Court. The matter emerged when the FBI wanted to access the apple cell phone of a terrorist, and they used a third party to help break the code of the phone that they could not. For the FBI to do all this, there was no law to do so, as it violated the suspect's right to privacy under the 4th amendment of the US Constitution. Apple took this matter to court to protect the privacy of its user and won the case against the FBI. Toyama (2015) argues that societies and governments are not taking digital threats so seriously. Still, they should be mindful of what will happen when private actors have control of all people's data in this age of "Digital Wild West" (Toyama 2015).

The compelling issue emerging out of the legal battle between Apple and the FBI regarding what is ethical and not regarding encryption and decryption now transcends the borders reaching Europe, Asia, and other parts of the civilised world. For example, British lawmakers press tech companies hard to waive privacy protection for national security. At the same time, French political leaders envisage stricter anti-terrorism laws to criminalise the refusals of tech giants to provide them with encrypted information (Vadhwa 2016). A similar debate on privacy issues surfaced when the government of Pakistan passed the Pakistan Electronics Crime Act in 2016.

Vadhwa (2016) aptly observes that technology and law sometimes conflict because technology proliferates faster than the law. Often, lawmakers are under-informed, misinformed, and ill-informed about the different roles and functions of different technologies in different spheres of society. Similarly, info-tech giants either fail to understand or prefer to reap financial profits against the societal impacts of the products they introduce. What happens if hackers or terrorists attack Facebook or Apple head offices in Silicon Valley? Undoubtedly, they will change their opinions about privacy and confidentiality versus national security and public safety (Vadhwa 2016). To reach a consensus on strategic legislation to determine what is right or wrong, it will take contemporary societies decades (Vadhwa 2016).

Consequently, law enforcement faces a legal and ethical crisis to handle the 'digital Wild West. Governments and law enforcement departments feel sensitised to the legal limitations to regulate the use of technology in society and work on policing solutions to this exponential crisis of policing. Police use of technology increases police effectiveness and impacts civil liberties, thus linking police effectiveness with the public perceptions of police, write Neyroud and Disley (2008). Most police officers have watched a "fly-on-the-wall" (BBC Documentary 2017), highlighting insights and applications of science and technology in police operations and investigations. Advances in DNA technology, artificial intelligence, telemetry, forensics, the internet of things (IoT), social media, and artificial intelligence (AI) have played a pivotal role in transforming policing worldwide (Christopher, 2016). With the complexities of crime, liquidation of the statutory controls, blurring of borders due to global connectivity, our police departments in Pakistan must ensure that they have the right technology for tackling crime locally, nationally and internationally.

Police reform campaigns in Pakistan must include technological adoption as a strategic move to develop policing for 21st century Pakistan. In this connection, it is suggested that there are many technologies that police officers apply to the police, and each toolkit has its utility. I am not suggesting the forensic here because our police are already doing it, and it needs to be expanded only.

- First, remote control robotic cameras (RCRCs) with an electric motor and unique wheels are used by police at places or crime scenes where it is riskier for police officers to reach safely.
- Second, hand-held lasers (HHC) or spectroscopy devices are essential toolkits for crime scene investigators to determine the "chemical composition" of unknown substances very expeditiously and protect officers from exposure to harmful substances.
- Third, to save money and ensure the safety of police officers, many police officers worldwide use drone systems (UAS-drones) to search suspects, obtain information, and survey disaster areas. However, public privacy issues in democratic societies have made expanding the use of drones in policing slower.
- Fourth, to respond quickly to the firing spot, provide rapid assistance to the victim, and track the suspects, the Gunshot Detection System (GDS) or Shoot-Spotter with sensitive audio sensors help police officers to identify the accurate location of where a gun is fired.
- Fifth, Thermal Imaging refers to a "heat Picture" that enables the police officers to analyse the thermal view of the surrounding of the crime scene in the darkness, fog, snowfall, and dusty environment for locating suspects, tracing victims, conducting search and carrying out a rescue mission.
- Sixth, police tech industries have developed a GPS Vehicle Pursuit Dart, enabling police officers to chase suspect cars by shooting a "special GPS-equipped dart". This device would be sticking to a fleeing vehicle by which it could be traceable by the police without making any frantic pursuit causing public insecurity, inconvenience and panic.

- Seventh, automatic license plate recognition (APLR) linked with the integrated CCTV database can read vehicle number plates and generate system alerts if the vehicle is the suspicious or desired owner, process such numbers or letters against the established database.
- Eighth, body-worn cameras that have been adopted by many police departments globally are valuable tools for ensuring transparency in police work, accountability of officers, deterrence to police abuse of authority and an increase in public confidence or trust in the police.
- Last is one small piece of law enforcement called Tablet or i-Paid, which allows police officers excellent mobility, accessibility, and versatility. The tablet enables a police officer to perform office and field jobs simultaneously. The cops on duty can file accident or incident reports wirelessly and access critical crime information through a database, crime scene photos, and CCTV in real-time.

Technology improves police service delivery and increases efficiency. For example, the cameras by police officers have reduced 93 per cent of complaints against police officers. They have also served as a solid deterrent to police misuse of authority, thus unveiling the study conducted by the University of Cambridge. The report admits that the videos, audios, and photos recorded and taken on the spot are also used as evidence to sift the grain from the grass (White et al., 2020).

It is ironic that in Pakistan's policing demographics, more significant scepticism and resistance to change still exist. The report released by Accenture on 26 September 2018 on "Reimagining the Policing Workforce: Future Vision" warns that in the wake of digital threats, police forces worldwide need to reinvent 'workforce strategies, skills and structures'. Suppose the police want to stay valuable and relevant. In that case, they must explore the flexible workforce and well-defined partnerships with all stakeholders with strategic nuclei characterised by strong interpersonal, communication, and collaboration skills. Police leaders also need softer skills, including innovation, creativity, empathy, accessibility, and inclusivity (Accenture Report 2018).

Thus, in this connection, Pakistan should establish a National Centre for Law Enforcement Technology Evaluation (NCFLETE) without any delay. Such a technology evaluation centre must be tasked with researching and evaluating technologies and formulating sustainable strategic policing solutions in Pakistan. Second, Pakistan's efforts in geo-tagging essential and sensitive places, registering mobile Sims, and establishing fingerprints at NADRA are appreciable. Still, there is a dire need of establishing a DNA database by NADRA. NADRA must take blood samples from all those who apply for an identity card or B-form in the same way they take fingerprints samples. In this way, we could effectively identify criminals and victims.

11.9. Formulation of Media Strategy for Police

In modern liquid times (Bauman 2007), the voluminous data and the large body of knowledge keep multiplying and pose a potential challenge to law enforcement for positioning and presenting their stance effectively (Chan 2003). To achieve this, police forces in Pakistan, as everywhere globally, are bound to reinvent their content and conversation about crime, violence, radicalism, order, safety, security, and peace to stay relevant and current (Crump 2011). The police should keep the public posted about what they do to gain public confidence. Change-driven postmodern society can undermine the status quo of traditional fixed roles, structuralism, and determinism (Lyotard 1984). Therefore, the police should re-imagine media and communication strategies to instrumentalise change and facilitate continuity (Kratcoski, 2017).

Police organisations need to strategize their media policies institutionally and formally (Baloch, 2016). The reasons for urgency lie in the fact that there is no policing mechanism of formal media response in Pakistan, nor are there any research, policy, or standard operating procedures for handling media challenges. The media runs after crime information and news from the police (Avery and Graham 2013.) On the contrary, police leadership follows the "no comments" approach of hiding and blinding. This approach further allows disinformation and rumours to increase, making things worse and unmanageable.

In the 21st century, police-media relations are changing, diverse, complex, symbiotic, and temporary (Chermak & Weis 2002). The equation of police with media lacks permanency, unity, and simplicity (ibid). Both the police and media are inevitable for each other. The police need media cooperation to engage communities, sensitise them to criminal threats, and publicise police performance (Ibid). In contrast, the media needs police for quick information about incidents of crime and police work, most importantly, to obtain valued data to generate their content, headlines, and stories forever curious and knowledge-hungry public (Christopher, 2016).

However, police media relations are tense, tricky, and sometimes even conflicting, often fluctuating (McCarthy, 2019). The new media or social media emergence of citizen journalism and the redefinition of police roles and new professionalism of the police have led to newer stages and equations in police-media relations (Jewkes 2011). The newer equation is more formalised and challenging in nature and

239

scope. Social media has facilitated police to become the media in their own right, create content at will to counter-rumour, propaganda, and misinformation, and engage communities to deliver services and build images (Baloch 2016). Social media helps police publicise their excellent work and engage the community and other stakeholders. Proliferating social media and increasing police reality shows have given police more access to the general public, where police are readily available through networking on WhatsApp and Twitter for speedier responses to people needing police help or assistance (Baloch 2016). Thus, social media adoption by police has enabled police to strengthen public trust in their police, encourage transparency in procedures, and gain legitimacy as a public service based on the rule of law (ibid).

Social media has drastically changed how Pakistani millennials interact and converse in the recent decade. The new media has dramatically facilitated the participation of people in national conversations on critical national issues, including policing. It stands to reason that social media represents massive transformations in communications and social networking (Christopher 2016). Although social media can facilitate interaction between the police and the public, police and law enforcement agencies are slower in formulating their social media strategy in Pakistan (Baloch 2016). Moreover, the government of Pakistan has not yet formulated a national social media policy. It is aptly pointed out that "embedding social media into police communications is challenging, and the technology itself will not bring about the organizational and cultural changes needed to transform police-citizen engagement' (Bullock 2018). Police departments must have a full-fledged media department with focal and qualified media and information officers at national, provincial, and district levels to communicate well with journalists looking for information about crime incidents, registration of cases, progress investigations, and Police successes. In this way, the police need to create the most formal social media platforms for communication and conventional media. Social media policy for law enforcement could offer a procedurally sound strategy for police to market and publicise their excellent work and share their efforts with the public in an organised manner (Baloch, 2016).

Every police officer on duty or not directly linked to or linked with the matter under media query should not be allowed to talk to media, nor should media talk to unconcerned and unauthorised persons in the police. Only authorised media representatives or a notified team of the concerned police department should talk to the media in a more formalised, professional, calculated, rehearsed, and articulated way with a balanced content, firm tone, and composed posture (Baloch 2016). Such authorised officers should not be uniform police officers but hired professionals in strategic communications with separate cadres, pay packages, and career tracks appointed through public service commissions at federal and provincial levels. To this end, any modern police law in the making must incorporate a police media strategy containing detailed procedures and key performance indicators for police-media relation strategists. The media strategy should constitute a cardinal part of strategic policing to hammer out a dynamic, transparent, and effective ecosystem of partnerships to build peace in society.

11.10. Forging the Ecosystem of Partnerships in Policing

Pakistan needs to build a law enforcement ecosystem of partnerships to enhance police collaboration, coordination, legitimacy, transparency, and tech efficacy. Police should forge strategic partnerships with local stakeholders, community, law enforcement networks, intelligence agencies, paramilitary forces (rangers), military police, armed forces, judiciary, financial institutions, banks, economic, regulatory bodies, revenue and tax authorities(FBR), audit and accounts departments, media, academia, business forums, international law enforcement institutions such as UNO, Interpol, NCA, AFP, FBI, CARIN, Egmont, ICJ, ICIJ, Corrections, Europol, Frontex, biotech, and Info-Tech biotech giants such as Facebook, Google, Twitter, Instagram, Wiki, Microsoft, and Apple (Bowling and Sheptycki 2010). In Pakistan, there is a continuing need to hammer out partnerships with financial institutions and banks such as the State Bank of Pakistan and tax departments such as the Federal Board of Revenue and other private banks to share suspicious transactions and other financial intelligence. Such partnership networks are strategic for effectively dealing with financial crimes such as terrorist financing, money laundering, identifying or tracing illegal assets, human trafficking, and so on (Perriment 2019).

It is now inevitable and unproductive to delay the development of strategic partnerships with the Ministry of Science and Technology or provincial departments of technology. Punjab police partnered with Punjab technology agency to develop a strategic plan to adopt law enforcement technologies in every police department. Police in Pakistan should also make the most of the experience and knowledge regarding using the technology available with our partners internationally. The example of the Staffordshire County Police in the UK has cultivated policing solutions by appointing Boeing as their IT partner (Perriment 2019). Many international companies, especially Chinese and national companies, have considerable expertise in Pakistan's sustainable law enforcement technological solutions. Police leadership in liaison with some enlightened political leadership should convert the present policing challenge into a promising opportunity (Perrott & Trites, 2017). The postmodern

241

policing requirements, as discussed in detail in Chapter 10, make us realise that policing no longer remains a police exclusivity and forging strategic partnerships with public and private stakeholders is the only way forward for police in Pakistan.

11.11. Focusing Public Service Delivery in Policing

To ensure public service delivery to the utmost public satisfaction, it is essential to identify the services, processes, mechanics, mechanisms, and actors involved in police service delivery. The services that police deliver and should deliver theoretically and practically include registration of complaint (FIR), issuing certificates or verifications, investigations of the crime, prevention and detection of crime, assistance to crime victims, responding to emergencies, rescuing people in disasters, and so on. There are two types of contact that police and their populations establish. In one case, the people go to the police station for registration of crimes or issuance of some verification, while in the other case, police respond to the public call for help and intervention (Spohn & George, 2020). However, communication between the police and the public occurs directly and indirectly on the telephone and social media forums/websites. For example, when a victim or his nearest relative or friend in case of a murder incident approaches the police station for registration of the criminal case, police officers deal with the victim or his family in a particular manner that is either nicer or disappointing (Ibid).

Similarly, how police deal with the accused or suspects they arrest and detain at the police station is a crucial determinant of service delivery by the police (Ibid). The other aspect of police conduct transpires when police respond to a call of emergency and visit the place of incident or crime scene. How professional the police come out of their physical and verbal response (Hutta 2019). In this regard, how police deal with the public (both victims and suspect) at the police station and the crime scene and during emergency rescue is instrumental in understanding police attitude and working culture (Ibid).

In police-public interaction, the police are either in control mode or helping mode. The control mode is reflected through authoritarian police attitudes, which tend to be powerful government agents (Sheptycki 2010). The authoritarian attitude alludes to police refusals to accept public complaints, use of delaying tactics, show aggressiveness, application of abusive language, avoidance of responsibility, demands for the bribe, and employment of discrimination (Wallace et al., 2020). However, the helping mode of policing refers to cordiality, responsiveness, courtesy, friendliness, humanity, democracy, transparency, and integrity (Hutta 2019). Unfortunately, the police in Pakistan are notorious for their authoritarian conduct, which needs to be changed.

In this regard, nothing works well than changing the old blood of police stations and a police constabulary that makes direct contact with the people in all such situations (Sheptycki 2010). With all other problems facing our police in Pakistan, the dysfunctional nature of police stations and the low status of constables ranks high in all police inefficiency and poor performance. All reforms and reorganizations in the Pakistan police have been top-centric, lacking focus on improving many constabularies and police stations, which are the core components of the police that interact with the public (Maguire et al., 2020). Care for a constabulary's wellness needs to be taken at the required level (Ibid). Instead of spending on capacity building and improving working conditions, police leadership always prefers to create new parallel structures with newer nomenclatures that produce nothing except for increasing the cost of policing in Pakistan.

The creation of the new 24/7 services centres is not a bad thing, nor should it be discouraged or opposed. However, the creation of parallel structures fails to attend to institutional soundness and sustainability because of the improper use of meagre funds available to the police. For example, instead of improving police stations and the constabulary serving there, police departments have created new police units and new facilitation centres-variously coined as Khidmat Centres in Punjab (PP website) and police assistance lines in the KP (KPP website). Keeping in mind the cost of maintaining parallel structures of policing and neglecting one component at the altar of the other is not advisable for developing countries such as Pakistan, which face severe financial and budgetary issues. Therefore, building one structure and disbanding others should be the way forward.

Parallel police structures that serve the same purpose are arguably dispensations in maximal utilization. It would have had a more significant impact on public service delivery if the same funds' police stations and the low status of constabulary working there had been improved. Every police station could have been converted into police public service centres with all advanced technology and educated staff, enhancing the levels of the education of constables to graduation, as is the case in UK police departments (Perriment 2019). In the UK, every police chief has to join the police as a constable and then grow with specialism through a rigorous system of examinations and interviews at the specified time to attain specific certifications and accreditations (Ibid). The fittest officers outshine and go up through what they call fast tracks. This dispensation makes sense in policing. The police system, which focuses on constables and police stations, works well in public service delivery. The duplicate roles and parallel structures overlapping operationally and overcharging in financial terms are good for nothing other than mere experimentation. Thus, all facilitation centres of police in Pakistan should be merged in police stations having all state-of-the-art facilities to assist and help the public in a befitting way and utilise the police budget at best with measurable impacts. Second, constables' academic, professional, and social profiles need to be enhanced through elaborate and well-thought-out recruitment systems, promotions, postings, and handsome pay packages.

11.12. Conclusion

Policing in Pakistan undergoes an unprecedented crisis of legitimacy, integrity, technology, inclusivity, the rule of law, democracy, accountability, transparency, innovation, and professional specialism. This unprecedented crisis poses an existential threat to Pakistan's cultural, societal, and political norms and systems; hence, it has become street gossip. This study finds a range of gaps in organisational culture, operational mandate, police governance, infrastructure, budgets, human resource management, training strategies, unclear policing policy, missing strategic vision, outlived police law, and fragile ecosystem of partnerships. This study has tracked the simmering debate on policing, especially the reforming police, to balance Pakistan's state authority and civil liberty. Policing experts and stakeholders maintain that the conversation on policing needs to be rationalised by specific, measurable steps and physical interventions. The challenge of the 21st-century law enforcement crisis was birthed by the change management of the organisational culture of policing in terms of societal innovations and global cultural transformations during the post-modern era. The change crisis characterises the liquidation of state power and monopoly on political narratives. The dilution of state power has created a crisis of statehood which allows the growth of diverse forms of the multiple power structures of non-state actors and the forces of globalisation to encroach upon the state's sovereign domain.

This discourse also reveals that good policing is good until it serves the communities. It serves the communities only when we see our police are easily accessible to the people in trouble and only when our police respond quickly to the people needing help. Policing helps avoid further loss of property, life, and liberty. We need our police to cultivate will and capacity to accomplish the tasks through exemplary and new police professionalism based on the core values of integrity, meritocracy, autonomy, accountability, legitimacy, transparency, organisational justice, due process, national coherence, and community support. The community always supports the police when they find them responsive, responsible, helping, cooperative, friendly, impartial, and thoroughly professional who can deliver (McCarthy 2019). Service delivery is the core benchmark of the best performance of police, which further cultivates public trust and helps build a better public image of the police.

Chapter: 12

Problems & Prospects

Chapter Brief

This chapter identifies the reasons and rationale behind reimagining policing in Pakistan. It also identifies the problems in transforming police (Katz & Maguire 2020) in Pakistan (Suddle 2012). It underscores the need to realign the process of police reform, change, and innovation with postmodern strategic policing developments. It argues that reforms should address the ground realities of policing, which it has neglected [in Pakistan], and innovations in policing may be guided by independent research (Clark 2005). To reduce the cost of policing in times of budgetary cuts and deficits, it emphasises more innovative and more cost-effective ways (Weisburd & Braga 2006). Finding the importance of police training and education in building capacity and character, this study calls for the inculcation of professional skills and toolkits. Professional integrity and legitimized authority of police officers can help them handle the strategic challenges of expanding police mandates, proliferating crime, violence, vandalism, and the magnitude of risks that policing societies involve (Cordner 2021). Policing in Pakistan requires networked coherence in national security, public safety, counterterrorism, and maintenance of public order through strategic policing approaches and a viable ecosystem of partnerships among stakeholders (Lyons 2002). Strategic policing meets these requirements well for consolidating integrated policing systems at different levels and concludes the chapter.

12.1. Introduction

Why and how transforming police for the government into police for the people has become a significant goal and existential challenge for struggling democracy in Pakistan? This book has attempted to answer the preceding question. Pakistan's experience with problems in police reforms, reorganization, innovations, and identification of fundamental challenges and opportunities to transform policing in Pakistan, the book offers the prospect of dealing with the challenges of aligning police mandates with capacity, challenges with opportunities, changes in society with police reform, state authority with civil liberty, legal dictates with cultural expectations, authoritarian power with democratic strength, and so on. This study has explored the rationale behind why policing in Pakistan needs to be reimagined. The analysis method involves revisiting preceding chapters, which can help draw some takeaways. This chapter unfolds takeaways in terms of expanding the mandate and proliferating mission of the police (Weisburd & Braga 2006) in the wake of the rise of risk society characterised by violence, complexity, uncertainty, and anxiety (Beck 1992), obscenity, technology, connectivity, and virtuality (Toyama 2016). Takeaways also identify some daunting challenges facing police in postmodern settings and encompass ideas for the reformers (Gravelle & Rogers 2014) to make most of the available opportunities for police reform and innovation in Pakistan.

12.2. Problems and Prospects

Conversation on reimagining policing in Pakistan reveals that the 21st century witnessed much faster and more drastic changes in policing and police organisations (Gravelle & Rogers 2014). The 9/11 revolution in thinking about managing violent crime led to a new discourse on law enforcement, criminal justice, and governance (Junkerman & Masakazu 2005). The expansion of police mandates has underscored the need to review and rethink policing in Pakistan in the context of the innovations that have taken place worldwide. Ostensibly, the Police Order 2002 in Pakistan envisaged a paradigmatic revolution in policing, corroborating the developments in contemporary policing, but, unfortunately, it could not be implemented (Abbas 2012). Even if fully implemented, PO-2002 is limited in scope to address postmodern challenges and requires thorough revisions. Police reforms in Pakistan have not been carried out in congruence with security and criminal justice sector reforms. Therefore, Pakistan's police reform projects remained more or less in discussions and on papers with only marginal success in the case of KPPA 2017 and Punjab police experiences with science and technology. However, policing in Pakistan has introduced new models such as the National Highways and Motorway Police. In light of these developments (Part II of this book), policing in Pakistan needs to be reimagined.

Although not implemented, this study found that, though not implemented, the Police Order 2002 incorporated the principles of modern, responsible, responsive, people-centric, community-oriented, specialized, and accountable policing under legitimate democratic and institutional controls (Suddle 2015). The failure in the widespread implementation of PO-2002 in Pakistan produced no significant outcomes as it promised (Abbass 2012). In its character, PO-2002 was the first revolutionary police order with strong democratic roots in Pakistan's legal landscape after the 1861 police dispensations (Ibid).

This book chapters on 'police reforms and reorganisations' have noted that the Police Order-2002 incorporated new features of the postmodern requirements of policing. First, the proposed law tried to translate many of the best practices from policing worldwide into new police dispensations in

247

Pakistan (using evidence from Britain, America, Canada, Japan, and others). Second, it addressed the fundamental concerns of the police and the people within a democratic society (Petzschmann's 2010 report 'Pakistan's Police Between Centralization and Devolution). Third, PO-2002 expanded the primary mission of the police from crime management to public safety and protection of the fundamental human rights of citizens as the primary duty of a police officer. Fourth, it also stood clear and categorical against any political interference in policing. Fourth, it promised to bolster civilian democratic oversight by making the police answerable to institutions built on public mandates rather than the bureaucratic and authoritarian mechanisms of the state. Fifth, Police Order 2002 emphasised specialisation in the police department regarding investigation, security, law and order, and public safety by doing away with the traditional paramilitary model based on a generalisation of functions. Fifth, it focused on functional divisions with administrative autonomy in police policy and practice. Finally, PO-2002 established a clear link between career growth and service delivery or a substantial nexus between professionalism and performance. Therefore, the practical potential of PO-2002 has made it a central point of discussion on transforming police in Pakistan.

The proposed transformation of police organisation towards autonomy, efficiency, and public service fell in the discomfort zone of many feudalistic and authoritarian power circles. As a result, the status quo advocates began to pick holes in new police formations and succeeded in reversing it and reviving the colonial framework of 1861. Hassan Abbass (2012) maintains that the Police Order 2002 was an institutional and constructive effort towards police autonomy, and he summarised the following paragraph as to why Police Order 2002 failed to sustain.

"The fact that [PO-2002] the Order failed as a result of politicians seeking to consolidate their influence demonstrates how the lack of political will remains one of the crucial obstacles to reform. Of course, this problem extends to the police leadership, which has, by and large, struggled to exhibit the qualities needed to push reform forward. However, not every shortcoming of the police is attributable to a lack of political will. Internal professionalism and competence can enhance the capacity of police to defy unlawful instructions coming from any powerful institution or individual" (Abbass, 2012).

However, as we have recorded in Chapter 5 on police reorganisations, the early amendments of 2004 and 2006 disfigured the original shape of the police order. These amendments changed the appointment procedure of provincial police officers (the Inspector General) and their powers to appoint district police officers. It also altered the composition of public safety commissions at all three levels (district, provincial, and federal) by reducing the strength of independent members and increasing the number of political appointees in PSCs (see Chapter 05 of this book).

By J.J. Baloch (2022)

This discourse has also confirmed that, in recent years, the debate around police reforms has gained momentum in Pakistan. In May 2018, the former Chief Justice of Pakistan's Supreme Court, Mr Justice Saqib Nisar, constituted the police reform committee (PRC-2018) under the stewardship of the former Inspector General of Police, Afzal Ali Shigri. The PRC's subsequent report (2019) on police reforms favoured the revival of the 2002 Police Order in its original tone. In essence, it advocated for a model police law that prioritised police accountability, improvements in the quality of investigations, alternative dispute resolutions, and urban policing models for big cities such as Karachi, Lahore, Peshawar, Quetta, and others. In addition, the PRC-2018 mandate suggests legislative reforms on policing terrorism and public service delivery by the police.

In addition to these efforts, previous decisions by superior courts have tried to deal with complex procedures around the appointment and removal of police chiefs, especially in the wake of legal debates on the issue of the constitutionality of police. Whether policing is a federal or provincial subject has been taken up by the Association of Former Inspectors General of Police (AFIGP) during early 2017-18. In January 2019, the Supreme Court of Pakistan passed a short order declaring that policing is a "concurrent subject" and not a provincial domain exclusively. The Supreme Court ordered the provinces to bring their provincial police laws congruent with the Police Order 2002. The Sindh government has also developed a new Police Order 2019, which offers a police structure mixing Police Act 1861 and PO-2002, resulting in perpetual confusion.

The ruling party, Pakistan Tehreek-e-Insaaf, also placed police reform on top of their electoral agenda during the 2018 general elections. Shortly after coming to power in 2018, the PTI announced the constitution of the police reform commission under the stewardship of the former Inspector General of Police KP, the late Nasir Khan Durrani. However, Durrani resigned due to differences with the government over how the latter was posting and transferring provincial police officers, revealing flaws in approaches to reform the policing system in Pakistan (Dawn, Feb.4, 2019). The Punjab Police Reform Committee was subsequently dissolved. Instead, the federal government constituted a new Federal Police Reform Committee led by the bureaucracy that scripted the purpose of police reforms to envisage "the police-for-the-government" (Dawn, Feb.4, 2019) instead of making it the police-for-the-people. However, PO 2002 provided for administrative and financial autonomy of police. The change in the police reform paradigm doomed Pakistan's agenda of transforming the police (Dawn, Feb 4, 2019). These developments reveal that although there has been an increased momentum for reforming the police in Pakistan, these reforms are still to be implemented and taken seriously. Therefore, the prevailing state of the policing crisis calls for reimagining policing in Pakistan.

Discussions in parts two and three of this book reveal that policing in Pakistan reflects fragmented structures and disparate operational networks that hardly seem well organized and smartly cohesive except in mandate or mission. The policing mandate remains the same and includes crime management, maintenance of law and order, counterterrorism, provision of services, emergency response, rescue, security, and protection (Bowling &Sheptycki 2010). However, policing organisations and agencies differ in their capacities to fulfil their responsibilities, perform their duties, and achieve their missions (ibid). The gaps in service delivery by police seem perspicuous. Thus, policing landscape shows weak institutional links between provincial police organisations over the issue of diverse legal frameworks and orders of the police departments in Pakistan (PRC 2019).

Fragmentation in the legal structures of police formations poses operational and institutional challenges (Sung, 2001). Fragmentation in police organisations undermines police policing capacity to control crime and disturb networked coherence in police functioning (Lacy 2020). This proposition is true for policing in Pakistan. The fragmented institutional landscape offers a well-timed opportunity for many vested interest groups to keep the police paralysed and under control by resisting change, innovation, and reform in policing (Suddle 2012). The previous chapters in this book record police governance and reform politics to confirm this contention (refer to Chapter 09 on police governance). Indeed, police departments have hosted many specialist stakeholders such as technology experts, forensic scientists, law scholars, and risk analysts to become part of the support base of core policing functions in the age of big data and surveillance (Bain 2016). However, unlike CPLC and other non-police forums in Pakistan, these new components remain limited to their exclusive domain of expertise without making any useless efforts to take control of the police functions by creating duplicate structures. Thus, fragmentation combined with plural policing trends stands in the way of police transformation (Jones & Newburn 2002) in Pakistan to attain functional soundness and institutional coherence.

Insights into this discourse on reimagining policing in Pakistan have also unearthed that policing no longer remains police or state exclusivity not because of any conspiracy or malafide but because of the postmodern conditions of the development in human societies and civilisations (Katz & Maguire 2020). The introductory chapter in this book has recorded that police and policing are two different things: the former alludes to uniformed sworn officers tasked with carrying out mandated responsibilities in a well-laid-out procedure by rules, while the latter refers to a function of controlling disorder, crime, and violence in best suitable ways (Reiner 1992). Policing is an age-old social institution of socialisation that starts with a mother who tries to teach her newborn baby about her culture and language (Baloch 2019 and 2016). On the contrary, police as an organised institution is the 19th-century product (Clockars 1985). However, since the formal institution of police has emerged, police have claimed to be their core function (Cooper 2011). Now, diverse conditions, times, and changed environs have diversified both police and policing. Many stakeholders from various backgrounds, including the community, public sector, and private companies, play a cardinal role in policing (Jones and Newburn 2006).

Police in Pakistan is slow and hesitant to adopt this emergent narrative of inclusive, networked, and strategic partnerships in policing. Here, the police seem to have xenophobia from outside police organisations (Braga & Winship, 2006). This xenophobic approach to the police is strong resistance to police transformation from a colonial model to a community-oriented service (Kratcoski, 2017). Likewise, the police working culture in Pakistan has been an inward-looking and stand-alone institution that always tries to solve their problems in isolation (Caless 2011). However, the attitudes and perspectives of the new demographics of millennials (Ipsos, 2018) in police are remarkably positive in accepting change and reform. In addition, it is evident from the experience that gender streamlining of new police demographics could help in oiling the turbulent movements of policing transformation in Pakistan. Similarly, the rise of new demographics at top leadership levels will add new dynamism (Kauppi & Madsen 2013) to police professionalism. It is new policing mechanics inviting change, reform, and innovation through inclusive and strategic approaches that are the need of the hour (Perrott & Trites 2017).

Noticeably, the content on policing reorganizations and innovations in Pakistan, as produced in Chapters 5 and 6, respectively, transpires the politics of policing (Deflem 2016). The developments refer to the external political environment in which the police reforms and policing developments have been set, which is also a substantial obstacle in transforming policing to a postmodern perspective (Katz & Maguire, 2020). As already discussed in detail, the postmodern condition of human societies aligns well with strategic policing approaches because strategic policing imbibes and encourages an integrated ecosystem of partnerships (Sweetman 1999). However, traditionally, policing in Pakistan, as inherited from the British colonial regime in India, has remained the government's coercive arm (Suddle 2012). As a result, community-oriented and problem-solving approaches in policing have not been developed in Pakistan. Therefore, no well-timed spadework for transforming police to postmodern strategic dispensation has been done in Pakistan; police reformers should address this substantial impediment to transforming police.

The perpetuating crisis of statehood caused by slow constitutional developments and democratic setbacks has not allowed the transfer of power to the people in Pakistan (McGrath, 1996). Many analysts believe that Pakistan gained independence to ensure civil liberties and fundamental freedoms of the people, but the democratic process in Pakistan has been inconsistent. Thus, the independence of governments- dominated by elitist heredity- from colonial power falls short of being defined as a nation's freedom (Ayaz 2013). Consequently, political instability and democratic deficit products continue to wash away the chances of civil, political, social, economic, and cultural progress in Pakistan (Ibid). To find a way forward for policing transformation towards police-for-the-people, the people of Pakistan must attain their sovereignty, which remains hijacked by actors other than the people in Pakistan (McGrath, 1996). As a pre-condition, only sovereign people can claim democratic police oversight, inclusive policing, and police for the people (Bayley, 2006, 1998).

Besides this, continuous political tossing between paralysed civilian democracies and strong military dictatorships has caused Pakistan to develop a 'hybrid state system'. In the hybrid state, the governments are "as an artificially bolstered civilian vessel of the military-establishment, propped up so that the latter can sustain its political influence within a semblance of democracy and without the controversial complexities of direct intervention" (Paracha 2020). The hybrid regimes refer to dual systems of power which are characterised by democratic and authoritarian conflicts, civil and military tensions, secular and religious divide, federal and provincial tussles, rich and poor struggle, sectarian and ethnic violence, white and black economies', legal and cultural dilemmas, and state and non-state authoritative claims. This divide and fragmentation signify postmodern conditions (Jordan & Weedon, 1995). Interestingly, the normative outcomes of hybrid structures and narratives are not productive and conclusive enough to end the crisis of statehood in Pakistan (Taqi, 2020) and (Chaudhry 2021). The policing transformation in Pakistan will remain a mirage until the hybrid nature of our statehood is fixed with coherence and common interests through the rule of law because policing transformation is subject to rethinking governance and statehood in Pakistan on democratic lines (Hussain 2019).

12.3. Rationale Behind Reimagining Policing

Parts 1 and 2 in this book on police developments, challenges, and opportunities find that old-fashioned policing in Pakistan needs to be revisited in the context of the developments in the different realms of society, governance, criminal justice, policing, and technology. Additionally, this study found a range of factors that undermine police legitimacy in Pakistan. Identified factors call for reimagining policing in Pakistan and offer an understanding of the policing crisis in Pakistan.

This conversation reveals that the police in Pakistan have been facing a serious crisis of public trust deficits (Shigri 2012). Citizens in Pakistan essentially believe that the police are incapable of combating crime, violence, disorder, and terrorism. Public dissatisfaction with service delivery is evident in Pakistan (Shigri, 2018). The primary police task of protecting citizens' lives, property, and liberty remains unaccomplished and clouded with frowsy public doubts (Khosa 2018). The public perception is that instead of being the source of the solution, the police are 'part of the problems' (Vitale 2017) of crime, corruption, violence, vandalism, extortion, torture, and extra-judicial killings. However, this is not a truth-packed perception and needs thorough introspection, for which all possibilities of wilder imaginations have to be applied to find out the way forward.

The foremost reason is the problem of the police's capacity to deliver and perform to a minimum satisfaction of the people. The deteriorating recruitment and evaluation criteria and the poor educational and training standards of the police have caused police inefficiency (Nekokara 2016). In Pakistan, almost all police training institutions, including the National Police Academy, still follow outdated modules that have lost their relevance and effectiveness in the fast-changing environment in which the police operate (AFIGP 2017). Entire training and instructional materials require sophistication and postmodernisation. The failure of the police to deliver better public service and meet public expectations renders it a liability (Accenture, 2019). Police in Pakistan have limited capacity to deliver service to the people's satisfaction. Therefore, following the steps recommended in Chapter 11 on Policing Reimagined, police should build their capacity through reform and innovation.

Notably, the police officer's loss of pride and sense of belonging to the police institution dilutes police morale. The feeling of inspiration that the congenial working environment and the ownership of police by their leadership ought to cultivate in their ranks has lost its 'oomph' (Khosa 2016). The poor working environments and the psychological impact cause the negative public image of the police.

Reimagining Policing in Pakistan

Similarly, the distance of police leadership and the public at large from the constabulary result in chronic inefficiency of police to deliver. As a result, the general environment of mistrust between other security institutions, the criminal justice system, and the police collectively constitute the fundamental reason for the police to lose their professional competence (Baloch 2016) and their sense of self-legitimacy (Brodeur 2011). Police officers' loss of pride in policing signifies reimagining policing in Pakistan to revive integrity, accountability, democracy, and transparency through the adoption of 'new police professionalism' (Stone & Travis 2011).

Furthermore, corruption at all levels in the police in Pakistan has corroded the idea of policing as the provision of public services (Khalid 2017). Police are different from other state departments because of their exposure to and interaction with the public (Reiner 2000). Almost all social class categories interact with the police for various reasons (Bowling and Sheptycki 2010). In this way, ordinary people know more about police corruption than other departments. People are frequently victims or participants in institutional malpractices (Khalid 2017). The internal and external police accountability systems, as discussed in Chapter 09 of this book on police governance, lack transparency, objectivity, democracy, strategic management, and merit. Thus, the persisting bribe-taking culture influences how people perceive police (Shigri 2012). Thus, the corruption factor has a dead-locked police transformation in Pakistan.

Outdated Police laws have lost their relevance and currency while policing in Pakistan is still grounded in the 1861 Police Act, a colonial relic (Baloch 2019). Pakistani society, like others, has transformed from a rural agrarian to an urbanized, in which over 50% of the population lives in big cities with enhanced literacy rates (Census-2017). Gender streamlining, democratic tendencies, liberal economy, digital algorithm, demographic displacements, youth demographics, religious intolerance, political militancy, and mob vandalism (Dharnas) have redefined social change in Pakistan (Baloch 2019). These changes in Pakistan's social structure reiterate the need for change and reform in police laws, a kind of reform that demands reviewing policing laws, regulations, procedures, practices, and organisational frameworks. This study recommends eleven strategic steps in Chapter 11 to transform policing in Pakistan on democratic and postmodern lines.

Similarly, the authoritarian and coercive organisational culture of policing continues to prevail and is one of the core reasons for its malaise. There is little space for consultation, discussion, or deliberation within the hierarchy within such an organisational culture. However, the central argument of Katz and Maguire (eds.2010) rests on the adoption of technology, strategic partnerships, policing by consent, research, evidence-based decision-making, reducing the use of force, efficient service delivery, procedural justice, protection of human rights, due process, and organizational justice. Sutton (2012) also identified some of these steps as the primary benchmarks of strategic police leadership and effective organizational communication. Unfortunately, in the absence of strategic leadership and organizational communication, the 'boss is always right' narrative prevails, resulting in police bosses running official affairs based on their interests and perspectives. Police in Pakistan could claim no exemption from this authoritarian organizational environment, which this study has stipulated as one of the leading impediments to transforming the police in Pakistan.

Police legitimacy is crucial in policing, and Pakistan's coercive police regime compromises it (Cockcroft, 2019). To address deep-laid malpractices, policing needs to be reimagined to make it a community-oriented and forward-looking public service, wherein the police are required to protect, not violate, the fundamental rights of the people (Palmiotto 2001). In this regard, this study proposes the incorporation of changing police officers' traditional role of warriors to guardians of fundamental rights under the police-for-the-people paradigm (MacLean et al., 2021).

Performance evaluation standards of the police need to be revisited as well. The performance evaluation standards of the police in Pakistan are subjective, vague, and discriminatory (Nekokara, 2016). There is a need to introduce a new empirical method of evaluation and assessment to improve police performance. People who outperform and sacrifice their lives in the line of duty are frequently sidelined and neglected by police leadership and the government alike because of the prevailing culture of nepotism and favouritism in Pakistani society (Baloch 2019). However, in the postmodern dispensations of governance and management (McLaughlin & Murji 1999), police organisations prioritise performance, service delivery, equal opportunities, accountability, and transparency, which are the essential cornerstones of new police professionalism (Travis and Stone 2011). New police professionalism is crucial for ensuring good police work, and good police officers are rewarded without distinction. Unfortunately, in this admirable arena, policing in Pakistan lags far behind.

Additionally, policing has been a deeply politicised profession in Pakistan, which compromises the impartiality and objectivity of police officers and leaders. Nekokara (2016) believes that policing can never be neutral and that political leadership at the provincial level decides what kind of leadership, resources, and oversight mechanisms are available (Reiner 2010) to provincial police departments in Pakistan. However, tracing the origins of politicisation in police, Babakhel (2019) alludes to the establishment of the "Special Branch" in colonial Calcutta (India) by Sir Charles Tegart during the 1870s as the intelligence wing of the police to monitor the political activity of local nationalist leaders and followers in British India. It is one of the earliest examples of policing in the subcontinent being instrumentalised to control dissent, opposition, and political resistance (Ibid). The police were further empowered under the Criminal Tribes Act of 1871 to control and subjugate the 'natives' (Babakhel 2019). In the post-independence period, this coercive system failed to evolve and reform. Police Order 2002 provided for the depoliticisation of police in its preamble, but 2004-6 amendments in PO 2002 doomed this objective. Police veterans, including Suddle (2015) and Shigri (2012), consider the bureaucratic and political leg-pulling of police reformers as the leading factor in the colossal and continued politicisation of policing.

Moreover, the police in Pakistan lack the appropriate counterterrorism capacity to combat religious militancy (ICGR-271, 2015). Pakistan has been central to the global war on terrorism for almost two decades (Yusuf, 2014). This multilayered and multi-actor phenomenon places the police and other law enforcement agencies on the frontlines, with thousands of officials falling victims to terrorist attacks since 2001 (ICGR-271, 2015). The first counterterrorism policy, the National Action Plan, was designed in 2014, but it is limited to and based on vague doctrine (see Chapter 07 of this book). Pakistan has yet to draft, adopt, and implement a coherent and comprehensive counterterrorism policy that takes on board different strategic stakeholders, including civil society and state institutions. In the absence of such comprehensive policies, the police will remain unable to counter religious militancy and terrorism (Newman & Clarke, 2008) at home.

No less critical remains the excessive dependency of the Pakistani police on outmoded crime investigation and policing methodologies. The volume and speed of reform, change, and police innovation clearly shows that police in Pakistan still depend on manual and traditional methods of crime investigations, security management, counterterrorism, and counter-extremism. Despite investments in technology and social media initiatives, the police are yet to learn how best to utilise and operationalise these tools (Baloch 2016). Moreover, there is a lack of policy guidelines on how to use law enforcement technology to prevent or detect crime and protect human rights. However, social media has emerged as a new battleground (Jehangir 2019) or what Goodman-2015 describes as fifth and new war zones after traditional land, air, sea, and space for normative conflicts (Christopher 2016) in Pakistan. In the last decade, people in Pakistan have embraced technology and new media, but our government and police are yet to adopt this new change (Jahangir 2019).

By J.J. Baloch (2022)

Technology deficit in policing is one of the leading impediments to transforming policing to consider the demands and requirements of the people (Baloch 2016).

Above all, police reforms in Pakistan need to merge into criminal justice (ICGR-160, 2008) and security sector reforms because police reforms would not produce desired outcomes unless both sectors are reformed (Sedra 2017). Policing is one of the criminal justice and security sectors (ICGR-196, 2010). Improvements in police work and performance will remain meaningless unless similar level reforms are introduced in prosecution, adjudication, and correction components of criminal justice (PRC 2019) and other law enforcement networks. The low conviction rates in the heinous crime, especially terrorism and human rights violations, are always referred to as poor police investigations (ICGR-196, 2010) and lack detailed improvements in counterterrorism mechanisms. However, it is not only poor police investigations but also the performance of prosecution, the interest of complainants and their witnesses, and the performance of trial courts do matter in the overall efficiency of the criminal justice system. Similarly, the issues of national security, terrorism, extremism, and violence in society put tremendous pressure on governments and legislatures to grant more pervasive and absolute powers to their police forces. Postmodern research contextualises postmodern policing on the grounds of the asymmetrical threats of security and terrorism (McLaughlin & Murji 1999), not only based on conventional criminal law enforcement (Bowling and Sheptycki 2010).

In contemporary Pakistani society, crimes including drugs, murders, rapes, kidnappings, terrorism, mob violence, and cybercrimes are at an all-time high. Therefore, the chain of command in the police should receive plenty of care and respect. Proper action demands clear and concise orders from the chain of command. Heightened awareness of digital era crimes has substantially developed in the last few decades, and it has modified law-enforcement methods, procedures, strategies, and policies (Newman & Clarke 2008). Crucial in this change remains the thin chain of command, which creates ambiguity for police regarding what to do and not to do in certain policing circumstances. To deal with terrorism (LaFree, 2012) and mob violence situations effectively (Maguire et al., 2020), police reforms should include matters of the chain of command.

Finally, policing policies and research are neglected. For example, Nekokara (2017) links the poor performance of police in terms of service delivery and citizen satisfaction with their poor training, which is a direct result of the lack of research on how to redesign training for different ranks within the police (Millie & Das 2008). There is also a shortage of research on the patterns and trends in crime. Moreover, no empirical study has been conducted on police policy and policing strategies that could suit Pakistan's socio-political environments for police to produce better results. What works is to redesign police training (Bayley 1998) in the light of postmodern research (McLaughlin & Murji 1999) and developments in human rights literature (Siddiki and Detho 2014).

Therefore, these and many other problems and challenges of similar nature have necessitated reimagining policing in Pakistan. To scrutinise the mandate, capacity, performance, and impacts of policing within the context of society at this particular point of time and the particular evolutionary stage of cultural development in Pakistan is a crucial step (Chaudhry, 1990). Reimagining policing considers policing a cultural phenomenon. Unfortunately, the police in Pakistan remain aligned with the 19th and the 20th-century modernist ideas of structuralism, determinism, and one-size-fits-all solutions, which, according to Guild and Geyer (2008), have lost their validity and viability in contemporary times, which indicates the following developments and transformation in policing (White & Gill, 2013).

12.4. The Way forward

The rediscovery of the role of policing in postmodern societies is possible in the new mission and mandate of the police (Weisburd & Braga, 2006). The primary mandate or mission of the police has expanded in a meaningful way, from crowd control and crime management to public safety, national security, and counterterrorism (Ibid). In Pakistan, the mission has changed, but the institutional mechanism with a legal mandate to realise the aims and objectives for setting standards is missing (PRCR 2019). This study stipulates that legged-far-behind police formations in Pakistan call for penning down a narrative equal to the magnitude of change and challenge. Pakistan can hardly achieve its political stability, social cohesion, sectarian or ethnic harmony, and economic security without transforming its police. Law enforcement in Pakistan is marred by the lack of resources, insufficient technological equipment, unavailability of specific human resources, the presence of political meddling, and bureaucratic cloning. Nevertheless, the police play a critical role as the first line of defence against threats of terrorism and insurgencies (Newman & Clarke, 2008). This discourse finds that effective police and intelligence work, rather than military force, can deliver better counterterrorism results.

Chapter ten of this book records the reasons why strategic policing (Hendrix et al., 2017) is the best option for us to realize our policing to postmodern conditions (Lyotard 1884). From time to time, new challenges to society's order have reinvented new policing strategies (Weisburd and Braga 2006).

However, this study has summarised all 11 strategies and some additional strategies into a new model that experts call the strategic policing model (SPM). In the SPM, police are equipped with the latest technology of telemetry, biometrics, forensics, and digital solutions and work in partnerships. The strategic policing approach follows a networked way of coordinating and working with the communities they serve, law enforcement departments, political organs, business associates and intelligence agencies, academia, media, NGOs, and other strategic stakeholders (Jones 2009). In this particular arena, police organisations in Pakistan are yet to evolve a permanent framework of collaborative work under strategic policing (Katz & Huff, 2020) model in a postmodern setting (Palmer et al., 2012). Therefore, the police reform agenda in Pakistan should incorporate strategic policing as the preferable model to align police transformation from colonial to postmodern policing.

Correspondingly, the change in strategies has underscored the shift in the policing toolkits used in the investigation, surveillance, intelligence, communication, operations, and security domains (Sedra 2017). The adoption of technology by many police departments worldwide has become an inevitable challenge involving budgetary and political matters (Stroshine, 2021). Many police departments in Pakistan have either adopted or are on their way to embracing the new technology, although to a varying degree, and benefit from what we understand as technological solutions to crime and violence in society (see Chapter 06 of this book). In Pakistan, safe city projects, forensic setups, biometric networking, digital currency, criminal databases, mobile SIM registrations, and many other technologies of the same nature are examples in point (Ibid). This conversation indicates that the security knowledge industry and security technology are more likely to expand in Pakistan, given the challenges. However, many experts fear the possible digital divide due to unequal access and distribution of technology among people from different backgrounds. This marginalisation of some segments of society could lead to segmentation, fragmentation, and divide within the society-a stage that facilitates crime and violence and hence emphasises police transformation. Analysis in preceding chapters underlines that prospective policing transformation in Pakistan should take the aspect of 'technological wild west' (Toyama, 2016) seriously and carefully and build police capacity to manage law enforcement technology rather than depending on external non-police actors.

This situation further compounds when 'inequality of rights, responsibilities, and resources' arises. At this stage, governments and civil societies experience recurring tensions of value conflicts caused by technology access inequalities (Toyama, 2016). Three crucial factors, including improving police effectiveness, managing information, meeting the demands of accountable, accessible, and responsive policing, have determined the use of technology in policing in recent years (Stroshine, 2020). First, technology adoption in policing has changed the way police officers think and perform their job activities, thereby changing their organisational culture altogether (Ibid). Technology is essential for the survival and success of the organisation and has become an existential issue for almost all government departments (Ibid). Therefore, the embrace of technology by the police would be invincible and crucial for transforming policing (Katz and Maguire, 2020) in Pakistan.

This conversation has also found that Pakistan is undergoing heavy pressure from civil libertarians and the media to reframe its policing laws to transform its police organisations as agencies of social service primarily tasked with protecting the lives, property, and liberty of the people. However, unfortunately, this will take time to reach an idealistic stage, although the freelance segments of our society are working hard to set the direction and pace of reforms in the Police (PRCR-2019). Strengthening community trust and relationships is the core theme of 21st century policing (Gravelle & Rogers, 2014). The Final Report (2015) by President's Task Force on 21st Century Policing in the United States suggests four main areas where law enforcement in the future will require attention, reform, and focus. The first four pillars of 21st century policing are based on the Taskforce: a) building trust and legitimacy, b) policy and oversight, c) technology and social media, and d) community policing and crime prevention. Unfortunately, public-Police relationships are tainted by public mistrust in Pakistan (Shigri, 2016).

"Unable to exorcise its nightmarish traits inherited as the colonial legacy, police in Punjab [and also in entire Pakistan] are still seen as a public-frightening rather than a public-friendly organisation, which continues to promote a sense of fear rather than security and wellbeing of the population. This image has perpetuated a widespread mistrust between police and the general masses" (PRCR, 2019).

Thus, policing transformation to suit postmodernity involves thinking beyond the state and governments and inviting multiple stakeholders and partners from diverse backgrounds, as discussed in the relevant chapter on community relations.

In the environment of change and controversies surrounding it, police governance is a severe issue that requires proper understanding in Pakistan, which I have discussed in Chapter 09 on police governance in this book. We found that grounds for the changes in the areas of the fundamental mission of the police, the proliferation of its strategies, technological advancements, and relationships with communities necessitate and underscore the need for more operational and financial autonomy for police without any political interference. Unfortunately, despite the lack of public demand to allow certain levels of autonomy- political, administrative, and economic- the Police Service of Pakistan struggles to encapsulate neutrality and impartiality. Due to an alarmingly increase in heavy bureaucratic and political campaigns to keep police departments dependent and under their controls through legislative and administrative instruments, it transpires. It will take some time to bring the process of the democratisation of police governance back on track. The professional, logistical, and financial maintenance of the police force remain weak because the elite governing manoeuvre takes full advantage of the police weaknesses and vulnerabilities and hence resist change, reform, and innovation in policing ways. Policing the police constitutes the cardinal part of policing transformation in Pakistan, and we found that democratic police oversight (Decker & Sjarback, 2020) is the only way forward for developing police-for-people dispensation.

The misplaced and outlived systems of performance evaluation of police and protection of police officers' human rights in Pakistan have rendered police officers to experience a 'deadly hesitation in using legitimate force in carrying their duties. Linked with this is the avoidance of using force, even when required by law to use. Islamabad police during grand Dharnas (violent crowd situations) have observed prudent restraint in using force to their peril. Still, those who used it unplanned got under fire in the model town case Lahore and those who failed to do in the Benazir murder case received a seventeen years imprisonment sentence. The same happened in recent TLP Dharnas with the Punjab police. Many have lost jobs, others get to jail, and the rest are ambivalent. In this regard, it is crucial to develop clarity on the appropriate use of a legitimate force (not a lethal force). Worldwide, police departments worldwide use equipment such as rubber bullets, water guns, gas, and other softer measures to disperse the mob. In Pakistan, we need to develop SOPs training and make necessary equipment available for the safety of the public and officers. Still, hair-raising is the government compromises cases against political leaders carrying out mob violence. Such laxity and political expediency on the part of governments create a severe crisis of the rule of law and due process. Police, on their own, cannot handle these issues because they are trained or equipped and not yet protected by law to make decisions on the use of legitimate force and get violators adequately prosecuted. In this context, Chapter nine has proposed the development of professional specialism in Pakistan's police forces under a strategic policing model for handling unruly mobs (see Chapter 11).

This study identifies that gender streamlining at all police human resources and leadership levels is essential for transforming police to postmodern policing. The persistent segregation patterns of employment limit women to a narrow range of occupations and industries; however, in the 21st century, gender balance in policing and criminal justice (Gravelle & Rogers, 2014) has become one of the best practices in policing and criminal justice systems worldwide (Katz & Maguire, 2020). However, there is resentment and antagonism towards working women and employment equity initiatives in male-dominated government sectors in developing countries such as Pakistan. Women face multiple obstacles while entering the public sphere for employment because of unsafe working environments. These obstacles can be categorised as socio-cultural, religious, ideological, or institutional. Due to the socialisation process, these are firmly embedded in women's lives (Baloch, 2019). The gendered socialisation of males and females creates a gender division of labour, due to which women are excluded from the public sphere. Gender inequalities decline across different regions, cultures, and traditions.

On the contrary, the growth of gender inequality is more evident in Pakistan, where the population is increasing rapidly. Women play a unique and vital role in all professions, especially in the police force, but this potentially valuable human resource is underutilized. The situation regarding gender equality in the police force is getting better but not even satisfactory in Pakistan. Women encounter enormous difficulties as they think of the police as their career. Most institutions are working under male dominance and, consequently, have been shaped according to the needs of males. This discourse proposes more intake of female police officers to change police demographics in Pakistan as a way forward to transforming policing.

Worldwide, police services worldwide embrace new professionalism based on transparency, accountability, democracy, legitimacy, the rule of law, and national security (Travis and Stone 2011). These policing principles form the core of postmodern policing development (Lint, 1999). Good relations between police and the public through easy access and rapid response offered by police organisations to their respective communities build images and improve their performance (Christopher, 2016). Police service in Pakistan should explore the essence of new police professionalism and incorporate its fundamental principles in policing practices and reforms. The strategic policing model, a postmodern invention, promises constructive partnerships among different stakeholders in policing and welcomes integrated and networked approaches (Hendrix 2017).

12.4. Conclusion

Policing in Pakistan and the world is at crossroads. Strategising policing transformation through innovation, reform, and reorganisation at this juncture is crucial and challenging. Postmodern developments in science, technology, research, media, and scholarship call for new thinking on policing in the context of postmodern theory, practice, and new social contact to redefine the mission and mandates of police, refine police-public relations, reinvent the role of police, rethink police training and education, and reimagine policing strategies for controlling crime, managing police resources, ensuring security, countering terrorism, and delivering services to the people in emergencies and problems(Katz & Maguire 2020). Partnerships between policing practitioners, educators, researchers, students, and anyone linked to governance, social work, human rights, and policing are the postmodern strategic requirements for responding to the challenges and issues of contemporary policing (Katz & Maguire 2020). This study argued that postmodern policing is embedded in broad changes in global and state systems, transitional societies, and expanding police mandates (Sheptycki, 1998). Therefore, strengthening the human security narrative through postmodern strategic policing, which involves the essence of new policing strategies, can go a long way to foster lasting peace and sustainable security.

This conversation endeavoured to find prospects of policing continuity by exploring ways and means to conceptualise responses to the challenges of change in policing, society, governance, policy, strategies, and thinking on these concepts (Kratcoski, 2017). Noticeably, the study found that police keep changing their ways of dealing with crime and criminals (Amicelle et al., 2021). In line with this, the continuous transformation of communities they serve, their societies, and their governments (Katz & Maguire 2020), police in Pakistan must change and reform in unity with their changed postmodern environments and requirements. Policing has undergone significant changes and innovations after the 2002 police order in Pakistan. The previous chapters on police developments recorded police reforms and innovations in new mandates, use of police technology, community involvement, strategic counterterrorism approaches, and broader collaboration between police and non-police actors in combating terrorism and new national security threats. We observed that the integrated models and networked partnership systems suit postmodern strategic policing design more than the one-size-fits-all narrative of coercive and authoritarian policing approaches. Therefore, limiting police authority and protecting people's civil liberties remained at the heart of this conversation on reimagining policing in Pakistan.

Discussions in this study have found that postmodern developments in policing worldwide, both on the sides of theory and practice, reiterate that policing no longer remains police or state exclusivity or a coercive arm of the government. Policing has emerged as a cultural phenomenon and the rule of

Reimagining Policing in Pakistan

law institutions that have developed a normative culture of collaboration, cooperation, integration, sharing and caring for all community members without distinction, discrimination, and unequal treatment (Schafer et al., 2012). Postmodern policing acknowledges legal and democratic limits to police authority (Hornberger, 2011). It emphasises inclusive, pluralistic, and gendered approaches (Cunningham, 2021) to forge strategic partnerships with public and private stakeholders at national, transnational, and international levels (Perrott & Trites, 2017). The postmodern strategic policing paradigm stipulates a reduction in the use of force, better public service delivery, employment of therapeutic measures, procedural justice, strategic partnerships, gender balance in police demographics, use of technology, and policing by consent. The elements of new police professionalism, including accountability, transparency, democracy, the rule of law, and legitimacy (Stone & Travis 2011), signify postmodern strategic policing that this discourse advocated for Pakistan. To realign policing in Pakistan with the new police professionalism, policing experts need to make their all-out efforts to chalk out the police transformation plan as provided in Chapter 11 of this book. The primary purpose is to set the direction of thinking about transforming policing in Pakistan through the rediscovery of the new strategic role and mandate of police officers and leaders in the emerging peace and security industry of governance.

This study takes away the point that no society can ever progress if its government fails to dispense justice and establish peace within its territory. Politics is, therefore, a lifeline of the socio-cultural, politico-economic, and civil progress of civilization (Wolin, 2016). Politics of policing, which has an integral part of governance, has had two shapes: power politics (control and strict mode) and popular politics (democratic, deliberative, inclusive, and consultative). Balancing authority with liberty is the core task police transformation needs to embed in Pakistan. However, the normative dilemma of all postmodern states, including Pakistan, emerges when coercive police or military authority is used to devalue human life in the name of preserving it (Baloch, 2017c). In this state of politico-ethical crisis within societies, governments justify means to achieve the ends, and the question of how to fight violence outweighs why to fight it (ibid). Despite public pressures and academic arguments on the lesser use of authoritarian tactics and taking due care of human rights and fundamental freedoms of the people, governments allow police to use force in the name of establishing peace and protecting life, liberty, and property of citizenry (Hornberger, 2021). In Pakistan, the politics of policing for using police authority against political elements have become commonplace in popular political culture (Shigri 2012). Indeed, policing and politics are inseparable (Maguire & Okada, 2011. I have defined police in the introductory chapter but using police as an instrument of control and compliance instead of an institution of public service delivery (Suddle, 2015) is devastating for struggling democracies such as Pakistan. Thus, the politics of policing in Pakistan appears different from the constructive political engagement of the community based on policing by consent organised under democratic police oversight mechanisms for better public service delivery and accountability of police (Deflem, 2016). No government can ensure good governance unless its police are efficient and effective in public service delivery and in enforcing the spirit of the law (Goodin, 2012). Hence, reforming the police and policing while keeping in mind the dark side of the politics of policing must be the cornerstone of all visionary governments and political leadership (Bowling and Newburn 2006), including Pakistan. However, the constant crisis of statehood signifying the crisis of establishing constitutional, federal, and democratic governments both in theory and in practice, maintaining balance in authority and liberty (Hof & Groothuis 2011) continues to cripple Pakistani political leadership. It prevents them from making the police capable, independent, and accountable in a procedurally just way (PRCR, 2019).

The new trends in politics, policing, and crime have enhanced political awareness in the Pakistani population and better informed them about civil rights, liberties, and privileges (Ayaz 2013). Consequently, politicians have realized that police reforms and restructuring are crucial for public relations and political point-scoring. The project of transferring policing in Pakistan seems challenging to materialise in prevailing pollical circumstances because of the resistance posed by vested interests across many segments of our society (Suddle, 2012). However, the solid postmodern challenges of crime, violence, and innovations in contemporary postmodern governance worldwide offer police a millennial opportunity to shift from a warrior role to the guardians of the people's fundamental rights and civil liberties. Policing no longer remains police exclusivity but rather a shared function between many stakeholders tied in a well-defined eco-system of partnerships which, this discourse has argued, is the future of policing in the postmodern age. Postmodern strategic policing ensures higher freedom, protection of human rights, and democratic engagement. It values diversity, disagreements, and dissent as sources of strength and progress.

The change creates the need for reform and innovation. It calls for romantic imaginations and reimaginations to the broadest extent. This book is just an academic effort made by a practitioner to break the ice by setting the direction of a meaningful strategic conversation on police transformations to post-modern strategic lines in Pakistan. The trickiest proposition for policing in Pakistan is to perform a balancing mechanism between the state and the people by perfectly presuming the role of the guardian of the people's fundamental rights. This approach can redefine the social contract between the civil and political elements of Pakistan's society, in which the authority of the state will serve and protect the populace. Therefore, transforming policing from police-for-the-government dispensation to a police-for-the-people is undoubtedly a daunting challenge for struggling democracy in Pakistan. The future of democracy and civilian ascendency depends mainly on achieving this task, indeed an existentialist challenge for libertarians and proponents of human rights. Policing, as an instrument of power and control, has become a contested function of the state; It no longer remains a state or police exclusivity in a postmodern society. Therefore, the police in Pakistan need to transform their coercive and authoritarian model to postmodern dispensation. As a result, policing may adopt a strategic, deliberative, and inclusive network of partnerships with local and international public and private stakeholders.

Bibliography

Aafani, A.A. (2012) Perspectives on Police Reforms on Gilgit-Baltistan' in Abbass, H. (ed) (2012) *Stabilising Pakistan Through Police Reforms* pp. 120-21 [Online] Available at https: //asiasociety.org/files/pdf/as_pakistan_police_reform.pdf (Accessed: 11 November 2017)

Abbas, H. (2009) Police & Law Enforcement Reform in Pakistan: Crucial for Counterinsurgency and Counterterrorism Success, Belfer Center [Online] Available at https://www.belfercenter.org/publication/police-law-enforcement-reform-pakistan-crucial-counterinsurgency-and-counterterrorism, Accessed on 28 October 2021

Abbass, H. (2009) 'Police & Law Enforcement Reform in Pakistan: Crucial for Counterinsurgency and Counterterrorism Success' *Institute for Social Policy and Understanding, Belfer Centre for Science and International Relations* [Online] Available at https://www.belfercenter.org/publication/police-law-enforcement-reform-pakistan-crucial-counterinsurgency-and-counterterrorism, (Accessed: 24 March 2018)

Abbass, H. (2011) 'Reforming Pakistan's Police and Law Enforcement Infrastructure', Special report 266, February 2011, published by *United States Institute of Peace*. The author is a former officer of the Police Service of Pakistan.

Abbass, H. (ed) (2012) Stabilizing Pakistan through Police Reform, *Asia Society*: A report by Independent Commission on Pakistan Police Reforms, New York Email: globalpolicy@asiasociety.org www.asiasociety.org [Online] Available at https://asiasociety.org/files/pdf/as_pakistan_police_reform.pdf (Accessed: October 20, 2017)

Accenture Report (2018) 'Reimagining the Police Workforce: Future Vision' an *Accenture Report* dated 26 September 2018

Acemoglu, D., Robinson, J.A. (2012) *Why Nations Fail*, New York: Crown Publications

Adams, G.B. and Balfour, D.L. (1998) *Unmasking Administrative Evil*, London: Sage

Afzal, M. (2021) 'Terrorism in Pakistan has declined, but the underlying roots of extremism remain' *BROOKINGS.EDU*. (15th January 2021) [Online] Available at https://www.brookings.edu/blog/order-from-chaos/2021/01/15/terrorism-in-pakistan-has-declined-but-the-underlying-roots-of-extremism-remain/, accessed on 30th October 2021

Ahmad, I. (2012) 'The Federal Investigation Agency' in Abbass, H. (ed) (2012) *Stabilizing Pakistan through Police Reform, Asia Society's* report by the independent commission on Police Reforms, pp. 99-103 [Online] Available at https://asiasociety.org/files/pdf/as_pakistan_police_reform.pdf (Accessed: 23 February 2018)

Ahmad, I. (2013) *Pakistan, the Garrison State: Origins, Evolution, and Consequences-1947-2011*, Karachi: Oxford University Press

Ahmad, S. (2012) 'Police Reforms in Balochistan' in Abbass, H. (ed) (2012) *Stabilising Pakistan Through Police Reforms* pp. 113-119 [Online] Available at https://asiasociety.org/files/pdf/as_pakistan_police_reform.pdf (Accessed: 17 November 2017)

Ahmad, S. (2020) 'Pakistani Policewomen: Questioning the Role of Gender in Circumscribing Police Corruption', *Policing and Society, An International Journal of Research and Policy*, vol, 30, issue 8, published on 13 September 2020 [Online] Available at https://www.tandfonline.com/doi/abs/10.1080/10439463.2019.1611820 (accessed 20 October 2021)

Alagappa, M. (2002) *Coercion and Governance: The Declining Political Role of Military in Asia*, Stanford, California: Stanford University Press

Albrecht, J. F., Dow, M.C., Plecas, D., and Das, D.K. eds. (2018) *Policing Major Events: Perspectives from Around the World*, NY, Routledge

Alexander, C. (2000) The *Asian Gang: Ethnicity, Identity, and Masculinity, Oxford*: Berg

Allen, J., Edmonds, S., Patterson, A. and Smith, D. (2006) 'Policing and the Criminal Justice System – Public Confidence and Perceptions: Findings from the 2004/05 *British Crime Survey*, London: Home Office Online Report 07/06

Amicelle, A., Boucher, K. C., Dupont, B., Mulone, M., Shearing, C., and Tanner, S. eds. (2021) *The Policing of Flows: Challenging Contemporary Criminology*, NY, Routledge

Andreas, P. and Nadelmann, E. (2006) Policing *the Globe: Criminalisation and Crime Control in International Relations*, New York: Oxford University Press

Appleton, M. (2005) 'The Political Attitudes of Muslims Studying at British Universities in the post-9/11 world (Part 1)' *Journal of Muslim Minority Affairs* 25(2): 171-191.

Arnold, D.J. (1986) *Police Power, and Colonial Rule: Madras 1859-1947,* Delhi: Oxford University Press

Atran, S. (2003) 'Genesis of Suicide Terrorism', *Science* 299(5612): 1534-1539.

Avery, E. and Graham, M. (2013) 'Political public relations and the promotion of participatory, transparent government through social media, *International Journal of Strategic Communication*, Vol-07(4): pp. 274-291 [Online] Available at https://www.tandfonline.com/doi/abs/10.1080/1553118X.2013.824885 (Accessed: 28 January 2019)

Ayaz, B. (2013) *What is Wrong with Pakistan,* India: Hay-House

Ayaz, K. (2018) Discussions and data received from Mr Ayaz who deals with public complaints at the National Cyber Crime Response Centre at Islamabad dated 21st November 2018 at NRC3 Headquarters Islamabad

Babakhel, A.M. (2016b) 'Hullabaloo of Police Reforms', Daily *the Express Tribune*, 23 September 2016, [Online] Available at https://tribune.com.pk/story/1186658/hullabaloo-police-reforms/ (Accessed: 03 October 2017)

Babakhel, M.A. (2015) 'Intelligence-led Policing', *Daily the Express Tribune*, 7 May 2015 [Online] Available at https://tribune.com.pk/story/882523/intelligence-led-policing Accessed on 13 September 2021

Babakhel, M.A. (2016a) *Pakistan: In-between Extremism and Peace*, Bloomington-Indiana USA: Xlibris Publishers

Babakhel, M.A. (2021) Policing the Police, published in daily dawn (1st January 2021) [Online] Available at https://www.dawn.com/news/1599020 (accessed on 25 June 2021)

By J.J. Baloch (2022)

Baig, M.A. (2015) National Action Plan, *Daily Dawn*, 12 January 2015 [Online] Available at https://nation.com.pk/12-Jan-2015/the-national-action-plan (Accessed: 12 April 2017)

Bain, A. (ed.) (2016) *Law Enforcement and Technology: Understanding Use of Technology in Policing* London: Palgrave Macmillan

Balko, R. (2013) *Rise of the Warrior Cop: The Militarization of American Police Force*, New York: Public-Affairs Books

Baloch, J.J. (2016) *The Power of social media & Policing Challenges* Karachi: Read & Write Publishers

Baloch, J.J. (2017a) *Whiter than White: The Daughter of the Land of Pure*, Leicestershire, UK: Matador Publications

Baloch, J.J. (2017b) 'Radicalization of Youth' [Online] Available at javedjiskanibaloch@wordpress.com

Baloch, J.J. (2017c) 'Ethical Dilemma of Postmodern State' [Online] available at javedjiskanibaloch@wordpress.com

Baloch, J.J. (2019) *Sociology in the 21st Century: A Perspective of Pakistani Society*, Karachi: Paramount Books, PP. 61-67

Balochistan Police Act 2011-Revival of 1861 Police Act & Repeal of 2002 Police Order

Banton, M. (1964) *The Policeman in the Community*, London: Tavistock

Banton, M. (1971) 'The Sociology of the Police' *Police Journal*, 44: pp. 225-244

Banton, M. (1973) 'The Sociology of the Police II', *Police Journal*, 46: pp. 241-262

Banton, M. (1975) 'The Sociology of the Police III', *Police Journal*, 48: pp. 298-312

Barratt, R. sir (1990) 'Review of Aspects of Policing in Pakistan", Report Published by UK Home Office available at National Police Academy library Islamabad

Baudrillard, J. (1981) *Simulacra and Simulations*, New York: Semiotext(e)

Baudrillard, J. (1996) *The Perfect Crime*, London: Verso Books

Bauman, Z. (1997) *Postmodernity and its Discontents*, London: Polity Press

Bauman, Z. (2000) Social Issues of Law & Order, *British Journal of Criminology*, 40, (2) PP. 205-221

Bauman, Z. (2007) *Liquid Times: Living in an Age of Uncertainty* Cambridge: Polity Press

Bayley, D.H. (1998) *What works in Policing,* New York: Oxford University Press

Bayley, D.H. (2006) *Changing the Guard: Developing Democratic Police Abroad*, New York: Oxford University Press

Bayley. D.H. (2001) Democratizing the Police Abroad: what to do and how to do it, Issues in International Crime US Department of Justice, Office of Justice Programs, *National Institute of Justice-Political Science* June 2001 [Online] Available at https://www.politieacademie.nl/kennisenonderzoek/kennis/mediatheek/PDF/44640.pdf (Accessed: 22 January 2017)

BBC (2001) 'Who is Richard Reid?' *BBC online* (28/12/01).

BBC (2007) 'A Police State? The Issues', *BBC online* (08/02/07).

BBC (2007) 'Woman in UK 'groomed' as bomber', *BBC online* (11/06/2007).

BBC (2008) 'Five Students Win Terror Appeal', *BBC online* (13/02/08)

BBC Documentary (2017) Cops with Cameras, UK Police Documentary, *YouTube Video* [Online] Available at https://www.youtube.com/watch?v=GPxAQHsUJeY (Accessed: 23 January 2019)

Beck, U. (1992) *Risk Society: Towards a New Modernity*, London: Sage

Beckman, K.A., Gibbs, J.C., Beatty, P.D. and Canigiani, M. (2005) 'Trends in Police Research: A Cross-Sectional Analysis of the 2002 Literature', Police Practice and Research: *An International Journal*, 6(3): 193–329.

Beene, C. Capt. (1992) *Police Crowd Control*, Colorado: Paladin Press

Bell, P., Dean, G. & Gottschalk, P. (2010). Information management in law enforcement: The case of police intelligence strategy implementation. International *Journal of Information Management*, 30, 220-350.

Berg, E.M., Dean, G., Gottschalk, P. & Karlsen, T.J. (2008). Police management roles as determinants of knowledge sharing attitudes in criminal investigations, *International Journal of Public Sector Management*, 21, 240-295.

Bergquist, W. (1993) *The Postmodern Organisation: Mastering the Art of Irreversible Change*, San Francisco: Jossey Bass

Berry, J. (2009) 'Reducing Bureaucracy in Policing', a *Home Office Report, UK*. [Online] Available at https://webarchive.nationalarchives.gov.uk/20100408132736/http://police.homeoffice.gov.uk/publications/police-reform/reducing-bureaucracy-policing2835.pdf?view=Binary

Bichler, G., Christie-Merrall, J., & Sechrest, D. (2011). Examining juvenile delinquency within activity space: Building a context for offender travel patterns. Journal of Research in Crime and Delinquency, 48(3), 472-506 [Online] Available at DOI: 10.1177/0022427810393014, Accessed 20 December 2020

Bittner, E. (1970) *The functions of the police in modern society*, Maryland: Chevy Chase, National Institute of Mental Health
Blake, C., Sheldon, B., Strzelecki, R. and Williams, P. (2012) *Policing Terrorism*, London, Sage Publications

Blick, A., Chaudhury, T., and Weir, S. (2006) *The Rules of the Game: Terrorism, Community and Human Rights*, London: Joseph Rowntree Reform Trust

Boer, D. M (2018) *Comparative Policing from a Legal Perspective*, Cheltenham UK: Edward Elgar Publishing, Inc.

Bond, M. (2016) 'CompStat: Policing Strategies' – *e-Roll Call Magazine*. [Online] Available at https://andragogytheory.com/2016/01/14/compstat-policing-strategies/ Accessed: 06 March 2018)

By J.J. Baloch (2022)

Bowling, B. and Newburn, T. (2006) 'Policing and National Security. Paper presented at the London-Columbia *'Police, Community and Rule of Law' workshop,* London 16th-17th March 2006

Bowling, B. and Sheptycki, J. (2012) *Global Policing,* London: Sage

Braga A.A. (2014) 'Pulling Levers Policing' in Bruinsma G. and Weisburd D. (ed.) *Encyclopaedia of Criminology and Criminal Justice,* Springer, New York, NY, [Online] Available at https://link.springer.com/referenceworkentry/10.1007/978-1-4614-5690-2_173 (Accessed: 05 March 2018)

Braga, A. and Weisburd, D. (2006) 'Problem-oriented Policing: The Disconnect between Principle and Practice' in *Police Innovations: Contrasting Perspectives* (eds.) Weisburd, D. & Braga, A.A. (2006), New York: Cambridge University Press, pp. 133-154

Braga, A. and Weisburd, D. (2012) The Effects of Focused Deterrence Strategies on Crime: A Systematic Review and Meta-Analysis of the Empirical Evidence, *in Journal of Research in Crime and Delinquency* vol-49 (3). [Online] Available at https://journals.sagepub.com/doi/abs/10.1177/0022427811419368 (Accessed: 13 May 2018)

Braga, A., Flynn, E., Kelling, G., and Cole, C. (2011) *Moving the Work of Criminal Investigators towards Crime Control,* New Perspectives on Policing, Cambridge: Harvard Kennedy School

Braga, A., Papachristos, A. and Hureau, D. (2012) Hot Spots Policing effects on Crime, *Campbell Systematic Reviews,* 2012:8, [Online] Available at http://www.campbellcollaboration.org/media/k2/attachments/Braga_Hot_Spots_Policing_Review.pdf (Accessed: 26 September 2018)

Braga, A.A and Weisburd, D. (2006) 'Conclusion: Police Innovation and Future of Policing' in *Police Innovations: Contrasting Perspectives* (eds.) Weisburd, D. & Braga, A.A. (2006), New York: Cambridge University Press, pp.339-350

Braga, A.A. (2006) 'Policing crime hot spots' in B. Welsh and D. Farrington, eds. Preventing Crime: *What Works for Children, Offenders, Victims, and Places,* P. 179-193? Great Britain: Springer.

Braga, A.A., and Weisburd, D. (2006) Problem-Oriented Policing: The Disconnect between Principle and Practice, in Weisburd and Braga (ed.) (2006) *Police Innovations: Contrasting Perspectives,* Cambridge: Cambridge University Press, Part III pp. 133-152

Braga, A.A. and Winship, C. (2006) 'Partnerships, Accountability and Innovation: Clarifying Boston's Experience with Pulling Levers' in *Police Innovations: Contrasting Perspectives* (eds.) Weisburd, D. & Braga, A.A. (2006), New York: Cambridge University Press, pp. 171-190

Bratton, W. (1998) *Turnaround: How America's top cop reversed the crime epidemic,* New York: Random House

Briggs, R., Fieschi, C., and Lownsbrough, H. (2006) *Bringing it Home: Community-based Approaches to Counterterrorism,* London: Demos

Brodeur, J.P. (2007) 'High Policing and Low Policing in post 9/11 times', Policing: *A Journal of Policy and Practice* 1(1): pp. 25-37 [Online] Available at https://doi.org/10.1093/police/pam002 published on January 1, 2007 (Accessed: 22 April 2018)

Brodeur, J.P. (2011) *The Policing Web,* Oxford: Oxford University Press

Bueermann, J. (2012) 'Being Smart on Crime with Evidence-based Policing', Strengthen *Science, Advance Justice, published by National Institute of Justice Journal Vol-269*, [Online] Available at https://nij.gov/journals/269/Pages/evidence.aspx (Accessed: 06 March 2018)

Buerger, M.E. and Mazerolle, L.G. (1998) Third-party policing: A theoretical analysis of an emerging trend, *Justice Quarterly*, 15 (2), pp. 301-327, [Online] Available at DOI: 10.1080/07418829800093761 (Accessed: 14 May 2018)

Bullock, K. (2018) 'The Police Use of Social Media: Transformation or Normalisation?' *Social Policy and Society*, 17(2) pp. 245-258. [Online] Available at https://www.cambridge.org/core/journals/social-policy-and-society/article/police-use-of-social-media-transformation-or-normalisation/19E5C6727038F01129B51CE4287D0FFB (Accessed: 12 January 2019)

Burke, J. (2008). The Not-so-winnable War against Terrorism, *Guardian.co.uk*, 19th July 2008.

Burleigh, M. (2008) *Blood and Rage: A Cultural History of Terrorism*, London: Harper Collins

Byrne, J. (2009) The New Generation of Concentrated Community Supervision Strategies: Focusing Resources on High-Risk Offenders, Times, and Places. (Washington, DC: A Report for the Public Safety Performance Project, the *Pew Charitable Trusts*).

Byrne, J., and Rebovich, D. (2007) *The New Technology of Crime, Law and Social Control Monsey*, New York: Criminal Justice Press

Caless, B. (2011) *Policing at the Top: The Roles, Values, and Attitudes of Chief Police Officers* New York: Polity Press

Center for Research and Security Studies (2015) Counterterrorism and Pakistan Police: Capacity and Challenges [Online] Available at https://crss.pk/wp-content/uploads/2010/07/Counter-Terrorism-and-Pakistan-Police.pdf (Accessed: 02 January 2018)

Chan, J. (2001) The Technology game: How information technology is transforming police practice, *Journal of Criminal Justice*, 1:139-159

Chan, J. (2003). Police and new technologies, in Newburn, T. (ed.), *The Handbook of Policing*, Cullompton: Willan.

Chapman, B. (2016) 'Research on the Impact of Technology on Policing Strategy in the 21st Century' Final Report, *National Institute of Justice-Police Executive Research Forum* (May 2016) [Online] Available at https://www.ojp.gov/pdffiles1/nij/grants/251140.pdf (accessed on 15 October 2021)

Charrier, K. (2010) 'Strategic Management in Policing: The Role of the Strategic Manager', *Police Chief Magazine*, published 20 July 2010 [Online] Available at https://www.theiacp.org/sites/default/files/all/s/Strategic%20Management%20in%20Policing.pdf (accessed on 21 August 2021)

Chaudhry, M.A.K (1990) The Police Reforms Implementation Committee Report available at National Police Academy library Islamabad

Chaudhry, M.A.K (1997) *Policing in Pakistan*, Lahore: Vanguard

Chaudhry, S. (2021) Politics' Raison D'etre, Express tribune (29 October 2021) [Online] Available at https://tribune.com.pk/story/2326783/politics-raison-detre, Accessed on 30th October 2021

By J.J. Baloch (2022)

By J.J. Baloch (2022)

Chaudhury, T. (2007) *The Role of Muslim Identity Politics in Radicalisation*, London: DCLG

Chermak, S. and Weiss, A. (2002) 'Identifying Strategies to Market Police in the News', *US Department of Justice*, [Online] Available at https://www.ojp.gov/pdffiles1/nij/grants/194130.pdf (accessed on 4 January 2020)

Choongh, S. (1997) *Policing as Social Discipline*, Oxford: Clarendon Press

Christopher J. S. (2016) *Policing and social media: Social Control in an Era of New Media* New York: Lexington Books

Clamp, K. & Paterson, C. (2017) *Restorative Policing: Concepts, Theory, and Practice*, New York: Routledge

Clancy, A., Hough, M., Aust, R. and Kershaw, C. (2001) Crime, Policing and Justice: The Experience of Ethnic Minorities.' Findings from the 2000 *British Crime Survey*, London: Home Office

Clarke, R. V. (1997) *Situational Crime Prevention: Successful Case Studies*, Albany, New York: Harrow and Heston

Clarke, V.R. and Newman, G.R (2007) 'Police and the Prevention of Terrorism', in *Policing: A Journal of Policy and Practice*, Vol-1, (1), 1 January 2007, pp. 9 [Online] Available at https://academic.oup.com/policing/article-abstract/1/1/9/1533918 (Accessed: 12 March 2018)

Clear, T. (2007) *Imprisoning Communities: How Mass Incarnation Makes Disadvantaged Communities Worse*, Oxford: Oxford University Press

Clockars, C.B. (1985) *The Idea of Police*, California: Sage Publications

Cofan, S.M., and Baloi, A.M. (2017) Intelligence Analysis: A Key Tool for Modern Police Management-The Romanian Perspective, Chapter 7, in Eterno, J.A, Verma, A., Das, A.M, & Das D.K (2017) *Global Issues in Contemporary Policing*, New York: CRC Press

Cohen, L. E., and M. Felson (1979) Social Change and Crime Rate Trends: A Routine Activity Approach, American *Sociological Review* 44, 588-605.

Cohn, A.W. (1978) *The Future of Policing*, London: Sage

Cole, D., and Lobel, J. (2007) *Less Safe, Less Free: Why America is Losing the War on Terror*, New York: The New Press

College of Policing UK (2020) How we help you to pursue a specialist role in policing (21 November 2020) [Online] Available at https://www.college.police.uk/article/specialist-learning-cpd-in-focus (accessed on 6 November 2021)

Colvin, C. (2001) *Evaluation of innovative technology: Implications for the community policing roles of law enforcement officers*, San Francisco: Psychology Department, San Francisco State University

Community Policing in Pakistan: An Assessment, Published in November 2014 by *Centre for Peace and Development Initiative-CPDI*

Concept Paper on PPIC3 Centre Programme (2015) The Future of Punjab Police, [Online] Available athttps://psca.gop.pk/PSCA/wp-content/uploads/2016/04/Concept-Paper.pdf (Accessed: 10 June 2018)

273

Constable, P. (2011) *Playing with Fire*, London: Random House

Constantine (1961) Police Commission Report 1960-61 available at National Police Academy Islamabad Library

Constitution of Pakistan-1973, Rawalpindi: Pakistan Law House

Constitutional Petition-CP-7097 (2016) Sindh High Court accepts the rights of Sindh government to legislate on Police matters [Online] Available at
http://sindhhighcourt.gov.pk/news_notifications/source_files/Police_Act_Case--CP_7097-2016.pdf (Accessed: 02 February 2017)

Cooper C.C. (2011) 'Contemporary Policing: Police Work in the 21st Century' in *Critical Issues in Crime and Justice*, (eds.) Maguire, M. and Okada, D. (2011) California, USA: Sage Publications, pp.217-231

Corbett, R., and Marx, G. (1991) Critique: No Soul in the New Machine: Techno-fallacies in the Electronic Monitoring Movement, *Justice Quarterly*, 8(3):259-301

Cordner, G. (2021) 'How police education and training can contribute to violence reduction' Police 1, [Online] Available at https://www.police1.com/police-training/articles/how-police-education-and-training-can-contribute-to-violence-reduction-oU4x5bz48otQTK4y/ (accessed on 8th November 2021

Coulon, J. (1998) Soldiers of Diplomacy: The United Nations, Peacekeeping, and The New World Order, Toronto, Canada: Toronto University Press (Originally published in French and translated by Aronoff, P. and Scott, H. in English)
Country Reports on Terrorism-2019, *U.S. Department of State* (2019) [Online] Available at https://www.state.gov/reports/country-reports-on-terrorism-2019/, accessed on 30th October 2021

CPDI Report (2014) 'Community Policing in Pakistan: An Assessment' Published in November 2014 *Centre for Peace and Development Initiative-CPDI, Islamabad* [Online] Available at http://www.cpdi-pakistan.org/wp-content/uploads/2014/12/Community-Policing-in-Pakistan-An-Assessment.pdf (Accessed: 10 January 2017)

CPLC Statistics published at Pakistan Today website [Online] Available at
https://www.pakistantoday.com.pk/2018/05/07/214-motorcycles-2576-phones-snatched-in-april-cplc/ (Accessed: 19 December 2018)

CPLC Website http://www.cplc.org.pk (Accessed: 14 November 2018)

CPLC-Citizen Police Liaison Committee Karachi website http://www.cplc.org.pk (Accessed: 14 November 2018)

Craig, P. (2011). Adding value: A review of the international literature on the role of higher education in police training and education, *Police Practice and Research*, 12 (4), 286-297 [Online] available at http://shura.shu.ac.uk/9114/1/Paterson_-_Adding_Value_PPR_%28final%29.pdf, (accessed on 38 January 2020)

Crank, J. (2003) *Imagining Justice*, Cincinnati USA: Anderson

Crank, J. Irlbeck, D., and Koski, C.M. (2011) 'Police Theory' in *Critical Issues in Crime and Justice*, (eds.) Maguire, M. and Okada, D. (2011) California, USA: Sage Publications, pp. 197-216

Crenshaw, M. (1995) 'Thoughts on Relating Terrorism to Historical Contexts' in M. Crenshaw (ed.) *Terrorism in Context*, Pennsylvania: Pennsylvania State University Press

Crick, B. (2007) *In Defence of Politics*, 5th ed. Chennai, India: Continuum Publishers

By J.J. Baloch (2022)

Crimes on rising in the capital as over 700 safe city cameras dysfunctional article BY BILAL SABRI, (LAST UPDATED JUNE 5, 2018) [Online] Available at https://www.pakistantoday.com.pk/2018/06/05/crimes-on-rise-in-capital-as-over-700-safe-city-cameras-dysfunctional/ (accessed on 14 June 2018) the visit of ASP Batch 44th

Crimes on rising in the capital as over 700 safe city cameras dysfunctional article BY BILAL SABRI, (LAST UPDATED JUNE 5, 2018) [Online] Available at https://www.pakistantoday.com.pk/2018/06/05/crimes-on-rise-in-capital-as-over-700-safe-city-cameras-dysfunctional/ (Accessed: 14 June 2018)

CrimeSolutions.gov. 'Hot Spots Policing' National Institute of Justice-NIJ. Practice Profile. [Online] Available at https://www.crimesolutions.gov/PracticeDetails.aspx?ID=8 (Accessed: 04 March 2018)
Criminal Justice Research, Technology, and Strategic Planning in Policing, [Online] available at http://criminal-justice.iresearchnet.com/system/technology-and-strategic-planning-in-policing/, Accessed 1 January 2021

Cronin, A. (2006) How al-Qaida Ends: The Decline and Demise of Terrorist Groups, *International Security* 31(1): 7-48

Croteau, D. (1995) Politics and the Class Divide: Working People and the Middle-Class Left, Philadelphia: Temple University Press

Crump, J. (2011) 'What are the police doing on Twitter? Social media, the police and the public', *Policy and Internet*, 3, 4, Article 7, [Online] Available at www.policyandinternet.org, (accessed 21 January 2019)

Cunningham, E. (2021) *Women in Policing: Feminist Perspectives on Theory and Practice*, NY, Routledge

Czwarno, M. (2006) Misjudging Islamic Terrorism: The Academic Community's Failure to predict 9/11, *Studies in Conflict and Terrorism*, 29(7) pp. 657-678

David, H. Clifford, B. Shearing (2008) 'The Future of Policing', *Law & Society Review*, 30, (3) pp. 585-606, [Online] Available at https://pdfs.semanticscholar.org/1ada/ce8b143e114ab58c0d977b1765be0941a2b3.pdf (Accessed: 16 January 2019)

Davies, D. (2021) 'Surveillance and Local Police: How Technology Is Evolving Faster Than Regulation', *NPR*, published on 27th January 2021 [Online] Available at https://www.npr.org/2021/01/27/961103187/surveillance-and-local-police-how-technology-is-evolving-faster-than-regulation (accessed on 27 October 2021)

Davies, H. and Murphy, G. (2002) Protecting your Community from Terrorism: The Strategies for local Law Enforcement, Police Executive Research Forum, Community Oriented Policing Services-COPS US Department of Justice available at https://www.policeforum.org/assets/docs/Free_Online_Documents/Terrorism/community%20policing%20and%20terrorism%20vol.%202%202004.pdf (accessed on 24 February 2016)

Dean, G. (1995) Police reform: rethinking operational policing? *American Journal of Criminal Justice*, Volume 23, Issue-4, pp. 337-47 [Online] Available at https://www.sciencedirect.com/science/article/pii/004723529500024K (Accessed: November 2017)

Decker, S.H., and Sjarback J.A. (2020) Options for Increasing Civilian Oversight of the Police, Chapter 6, in Katz, C.M. and Maguire, E.R. eds. (2020) *Transforming the Police: Thirteen Key Reforms*, Long Grove Illinois, USA, Waveland Press, Inc. pp. 113-125

Definitions of terrorism - Wikipedia. [Online] Available at
https://en.wikipedia.org/wiki/Definitions_of_terrorism (Accessed: 25 November 2018)

Deflem, M. (2004) *Policing World Society: Historical Foundations of International Police Cooperation,* New York: Oxford University Press

Deflem, M. (ed) (2016) *The Politics of Policing: Between force and Legitimacy,* Bingley UK: Emerald Group Publishing

Delahunty, J.G., Taitz, M., Coker, C.S., and Nguyen, I. (2017) Using Complaints against the Police to Improve Community-Police Relations, Chapter 5, in Eterno, J.A, Verma, A., Das, A.M, & Das D.K (2017) *Global Issues in Contemporary Policing,* New York: CRC Press, pp. 97-120

Derrida, J. (1967/1997) *Of Grammatology,* Baltimore: Johns Hopkins University Press

Diamond, L. (2008) *The Spirit of Democracy: The Struggle to Built Free Societies Throughout the World,* MacMillan Publishers

Din, I. (2006) *The New British: The impact of Culture And Community on Young Pakistanis,* Ashgate: Aldershot

Discussion Club on Pakistan defence (2016) Pakistan Fails to Implement NAP [Online] Available at http://defence.pk/threads/pakistan-fails-to-implement-nap.418778/page-2 (Accessed: 23 December 2017

Discussions with Lady Police Officers of 44th Batch (December 2017) at NPA regarding their Personal Experiences and also regarding their female subordinate officers

Dorius, S. & Firebaugh, G. (2010) Trends in Global Gender Inequality, *Social Forces* 88 (5)-1941-1968

Doyle, Sir, A., C. (1993) *Case-Book of Sherlock Holmes & His Last Bow,* Hertfordshire, UK: Wordsworth Classics, www.wordsworth-editions.com

Dunham, R.G., Alpert, G.P., and MacLean, K.D. eds. (2021) *Critical Issues in Policing: Contemporary Readings,* 8th edn. Illinois USA, Waveland Press, Inc.

Dunnigham, C. and Norris, C. (1999) The Detective, the Snout, and the Audit Commission: The Real Costs in Using Police Informants', *The Howard Journal* 38(1) pp. 67-86, [Online] Available at https://onlinelibrary.wiley.com/doi/pdf/10.1111/1468-2311.00117 (Accessed: 12 August 2016)

Durkheim, E. (1952) *Suicide: A Study in Sociology,* London: Free Press

Eck, J.E. (2006) 'Science, Values and Problem-oriented Policing: Why Problem-oriented Policing' in *Police Innovations: Contrasting Perspectives* (eds.) Weisburd, D. & Braga, A.A. (2006) New York: Cambridge University Press, pp. 117-132

Editorial on 'Police Politicisation' published in *daily Dawn* dated 11 October 2018 [Online] Available at https://www.dawn.com/news/1438271 [Accessed: 22 March 2019]

Editorial 'Police Reforms' Published in *Dawn*, February 4th, 2019 [Online] Available at https://www.dawn.com/news/1461710 (accessed on 24 February 2019)

Editorial, 'Good, Bad, and Indifferent, *The Express Tribune*, 31 December 2015

By J.J. Baloch (2022)

Edwards, C. (2005) *Changing Policing Theories for 21st Century Societies*, 2nd edition, USA: Federation Press

Eighteenth Amendment to the Constitution of Pakistan (2010), [Online] Available at https://en.wikipedia.org/wiki/Eighteenth_Amendment_to_the_Constitution_of_Pakistan (Accessed: 12 April 2018)

Eisler, R. (2003) *The Power of Partnership: Seven Relationships that Will Change Your Life* California: New World Library, Chapter-5 pp. 123-157

Ekengren, M. and Simons, G. (2010) *The Politics of Security Sector Reform: Challenges and Opportunities for European Union's Global Role*, New York: Routledge

Elahi, N. (2017) 'Countering Crime with Intelligence, *Daily Times*, 8th August 2017 [online] Available at https://dailytimes.com.pk/121808/countering-crime-with-intelligence/ Accessed 15 September 2021

Elliott, A. and Urry, J. (2010) *Mobile Lives*, New York: Routledge

Ericson, R.V., Haggerty, K.D. (1997) *Policing the Risk Society* Oxford: Oxford University Press

Eterno, J.A, Verma, A., Das, A.M, & Das D.K (2017) *Global Issues in Contemporary Policing*, New York: CRC Press

Fair, C.C. and Ganguli, S. (2014) *Policing Insurgencies: Cops as counterinsurgents*, New York: Oxford University Press

Farmer, J.D. (1997) *Leopards in the Temple: Bureaucracy and the Limits of the 'In-between'*, in Administration *and Society* (39) 4, pp. 449-474

Ferguson Police Investigation (2015) A report by Ferguson Police Department' to U.S Justice Department, 04 March 2015 [Online] Available at https://www.justice.gov/sites/default/files/opa/press-releases/attachments/2015/03/04/ferguson_police_department_report.pdf (Accessed: 28 February 2019)

Ferguson, A.G. (2017) *The Rise of Big Data Policing: Surveillance, Race, and the Future of Law Enforcement*, New York: NYU Press

Ferreira, B.R. (1996) 'The Use and Effectiveness of Community Policing in a Democracy' *National Criminal Justice Reference Service* Washington D.C. [Online] Available at https://www.ncjrs.gov/policing/use139.htm (Accessed: 23 March 2018)

FIA Act, (1974) VIII OF 1975, An Act to provide for the constitution of a Federal Investigation agency in Gazette of Pakistan, Extra-ordinary, Part-I, 17th January 1975 [Online] Available at https://www.fia.gov.pk/act (accessed on 25 September 2020)

Final Report (2015) of Present Obama's Task Force on the 21st Century Policing [Online] Available at http://noblenational.org/wp-content/uploads/2017/02/President-Barack-Obama-Task-Force-on-21st-Century-Policing-Implementation-Guide.pdf (Accessed: 28 December 2017)

Flanagan, R. (2007) The Independent Review of Policing, London: *Interim Report, Home Office*

Foster, J. (1999) *Docklands: Cultures in Conflict, Worlds in Collision*, London: UCL Press

Foster, R. E. (2004) *Police Technology* London: Pearson

Foucault, M. (1980) *Power/Knowledge*: *Selected Interviews and Other Writings* (from 1972 to 1977 conducted by Gordon, Marshall, and others), New York: Pantheon Books

Foucault, M. (1995) *Discipline and Punish: The Birth of the Prison*, New York: Vintage Books

Fraser (1902-3) Report of the Indian Police Commission, Available at National Police Academy Library, Chapter 1 p. 6

Freedom House (2016) Pakistan-Freedom in the World-Report, [Online] Available at https://freedomhouse.org/report/freedom-world/2016/Pakistan (Accessed: 24 January 2018)

Friedman, R.R. (1992) *Community Policing: Comparative Perspectives and Prospects* New York: Palgrave Macmillan

Friedman, T.L. (2006) *The World is Flat*, New York: Farrar, Straus, and Giroux

Fritsvold, E. (2021-a) 'Going Beyond the Bachelor's: Why Police Officer Education is So Important', Law Enforcement and Public Safety, University of San Diego, [Online] Available at https://onlinedegrees.sandiego.edu/why-police-officer-education-is-important/ (accessed on 5th November 2021)

Fritsvold, E. (2021-b) 'A Firsthand Account on the Importance of Education for Law Enforcement and Public Safety, University of San Diego, [Online] Available at https://onlinedegrees.sandiego.edu/importance-education-law-enforcement/ (accessed 5th November 2021)

Fukuyama, F. (2004) *The End of History and the Last Man* New York: Free Press

Fukuyama, F. (2014) *Political Order & Political Decay*, London: Profile Books

Gabol, I. (2021) '3 policemen martyred, several injured in a clash with TLP protesters in Lahore' daily Dawn published on 22 October 2021 [Online] Available at https://www.dawn.com/news/1653381 (accessed on 6 November 2021)

Garcia, V. (2021) *Women in Policing around the World: Doing Gender and Policing in a Gendered Organization*, NY, Routledge

Gardner v. Broderick, 392 U.S. 273 (1968) Supreme Court of the United States of America available at https://supreme.justia.com/cases/federal/us/392/273/ (accessed on 22 January 2019)

Garrity v. New Jersey, 385 U.S. 493 (1967) Supreme Court of the United States of America available at https://supreme.justia.com/cases/federal/us/385/493/ (Accessed: 22 January 2019)

Gary, E. (2014) 'The police executive and governance: Adapting police leadership to an increase in oversight and accountability in police operations' published in *Salus Journal* (2), No. 1, PP. 2-18. [Online] Available at https://search.informit.com.au/documentSummary;dn=748160878099450;res=IELHSS> ISSN: 2202-5677 [Accessed: 22 June 2019]

Gauhar, A. (1997) 'How Intelligence Agencies Run Our Politics', The Nation, published on 4th September 1997

Gavender, G. & Jurik, N.C. (2012) *Justice Provocateur*, Chicago: University of Illinois Press

By J.J. Baloch (2022)

Geoghegan, S. (2006) 'CompStat Revolutionizes Contemporary Policing', Published in *Law and Order of Hendon Media Group*. Issue of April 2006. [Online] Available at http://www.hendonpub.com/resources/article_archive/results/details?id=3759 (Accessed: 05 March 2018)

Ghous, K. (2016) 'National Economic Policy' *NIM Karachi Lecture* dated 25th August 2016 (SMC CLASS)

Gibbins, J. (1998) 'Postmodernism, Poststructuralism, and Social Policy' in *Postmodernity and the Fragmentation of Welfare* edited by John Carter, 3rd ed. London: Routledge

Giddens, A. (1990) *The Consequences of Modernity*, Stanford, CA: Stanford University Press

Giddens, A. (1991) *Modernity and Self Identity: Self and Society in the Late Modern Age*, Cambridge: Polity Press

Gilmour, S. (2007) 'Why we trussed the police: police governance and the problem of trust', *Thames Valley Police, Kidlington, Oxfordshire*, OX5 2NX, UK. email: stan.gilmour@thamesvalley.pnn.police.uk published 8 February 2007 [Online] available at https://www.researchgate.net/profile/Stan-Gilmour-2/publication/238340996_Why_We_Trussed_the_Police_Police_Governance_and_the_Problem_of_Trust/links/564c451308ae3374e5de4e38/Why-We-Trussed-the-Police-Police-Governance-and-the-Problem-of-Trust.pdf, (accessed on 28 February 2021)

Glensor, R. W., and Peak, K. J. (2005) Strategic IT planning. Issues in IT: A reader for the busy police chief executive, Washington, DC: *Police Executive Research Forum*

Goldsmith, A. and Sheptycki, J. (2007) *Crafting Transnational Policing: Police Capacity Building and Global Police Reforms*, Portland: (Hart Publishing) Bloomsbury

Goodin, R.E. (2012) *Innovating Democracy: Democratic Theory and Practice after the Deliberative Turn*, Oxford: Oxford University Press

Goodman, M. (2015) *Future Crime: Inside the Digital Underground and the Battle of our Connected World* New York: Penguin Random House

Gravelle, J. and Rogers, C. (ed.) (2014) *Researching the Police in the 21st Century, International Lessons from the Field*, London: Palgrave Macmillan

'Guidebook on Democratic Policing' (2008) 2nd Ed. May, Vienna: *Organisation for Security and Co-operation in Europe-OSCE Secretary-General*, [Online] Available at https://www.osce.org/secretariat/23804?download=true (Accessed: 16 June 2017)

Guild, E, & Geyer, F. (2008) *Security Versus Justice: Police and Judicial Cooperation in the European Union*, Great Britain: Ashgate Publishers

Guttmann, A. & Thompson, D. (2004) *Why deliberative democracy?* Princeton-New Jersey: Princeton University Press

Haass, R. N. (2013) Resident Council on Foreign Relations Independent Task Force Report No. 70, USA

Haider, Z. (2012) Police Image and the Media' in Abbass, H. (ed) (2012) *Stabilising Pakistan Through Police Reforms* pp. 92-93 [Online] Available at https://asiasociety.org/files/pdf/as_pakistan_police_reform.pdf (Accessed: 23 December 2017)

279

Haines, Stephen G. (2000) The systems thinking approach to strategic planning and management. Boca Raton, FL: CRC Press

Hameed, Z. (2015) *Changes in Pakistan's Counterterrorism Legal Regime: Challenges, Prospects, and Recommendations*, New America, available at https://na-production.s3.amazonaws.com/documents/changes-in-pakistans-counter-terrorism-legal-regime.pdf (Accessed: 25 May 2016)

Hanania, J.M. (2018) *Architecture of a Techno democracy*, USA: www.technodemocracy.us.

Handbook on police accountability, oversight, and integrity (2011) New York: UNITED NATION

Hanggi, H. and Tanner, F. (2005) Promoting Security Sector Governance in EU Neighbourhood, *Chaillot Paper No. 80*, July 2015, New York: Institute for Security Studies

Harari, Y.N. (2018) *21 lessons from the 21st Century* London: Jonathan Cape Publishers

Hashmi, F. (2018) 'Dispute Resolution Council Settles 727 disputes in First Quarter' *Urdu-Point*, dated 05th April 2018, [Online] Available at https://www.urdupoint.com/en/pakistan/the-dispute-resolution-councils-drcs-settle-305155.html (Accessed: 24 December 2018)

Hassan, R. (2018) Pakistan's Civil-Military Relations, Yale Global Press [Online] Available at https://yaleglobal.yale.edu/content/pakistans-civil-military-relations (Accessed: 25th April 2019)

Hayat, A. (1985) Police Reforms Committee Report 1985 Original documents available at National police Academy Islamabad Library

Heatherton, C. & Jordan T.C. (2016) *Policing the Planet: Why the Policing Crisis Led to Black Lives*, New York: Verso Books

Hendrix, J.A. (2017) Strategic policing philosophy and the acquisition of technology: findings from a nationally representative survey of law enforcement, published in *Policing and Society: An International Journal of Research and Policy* on 7th May 2017. [Online] Available at https://www.tandfonline.com/doi/abs/10.1080/10439463.2017.1322966?src=recsys&journalCode=gpas20 (Accessed: 20 January 2019)

Hendrix, J.A., Taniguchi, T., Strom, K.J., Aagaard, B. and Johnson, N. (2017) Strategic policing philosophy and the acquisition of technology: findings from a nationally representative survey of law enforcement, Policing and Society, 29:6, 727-743, DOI: 10.1080/10439463.2017.1322966 [online] (Accessed on 14 October 2021)

Henry, V.E. (2002) *The CompStat Paradigm: Management Accountability in Policing, Business and the Public Sector,* (1st edition), New York: Looseleaf Law Publications, pp. 235-325
Herbert, S. (2007) Citizens, Cops, and Power: Recognizing the Limits of Community, *Law and Society Review* (March 2007) [Online] Available at https://www.researchgate.net/publication/249479428_Citizens_Cops_and_Power_Recognizing_the_Limits_of_Community_by_Steve_Herbert, accessed on 20 October 2021

Heyer, G. D. (2016) *Delivering Police Services Effectively,* London: Taylor & Francis Group, CRC Press

Hof, S. and Groothuis, M.M. (2011) *Innovating Government: Normative, Policy and Technological Dimensions of Modern Government*, T.M.C. Asser Press

Holmes, J. R. (2006) *Theodore Roosevelt and World Order: Police Power in International Relations*, Washington, DC: Potomac Books, Inc.

By J.J. Baloch (2022)

Holton, R.J. (2014) *Global Inequalities*, Basingstoke: Palgrave Macmillan

Home Office UK (2013) 'Reducing Bureaucracy Programme in Policing' [Online] Available at
https://webarchive.nationalarchives.gov.uk/20100408132736/http://police.homeoffice.gov.uk/publications/p
olice-reform/reducing-bureaucracy-policing2835.pdf?view=Binary (Accessed: 13 January 2019)

Home Office, UK (2015) The Strategic Policing requirement. [Online] Available at
https://assets.publishing.service.gov.uk/government/uploads/system/uploads/attachment_data/file/417116/
The_Strategic_Policing_Requirement.pdf (Accessed: 01 March 2019)
Hornberger, J. (2011) *Policing and Human Rights: The Meaning of Violence and Justice in the
Everyday Policing of Johannesburg*, NY, Routledge

HRW Report (2016) The Crooked System: Police Abuse and Reforms in Pakistan [Online] Available at
https://www.hrw.org/sites/default/files/report_pdf/pakistan0916_web.pdf (Accessed: 21 January 2017)
http://www.humanrightsinitiative.org/publications/police/feudal_forces_reform_delayed_moving_from_forc
e_to_service_in_south_asian_policing.pdf (accessed on 12 May 2017)

Hu, L. (2010). Same bed, but different dreams? Comparing retired and incumbent police officers' perceptions
of lost knowledge and transfer mechanisms. *Crime Law Social Change*, Volume-53, pp. 313-410

Huey, L. and Mitchell, R.J. (2019) *Evidence-Based Policing: An Introduction*, Bristol, UK: Policy Press, pp. 03-51

Huggins, M.K. (1997) From bureaucratic consolidation to structural devolution: Police death squads
in Brazil, *Policing and Society*, (7) 4, pp. 207-234, [Online] Available at DOI:
10.1080/10439463.1997.9964775 (accessed on 28 October 2021)

Hughes, V. & Love, P. (2004) Toward cyber-centric management of policing: back to the future with
information and communication technology, *Industrial Management & Data Systems*, Volume- 104, pp. 604-
612

Hunt, G. (2007) *The Rules of Modern Policing*, London: Bantam Press

Hunter, R.D. (1990) Three Models of Policing, in 13 Police Study International Review, Police Division 118
[Online] Available at
https://heinonline.org/HOL/LandingPage?handle=hein.journals/polic13&div=24&id=&page= (accessed on 5
November 2021)

Hussain, I. (2018) *Governing the Ungovernable: Institutional Reforms for Democratic Governance*, Karachi:
Oxford University Press, pp.210-263

Hussain, S.E. (2012) 'Myths about Terrorism in Pakistan' in Abbass, H. (ed) (2012) *Stabilising Pakistan Through
Police Reforms* pp. 43-48 [Online] Available at https://asiasociety.org/files/pdf/as_pakistan_police_reform.pdf
(Accessed: 15 December 2017)

Hutta, J.S. (2019) From sovereignty to technologies of dependency: Rethinking the power relations
supporting violence in Brazil, *Political Geography*, March 2019 (69), pp. 65-76 [Online] Available at
https://www.sciencedirect.com/science/article/abs/pii/S0962629817300884?via%3Dihub (accessed
28 October 2021)

Hyder, M. (2016) 'Terrorism & Extremism', *Lecture at National Institute of Management-NIM Karachi*, 31
December 2016

281

ICG Report 160 (2008) 'Reforming Judiciary in Pakistan' by International Crisis Group (ICG) Asia Report, 160 16 October Brussels [Online] Available at https://www.crisisgroup.org/asia/south-asia/pakistan/reforming-judiciary-pakistan (Accessed: 13 January 2018)

ICG Report 196 (2010) 'Reforming Pakistan's Criminal Justice' by *International Crisis Group (ICG) Asia Report, 196,* 06 December 2010, Brussels [Online] Available at https://www.crisisgroup.org/asia/south-asia/pakistan/reforming-pakistan-s-criminal-justice-system, The report says that dysfunctional Criminal Justice of Pakistan is a serious threat to domestic, regional and international security. (Accessed: 13 January 2018)

ICG Report 271 (2015) 'Revisiting Counter-terrorism Strategies in Pakistan: Opportunities and Pitfalls', *International Crisis Group Report 271 /Asia,* dated 22 JULY 2015 [Online] Available at https://www.crisisgroup.org/asia/south-asia/pakistan/revisiting-counter-terrorism-strategies-pakistan-opportunities-and-pitfalls (Accessed: 23 August 2016)

ICG Report-29 (2018) 'China-Pakistan Economic Corridor: Opportunities and Risks' in *International Crisis Group Report No. 29,* ASIA dated 29th June 2018 [Online] Available at https://www.crisisgroup.org/asia/south-asia/pakistan/297-china-pakistan-economic-corridor-opportunities-and-risks (Accessed: 02 December 2018)

ICG-Report (2014) 'Policing Urban Violence in Pakistan', Brussels [Online] Available at https://www.crisisgroup.org/asia/south-asia/pakistan/policing-urban-violence-Pakistan (Accessed: 28 February 2018)

Imam, S.K. (2019) 'Operational Planning and Post Operational Response or SOP for Police Operations' *Sindh Police* [Online] Available at file:///C:/Users/hp1/Downloads/SOP%20for%20Police%20operations.pdf (Accessed: 20 February 2019)

Iman, S.K. (2011) *Problems of Governance in Pakistan: A Case Study of Police Administration,* Islamabad: International Islamic University, pp. 60-164.

Information and Data provided by *Mr Ayaz Khan Deputy Director* Cyber Crime Response Unit of FIA Islamabad on request on 21st November 2018

Innes, M., Abbott, L. Lowe, T. and Roberts, C. (2007) *Hearts and Minds and Eyes and Ears: Reducing Radicalisation Risks Through Reassurance-Oriented Policing,* London: ACPO

Ipsos (2018) 'Millennials in Pakistan', in *Game Changers Series of Survey Research* that published in May 2018. This survey report draws on Pakistani Millennials as the country's most important as well as the most disruptive segments

Iqbal, K. (2016) 'National Action Plan, Loops, and holes' *The Nation,* 14 September 2016 [Online] Available at https://nation.com.pk/14-Sep-2015/nap-loops-and-holes (Accessed: 18 November 2016)

Iqbal, N. (2019) 'Police Autonomy as Important as Independence of Judiciary: CJP' Published in *Daily Dawn* (4 October 2019) [Online] Available at https://www.dawn.com/news/1508864 (Accessed on 10 December 2020)

Irwin, J. (2005) *The Warehouse Prison: Disposal of New Dangerous Class,* Los Angles: Roxbury

Jabri, P. (2019) 'Government Striving to Provide Easiness, facilitates to overseas Pakistanis', reported in *Business Recorder,* 26 February 2019 [Hotline] available at https://www.brecorder.com/2019/02/26/477333/govt-striving-to-provide-easiness-facilities-to-overseas-pakistanis-pm/ (Accessed: 28 February 2019)

By J.J. Baloch (2022)

Jackson, R. (2008) Conversations in Critical Studies in Terrorism – Counter-terrorism and communities: An Interview with Robert Lambert, *Critical Studies on Terrorism*, 1(2), pp. 293-308

Jahangir, R. (2019) How social media has become a War Zone for Competing Narratives published in monthly Herald Magazine of Pakistan on 02 January 2019 [Online] Available at https://herald.dawn.com/news/1398759

JAICA Report (1996) The Japanese Police Delegation Report prepared by National Police Agency, Japan in collaboration with *Japan International Cooperation Agency*-JAICA- 5-21 April 1996 available at National Police Academy library Islamabad

James, B., and Marx, G. (2011-3) Technological innovations in Crime Prevention and Policing: A Review of research on Implementation and Impact, Cahiers Politiestudies Jargang, 20: pp. 17-40 [Online] Available at https://www.ncjrs.gov/pdffiles1/nij/238011.pdf (Accessed: 18 November 2018)

Jeffersonquotes.com. These are taken from the discourse of American president Jefferson

Jenkins, R. (2002) *Social Identity*, New York: Routledge

Jewkes, Y. (2011) *Media and Crime*, London: Sage

Jobard, F. (2003) Raw facts and Narratives, *Policing and Society*, 13 (4), pp. 423-428

John, W. (2008) 'Resurgent Radicalism in Pakistan: A Case Study of Jamaat-ud-Dawa', CLAWS Journal, Winter 2008, Mr Wilson John is Senior Fellow, Observer Research Foundation, New Delhi.
Johnson, R. (2013) *Antiterrorism and Threat Response: Planning and Implementation*, Boca Rotan USA, CRC Press

Jonathan, Z. T. (2014) *Policing Terrorism, Crime Control, and Police-Community Relations*, Springer International Publishing

Jones and Newburn (2006) *Plural policing: A Comparative Perspective*, London, Routledge

Jones, M. (2009) 'Governance, integrity, and the police organization', *An International Journal of Police Strategies and Management* 32(2):338-350 [Online] available at https://www.researchgate.net/publication/235319123_Governance_integrity_and_the_police_organization, (accessed on 25 September 2021)

Jones, O.B. (2002) *Pakistan: Eye of the Storm*, India-Haryana: Penguin Books

Jones, T. & Newburn, T. (2013) Policy convergence, politics, and comparative penal reform: Sex offender notification schemes in the USA and UK. *Punishment and Society*, 15(5), pp. 439-467

Jones, T., and Newburn, T. (2002) The Transformation of Policing: Understanding Current Trends in Policing Systems, *The British Journal of Criminology* (42)1, Winter 2002, pp. 129-146 Published by Oxford University Press available at https://www.jstor.org/stable/i23637163 (accessed on 7 November 2021)

Jordan, G. and Weedon, C. (1995) *Cultural politics: Class, gender, race and the postmodern world*, Cambridge, MA: Wiley-Blackwell

Joyce, P. (2011) *Policing: Development and Contemporary Practice* London: Sage Chapter-9 pp. 208-230 and chapter-4, pp. 68-92

JTIC - Law Enforcement - Evidence-Based Policing. [Online] Available at https://www.justnet.org/law-enforcement/evidence-based-policing.html (Accessed: 06 March 2018)

Junkerman, J. and Masakazu, T. (eds.) (2005) *'Power and Terror', Post 9/11 Talks and Interviews of Noam Chomsky*, New York: Vanguard Press

Kalia, S. (2013) 'Bureaucratic Policymaking in Pakistan', The Dialogue, VIII (2) pp. 156-170 [Online] Available at http://www.qurtuba.edu.pk/thedialogue/The%20Dialogue/8_2/Dialogue_April_June2013_156-170.pdf (Accessed: 12 January 2018)

Kalyvas, S. and Luenia, S. (2005) 'Killing without dying: the absence of suicide missions' in D. Gambetta (ed.) *Making Sense of Suicide Missions.* Oxford: Oxford University Press

Katusa, M. (2014) The Colder War: How the Global Energy Trade Slipped from America's Grasp, Wiley Publishers

Katz, C.M. and Huff, J. (2020) Implement Collaborative Strategic Crime Control Initiatives Chapter 2 in Katz, C.M. and Maguire, E.R. eds. (2020) *Transforming the Police: Thirteen Key Reforms*, Long Grove Illinois, USA, Waveland Press, Inc. pp. 31-46

Katz, C.M. and Maguire, E.R. eds. (2020) Transforming the Police: Thirteen Key Reforms, Long Grove Illinois, USA, Waveland Press, Inc.

Katz, J. (1988) *Seductions in Crime: Moral and Sensual Attractions in Doing Evil*, New York: Basic Books

Kauppi, N. and Madsen, M.R. (2013) Transnational Power Elites: The New Professionals of Governance, Law and Security, New York, Routledge

Keane, T. and Hamilton, L. (2006) *Without Precedent: The Inside Story of the 9/11 Commission*, New York: Knopf

Kelling, George L., and Wilson, James Q. (1982) The Broken Windows: The Police and Neighbourhood Safety, *The Atlantic* [Online] Available at https://www.theatlantic.com/magazine/archive/1982/03/broken-windows/304465/ Accessed on 13 October 2021.

Kelty, S.F., Julian, R. & Ross, A. (2013). Dismantling the Justice Silos: Avoiding the pitfalls and reaping the benefits of information-sharing between forensic science, medicine, and law, *Forensic Science International*, 230, pp. 8-15

Kempe, H. (2015) *Police Corruption and Police Reforms in developing societies* New York: CRC Press, Taylor & Francis Group

Kennedy, D.M. (2006) 'Old Wine in New Bottles and the Lessons of Pulling Levers' in *Police Innovations: Contrasting Perspectives* (eds.) Weisburd, D. & Braga, A.A. (2006), New York: Cambridge University Press, pp. 155-170

Khair, T. (2012) *How to Fight Islamist Terror from the Missionary Position*, A Novel, New Delhi: Fourth Estate

Khaki, Dr. A., Haider, Y. (2015) 'Readings in Human Rights, *Foundation for Research & Development-FORD, Islamabad,* pp. 119-140

Khalid, S. (2017) *Theory and Practice of Police Corruption in Pakistan: Case Studies of Three Police Departments* Islamabad: Iqbal International Institute for Research and Dialogue

By J.J. Baloch (2022)

Khan, A. (2018) Discussions on National Police Bureau with Mr. Amjad Khan, PSP, who had served for more than three years as DIG/Director at the National Police Bureau

Khan, I. (2011) *Pakistan: A Personal History*, London: Trans-world Books, pp. 310-399

Khan, I. (2016) Charge Sheet Against NAP, *Daily Dawn*, 8th October 2016 [Online] Available at https://www.dawn.com/news/1280318 (Accessed on 13 April 2017)

Khattak, D. (2020) Whither the Pakistani Taliban: An Assessment of Recent Trends, *New America Foundation*, (31st August 2020) [Online] https://www.newamerica.org/international-security/blog/whither-pakistani-taliban-assessment-recent-trends/, accessed on 30th October 2021

Khera, S. (2014) *Freedom is not free*, New Delhi: Bloomsbury, pp. 162-219

Khosa, T. (2016) 'Sleeping on the Job', *Daily Dawn*, 22 August 2016 [Online] Available at https://www.dawn.com/news/1279081 (Accessed 12 November 2016)

Kiessling, H. G. (2016) 'Faith, Unity, Discipline-ISI of Pakistan, Noida, India: HarperCollins, pp. 13-90

Koch, B. and Bennett, T. (1993) Community Policing in Canada and Britain, *Research Bulletin* (34) (Summer 1993) pp. 36-42 [Online] Available at https://www.ncjrs.gov/App/Publications/abstract.aspx?ID=146120 (Accessed: 13 January 2017)

Kochel, T.R. (2011). Constructing hotspots policing: Unexamined consequences for the disadvantaged population and police legitimacy. Criminal Justice Policy Review, 22(3), 350-374, [Online] Available at https://www.ojp.gov/ncjrs/virtual-library/abstracts/constructing-hot-spots-policing-unexamined-consequences, Accessed 20 December 2020

Koenig, D.J. and Das, D.K. (ed.) (2001) *International Police Cooperation: A Global Perspective*, Lanham, Maryland: Lexington Books

Kolsky, E. (2010) *Colonial justice in British India* Cambridge: Cambridge University Press

KPK Government Website: Khyber Pakhtunkhwa Government website, History -March of Time, [Online] Available at http://kp.gov.pk/page/history_march_of_time (Accessed: 20 December 2018)

KP Police Website: Khyber Pakhtunkhwa Police Official Website [Online] Available at http://kppolice.gov.pk/ (Accessed: 20 December 2018)

Kratcoski, P.C. (2017) Policing Continuity and Change, Chapter 1, in Eterno, J.A, Verma, A., Das, A.M, & Das D.K. eds. (2017) *Global Issues in Contemporary Policing*, New York: CRC Press, pp. 3-32

Kuhn, T. (1962) *The Structure of Scientific Revolution*, Chicago: Chicago University Press

Kumar, K. (2015) Police and Politics: Autonomy and Accountability, Public Affairs And Governance 3(2):98 (January 2015) [Online] available at https://www.researchgate.net/publication/307792812_Police_and_Politics_Autonomy_and_Accountability, (accessed on 15 October 2021)

Kumar, V. (2017) Police Executive Leadership and Police Legitimacy, Chapter 2, in Eterno, J.A, Verma, A., Das, A.M, & Das D.K (2017) *Global Issues in Contemporary Policing*, New York: CRC Press, pp. 33-44

285

Kunjappan, S. (2021) Policing by Consent: Exploring the Possibilities of Functional Linkage between Local Police Station and Panchayat, Chapter 11, in Dunham, R.G., Alpert, G.P., and MacLean, K.D. eds. (2021) *Critical Issues in Policing: Contemporary Readings*, 8th edn. Illinois USA, Waveland Press, Inc. pp.221-238

Lacey, N. (2020) The fragmented US system means that the battle for criminal justice reform must be fought in multiple political arenas, published at *The LSE US Centre's daily blog on American Politics and Policy* (11 June 2020) available at https://blogs.lse.ac.uk/usappblog/2020/06/11/the-fragmented-us-system-means-that-the-battle-for-criminal-justice-reform-must-be-fought-in-multiple-political-arenas/ (accessed on 3 November 2021)

LaFree, G. (2012) Policing Terrorism, in Ideas in American Policing by *Police Foundation,* Number 15, July 2012 [Online] Available at https://www.policefoundation.org/wp-content/uploads/2015/06/Ideas_15_LaFree_1.pdf (Accessed on 12 July 2021)

Lang-worthy, R.H & Travis, L.F. (1994) *Policing in America: Balance of Forces*, New York: Macmillan

Lau, T. (2020) Predictive Policing Explained, Brennan Center for Justice, 1 April 2020, [Online] Available at https://www.brennancenter.org/our-work/research-reports/predictive-policing-explained, Accessed on 12 October 2021.

Lawrence, R. (2000) *The Politics of Force: Media and the Construction of Police Brutality*, Berkley: California University Press

Lawson, S.G., and Wolfe, S.E. (2021) Organisational Justice and Policing, Chapter 28, in Dunham, R.G., Alpert, G.P., and MacLean, K.D. eds. (2021) *Critical Issues in Policing: Contemporary Readings*, 8th edn. Illinois USA, Waveland Press, Inc. pp. 560-579

Lawteacher.net, (2018) 'Advantages and disadvantages of community policing' published online on February 02, 2018, Chapter 01, [Online] Available at https://www.lawteacher.net/free-law-essays/criminology/advantages-and-disadvantages-of-community-policing.php (Accessed 24 March 2018)

Lemieux, F. (2010) *International Police Cooperation: Emerging Issues, Theory, and Practice*, London: Routledge

Lemieux, F., Heyer, G. D., Das, D.K. eds. (2019) *Economic Development, Crime, and Policing: Global Perspectives*, NY, Routledge

Leong, N. (2013) 'Racial Capitalism' *Harvard Law Review 126 (8)*

Levi, L. (2007) 'State-centric Paradigm' in *Group for Study and Research on Globalisation* [Online] Available at http://www.mondialisations.org/php/public/art.php?id=25917&lan=EN (Accessed: 28 January 2019)

Levi, M. (2007) *On Nuclear Terrorism*, New York: The Council on Foreign Affairs

Lieven, A. (2011) *Pakistan: A Hard Country*, London: Penguin Books, pp. 83-248, & 405-488

Lint, W.D. (1999) A Postmodern Turn in Policing: Police as a Pastiche, International Journal of the Sociology of Law, (27), 2, pp. 127-152 [Online] Available at https://doi.org/10,1006/ijsl.1999.0085 (Accessed: 15 July 2019)

Lister, S.C. and Jones, T. (2016) Plural Policing and the Challenge of Democratic Accountability, in Lister, S.C., and Rowe, M. (eds.) *Accountability of Policing-Routledge Frontiers of Criminal Justice*, London, Routledge

Loader, I. and Walker, N. (2007) *Civilizing Security*, Cambridge: Cambridge University Press

Lobnikar, B., Mesko, G., and Modic, M. (2021) Transformations in policing-Two Decades of Experience in Community Policing in Slovenia, Chapter 10, in Dunham, R.G., Alpert, G.P., and MacLean, K.D. eds. (2021) *Critical Issues in Policing: Contemporary Readings*, 8th edn. Illinois USA, Waveland Press, Inc. pp. 199-220

Lodhi, M. (2011) *Pakistan Beyond Crisis State,* London: C Hurst & Co Publishers Ltd
Lowe, D. (2015) *Policing Terrorism: Research Studies in Police Counterterrorism Investigations,* London, CRC Press

Lowe, D., (2015) *Policing Terrorism: Research Studies into Police Counterterrorism Investigations,* London: Taylor & Francis Group, CRC Press

Lum, C, Koper, C. and Telep, C. (2011) The Evidence-Based Policing Matrix, *Journal of Experimental Criminology*, 7(1), pp. 3–26.

Lyons, W. (2002) 'Partnerships, information and public safety: Community policing in a time of terror', *Policing: An International Journal of Police Strategies and Management,* 25(3), pp. 530-542

Lyotard, J.F. (1984) the *postmodern condition: A report on knowledge.* Manchester: Manchester University Press.

MacLean, K., Wolfe, S.E., Rojek, J., Alpert, G.P., and Smith, M.R. (2021) Police Officers as Warriors or Guardians: Empirical Reality or Intriguing Rhetoric, Chapter 13, in Dunham, R.G., Alpert, G.P., and MacLean, K.D. eds. (2021) *Critical Issues in Policing: Contemporary Readings*, 8th edn. Illinois USA, Waveland Press, Inc. pp. 233-260

Macpherson, W. (1999) *Stephen Lawrence Enquiry: Report of an Inquiry by Sir William Macpherson of Cluny,* London: HMSO

Madsen, F. (2009) *Transnational Organised Crime,* London: Routledge

Magliocca, G. N. (2016) The Bill of Rights as a Term of Art, 92 Notre Dame Law Review 231 (9 November 2016), [Online] Available at SSRN: https://ssrn.com/abstract=2617811 or http://dx.doi.org/10.2139/ssrn.2617811 (accessed on 23 November 2021)

Maguire, E.R., Khade, N., and Mora, V. (2020) Improve the Policing of Crowds, Chapter 12, in Katz, C.M. and Maguire, E.R. eds. (2020) *Transforming the Police: Thirteen Key Reforms*, Long Grove Illinois, USA, Waveland Press, Inc. pp. 235-249

Maguire, E.R., Somers, L.J., and Padilla, K.E. (2020) Promoting Officer Health and Wellness, Chapter 11, in Katz, C.M. and Maguire, E.R. eds. (2020) *Transforming the Police: Thirteen Key Reforms*, Long Grove Illinois, USA, Waveland Press, Inc. pp. 213-230

Maguire, M., and Okada, D. (ed.) (2011) *Critical Issues in Crime and Justice,* California, USA: Sage Publications

Majid, A. (2020) The Impact of Leadership Style on Organizational Performance in Pakistan's Service Sector (December 8, 2020) [Online] Available at SSRN: https://ssrn.com/abstract=3807888 or http://dx.doi.org/10.2139/ssrn.3807888 (accessed on 23 November 2021)

Majoran, A. (2015) The Illusion of War: is Terrorism a Criminal Act or an Act of war, International Politics Review (3) pp. 19–27 [Online] Available at https://doi.org/10.1057/ipr.2015.9 (Accessed on 23 October 2021)

Malik, H. (2019) Law and Justice Commissions St to Issue Police reform Report Today, *the Express Tribune*, 14 January 2019. [Online] Available at https://tribune.com.pk/story/1887648/1-law-justice-commission-set-launch-police-reforms-report-today/ (Accessed: 28 February 2019)

Manning, P. (1992) 'Information technologies and the police' *Crime and Justice*, 15, pp. 349-398

Manning, P. (2005) 'The study of policing' *Police Quarterly*, 8(1), pp. 23-43

Manning, P.K. (2000). Policing new social spaces, in Sheptycki, J. (ed.), *Issues in Transnational Policing*, London: Routledge, pp. 177-200.

Manning, P.K. (2015) *Democratic Policing in a Changing World*, London: Routledge

Manningham, D. E. (2006) The International Terrorist Threat to the UK, *speech given at Queen Mary's College, London*, on 11 September 2006

Manningham, D.E. (2007) 'Partnership and Continuous Improvement in Countering Twenty-First Century Terrorism', *Policing: A Journal of Policy and Practice* 1, (1), 1 January 2007, pp. 43–45 [Online] Available at https://doi.org/10.1093/police/pam010 (Accessed: 25 May 2018)

Marenin, O. (2005) 'Building a global police studies community', Research Article *Police Quarterly*, pp. 102-136 [Online] Available at https://doi.org/10.1177/1098611104267329 (Accessed: 15 June 2018)

Marks, M., Wood, J., Ally, R, Walsh, T., and Witbooi, A. (2010) 'Worlds Apart? On the Possibilities of Police/Academic Collaborations', *Policing: A Journal of Policy and Practice,* 4(2): pp. 112–118

Martin, C. (2013) *'Terrorism as a Crime'. Counter-Terrorism Strategies in a Fragmented International Legal Order.* Cambridge, UK: Cambridge University Press, pp. 639–666

Martin, S.E. & Jurik, N.C. (2007) *Doing Justice, Doing Gender: Women in Legal & Criminal Justice Occupations,* California: Sage Publications, Inc.

Marx, G.T. (2007) 'The Engineering of Social Control: Policing and Technology', *Policing: A Journal of Policy and Practice*, Vol-1, (1), 1 January 2007, pp. 46–56, [Online] Available at https://doi.org/10.1093/police/pam001 (Accessed: 23 March 2018)

Mason, L. and Deflem, M. (ED) (2004) 'Terrorism and counter-terrorism: criminological perspectives, *Policing: A Journal of Policy and Practice* 1, (1), 1 January 2007, pp. 123–125 [Online] Available at https://doi.org/10.1093/police/pam018 (Accessed: 27 May 2017)

Mastrofski, S. (1999) *Policing for People*, Ideas in American Policing, Washington: Police Foundation

Mastrofski, S. (2006) 'Community Policing: A Skeptical View' in *Police Innovations: Contrasting Perspectives* (eds.) Weisburd, D. & Braga, A.A. (2006), New York: Cambridge University Press, pp. 44-76

Mawby, R. (2008) 'Models of policing' in T. Newburn (Ed.), *Handbook of Policing* (Second Ed.). Cullompton, Devon: Willan Publishing, pp. 17-46.

Maxson, C., Hennigan, K. and Sloane, D.C. (2021) Factors That Influence Public Opinion of the Police, National Institute of Justice (3rd June) http://www.ojp.usdoj.gov/nij [Online] available at https://www.ojp.gov/pdffiles1/nij/197925.pdf, accessed 30 October 2021

By J.J. Baloch (2022)

Maxwell, R. (2006) Muslims, South Asians, and the British Mainstream: A National Identity Crisis? *West European Politics*, 29(4): pp. 736-756.

Mazerolle, L. and Ransley, J. (2002) Third-party policing: prospects & challenges, Australian Institute of Criminology, Griffith University, available at https://researchrepository.griffith.edu.au/bitstream/handle/10072/9043/20297_1.pdf%3bsequence=1(Accessed: 05 March 2018)

Mazerolle, L. and Ransley, J. (2006) 'The Case for Third-Party Policing' in *Police Innovations: Contrasting Perspectives* (eds.) Weisburd, D. & Braga, A.A. (2006), New York: Cambridge University Press, pp. 191-206

McCarthy, M. (2019) Explaining community-level variation in police use of force: The influence of community characteristics and community-oriented policing on Australian officer's use of force, (a Ph.D. Research Thesis) published by Griffith University, Queensland, Australia [Online] Available at https://doi.org/10.25904/1912/2897 (accessed on 20 November 2021)

McCluskey, J. (2003) *Police Requests for Compliance: Coercive and Procedurally Just Tactics*, New York: LFB Scholarly Publishing

McConville, M. Sanders, A., and Leng, R. (1991) *The Case for the Prosecution*, London: Routledge

McGrath, A. (1996) *The Destruction of Pakistan's Democracy*, Karachi: Oxford University Press

McHenry, M.K. (2019) A Need for Change: The Importance of Continued Training and Education for Modern Day Police Officers, *Criminal Justice Institute*, [Online] Available at https://www.cji.edu/wp-content/uploads/2019/04/aneedforchange.pdf (accessed on 20 October 2021)

McLaughlin, E. (2007) *The New Policing*: London: Sage

McLaughlin, E. and Murji, K. (1999) The Postmodern Condition of the Police, *The Liverpool Law Review*, 21 (2-3) pp. 217-240 [Online] Available at https://doi.org/10.1023/A:1005637612120 (Accessed: 13 February 2019) McLaughlin, E., Murji, K (1999) The Postmodern Condition of the Police. *Liverpool Law Review* **21**, 217–240 [Online] Available at https://doi.org/10.1023/A:1005637612120, Accessed on 10 July 2021

McNamara, J. (2010) *The 21st Century Media (R) evolution*: Emergent Communication Practices, New York: Peter Lang Publishing

Meares, T. (2017) Policing and Procedural Justice: Shaping Citizens' Identities to Increase Democratic Participation, North-Western University Law Review, Yale University vol. (111) 6 [Online] Available at https://digitalcommons.law.yale.edu/cgi/viewcontent.cgi?article=6183&context=fss_papers (accessed on 1st November 2021)

Meares, T. (2017) Policing and Procedural Justice: Shaping Citizens' Identities to Increase Democratic Participation, (111) 6. Nw. U. Law Review, 1525 (2016-2017) [Online] Available at https://heinonline.org/HOL/LandingPage?handle=hein.journals/illlr111&div=53&id=&page= (accessed 23 November 2020)

Meares, T.L. (2006) 'Third-Party Policing: A Critical View' in *Police Innovations: Contrasting Perspectives* (eds.) Weisburd, D. & Braga, A.A. (2006), New York: Cambridge University Press, pp. 207-224

Mehmood, T. (2016) 'Energizing National Action Plan', *The Express Tribune*, 17 August 2016 [Online] Available at https://tribune.com.pk/story/1164056/energising-national-action-plan/ (Accessed: 01 May 2017)

Melchor C., Das, A.M., and Das, D.K. (2013) *The Evolution of Policing: Worldwide Innovations and Insights* Boca Raton, FL-USA: CRC Press

Mello, P.A. (2015) Democratic Peace Theory, The SAGE Encyclopedia of War: Social Science Perspectives, edited by Paul I. Joseph, Thousand Oaks: Sage, (25th September 2014) Available at SSRN: https://ssrn.com/abstract=2674255, (accessed 24 November 2020)

Mercer, T. (2019) Values in Today's Society, Published in *Youth First Blog* on 23 April 2019 [Online] Available at https://youthfirstinc.org/values-in-todays-society/#:~:text=Social%20values%20include%20justice%2C%20freedom,of%20power%2C%20greed%2C%20etc. (Accessed on 22 October 2021)

Mihailescu, C.A. and Murkami T.Y. (2018) *Policing Literary Theory, Boston* USA: Brill Sense Publishing

Miller, K. (2007) 'Racial Profiling and Postmodern Society: Police Responsiveness, Image Maintenance, and the Left Flank of the Legitimacy' *Journal of Contemporary Criminal Justice*, 23 (3) pp. 248-262
Millie, A. & Das, D. (2008) Conclusions, in *Contemporary Issues in Law Enforcement and Policing*, pages 199-202.

Ministry of Law, Justice, Human Rights and Parliamentary, [Online] Available at http://npb.gov.pk/wp-content/uploads/2014/08/police_order_2002.pdf (Accessed: 12 April 2018)

Minnaar, A. (2017) Cyber Crime, Cyberattacks, and Problems of Implementing Organisational Cybersecurity, Chapter 6, in Eterno, J.A, Verma, A., Das, A.M, & Das D.K (2017) *Global Issues in Contemporary Policing*, New York: CRC Press, pp.121-138

Mir, A. (2006) 'The True Face of Jihadis: Inside Pakistan's Network of Terror', New Delhi: Roli Books

Mir, A. (2018) The U.S. drone war in Pakistan revisited, The *Freeman Spogli Institute for International Studies, Stanford University*. [Online] Available at https://fsi.stanford.edu/news/us-drone-war-pakistan-revisited, (Accessed: 24 July 2018)

Mirza, S.A. (2018) Discussions with Mr. Saud Ahmad (PSP) on many occasions who always enlightened me with new ideas and information regarding the background of Sindh Police in terms of its history, heritage, and legacy

Mitha, Gen. (1970) *Police Reform Commission Report* available at National Police Academy Library, H/11, Islamabad

Moore, M.H. (2006) 'Improving Police Through Expertise, Experience and Experiments' in *Police Innovations: Contrasting Perspectives* (ed.) Weisburd, D. & Braga, A.A. (2006), New York: Cambridge University Press, pp.322-338

Morabito, M, (2008) 'The Adoption of Police Innovation: The Role of Political Environment' *Policing*, 31, pp. 466-484

Moran, R. & Newburn, T. (1997) *The Future of Policing*, London: Oxford University Press

By J.J. Baloch (2022)

Morgan, R. (1989) 'Police Accountability, Current Developments, and Future Prospects', in Weatheritt, M. (Ed.) *Police Research: Some Future Prospects*, Aldershot: Avebury: Police Foundation

Morris, J. (2006) *The National Reassurance Policing Programme: A Ten-site Evaluation*, Home Office Research Findings 273, London: Home Office:

Muhammad, I. (2016) Instability in Afghanistan: Implications for Pakistan, Journal of Political science and Public Affairs, 4, (3) pp. 1-6 [Online] Available at file:///C:/Users/hp1/Downloads/instability-in-afghanistan-implications-for-pakistan-2332-0761-1000213.pdf (Accessed: 28 February 2019)

Mulayim, S., Lai, M., (2016) *Translators Ethics for Police and Interpreters*, London: Taylor & Francis Group, CRC Press

Murray, J. (2005) 'Policing Terrorism: A Threat to Community Policing or Just a Shift in Priorities?' *Police Practice and Research* 6(4): pp. 347-361

Murray, T. (2021) Nearly Twenty Years on The Canadian Police Executive Community Revisited. *Policing: A Journal of Policy and Practice* 15:1 pp. 208-221

NACTA Act No. XIX of 2013 created National Counter Terrorism Authority-NACTA for national coordination among all law enforcement departments, organisations, agencies, both civilian and military, and also bring together an entire government under the prime minister's headship under one single roof for coordinating all responses to extremism and terrorism in Pakistan. The establishment of NACTA speaks volumes of the networked law enforcement model in Pakistan which this book tries to have explored as the newer trend in Policing here and abroad.

NACTA Website (at http://www.nacta.gov.pk/) "International Cooperation in Terrorism", [Online] available at http://www.nacta.gov.pk/Downloads/7.International%20Cooperation%20-%20Agreement%20and%20MOUS%20and%20Declerations.pdf. (Accessed: 17 April 2018)
Najam, D. (2021) Ability to dispense justice makes a leader legitimate, Express Tribune (28 October 2021) [Online] Available at https://tribune.com.pk/story/2326712/ability-to-dispense-justice-makes-a-leader-legitimate, accessed on 30 October 2021

NAP Statistics (2016) Government of Pakistan [Online] Available at http://infopak.gov.pk (Accessed: 13 December 2017)

Naqvi, H. (2016) 'Conversations of Revival of NACTA', Interview of Muhammad Ali Nekokara, *Daily Times*, 24 August 2016

National Counterterrorism Authority Act 2013 Document, [Online] Available at http://www.na.gov.pk/uploads/documents/1364795170_139.pdf (Accessed: 27 March 2017)

National Forensic Science Agency-NFSA Website: http://www.nfsa.gov.pk/ (Accessed: 18 September 2018)

National Police Academy-NPA Website: www.npa.gov.pk/. (Accessed on 24th August 2017)
Nawaz, S. (2016) Countering Militancy and Terrorism in Pakistan: The Civil-Military Nexus, Special Report US Institute of Peace, (www.usip.org October 2016) [Online] Available at https://www.usip.org/sites/default/files/SR393-Countering-Militancy-and-Terrorism-in-Pakistan-The-Civil-Military-Nexus.pdf, accessed on 30th October 2021

Nekokara, M.A (2016) 'Rickety Criminal Justice', *Daily Dawn*, 27 August 2016 [Online] Available at https://www.dawn.com/news/1280189 (Accessed 21 November 2016)

Nekokara, M.A. (2018) Discussions with Mr. Muhammad Ali Nekokara (2018 December) regarding the effectiveness and viability of the Islamabad Safe City projects as he had served as District Police Officers Islamabad in 2014-15 which had been very turbulent times for Islamabad because the city was in the grip of crowd violence.

Neocleous, M. (2014) *War Power, Police Power*, Edinburgh: Edinburgh University Press

Newburn, T. (2001) The Commodification of Policing: Security Networks in Late Modernity, *Urban Studies*, (38) 5-6, pp. 829-848 [Online] Available at https://doi.org/10.1080/00420980123025 (Accessed: 20 July 2019)

Newburn, T. (2015) Literature Review: Police Integrity and Corruption, London: HMIC

Newburn, T. (ed.) (2004) *Policing: Key Readings*, Cullompton: Willan

Newman, G.R. and Clarke, R.V. (2008) Policing terrorism: An executive Guide, US Department of Justice, Office of Justice Programs [Online] Available at https://www.ojp.gov/ncjrs/virtual-library/abstracts/policing-terrorism-executives-guide (Accessed on 14 October 2021)

Newsome, B. O., Stewart, J. W., and Mosavi, A. (2018) *Countering New(est) Terrorism: Hostage-Taking, Kidnapping, and Active Violence — Assessing, Negotiating, and Assaulting*, Boca Raton USA, CRC Press

Neyroud, P. (2007) 'Policing Terrorism', *Policing: A Journal of Policy and Practice* 1, (1), 1 January 2007, pp. 5–8, [Online] Available at https://doi.org/10.1093/police/pam006 (Accessed 01 March 2018)

NIJ (2017) Policing Strategies Strengthen Science & Advance Justice, published by *National Institute of Justice-NIJ* dated 17 July 2017. available at https://www.nij.gov/topics/law-enforcement/strategies/pages/welcome.aspx (Accessed: 22 January 2019)

Notification, F. NO 2/R/Police Law/ LJCP-2018, Government of Pakistan, Law, and Justice Commission, Supreme Court Building, Constitutional Avenue, Islamabad dated 15 May 2018

NPCC-National Police Chief's Council, Policing Vision 2025, sponsored by Association of Police and Crime Commissioners, United Kingdom [Online] Available at https://www.npcc.police.uk/documents/Policing%20Vision.pdf (accessed on 30th October 2021)

O'Neil, C. (2016) *Weapons of Math Destruction: How Big Data Increases Inequality and Threatens Democracy*, New York: Broadway Books

O'Neil, M. (2007) *Police Occupational Culture: New Debates and Directions*, Oxford UK: JAI Press

O'Reilly, C. ed. (2020) *Colonial Policing and the Transnational Legacy: The Global Dynamics of Policing Across the Lusophone Community*, NY, Routledge

Pakistan Railways Police Act (1977) An Act to provide for constitution and Regulation of Pakistan Railways, published in Gazette of Pakistan on 9th January 1977 [Online] Available at http://www.na.gov.pk/uploads/documents/1491542412_976.pdf (accessed 16 January 2019)

Pakistan Today (2018) Sahiwal Incident, *Pakistan Today*, 20th January 2018, [Online] Available at https://www.pakistantoday.com.pk/2019/01/20/sahiwal-incident-new-video-shows-ctd-cops-open-fire/ (Accessed: 20th February 2019)

By J.J. Baloch (2022)

Pakistan's Electronics Crime Act-PECA (2016) Passed by Parliament of Pakistan on 11 August and Promulgated on 14 August (Independence Day) 2016 by the Government [Online] Available at http://www.na.gov.pk/uploads/documents/1470910659_707.pdf (Accessed: 24 October 2018)

Pakistan's Security Report (2017) by *Pakistan Institute for Peace Studies* (PIPS). [Online] Available at http://pakpips.com/downloads/325.pdf (Accessed: 22 August 2018)

Pakistan's Security Report (2018)' by *Pakistan Institute for Peace Studies*. [Online] Available at https://www.pakpips.com/article/book/pakistan-security-report-2018 (Accessed: 20 February 2019)

PAL Launch Dawn Report (2017) 'Police Access Service Launched in Malakand as reported in *Daily Dawn*, 28th May 2017 [Online] Available at https://www.dawn.com/news/1335851 (Accessed: 12 November 2018)
Palmer, D., Berlin, M.M., and Das, D.K. (2012) *Global Environment of Policing*, London, Routledge

Palmiotto M.J. (2000) *Community Policing: A policing Strategy for the 21st Century*, Gaithersburg Maryland USA: Aspen Publishers

Palmiotto, M.J. (2001) *Police Misconduct: A Reader for the 21st Century* New York: Prentice-Hall

Palmiotto, M.J. (2010) Policing & Society: A Global Approach, New York, Delmar Cengage Learning

Panda, A. (2015) ' Afghanistan, Pakistan to Cooperate on Counter-Terrorism', *The Diplomat*, dated 18 May 2015, [Online] Available at http://thediplomat.com/2015/05/afghanistan-pakistan-to-cooperate-on-counter-terrorism/ (Accessed: 14 March 2018)

Pape, R. (2005) *Dying to Win: The Strategic Logic of Suicide Terrorism*, New York: Random House
Paracha, N.F. (2020) Smokers' Corner: 'Hybrid Regimes and their Discontents', *Daily Dawn*, published on 11 October 2020 [Online] Available at https://www.dawn.com/news/1584372 (accessed on 10 November 2021)

Pargeter, A. (2006) *Western Converts to Radial Islam: The Global Jihad's New Soldiers? Jane's Intelligence Review*, 18(8): pp. 20-27

Partick, C.H. (1972) *The Police, Crime, and Society*, Illinois: Charles C. Thomas Publications

Parvez, T. (2012) 'The National counterterrorism Authority' in Abbass, H. (ed) (2012) *Stabilising Pakistan Through Police Reforms*, pp. 62-67 [Online] Available at https://asiasociety.org/files/pdf/as_pakistan_police_reform.pdf (Accessed: 13 December 2017)

Parvez, T. (2015) 'An Obstacle to Police Reform: Brevity of Tenures', *IPR Brief published by Institute for Policy Reforms* in February 2015

Pasquale, F. (2015) The Black Box Society: The Secret Algorithms that Control Money and Information, New York, Harvard University Press

Patel, S. (2008) 'Feudal Forces: Reform Delayed, moving force to Service in South Asian Policing', *Commonwealth Human Rights Initiative* CHRI, [Online] Available at http://www.humanrightsinitiative.org/publications/police/feudal_forces_reform_delayed_moving_from_force_to_service_in_south_asian_policing.pdf (Accessed: 19 October 2017)

Paul, G., Shane, Sc, D. (1980) *People, and Police: A Comparison of Five Countries*, Missouri, USA: The C.V. Mosby Company,

Peace-Direct Report-Pakistan 2017 on 'Local Approaches to preventing Violent Extremism in Pakistan' based on Dialogue among 54 leading Pakistani experts on violent extremism [Online] available at https://www.peacedirect.org/wp-content/uploads/2017/03/Report-Pakistan-8-single-pages.pdf, accessed on 30th October 2021

Peak, K.J. and Glensor, R.W. (2017) Community Policing and Problem Solving: Effectively Addressing Crime and Disorder, 7th ed. London: Pearson

Pearson, G. (1983) *Hooligan: A History of Respectable Fears*. London: Macmillan
Perito, R. & Parvez, T. (2014) A Counterterrorism Role for Pakistan's Police Stations, Special Report, U.S Institute of Peace (www.usip.org) [Online] Available at https://www.usip.org/sites/default/files/SR351-A-Counterrerrorism-Role-for-Pakistan%E2%80%99s-Police-Stations.pdf, Accessed on 22nd March 2020

Perriment, K. (2018) Discussions with Mr Kevin Perriment, Consultant and Advisor with British High Commission Islamabad on Sustainable Criminal Justice Solutions of Home Office UK for Pakistan (December 2018 at FIA Academy Islamabad). Mr Kevin is leading a group of experts who work on the capacity building of the Federal Investigation Agency in the areas of transnational crime with a primary focus on financial crime such as money laundering, terrorist financing, cybercrime, and anti-corruption.

Perriment, K. (2019) Workshop on developing National Curriculum for financial investigations organised by UK funded Project named Sustainable Criminal Justice Solutions in collaboration with City of London Police (CoLP) and UNODC Pakistan and attended by FIA, NAB, and FBR representatives and led by Mr. Kevin Perriment-project Advisor, Mr. Joe and Mr. Rowan from National Crime Agency the UK at Marriott Hotel Islamabad Room: no-05, on 12th and 13th March 2019.

Perrott, S.B., and Trites, K. (2017) On the Acceptability of Closer Public-Private Policing Partnerships: Views from the Public Side, Chapter 3, in Eterno, J.A, Verma, A., Das, A.M, & Das D.K (2017) *Global Issues in Contemporary Policing,* New York: CRC Press, pp. 45-62

Perry Stanislas, P. (2021) The changing perceptions of St. Lucian policing: how St. Lucian police officers view contemporary policing. *Police Practice and Research* 22:1 pp. 337-354

Perry, W.L., McInnis, B., Price, C.C., Smith, S.C. and Hollywood, J.S. (2013) *Predictive Policing: The Role of Crime Forecasting in Law enforcement Operations,* Santa Monica, CA, USA: RAND, pp. 1-15

Peterson, D.S., and Das, D.K., eds. (2019) *Global Perspectives on Crime Prevention and Community Resilience*, NY, Routledge

Phillips, M. (2006) *Londonistan: How Britain is creating a terror state within*, New York: Encounter Books

Phillips, S. W., and Das, D.K. eds. (2017) *Change and Reform in Law Enforcement: Old and New Efforts from Across the Globe*, NY, Routledge

Pike, M. S. (1985) *The Principles of Policing,* London: Macmillan

PIPS Security Report, (2017) Pakistan's Annual Security Report *Pakistan Institute for Peace Studies (PIPS)* [Online] Available at http://pakpips.com/downloads/325.pdf (Accessed: 22 August 2018)

PIPS Security Report, (2018) Pakistan's Annual Security Report' *Pakistan Institute for Peace Studies PIPSs*, [Online] Available at https://www.pakpips.com/article/book/pakistan-security-report-2018 (Accessed: 20 February 2019)

By J.J. Baloch (2022)

Platt, L. (2007) Making Education Count: The Effects of Ethnicity and Qualifications on Intergenerational Social Class Mobility, *the Sociological Review*, 55(3): pp. 485-508

Police Act 1861 available at National Police Academy library Islamabad

Police Act 2017 KP available at National Police Academy library Islamabad

Police Executive Research Forum. (2008, May). Violent crime in America: What we know about hotspots enforcement. Critical Issues in policing series, Washington, D.C. [Online] Available at http://policeforum.org/library/critical-issues-in-policing-series/HotSpots_v4.pdf Accessed on 12 January 2021

Police Order 2002 as amended in 2004-6 and later on and as presented by PRC on 14 January 2019 in Supreme Court as Model Police Law 2018

Police Order 2002 available at National Police Academy library Islamabad

Police Order 2002, Ministry of Law, Justice, Human Rights and Parliamentary, [Online] Available at http://npb.gov.pk/wp-content/uploads/2014/08/police_order_2002.pdf (Accessed: 12 April 2018)

Police Reform Commission 1860 Report available at National Police Academy Library, Islamabad
Portland State University. Criminology and Criminal Justice Senior Capstone, "Implementing Hotspot Policing: A Review of the Literature" (2013). Criminology and Criminal Justice Senior Capstone Project. 4. [Online] Available at https://pdxscholar.library.pdx.edu/ccj_capstone/4

Prenzler, T. (2009) *Police Corruption: Preventing Misconduct and Maintaining Integrity*, Boca Raton USA, CRC Press

Prenzler, T., Hayer, G.D. (2015) *Civilian Oversight of Police: Advancing Accountability in Law Enforcement*, London: Taylor & Francis Group, CRC Press

Presentation by Mr. Tariq Parvez, ex-DG FIA and ex NC NACTA on Launching Ceremony 14th January 2019

Punch M (2003) 'Rotten Orchards: Pestilence, Police Misconduct and System Failure' *Policing and Society* 13 (2) pp. 171–96

Punjab Government's Safe Cities Project: Safer City available at https://digitalrightsfoundation.pk/safer-city-or-over-policing/(Accessed: 11 June 2018)

Puonti, A. (2004) 'Tools for collaboration: using and designing tools in inter-agency economic-crime investigations' *Mind, Culture, and Activity*, 11, pp. 133-152

Ramsey, L. (2018) Strategies for Inclusive and Responsive Police Accountability, Doctoral Thesis supervised by Eric Riedel, Ph.D., at University of Walden [Online] available at https://scholarworks.waldenu.edu/cgi/viewcontent.cgi?article=7375&context=dissertations, (accessed on 14 October 2021)

Rana, M.A. (2012) 'De-radicalisation and the Role of Police' in Abbass, H. (ed) (2012) *Stabilising Pakistan Through Police Reforms* pp. 57-61 [Online] Available at https://asiasociety.org/files/pdf/as_pakistan_police_reform.pdf (Accessed: 29 December 2017)

Rana, M.A. (2013) 'Perceptions of extremism' *daily Dawn*.com, 8 September 2013, [Online] Available at http://www.dawn.com/news/1041383. (Accessed: 12 July 2018)

Rana, M.A. (2016) 'Common Confusions', *Daily Dawn*, 14 August 2016 [Online] Available at https://www.dawn.com/news/1277432/common-confusions (Accessed: 25 January 2017)

RAND CORPORATION ARTICLE (2018) 'Helping Police Find Better Strategies to Fight Crime' 14 December [Online] Available at https://www.rand.org/blog/articles/2018/12/helping-police-find-better-strategies-to-fight-crime.html Accessed on 14 October 2021

RAND Report (2007) 'Building Moderate Muslim Networks' A study Report by RAND Corporations, *Centre for Middle East Public Policy* A California-based Think-tank [Online] Available at https://www.rand.org/content/dam/rand/pubs/monographs/2007/RAND_MG574.pdf (Accessed: 25 November 2016)

Rapoport, D. (1984) Fear, and Trembling: Terrorism in Three Religious Traditions, *American Political Science Review*, 78(3), pp. 658-677

Rasheed, I. (2017) 'Excerpts from Lecture of former and founder IGP of National Highways and Pakistan Motorway, Mr. Iftikhar Rasheed who founded NH&MP Police (NHMP). He delivered at *National Police Academy in 2017* to the 44th PSP batch

Ratcliffe, J. H. (2018) 'Strategic Policing', a blog in *Evidence-based policing, criminal intelligence, and crime science* published on September 18, 2018, [Online] Available at http://www.jratcliffe.net/blog/tag/strategic-policing/ (Accessed: 06 March 2019)

Ratcliffe, J.H. (2016) *Intelligence-Led Policing*, 2nd ed. London: Routledge, pp.66-85

Redmond, M. & Baveja, A. (2002). A data-driven software tool for enabling cooperative information sharing among police departments. *European Journal of Operational Research*, 141, pp. 660-678

Reid, J. (2013). Rapid Assessment Exploring Impediments to Successful Prosecutions of Sex Traffickers of U.S. Minors. *Journal of Police and Criminal Psychology*, 28, pp. 75-89

Reiner, R. (1992) Policing a Postmodern Society, *Modern Law Review*, 55 (6) (November 1992 issue), pp. 761-781

Reiner, R. (2010) *The Politics of the Police* (4th ed.) Oxford: Oxford University Press

Reiner, R. (2017) 'Is Police Culture Cultural?', *Policing: A Journal of Policy and Practice*, 11, (3), 1 September 2017, Pages 236–241, [Online] Available at https://doi.org/10.1093/police/paw046 (Accessed: 02 March 2018)

Reisig, M.D. (2020) Institutionalize Procedural Justice, Chapter 3, in 2 in Katz, C.M., and Maguire, E.R. eds. (2020) *Transforming the Police: Thirteen Key Reforms*, Long Grove Illinois, USA, Waveland Press, Inc. pp. 51-67

Reiss, A. (1992). Police Organisation in the Twentieth Century. *Crime and Justice*, 15: pp. 51-97

Riaz, O. (2018) 'Police: Autonomy and Accountability, *The Express Tribune*, 12 May 2018 [Online] Available at https://tribune.com.pk/story/1708354/police-autonomy-accountability/ (Accessed: December 2018)

Ribaux, O. (2019) 'Reframing Forensic Science and Criminology for Catalysing Innovation in Policing Practices', *Policing: A Journal of Policy and Practice*, vol-13, (1), 1 March 2019, pp. 5–11, Available at https://doi.org/10.1093/police/pax057 (Accessed: 10 March 2019)

Rich, P.B. (1990) *Race and Empire in British Politics*, Cambridge: Cambridge University Press

By J.J. Baloch (2022)

Richardson, L. (2006) *What Terrorists Want: Understanding the Terrorist Threat,* London: John Murray

Roberson, C., Das, D.K., & Singer, J.K. (2010) *Police Without Borders: Fading Distinction between Local and Global* New York: CRC Press

Robert E. W. & Sarah J. M. (2017) *Mirage of Police Reform: Procedural Justice and Police Legitimacy,* California, University of California Press

Roberts, P.C. Dr. (2014) How America was Lost: From 9/11 to Police/Warfare State, Atlanta, USA: Clarity Press, Inc.

Rogers, C. (2016) *Plural Policing: Theory and Practice,* Bristol, Policy Press

Rogers, C. (2017) *Plural Policing: Theory and Practice,* Bristol UK: Policy Press

Rosenbaum, D.P. (2006) 'The Limits of Hot-spot Policing' in Police Innovation: Contrasting Perspectives (eds.) Weisburd, D. & Braga, A.A. (2006), New York: Cambridge University Press, pp. 245-266

Roufa, T. (2018) Police Officers' Bill of Rights published in Technology and Trends at balance-Careers webpage updated November 2018 and available

Roufa, T. (2019a) The History of Modern Policing, *The Balance Careers,* [Online] Available at https://www.thebalancecareers.com/the-history-of-modern-policing-974587 (Accessed: 20 July 2019)

Roufa, T. (2019b) The Early History of Policing, *The Balance Careers,* [Online] Available at https://www.thebalancecareers.com/early-history-of-policing-974580 (Accessed: 19 July 2019)

Rowe, M. (2018) *Introduction to Policing,* 3rd edition, London: Sage publications

Rudy Giuliani along with his pick for Police Commissioner. [Online] Available at https://www.coursehero.com/file/p6u00hq/Rudy-Giuliani-along-with-his-pick-for-Police-Commissioner-Bill-Bratton-laid-out/ (Accessed: 06 March 2018)

Rumi, R. (2015) Charting Pakistan's Internal Security Policy, Special Report (May 2015), US Institute of Peace (www.usip.org) [online] available at https://www.usip.org/sites/default/files/SR363-Charting-Pakistans-Internal-Security-Policy.pdf, accessed 20 April 2021

Safe Cities Index (2017)' Security in a Rapidly Urbanising World, A Report from *Economist's Intelligence Unit* [Online] Available at https://dkf1ato8y5dsg.cloudfront.net/uploads/5/82/safe-cities-index-eng-web.pdf (Accessed: 12 March 2018)

Safe City Project manager *Mr. Nasir Akbar Khan* revealed in his presentation at Safe City Project Headquarters 2017 during The Punjab Safe City Authority statics 2017-18 [Online] Available at http://psca.gop.pk/PSCA/2018/10/02/psca-releases-ic3-performance-review-for-september-2018-2/ (accessed on 13 June 2018) Safe City Project manager Nasir Akbar Khan revealed in his presentation at Safe City Project Headquarters 2017 during the visit of ASP Batch 44th

Sageman, M. (2004) *Understanding Terror Networks,* Pennsylvania: University of Pennsylvania Press

Sampson, R., Raudenbush, S. and Earls, F. (1997) Neighbourhoods and Violent Crime, *Science,* Vol-277: pp. 918-924

Sanders, C.B. & Henderson, S. (2013). Police 'empires and information technologies: uncovering material and organisational barriers to information sharing in Canadian police services, *Policing and Society: An International Journal of Research and Policy*, Vol-23: pp. 243-260

Sardar, Z. (2006) *What Do Muslims Believe?* London: Granta

Sawyer, F., Sylvester Jr., Sagarin, E. (1972) *Politics and Crime*, New York: American Society of Criminology, Praeger Publishers

Schafer, J. A., Buerger, M. E., Meyers, R. W., Jensen III, C. J., and Levin, B. H. (2012) *The Future of Policing: A Practical Guide for Police Managers and Leaders*, Boca Raton USA, CRC Press, Routledge

Schafer, S. (1974) *The Political Criminal-The Problem of Morality and Crime*, London: Macmillan

Schmid, A. (2005) 'Prevention of Terrorism: Towards a Multi-pronged Approach', T. Bjorgo (ed.) *Root Causes of Terrorism: Myths, Reality, and Ways Forward*, Oxford: Routledge

SCJ (2009) Western Iowa Tech Launches Security Institute, *Sioux City Journal* [Online] Available at https://siouxcityjournal.com/special-section/local/western-iowa-tech-launches-security-institute/article_180427e2-ea93-5bb7-85ea-9575df53f33d.html (Accessed: 05 March 2018)

Scott, M.S. (2010) 'Policing and Police Research: Learning to Listen, With a Wisconsin Case Study', *Police Practice and Research: An International Journal*, 11(2): pp. 95–104

Scott, M.S. (2020) Improve Prevention of Police-Involved Harm through Sentinel Event Reviews, Chapter 8, in Katz, C.M. and Maguire, E.R. eds. (2020) *Transforming the Police: Thirteen Key Reforms*, Long Grove Illinois, USA, Waveland Press, Inc. pp. 157-170

Security in a Rapidly Urbanising World, A Report from *Economist's Intelligence Unit* [Online] Available at https://dkf1ato8y5dsg.cloudfront.net/uploads/5/82/safe-cities-index-eng-web.pdf (Accessed: 12 March 2018)

Sedra, M. (2017) *Security Sector Reform in Conflict-affected Countries: The Evolution of Model*, New York: Routledge

Shahzad, S.S. (2011) *Inside Al-Qaeda and the Taliban*, London: Pluto Press

Sharif, S. (2017-18) 'Assessing Forensic Science Landscape in Pakistan' in MIT *TECHNOLOGY REVIEW* no publications date shown [Online] Available at http://www.technologyreview.pk/assessing-forensic-science-landscape-pakistan/ (accessed on 10 December 2018)

Sharkey, P. (2018) *Uneasy Peace: The Great Crime Decline, the Renewal of City Life, and the Next War on Violence* New York: W.W. Norton

Sheldon, B. and Wright, P. (2010) *Policing and Technology*, London: Sage

Shepherd J.P, & Sumner S.A (2018) *Policing and Public Health Author Manuscript* dated 15 February 2018 [Online] Available at https://www.ncbi.nlm.nih.gov/pmc/articles/PMC5814117/ [Accessed: 11 January 2019]

Sheptycki, J. (1995) Transnational Policing and the Making of a Transnational State, *The British Journal of Criminology*, 35 (4) pp. 613-635, [Online] Available at https://doi.org/10.1093/oxfordjournals.bjc.a048550 (Accessed: 28th June 2019)

By J.J. Baloch (2022)

Sheptycki, J. (1998) 'Policing, Postmodernism, and Transnationalisation, *The British Journal of Criminology*, 38 (3) pp. 485-503 [Online] Available at https://doi.org/10.1093/oxfordjournals.bjc.a014259 (Accessed: 21 June 2019)

Sheptycki, J. (2000) *Issues in Transnational Policing*, London: Routledge

Sheptycki, J. (2002) Postmodern Power and Transnational Policing: Democracy, the Constabulary Ethics, and the Response to Global (in)security, *Geneva Centre for Democratic Control of Armed Forces-DCAF,* Working Paper Series-No. 19

Sheptycki, J. (2007) High Policing in Security Control Society, Policing: A Journal of Policy and Practice, 1 (1), pp. 70-79 [Online] Available at http://citeseerx.ist.psu.edu/viewdoc/download?doi=10.1.1.476.806&rep=rep1&type=pdf (Accessed: 22 November 2018)

Sheptycki, J. (2011) *Transnational Crime and Policing*, London: Routledge

Sherman, L., and D. Weisburd (1995) 'General Deterrent Effects of Police Patrol in Crime Hot Spots: A Randomized Study, *Justice Quarterly*, 12(4): pp. 625-648

Sherman, L.W. (2009) Evidence and Liberty: The Promise of Experimental Criminology, *Criminology, and Criminal Justice*, 9(1): pp. 2–28

Shigri, A.A. (2012) 'Police Corruption and Accountability, in Abbass (ed) *Stabilizing Pakistan Through Police Reforms, Asia Society*, A report by Independent Commission on Pakistan Police Reforms, New York Email: globalpolicy@asiasociety.org www.asiasociety.org, pp. 24-28

Shigri, A.A. (2019) Police Reforms: Way Forward, a report by *Police Reform Committee* constituted by Supreme Court of Pakistan (May 15, 2018) Presented to the Supreme Court on 14 January 2019, Page XV

Shohel, M.C., Gias Uddin, McLeod, J.P., and Silverstone, D. (2020) Police Education in the United Kingdom: Challenges and Future Directions, *Intech Open Book Series*, published: 17th August 2020, [Online] Available at DOI: 10.5772/intechopen.92705 (accessed on 13 October 2021

Siddiki, N.A. and Detho, I. (2014) *Protecting Human Rights: Training Module for Police Officers*, Karachi: Paramount Books

Silke, A. (2006) The Role of Suicide in Politics, Conflict, and Terrorism, *Terrorism and Political Violence*, 18: pp. 35-46

Silke, A. (2008) 'Holy Warriors: Exploring the Psychological Processes of Jihadi Radicalization', *European Journal of Criminology* 5(1): pp. 99-123

Silverman, E.B. (2006) 'CompStat's Innovation' in *Police Innovations: Contrasting Perspectives* (eds.) Weisburd, D. & Braga, A.A. (2006), New York: Cambridge University Press, pp. 267-283

Sindh Police Website: http://www.sindhpolice.gov.pk/

Singh, R. (2016) Pakistan's Counter-terrorism Challenge, Moeed Yusuf (ed)' *South Asia: Journal of South Asian Studies*, 38(4), pp. 857–858

Sirrs, O. L. (2017) *Pakistan's Inter-Services Intelligence Directorate*, New York: Routledge, pp. 109-288

Skogan, W. G. (2006) 'Asymmetry in the Impact of Encounters with the Police', *Policing and Society*, 16(2): pp. 99-126 [Online] Available at http://citeseerx.ist.psu.edu/viewdoc/download?doi=10.1.1.544.1978&rep=rep1&type=pdf (Accessed: 13 June 2019)

Skogan, W.G. (2006) 'The Promise of Community Policing', in *Police Innovations: Contrasting Perspectives* (eds.) Weisburd, D. & Braga, A.A. (2006), New York: Cambridge University Press, pp. 27-44

Sousa, W.H. and Kelling, G. L. (2006) 'Of "Broken Windows," Criminology and Criminal Justice' in *Police Innovations: Contrasting Perspectives* (eds.) Weisburd, D. & Braga, A.A. (2006), New York: Cambridge University Press, pp. 77-97

Spalek, B. (2007) Disconnection, and Exclusion: Pathways to Radicalism? in T. Abbas (ed.) *Islamic Political Radicalism: A European Perspective*, Edinburgh: Edinburgh University Press

Spohn, C., and George, S.S. (2020) Increase Efficacy of Police response to Sexual Assault, Chapter 13, in Katz, C.M. and Maguire, E.R. eds. (2020) *Transforming the Police: Thirteen Key Reforms*, Long Grove Illinois, USA, Waveland Press, Inc. pp. 253-267

Stanko, EA. (2009) 'Improving Policing Through Research', Policing: *A Journal of Policy and Practice*, 3(4): pp. 306–309

Stephens, D.W. (2010) Enhancing the Impact of Research on Police Practice, *Police Practice and Research: An International Journal*, 11(2): pp. 150–154

Stone, C. and Travis, J. (2011) 'Towards a New Professionalism in Policing', Executive Sessions on Policing and Public Safety series of *New Perspectives in Policing, March 2011 issue* published by the Institute of Justice, Harvard Kennedy School Program in Criminal Justice Policy and Management. [Online] Available at https://www.ncjrs.gov/pdffiles1/nij/232359.pdf (Accessed: 28 January 2019)

Stroshine, M.S. (2021) Technology in Policing: The Past, Present, and Future, Chapter 30, in Dunham, R.G., Alpert, G.P., and MacLean, K.D. eds. (2021) *Critical Issues in Policing: Contemporary Readings*, 8th edn. Illinois USA, Waveland Press, Inc. pp. 605-620

Suddle, S. (2012) Obstacles to Reform, Article in Stabilising Pakistan through Police Reform, *A Report by Asia Society independent Commission on Pakistan Police Reforms*, [Online] Available at https://asiasociety.org/files/pdf/as_pakistan_police_reform.pdf (accessed on 12 October 2018)

Suddle, S. (2015) 'Police System of Pakistan', Position Paper, published by *PILDAT www.pildat.com* in October 2015 [Online] Available at http://www.millat.com/wp-content/uploads/pdf/democracy/PoliceSystemofPakistan_PositionPaper.pdf, (Accessed: 25th June 2017)

Sung, H. (2001) The Fragmentation of Policing in American Cities: Toward an Ecological Theory of Police-Citizen Relations, *ResearchGate Publications* [Online] Available at https://www.researchgate.net/publication/258840114_The_Fragmentation_of_Policing_in_American_Cities_Toward_an_Ecological_Theory_of_Police-Citizen_Relations (accessed 2 November 2021)

Sunshine, J. and Tyler, T. (2003) The Role of Procedural Justice and Legitimacy in Shaping Public Support for Policing, *Law Society Review*, 37(3): pp. 513-548 [Online] Available at https://doi.org/10.1111/1540-5893.3703002 (Accessed: 23 January 2018)

Sutton, R.I. (2012) 'Good Boss, Bad Boss: How to Be the Best... and Learn from the Worst', 2nd ed. & first published in 2010, New York, Business Plus, Hachette Book Group

By J.J. Baloch (2022)

Sweetman, B. Dr (1999) Postmodernism, Derrida and Difference: A Critique in International Philosophical Quarterly, (XXXIX), 1, pp.5-18 [Online] Available at file:///C:/Users/hp1/Downloads/CJ%20Seminar%203%20-%20Working%20group%201%20CC%20-%20Postmodern%20Legal%20Theories.pdf [Accessed: 07 June 2019]

Tahir, M. (2012) 'The National Highways and Motorways Police' in Abbass, H. (ed) (2012) *Stabilising Pakistan Through Police Reforms*, pp. 94-98 [Online] Available at https://asiasociety.org/files/pdf/as_pakistan_police_reform.pdf (Accessed: 13 December 2017)

Tajik, S.H. (2012) 'Technology and Law Enforcement' in Abbass, H. (ed) (2012) *Stabilising Pakistan Through Police Reforms* pp. 73-77 [Online] Available at https://asiasociety.org/files/pdf/as_pakistan_police_reform.pdf (Accessed: 21 December 2017)

Tan, R. (2020) 'There's a reason it's hard to discipline police. It starts with a bill of rights 47 years ago-Washington Post, Democracy Dies in darkness, published on 29 August 2020 [Online] Available at https://www.washingtonpost.com/history/2020/08/29/police-bill-of-rights-officers-discipline-maryland/ (accessed 5th November 2021)

Taqi, M. (2020) Pakistan's Hybrid Regime: The Army's Project Imran Khan: With its latest power play, Pakistan's civilian-military regime might have bitten off more than it could chew, *The Diplomat Magazine* published on 1 October 2020 [Online] Available at https://thediplomat.com/2020/10/pakistans-hybrid-regime-the-armys-project-imran-khan/ (accessed on 8 November 2021)

Tarar, H. (2012) 'Leading Changes in Police Organisations' in Abbass, H. (ed) (2012) *Stabilising Pakistan Through Police Reforms* pp. 41-42 [Online] Available at https://asiasociety.org/files/pdf/as_pakistan_police_reform.pdf (Accessed: 13 December 2017)

Taylor, B., Koper, C., & Woods, D. (2011). A randomized controlled trial of different policing strategies at hotspots of violent crime, Journal of Experimental Criminology, 7, 149-181. [online] Available DOI: 10.1007/s11292-101-9120-6, Accessed on November 2020

Taylor, R.B. (2006)' Incivilities Reduction Policing, Zero Tolerance and Retreat from Coproduction: Weak Foundations and Strong Pressures' in *Police Innovations: Contrasting Perspectives* (eds.) Weisburd, D. & Braga, A.A. (2006), New York: Cambridge University Press, pp. 98-116

Telep, C.W. Bottema, A.J. (2020) Adopt Evidence-based Policing, Chapter 1 in Katz, C.M. and Maguire, E.R. eds. (2020) *Transforming the Police: Thirteen Key Reforms*, Long Grove Illinois, USA, Waveland Press, Inc. pp. 9-25

Terpstra, J. & Trommel, W. (2009) Police, materialization and presentational strategies, Policing: *An International Journal of Police Strategies & Management* 32:1, pages 128-143

Terrill, W. (2020) Reduce Use of Force, Chapter 4 in Katz, C.M., and Maguire, E.R. eds. (2020) *Transforming the Police: Thirteen Key Reforms*, Long Grove Illinois, USA, Waveland Press, Inc. pp. 73-89

Thatcher, D. (2001) 'Policing is Not a Treatment: Alternatives to the Medical Model of Police Research', *Journal of Research in Crime and Delinquency*, 38(4): pp. 287–413

The 21st Constitutional Amendment (2014) See the National Action Plan Contents or content of 21st constitutional amendment in the constitution of 1973 Pakistan for details or go to the concerned chapter titled "Policing Terrorism" to see a further detailed overview of NAP

The Economist (2015) What the Broken Window Policing is? 27 January 2015 [Online] Available at https://www.economist.com/the-economist-explains/2015/01/27/what-broken-windows-policing-is (Accessed: 25 August 2017)

The Economist report (2018) on 'Adoption of Technology by the Common Man' 24 November

The Police Act 1861, An Act for Regulation of Police in India [now Pakistan after Partition] vol No. V dated 22 March 1861 [Online] Available at http://www.ilo.org/dyn/natlex/docs/ELECTRONIC/104949/128182/F-1626591262/PAK104949.pdf (accessed on 19 June 2019)

The South Asian Terrorism Portal website database [Online] Available at https://www.satp.org/ (Accessed: 13 July 2018)

Thomas, E. Baker (1941) *'Effective Police Leadership: Moving Beyond Management'*, 3rd ed. New York: Looseleaf Law Publications

Thomas, G. (2014) Research on Policing: Insights from the Literature, *Police Journal: Theory, Practice, and Principles*, 87(1): pp. 1-20

Thornton, S. and Mason, L. (2007) Community Cohesion in High Wycombe: A Case Study of Operation Overt, *Policing: A Journal of Policy and Practice*, 1(1): pp. 57-60

Tom Cockcroft. (2019) Institutional hybridity and cultural isomorphism in contemporary policing. *International Journal of Police Science & Management* 21:4, pages 218-229

Toyama, K. (2015) *Geek Heresy: Rescuing Social Change from the Cult of Technology* New York: Public Affairs

Transparency International Report (2018) 'Corruption Perception Index, Transparency *International Pakistan Report 2018* [Online] Available at https://www.transparency.org/cpi2018?gclid=Cj0KCQiA5NPjBRDDARIsAM9X1GI-XKgFPigM7Vnozn0xm166f8ex7H7qJWsiF7sIN06FqxOw4CxJUHkaAkxEEALw_wcB (Accessed: 25 February 2019)

Trinkner, R., and Tyler, D.H. (2020) Build Momentum for Police Reforms through Organisational Justice, Chapter 10, in Katz, C.M. and Maguire, E.R. eds. (2020) *Transforming the Police: Thirteen Key Reforms*, Long Grove Illinois, USA, Waveland Press, Inc. pp. 195-208

Trojanowicz, R.C. and Bucqueroux, B. (1994) *Community Policing: How to get Started* Cincinnati, OH: Anderson Pub Co.

Tulini, B. (2019) Using Technology to Advance Police Legitimacy, *Benchmark Analytics* Blog, posted on 23 May 2019 [Online] available at https://www.benchmarkanalytics.com/blog/police-legitimacy-technology/ accessed on 20 October 2021

Tulsa Commission (2017) Findings and Recommendations on community Policing, City of Tulsa Police Department, USA [Online] Available at http://bloximages.newyork1.vip.townnews.com/tulsaworld.com/content/tncms/assets/v3/editorial/e/c4/ec4c93b2-0f63-53ba-b650-ac19d4f96d02/58c380f31590e.pdf.pdf (Accessed: 26 November 2018)

Tyler, T. (1990) *Why People Obey the Law,* New Haven: Yale University Press

Tyler, T. (2004) Enhancing Police Legitimacy, *the Annuals of the American Academy of Political and Social Science*, 593(1): pp. 84-99

By J.J. Baloch (2022)

U.S Department of Justice (2016a) 'Pakistan's Country Report on Terrorism' published by the United States Department of State Publication Bureau of Counterterrorism, Released in July 2017. [Online] Available at: https://www.state.gov/documents/organization/272488.pdf (Accessed: 03 December 2017)

U.S Department of Justice (2016b) Pakistan's Country Reports on Human Rights Practices for United States Department of State Bureau of Democracy, Human Rights and Labour, [Online] Available at https://www.state.gov/documents/organization/265758.pdf (Accessed: 25 March 2018)

Uchida, C.D. (2011) 'A History of American Policing' in *Critical Issues in Crime and Justice*, (eds.) Maguire, M. and Okada, D. (2011) California, USA: Sage Publications, pp.184-196

UN General Assembly resolution 34/169 of December 17, 1979, titled "*Code of Conduct for Law Enforcement Officials.*" UNGA Res. 60/288. (8th September 2006) The United Nations Global Counter-Terrorism Strategy, sixtieth session, Agenda items 46 and 120 [Online] available at https://documents-dds-ny.un.org/doc/UNDOC/GEN/N05/504/88/PDF/N0550488.pdf?OpenElement, (accessed 29th October 2021)

UNGA Resolution 34/169 (1979) Code of Conduct for Law Enforcement Officials, UN General Assembly 17 December 1979, [Online] Available at https://www.refworld.org/docid/48abd572e.html (Accessed: 23 January 2017)

UNODC (2011) Handbook on police accountability, oversight, and integrity Criminal Justice Handbook Series, New York [Online] Available at https://www.unodc.org/pdf/criminal_justice/Handbook_on_police_Accountability_Oversight_and_Integrity.pdf (Accessed: 12 January 2017)

UNRA (2017) 'Dreams Turned into Nightmares - Attacks on Students, Teachers, and Schools in Pakistan' *Pakistan's Country Report by ref-World, United Nations' Refugee Agency*, 27 March 2017, [Online] Available at http://www.refworld.org/type,COUNTRYREP,,PAK,50ffbce445,,0.html (Accessed:13 April 2018)

Vadhwa, V. (2016) Apple vs. FBI: The Tip of the Iceberg as Laws Cannot Keep up with Tech' published in *The Washington Post* dated 4 March 2016 [Online] Available at https://www.washingtonpost.com/news/innovations/wp/2016/03/04/apple-vs-fbi-the-tip-of-the-iceberg-as-laws-cant-keep-up-with-tech/?noredirect=on&utm_term=.d2d6450be6b9 (Accessed: 12 February 2019)

Verma, A., Das, D.K., and Abraham, M. eds. (2019) *Global Community Policing: Problems and Challenges*, NY, Routledge

Viotti, P., Opheim, M., and Bowen, N. eds. (2008) *Terrorism and Homeland Security: Thinking Strategically About Policy*, Boca Raton USA, CRC Press

Vitale, S.A. (2017) *the End of Policing* New York: Verso Books

Waddington; P.A.J. (2007) 'Policing Terrorism', *Policing: A Journal of Policy and Practice*, 1 (1), 1 January 2007, pp. 1–4, [Online] Available at https://doi.org/10.1093/police/pam007 (Accessed: 13 May 2018)

Walker, N. (2000) *Policing in a Changing Constitutional Order*, London: Sweet & Maxwell
Walker, S. (2006) Police Accountability: Current Issues and Research Needs, a paper published by the *U.S. Department of Justice and presented at the National Institute of Justice (NIJ)* Policing Research Workshop: Planning for the Future, Washington, DC, (November 28-29, 2006) [Online] Available at https://www.ojp.gov/pdffiles1/nij/grants/218583.pdf (accessed on 15 April 2020)

Walker, S. (2019) *The New World of Police Accountability*, 3rd edition, Sage Publications, Available online at https://sk.sagepub.com/books/the-new-world-of-police-accountability (accessed on 12 January 2020)

Wall, D.S., and Williams, M. eds. (2014) *Policing Cybercrime: Networked and Social-Media Technologies and the Challenges for Policing*, NY, Routledge

Wallace, D., Orosco, C., and Louton, B. (2020) Reduce Racial Inequality in Police Practice, Chapter 5, in Katz, C.M. and Maguire, E.R. eds. (2020) *Transforming the Police: Thirteen Key Reforms*, Long Grove Illinois, USA, Waveland Press, Inc. pp. 93-110

Walters, W. (2002) Deportation, Expulsion, and the International Police of Aliens, *Journal of Citizenship Studies*,6 (3), pp. 265-292, [Online] Published 01 Jul 2010, available at DOI: 10.1080/1362102022000011612 (Accessed: 25 July 2019)

Waseem, Z. (2018) 'Policing the Police', a cover story Published in *Newline Magazine* September issue [Online] Available at https://newslinemagazine.com/magazine/policing-the-police/ (Accessed: January 20th, 2019)
Waseem, Z. (2019) 'Brothers in arms? A police-paramilitary partnership in Karachi', *Policing and Society, An International Journal of Research and Policy* vol, 31 issues 2, published on 19 December 2019 [Online] Available at https://doi.org/10.1080/10439463.2019.1705824 (accessed on 9th November 2021)

Waters, I. (2007) Policing, Modernity and Postmodernity, *Policing and Society*, 17 (3) pp. 257-278 [Online] Available at DOI: 10.1080/10439460701497345 (Accessed: 28 May 2017)

Weatheritt, M. (1986) *Innovations in Policing*, Croom Helm: Beckenham
Webb, V.J., Katz, C.M., and Flippin, M.R. (2020) Build Police-researcher Partnership to Advance Policing, Chapter 9, in Katz, C.M. and Maguire, E.R. eds. (2020) *Transforming the Police: Thirteen Key Reforms*, Long Grove Illinois, USA, Waveland Press, Inc. pp. 175-189

Weisburd, D. (2011) 'The Evidence for Place-Based Policing', George Mason University, [Online] Available at https://cornerstone.gmu.edu/articles/2275 (Accessed: 04 March 2018)

Weisburd, D. and Braga, A.A. (2006) 'Hot-Spot Policing as a Model for Police Innovation' in *Police Innovations: Contrasting Perspectives* (eds.) Weisburd, D. & Braga, A.A. (2006), New York: Cambridge University Press, pp. 225-244

Weisburd, D. and Braga, A.A. (eds.) (2006) *Police Innovations-Contrasting Perspectives* London: Cambridge University Press

Weisburd, D., and L. Green (1995). Policing Drug Hot Spots: The Jersey City DMA Experiment, *Justice Quarterly*, 12(4) pp. 711-735

Weisburd, D., Mastrofski, S.D., Willis, J.J., and Greenspan, A.R. (2006) 'Changing Everything so that Everything Remains the Same: CompStat and American Policing' in *Police Innovations: Contrasting Perspectives* (eds.) Weisburd, D. & Braga, A.A. (2006), New York: Cambridge University Press, pp.284-304

Weisburd, D., S. Bush-way, C. Lum, et al. (2004). Crime Trajectories at Places: A Longitudinal Study of Street Segments in the City of Seattle, *The British Journal of Criminology*, 42(2): pp. 283-322.

Weiss, M. and Hassan, H. (2015) ISIS-Inside the Army of Terror, New York: Regan Arts, pp. 48-98

Wells, R. (2009) Intelligence-led Policing: A New Paradigm in Law Enforcement in *Public Agency Training Council Agency-PATC*. [Online] Available at http://www.patc.com/weeklyarticles/intelligence_policing.shtml (Accessed: 06 March 2018)

Welsh, B.C. (2006) 'Evidence-based Policing for Crime Prevention in *Police Innovations: Contrasting Perspectives* (eds.) Weisburd, D. & Braga, A.A. (2006), New York: Cambridge University Press, pp.305-321

Westmarland, L. and Conway, S. (2020) Police ethics and integrity: Keeping the 'blue code of silence, *International Journal of Police Science & Management-Sage* 2020, Vol. 22(4) 378–392 [Online] Available at https://journals.sagepub.com/doi/pdf/10.1177/1461355720947762 (accessed 6th November 2021)

What Works Centre for Policing (2017) What is evidence-based policing? [Online] Available at https://whatworks.college.police.uk/About/Pages/What-is-EBP.aspx (Accessed: 06 March 2018)

Whitaker, B. (1979) *The Police in society*, London: Eyre Methuen
White, M.D., Goud, J.E., and Todak, N. (2020) Implement a Body-Worn Camera Program, Chapter 7, in Katz, C.M., and Maguire, E.R. eds. (2020) *Transforming the Police: Thirteen Key Reforms*, Long Grove Illinois, USA, Waveland Press, Inc. pp. 129-152

White, A. & Gill, M. (2013) The Transformation of Policing: From Ratios to Rationalities. *British Journal of Criminology* 53:1, pages 74-93

Wiatrowski M.D. and Pino, N. (2016) *Democratic Policing in Transitional And Developing Countries*, London: Routledge

Wikipedia on Intelligence Bureau of Pakistan available at https://en.wikipedia.org/wiki/Intelligence_Bureau_(Pakistan) (Accessed on 22 March 2020)

Wilkinson, P. (2001) *Terrorism versus Democracy: The Liberal State Response*, Abingdon: Frank Cass

Wills, B. (2010) 'Why leadership in law enforcement is not about rank' published in *PoliceOne.com* on August 19, 2010, [Online] Available at https://www.policeone.com/leadership/articles/2364121-Why-leadership-in-law-enforcement-is-not-about-rank/ (Accessed: 10th February 2019)

Wilson, J.Q. (1975) *Thinking About Crime*, New York: Vintage

Wolin, S.S. (2016) *Politics & Vision: Continuity and Innovation in Western Political Thought*, London: Princeton University Press

Woolsey, J. (2004) Testimony in the Congress on 9/11 Incident

Writ Petition No.3151-P/2014 JUDGMENT, Date of hearing 5.4.2016, Announced on 20.4.2016 by Peshawar High Court on a petition filed by Petitioner(s) Muhammad Zafar Ali and ten others

Yetman, A. & Wilson, M. *(1995) Justice and identity: Antipodeans practices* Sydney: Allen & Unwind

Yetman, A. (1994). *Postmodern Re-visioning of the political*, New York: Routledge

Young, I. M (1990) *Justice and the politics of difference*, Princeton New Jersey: Princeton University Press

Young, J. M. (2007) *The Vertigo of Late Modernity*, London: Sage

Yusuf, M. (2014) *Pakistan's Counter-terrorism Challenge*, Washington: Georgetown University Press

Important Websites

Reimagining Policing in Pakistan

IB website https://pakistanforces.com/intelligence-bureau-ib/ (accessed on 20 April 2019)

NH&MP official website http://nhmp.gov.pk/ (accessed on 13 July 2018)

PP official website https://punjabpolice.gov.pk/police-jobs (accessed on 18 July 2019)

SP official website https://www.sindhpolice.gov.pk/ (accessed on 12 July 2019)

KPP official website https://kppolice.gov.pk/ (accessed on 15 July 2019)

BP official website https://balochistanpolice.gov.pk/ (accessed on 20 July 2019)

GBP official website https://gbp.gov.pk/ (accessed 25 July 2019)

IP official website https://www.islamabadpolice.gov.pk/ (accessed 26 July 2019)

AJKP official website https://police.ajk.gov.pk/ (accessed 28 July 2019)

NPA official website http://npa.gov.pk/na/ (accessed 15 January 2018)

PSCA official website https://psca.gop.pk/ (accessed 20 August 2019)

PFSA official website https://pfsa.punjab.gov.pk/ (accessed 12 July 2019)

NR3C official website http://www.nr3c.gov.pk/ (accessed 11 December 2019)

PRP website http://www.railways.gov.pk/ (accessed 13 May 2019)

NACTA official website https://nacta.gov.pk/ (accessed 14 July 2019)

NPB website http://www.npb.gov.pk/index.php/associations/ (accessed 19 February 2019)

Printed in Great Britain
by Amazon

77475641R00182